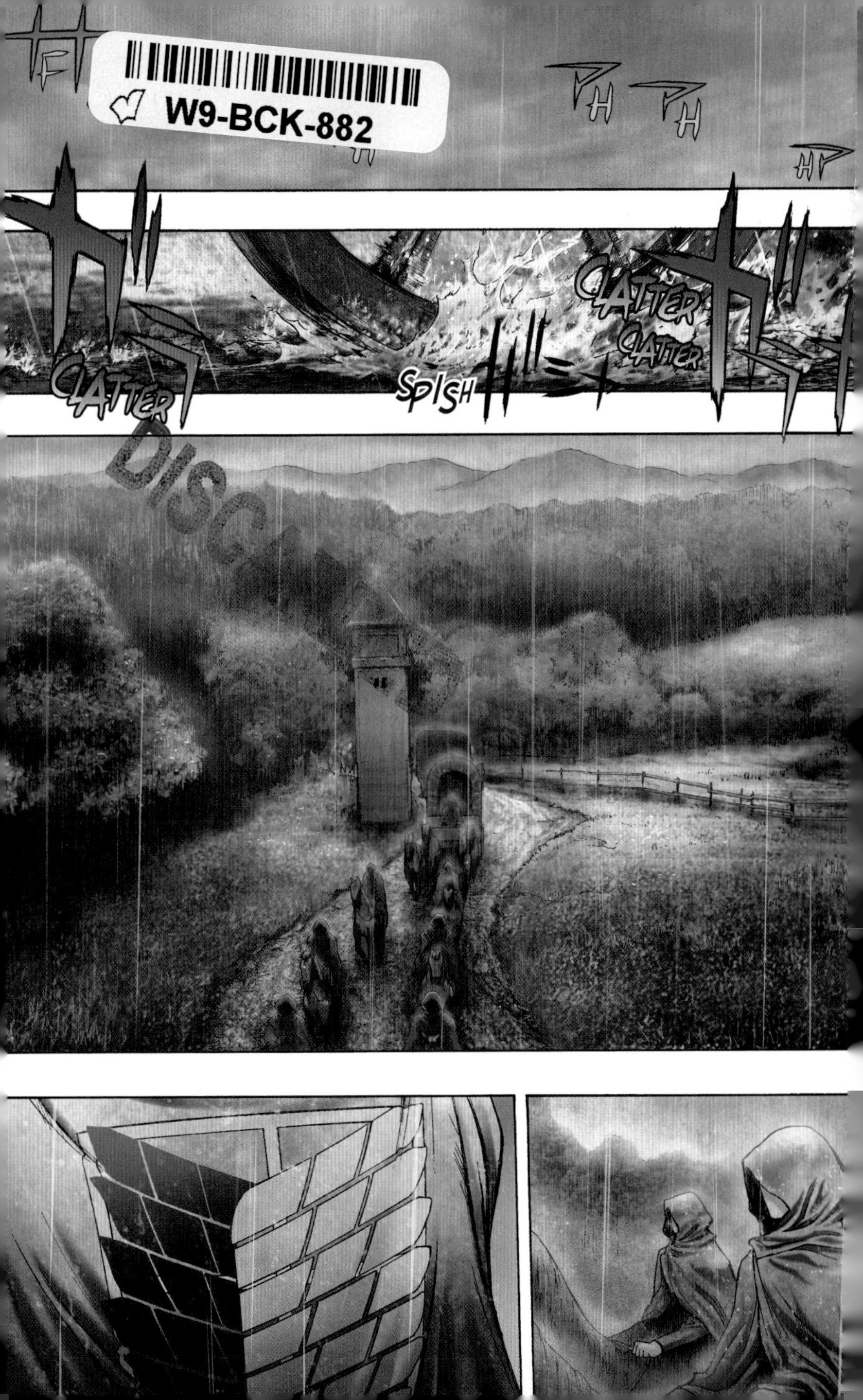
PH
PH
HP
CLATTER
CLATTER
SPISH
CLATTER

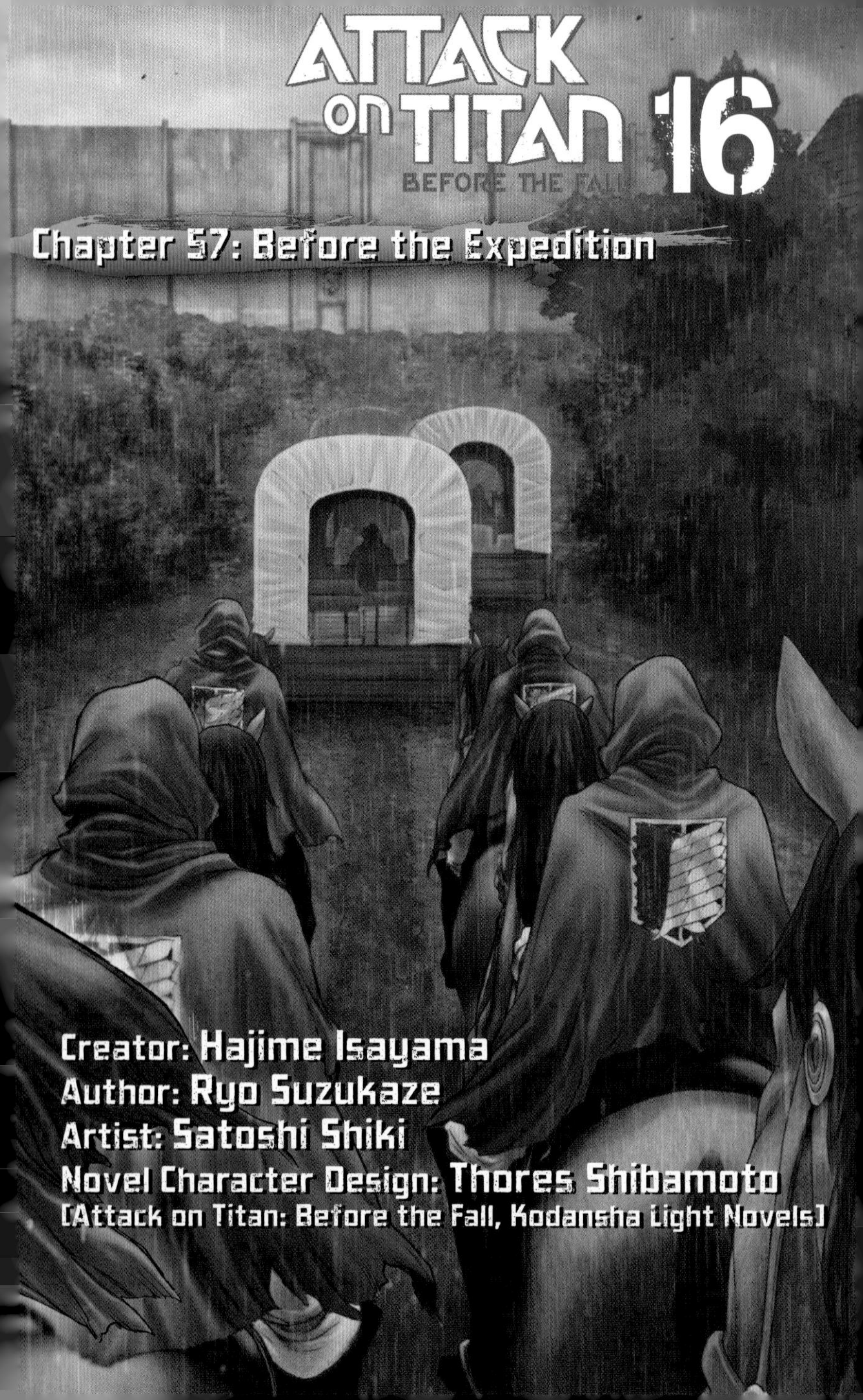
ATTACK ON TITAN
BEFORE THE FALL
16

# Chapter 57: Before the Expedition

Creator: Hajime Isayama
Author: Ryo Suzukaze
Artist: Satoshi Shiki
Novel Character Design: Thores Shibamoto
[Attack on Titan: Before the Fall, Kodansha Light Novels]

# STOP!

You are going the *wrong way!*

Manga is a *completely* different type of reading experience.

To start at the *BEGINNING,* go to the *END!*

That's right! Authentic manga is read the traditional Japanese way-from right to left, exactly the opposite of how American books are read. It's easy to follow: just go to the other end of the book, and read each page-and each panel-from the right side to the left side, starting at the top right. Now you're experiencing manga as it was meant to be.

A Kodansha Comics Trade Paperback Original
*Attack on Titan: Before the Fall* volume 16 copyright © 2018 Hajime Isayama/
Ryo Suzukaze/Satoshi Shiki
English translation copyright © 2018 Hajime Isayama/Ryo Suzukaze/Satoshi Shiki

Published in the United States by Kodansha Comics, an imprint of
Kodansha USA Publishing, LLC, New York.

Publication rights for this English edition arranged through
Kodansha Ltd, Tokyo.

First published in Japan in 2018 by Kodansha Ltd., Tokyo
as *Shingeki no kyojin Before the fall*, volume 16.

ISBN 978-1-63236-829-4

Character designs by Thores Shibamoto
Original cover design by Takashi Shimoyama and Kayo Hasegawa (Red Rooster)

Printed in the United States of America.

www.kodanshacomics.com

9 8 7 6 5 4 3 2 1
Translation: Stephen Paul
Lettering: Steve Wands
Editing: Lauren Scanlan
Kodansha Comics edition cover design by Phil Balsman

# HAPPINESS

## —ハピネス—

By **Shuzo Oshimi**

**From the creator of *The Flowers of Evil***

Nothing interesting is happening in Makoto Ozaki's first year of high school. HIs life is a series of quiet humiliations: low-grade bullies, unreliable friends, and the constant frustration of his adolescent lust. But one night, a pale, thin girl knocks him to the ground in an alley and offers him a choice.

Now everything is different. Daylight is searingly bright. Food tastes awful. And worse than anything is the terrible, consuming thirst...

**Praise for Shuzo Oshimi's *The Flowers of Evil***

"A shockingly readable story that vividly—one might even say queasily—evokes the fear and confusion of discovering one's own sexuality. Recommended." —The Manga Critic

"A page-turning tale of sordid middle school blackmail." —Otaku USA Magazine

"A stunning new horror manga." —Third Eye Comics

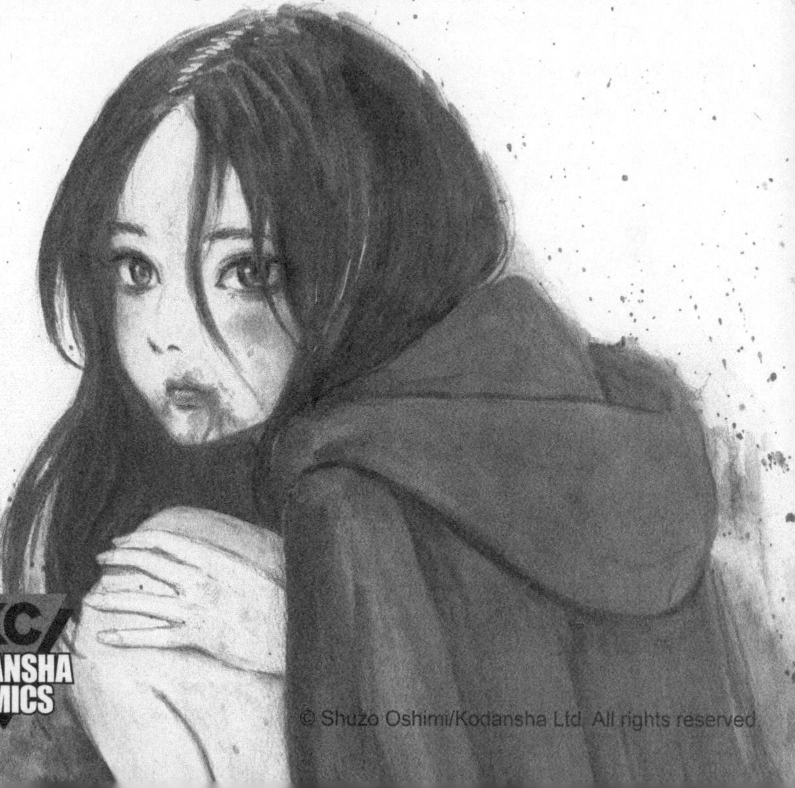

KC KODANSHA COMICS

# The Black Museum — The Ghost and the Lady

## By Kazuhiro Fujita

Deep in Scotland Yard in London sits an evidence room dedicated to the greatest mysteries of British history. In this "Black Museum" sits a misshapen hunk of lead—two bullets fused together—the key to a wartime encounter between Florence Nightingale, the mother of modern nursing, and a supernatural Man in Grey. This story is unknown to most scholars of history, but a special guest of the museum will tell the tale of *The Ghost and the Lady*...

### Praise for Kazuhiro Fujita's *Ushio and Tora*

"A charming revival that combines a classic look with modern depth and pacing... **Essential viewing both for curmudgeons and new fans alike.**" — Anime News Network

"**GREAT!** The first episode of *Ushio and Tora* captures the essence of '90s anime." — IGN

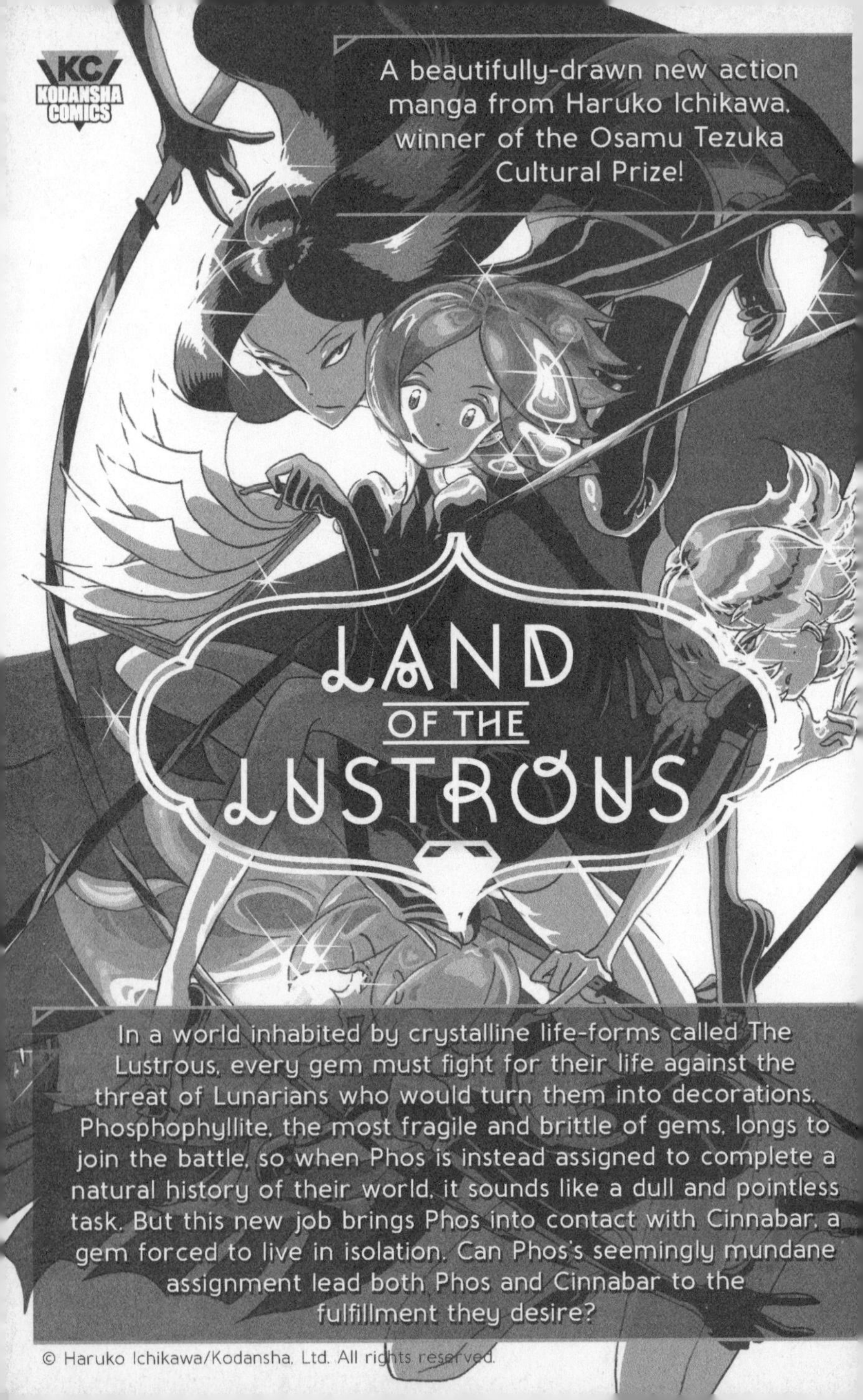
KC KODANSHA COMICS
A beautifully-drawn new action manga from Haruko Ichikawa, winner of the Osamu Tezuka Cultural Prize!
LAND OF THE LUSTROUS
In a world inhabited by crystalline life-forms called The Lustrous, every gem must fight for their life against the threat of Lunarians who would turn them into decorations. Phosphophyllite, the most fragile and brittle of gems, longs to join the battle, so when Phos is instead assigned to complete a natural history of their world, it sounds like a dull and pointless task. But this new job brings Phos into contact with Cinnabar, a gem forced to live in isolation. Can Phos's seemingly mundane assignment lead both Phos and Cinnabar to the fulfillment they desire?
© Haruko Ichikawa/Kodansha, Ltd. All rights reserved.

From the creator of *The Ancient Magus' Bride*
comes a supernatural action manga in the
vein of *Fullmetal Alchemist*!

# Frau · Faust

More than a century after an eccentric scholar made an infamous deal with a
devil, the story of Faust has passed into legend. However, the true Faust is not
the stuffy, professorial man known in fairy tales, but a charismatic, bespectacled
woman named Johanna Faust, who happens to still be alive. Searching for
pieces of her long-lost demon, Johanna passes through a provincial town, where
she saves a young boy named Marion from a criminal's fate. In exchange, she
asks a simple favor of Marion, but Marion soon finds himself intrigued by
the peculiar Doctor Faust and joins her on her journey. Thus begins the strange
and wonderful adventures of *Frau Faust*!

Japan's most powerful spirit medium delves into the ghost world's greatest mysteries!

Story by Kyo Shirodaira, famed author of mystery fiction and creator of *Spiral*, *Blast of Tempest*, and *The Record of a Fallen Vampire*.

Both touched by spirits called yôkai, Kotoko and Kurô have gained unique superhuman powers. But to gain her powers Kotoko has given up an eye and a leg, and Kurô's personal life is in shambles. So when Kotoko suggests they team up to deal with renegades from the spirit world, Kurô doesn't have many other choices, but Kotoko might just have a few ulterior motives...

# IN/SPECTRE

### STORY BY KYO SHIRODAIRA
### ART BY CHASHIBA KATASE

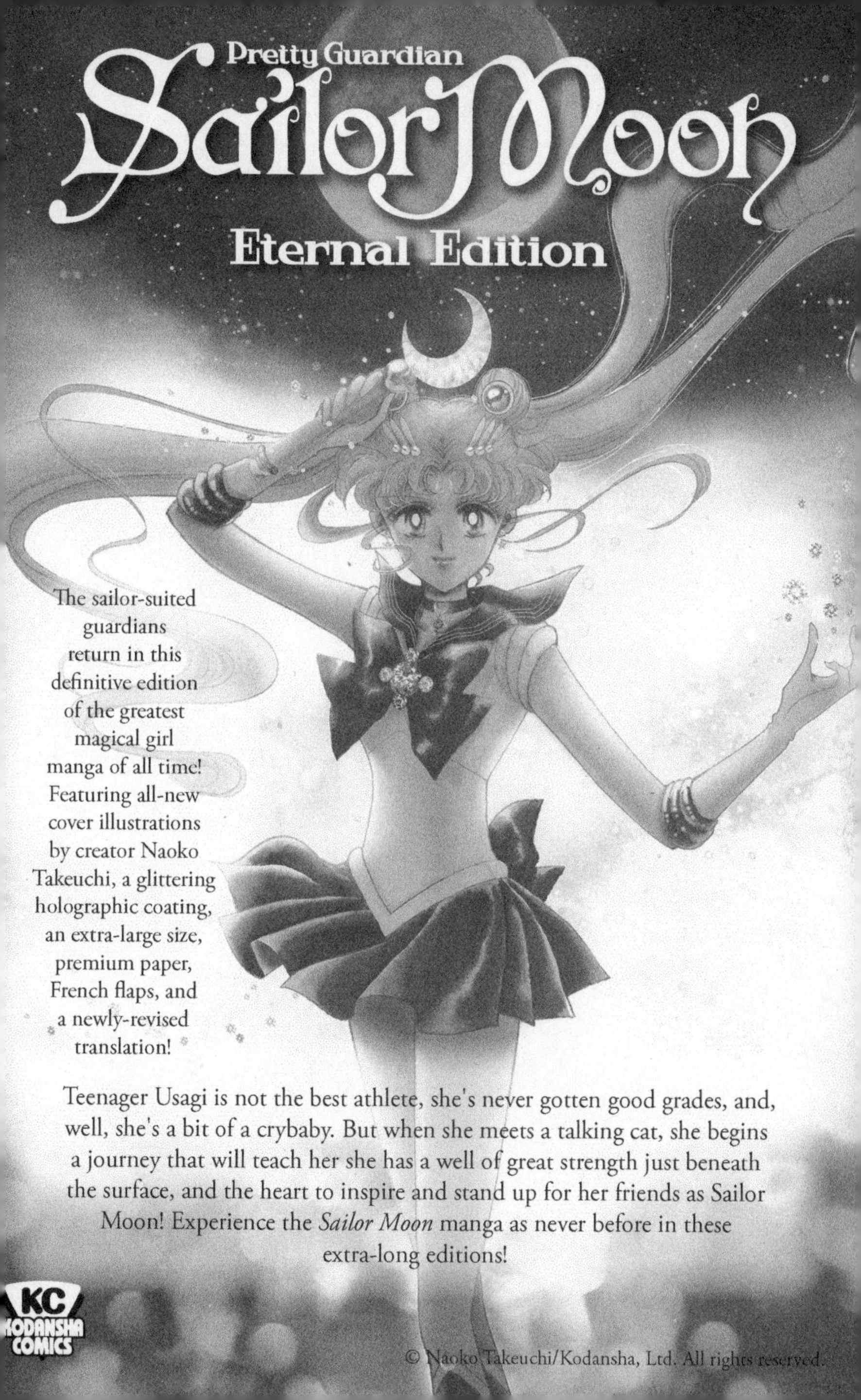
Pretty Guardian
Sailor Moon
Eternal Edition
The sailor-suited guardians return in this definitive edition of the greatest magical girl manga of all time! Featuring all-new cover illustrations by creator Naoko Takeuchi, a glittering holographic coating, an extra-large size, premium paper, French flaps, and a newly-revised translation!
Teenager Usagi is not the best athlete, she's never gotten good grades, and, well, she's a bit of a crybaby. But when she meets a talking cat, she begins a journey that will teach her she has a well of great strength just beneath the surface, and the heart to inspire and stand up for her friends as Sailor Moon! Experience the *Sailor Moon* manga as never before in these extra-long editions!
KC KODANSHA COMICS
© Naoko Takeuchi/Kodansha, Ltd. All rights reserved.

A new series from Yoshitoki Oima, creator of The New York Times bestselling manga and Eisner Award nominee *A Silent Voice*!

An intimate, emotional drama and an epic story spanning time and space...

# TO YOUR ETERNITY

An orb was cast unto the earth. After metamorphosing into a wolf, It joins a boy on his bleak journey to find his tribe. Ever learning, It transcends death, even when those around It cannot…

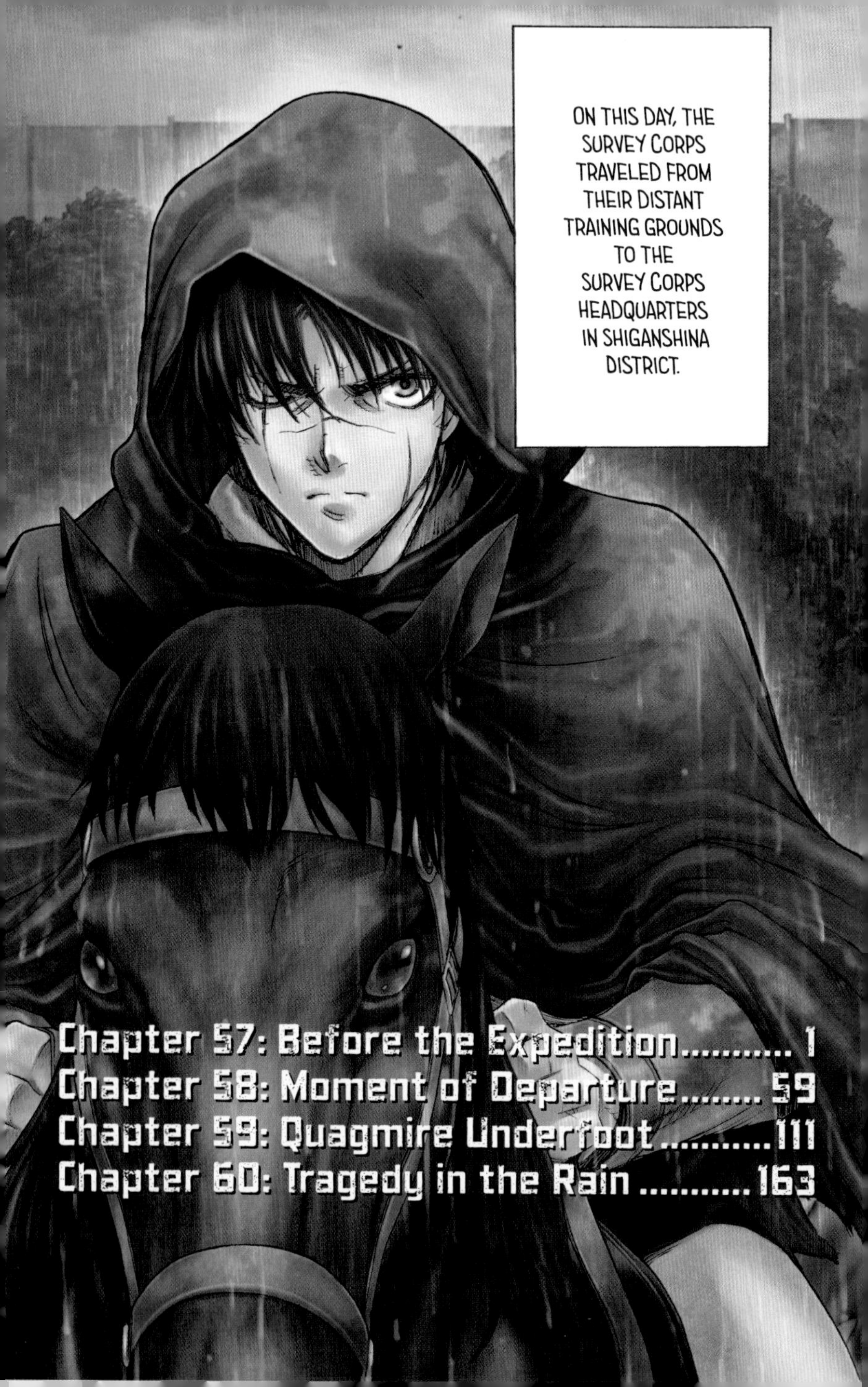
ON THIS DAY, THE SURVEY CORPS TRAVELED FROM THEIR DISTANT TRAINING GROUNDS TO THE SURVEY CORPS HEADQUARTERS IN SHIGANSHINA DISTRICT.

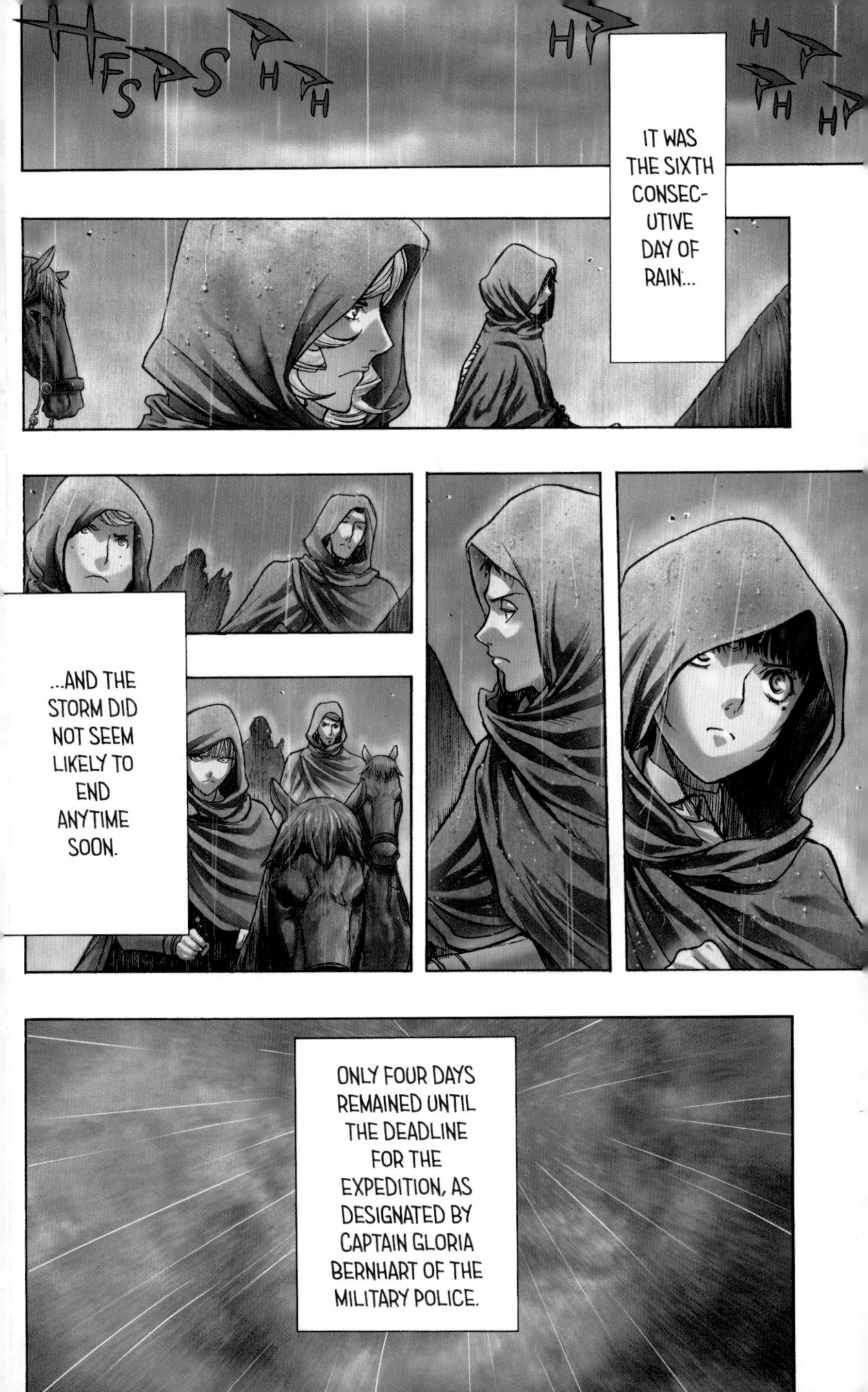
IT WAS THE SIXTH CONSEC-UTIVE DAY OF RAIN...
...AND THE STORM DID NOT SEEM LIKELY TO END ANYTIME SOON.
ONLY FOUR DAYS REMAINED UNTIL THE DEADLINE FOR THE EXPEDITION, AS DESIGNATED BY CAPTAIN GLORIA BERNHART OF THE MILITARY POLICE.

# Before the fall Character Profiles

## Kuklo

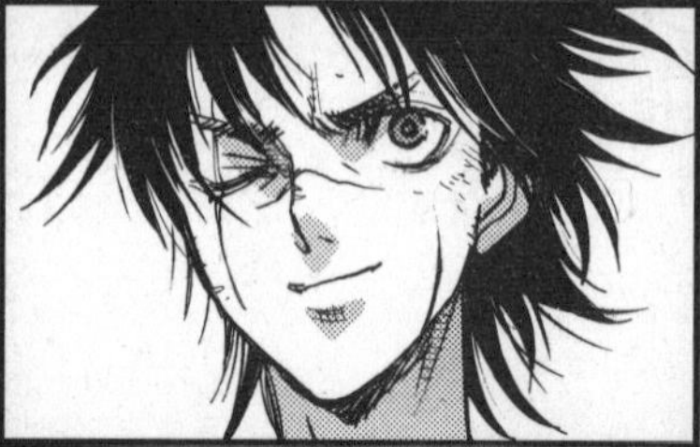

A 15-year-old boy born from a dead body packed into the vomit of a Titan, which earned him the moniker, "Titan's Son." He is fascinated with the Device as a means to defeat the Titans. Xavi defeated him in battle and left him for dead, until Rosa's group found and rescued him.

## Sharle Inocencio

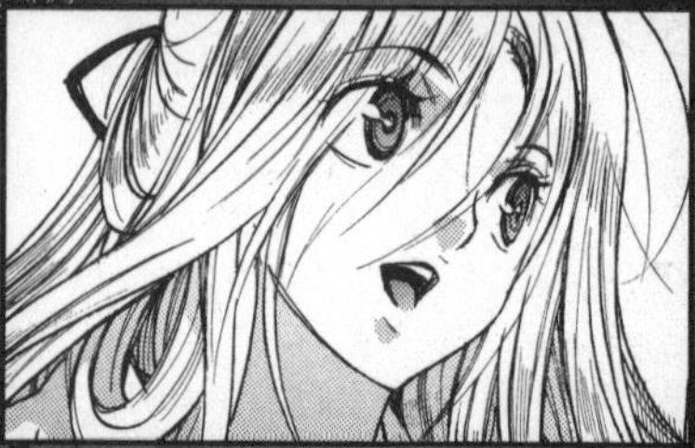

First daughter of the Inocencios, a rich merchant family within Wall Sheena. When she realized that Kuklo was a human, she taught him to speak and learn. She escaped her family home and went into the underground in search of Angel, inventor of the Device.

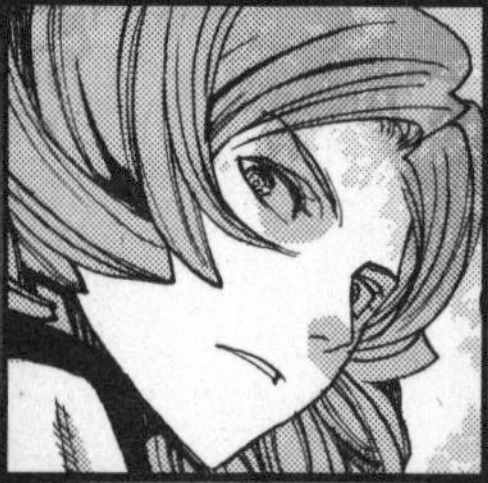

## Cardina Baumeister

Kuklo's first friend in the outside world, and his companion in developing the Device.

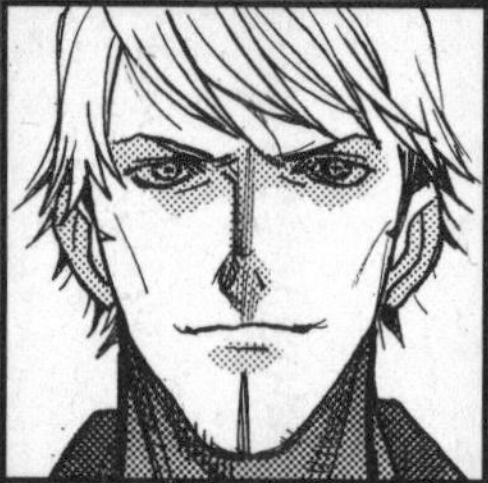

## Carlo Pikale

Jorge's son and current captain of the Survey Corps. Since they battled Titans together, he's had great respect for Kuklo.

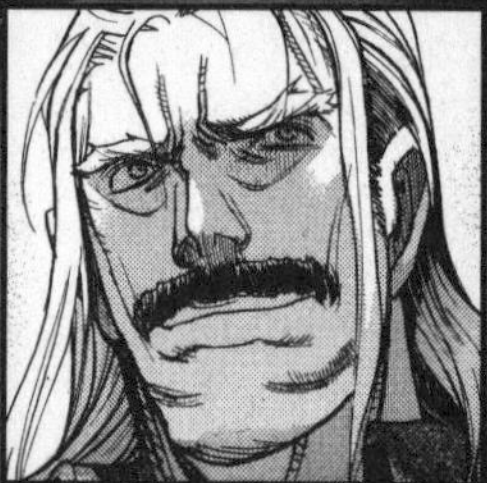

## Jorge Pikale

Training Corps instructor. A former Survey Corps captain who was hailed as a hero for defeating a Titan.

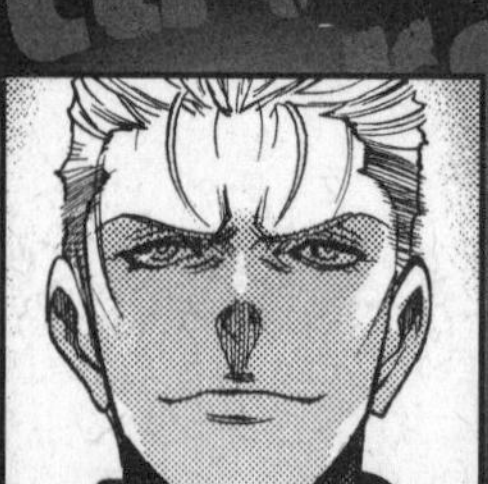

## Xavi Inocencio

Head of the Inocencio family and Sharle's brother. Member of the Military Police in Shiganshina District.

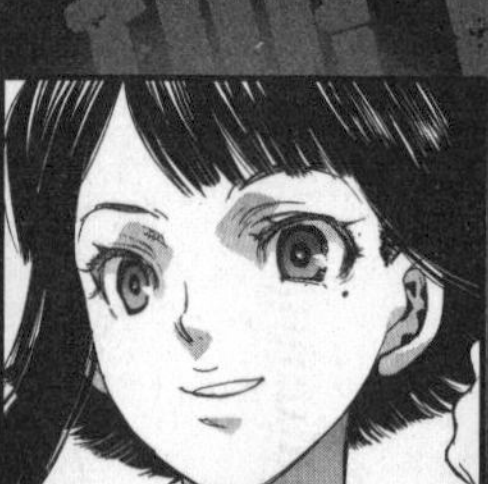

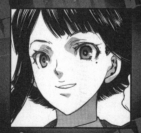

## Rosa Carlstead

The daughter of Maria and Sorum, Angel's longtime friends. She's in training now, hoping to enter the Survey Corps.

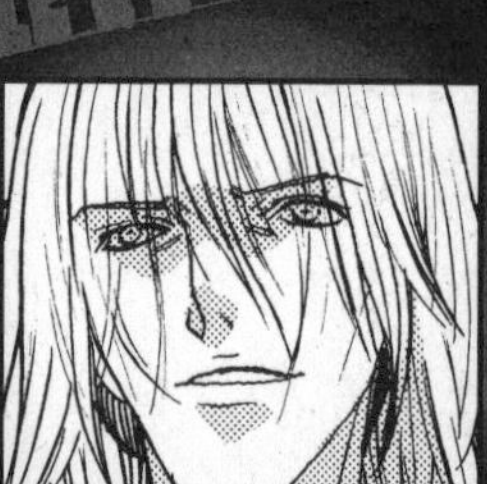

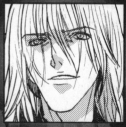

## Angel Aaltonen

A former inventor who developed a tool to fight the Titans 15 years ago, known simply as "The Device."

# The Story So Far

When a Titan terrorized Shiganshina District and left behind a pile of vomit, a baby boy was miraculously born of a pregnant corpse. This boy was named Kuklo, the "Titan's Son," and treated as a sideshow freak. Eventually the wealthy merchant Dario Inocencio bought Kuklo. Dario's daughter Sharle learned that he was human and not the son of a Titan, and decided to teach him the words and knowledge of humanity. Two years later, Kuklo escaped from the mansion along with Sharle, who was being forced into a marriage she did not desire.

In Shiganshina District, the Survey Corps was preparing for its first expedition outside the Walls in fifteen years. Kuklo snuck into the expedition's cargo wagon, but the Titan they ran across was far worse of a monster than he expected. He helped the Survey Corps survive, but inside the Walls he was greeted by the Military Police, who wanted the "Titan's Son" on charges of murdering Dario. In prison, he met Cardina, a young man jailed over political squabbles. They hoped to escape to safety when exiled beyond the Walls, but found themselves surrounded by a pack of Titans. The two boys escaped with their lives only thanks to the help of Jorge, a former Survey Corps captain. The equipment that Jorge used was the very "Device" that was the key to defeating the Titan those fifteen years earlier. Kuklo and Cardina escaped the notice of the MPs by hiding in the Industrial City, where they found Sharle. It was there that the three youngsters learned the truth of the ill-fated Titan-capturing expedition fifteen years earlier, and swore to uphold the will of Angel, the inventor of the Device.

Then, Kuklo and Cardina headed back to Shiganshina to test out a new model of the Device developed by Xenophon, Angel's friend and rival, but while they were gone, a rebellion by anti-establishment dissidents broke out in the Industrial City. Kuklo was able to slip through the chaos to rescue Sharle from the dissidents, but then Sharle's brother Xavi, now a member of the Military Police, arrived and turned his sword on Kuklo. Xavi won the battle by inflicting a grievous blow on Kuklo, who fell into the river and only survived thanks to the help of Rosa, the daughter of Sorum, who lost his life on the fateful expedition fifteen years earlier.

After a month and a half of recovery, Kuklo accepted Jorge's offer of an assistant instructor position with the Survey Corps. Sharle escaped Xavi's grasp and visited Angel, inventor of the Device, who unveiled the finished version, called the vertical maneuvering equipment. But not all of their news was good: the Survey Corps would have to embark on an expedition in just two months' time, and bring back proof that the vertical maneuvering equipment could vanquish a Titan, or the Corps would be disbanded. Captain Carlo decided to split the trainees in two: an elite training class that would use the limited equipment they could produce, and general trainees who would receive the typical Survey Corps regimen. Rosa wound up as a reserve member of the special training class, and overcame her fear of the Titans atop Wall Maria, passing the secondary selection test.

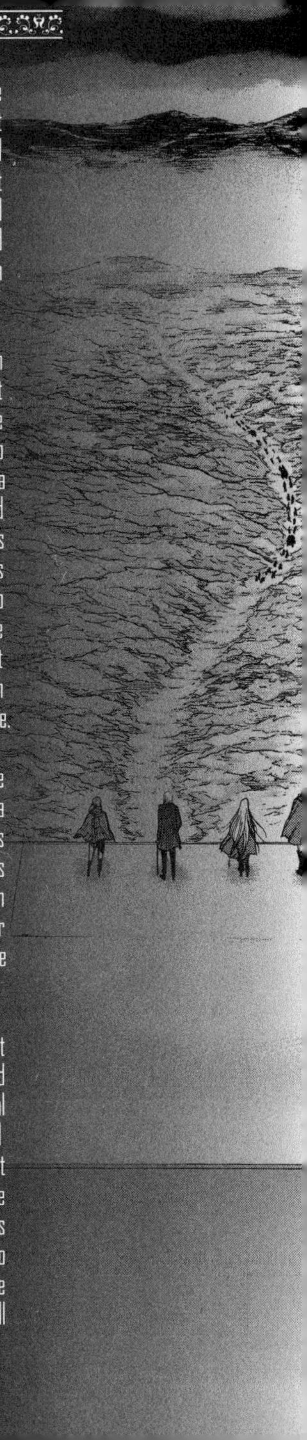

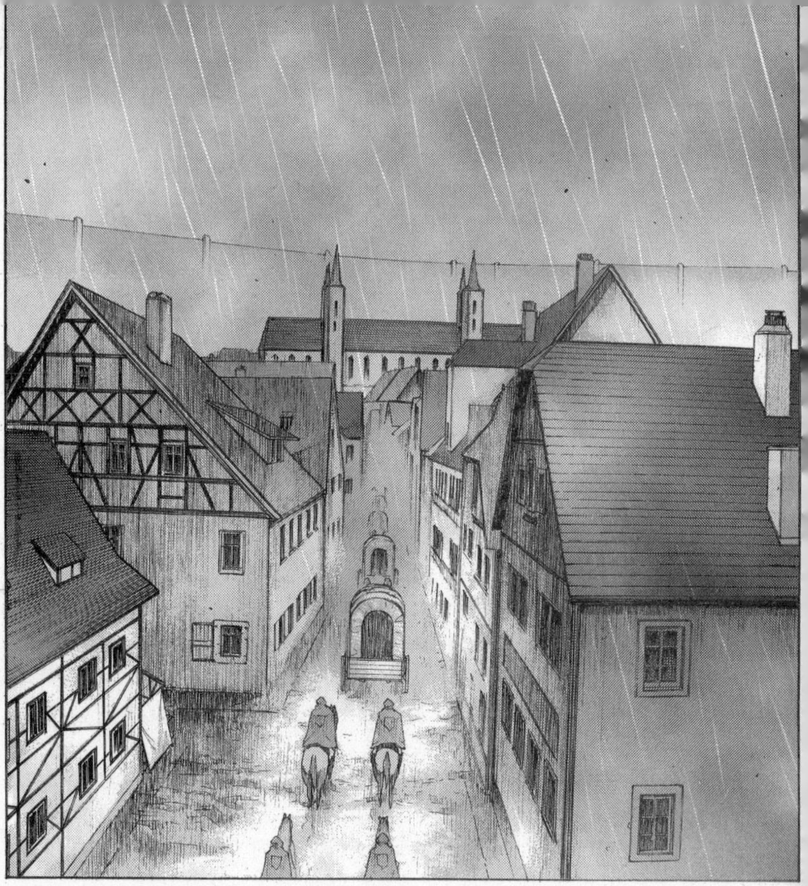
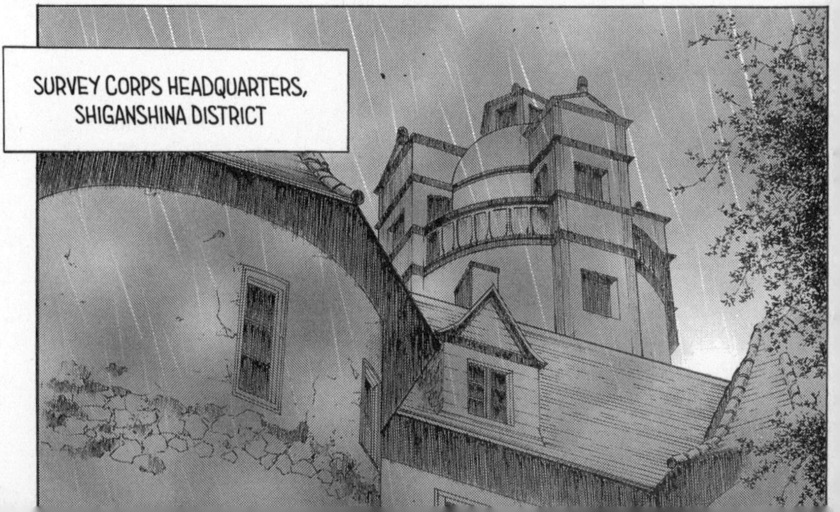
SURVEY CORPS HEADQUARTERS, SHIGANSHINA DISTRICT

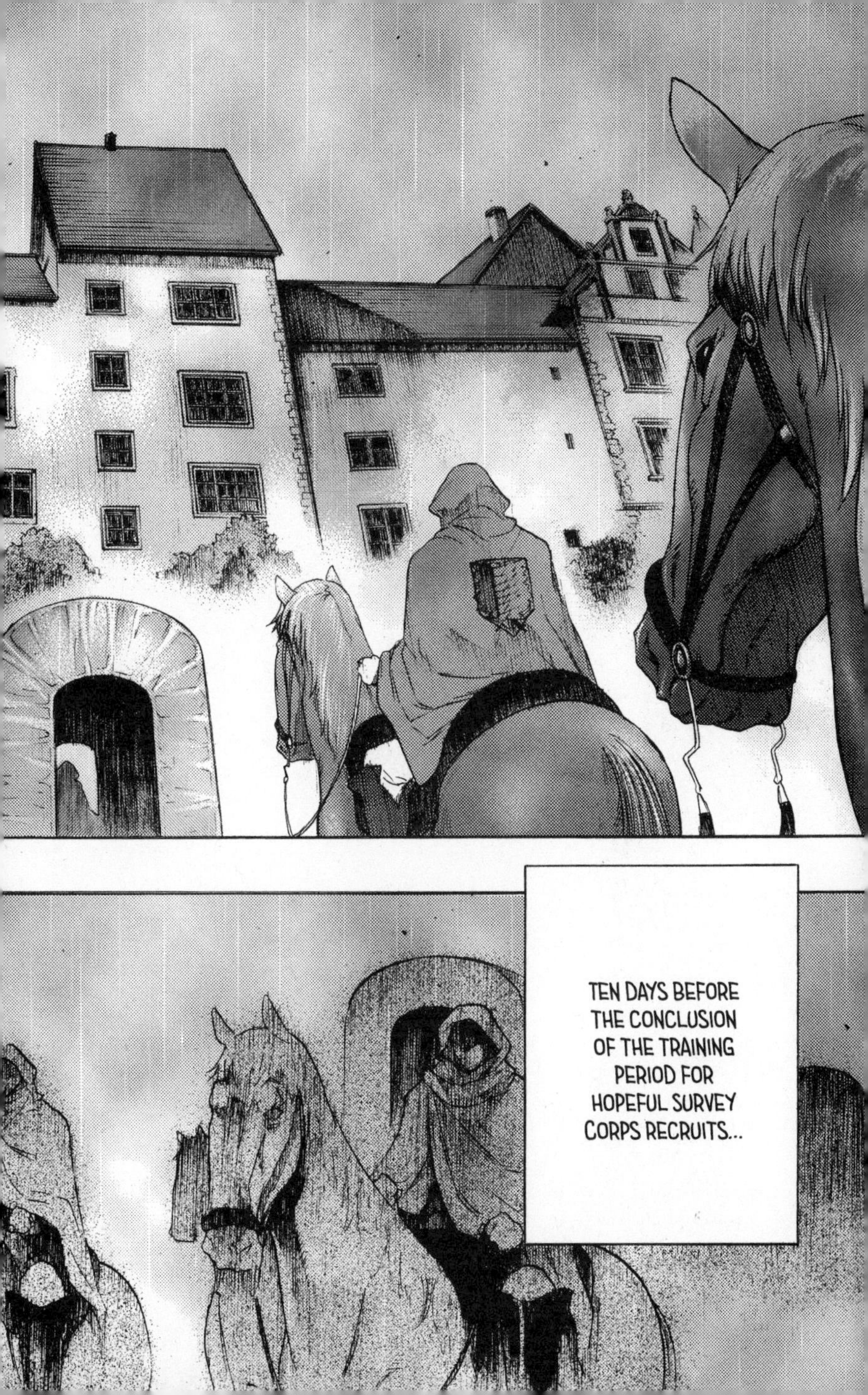
TEN DAYS BEFORE THE CONCLUSION OF THE TRAINING PERIOD FOR HOPEFUL SURVEY CORPS RECRUITS...

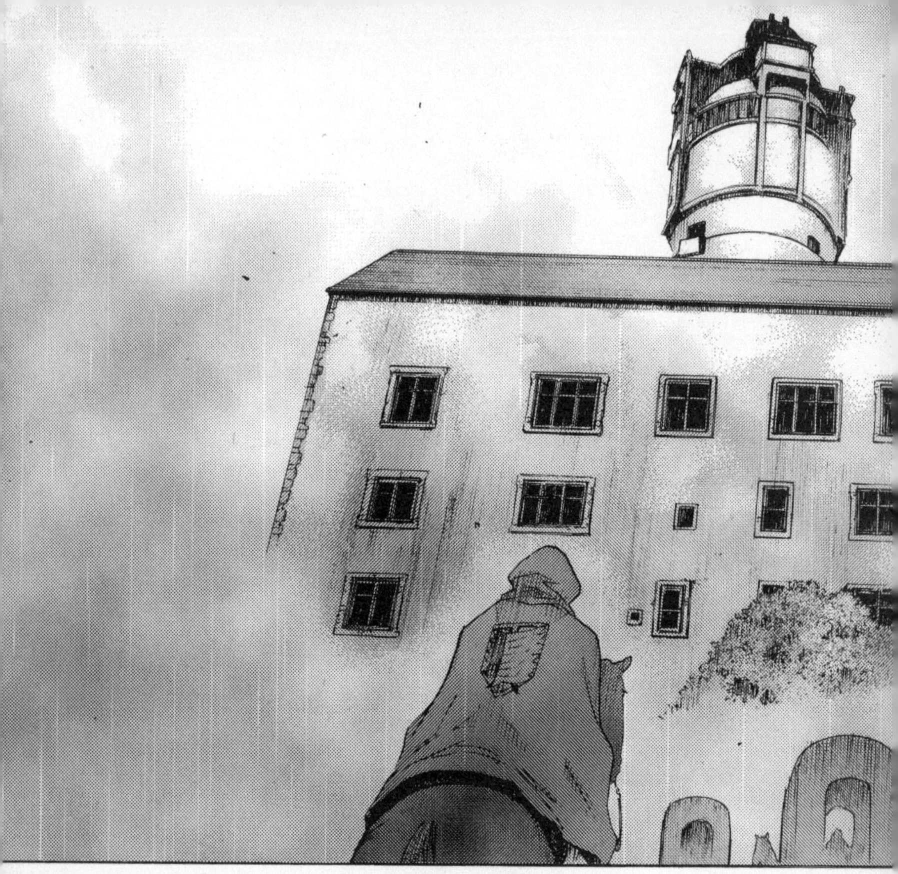
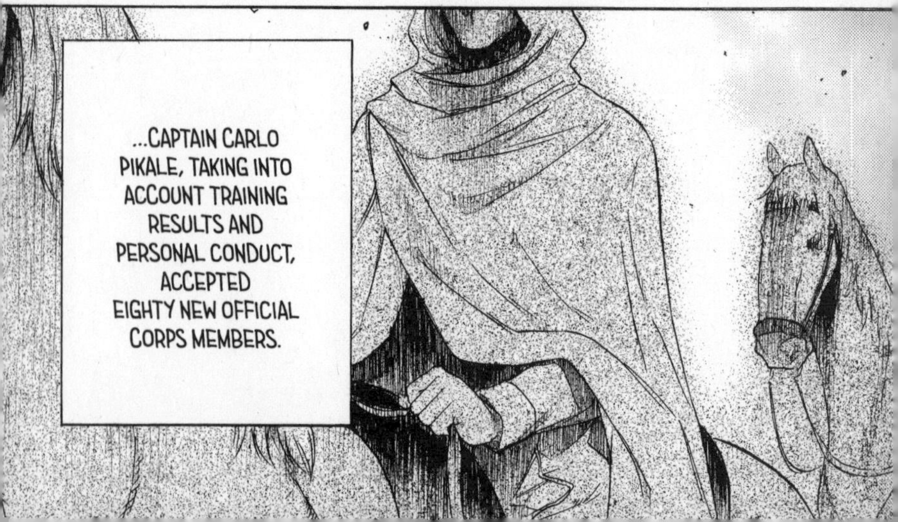
...CAPTAIN CARLO PIKALE, TAKING INTO ACCOUNT TRAINING RESULTS AND PERSONAL CONDUCT, ACCEPTED EIGHTY NEW OFFICIAL CORPS MEMBERS.

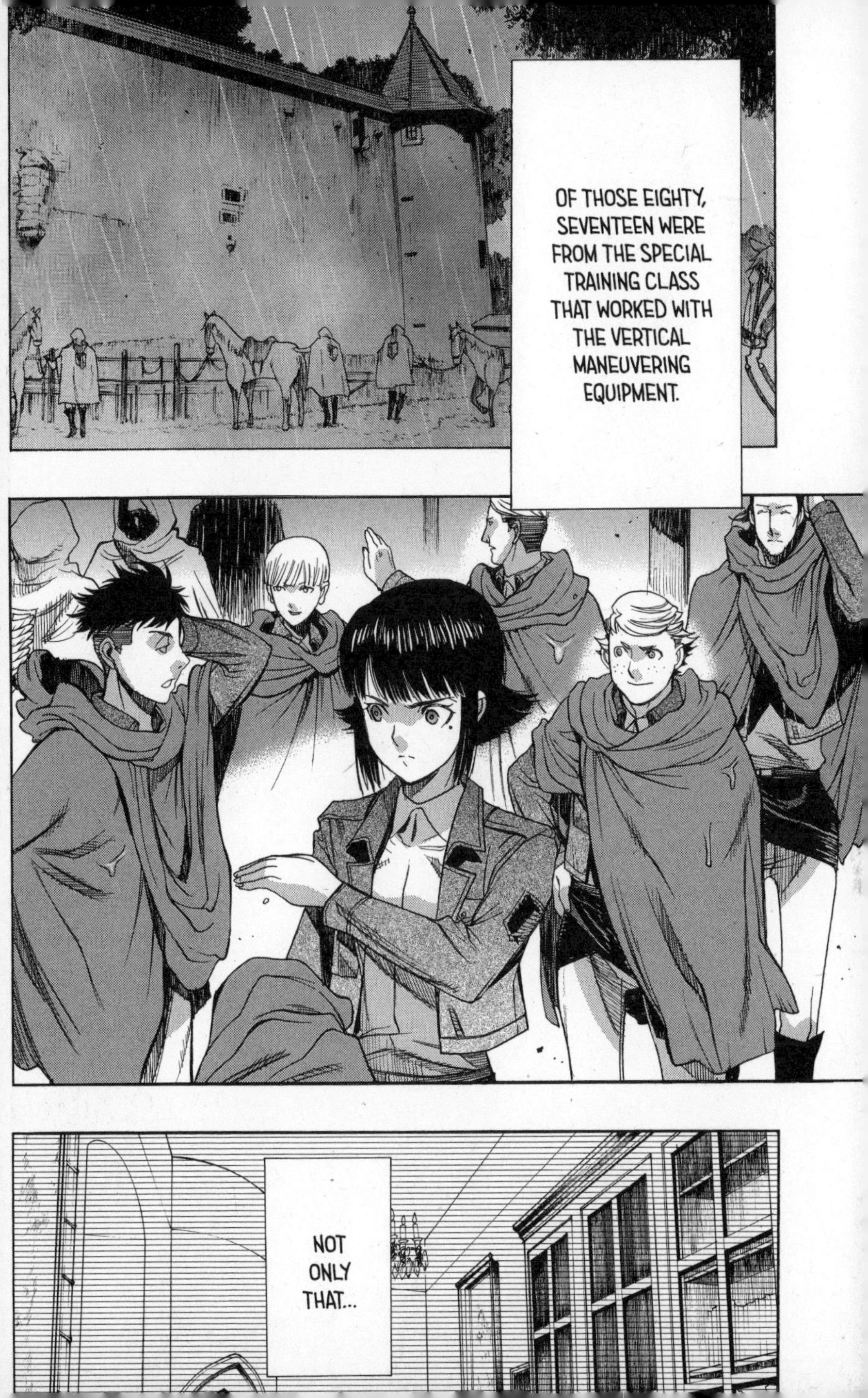
OF THOSE EIGHTY, SEVENTEEN WERE FROM THE SPECIAL TRAINING CLASS THAT WORKED WITH THE VERTICAL MANEUVERING EQUIPMENT.
NOT ONLY THAT...

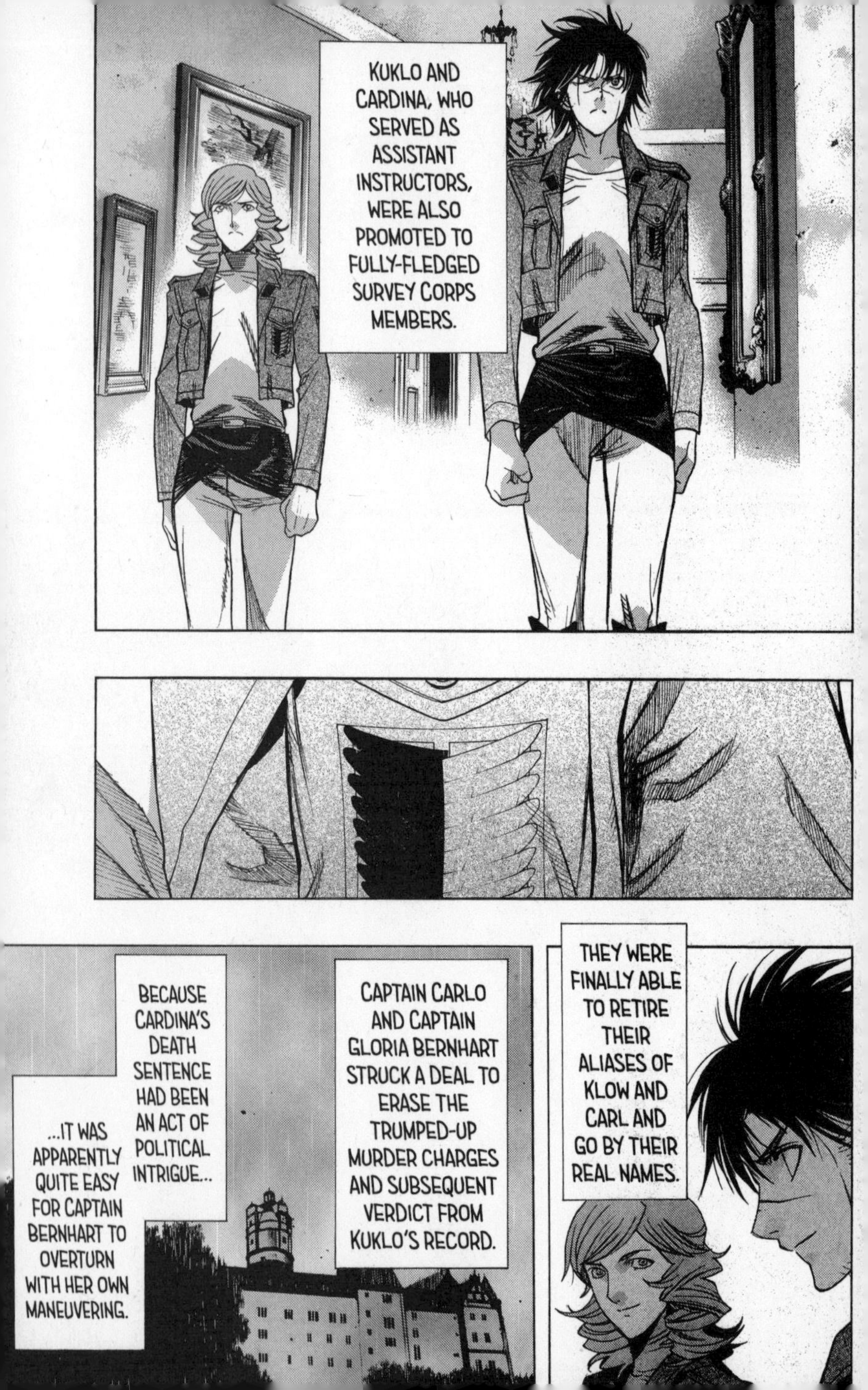
KUKLO AND CARDINA, WHO SERVED AS ASSISTANT INSTRUCTORS, WERE ALSO PROMOTED TO FULLY-FLEDGED SURVEY CORPS MEMBERS.
THEY WERE FINALLY ABLE TO RETIRE THEIR ALIASES OF KLOW AND CARL AND GO BY THEIR REAL NAMES.
CAPTAIN CARLO AND CAPTAIN GLORIA BERNHART STRUCK A DEAL TO ERASE THE TRUMPED-UP MURDER CHARGES AND SUBSEQUENT VERDICT FROM KUKLO'S RECORD.
BECAUSE CARDINA'S DEATH SENTENCE HAD BEEN AN ACT OF POLITICAL INTRIGUE...
...IT WAS APPARENTLY QUITE EASY FOR CAPTAIN BERNHART TO OVERTURN WITH HER OWN MANEUVERING.

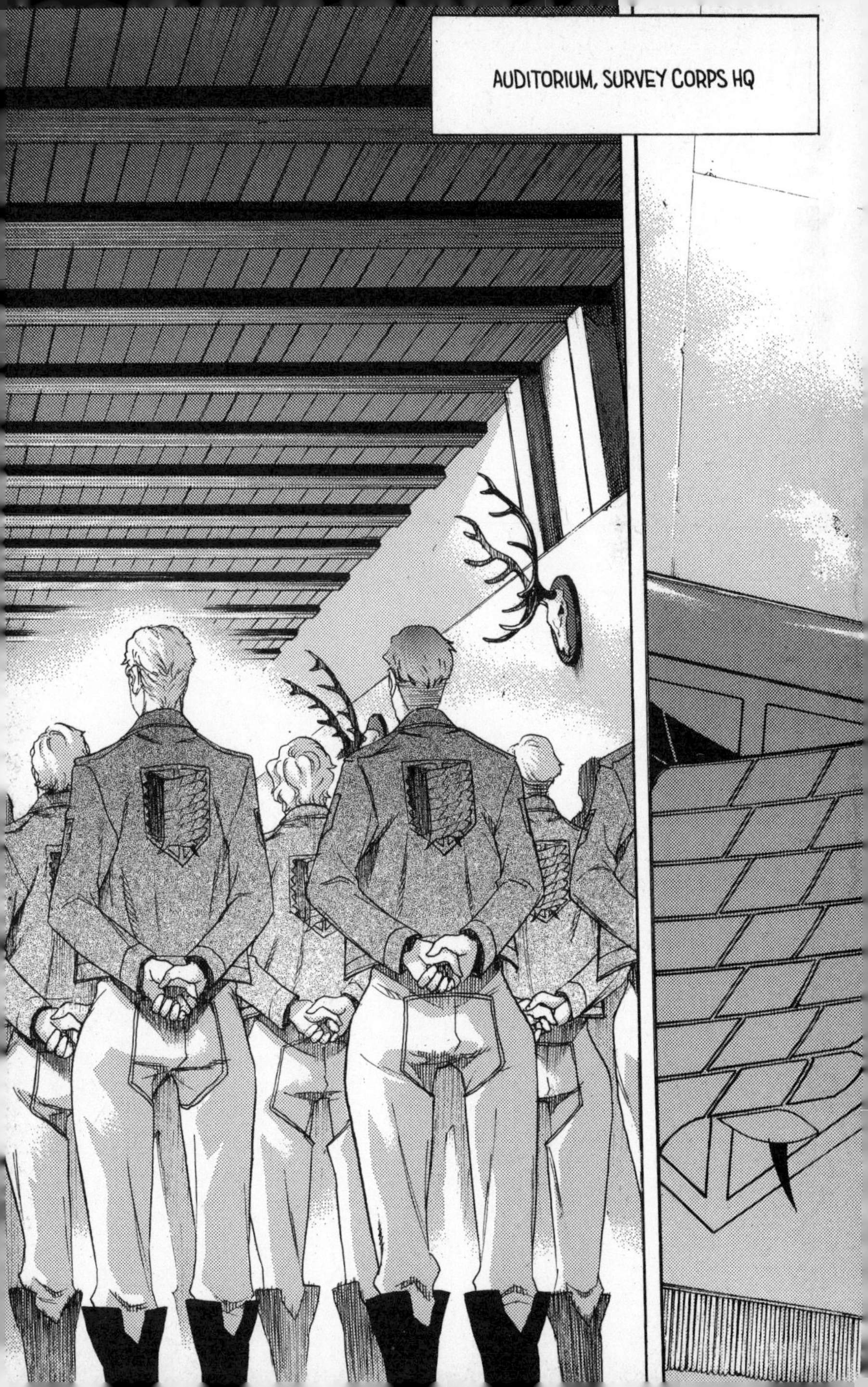
AUDITORIUM, SURVEY CORPS HQ

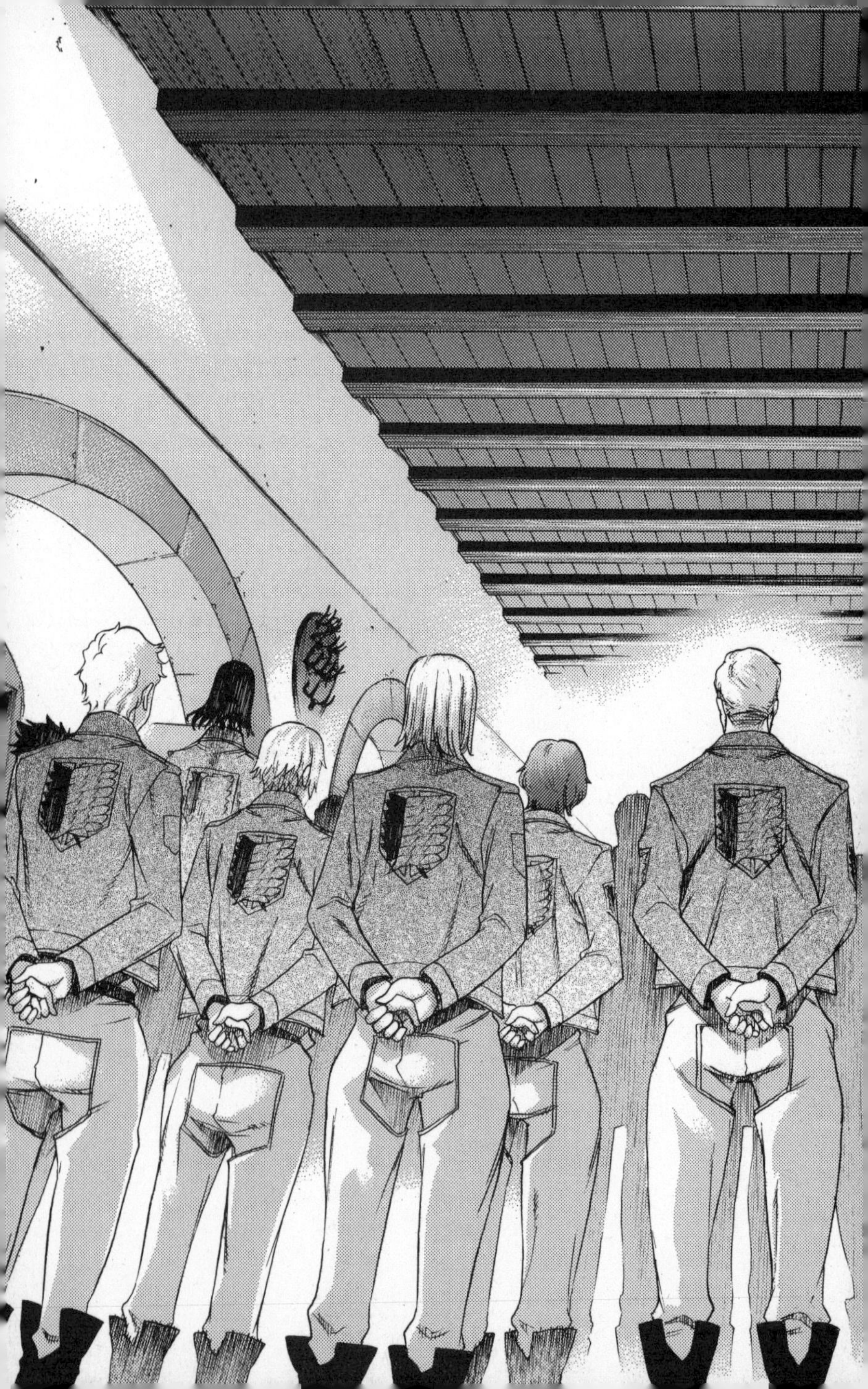

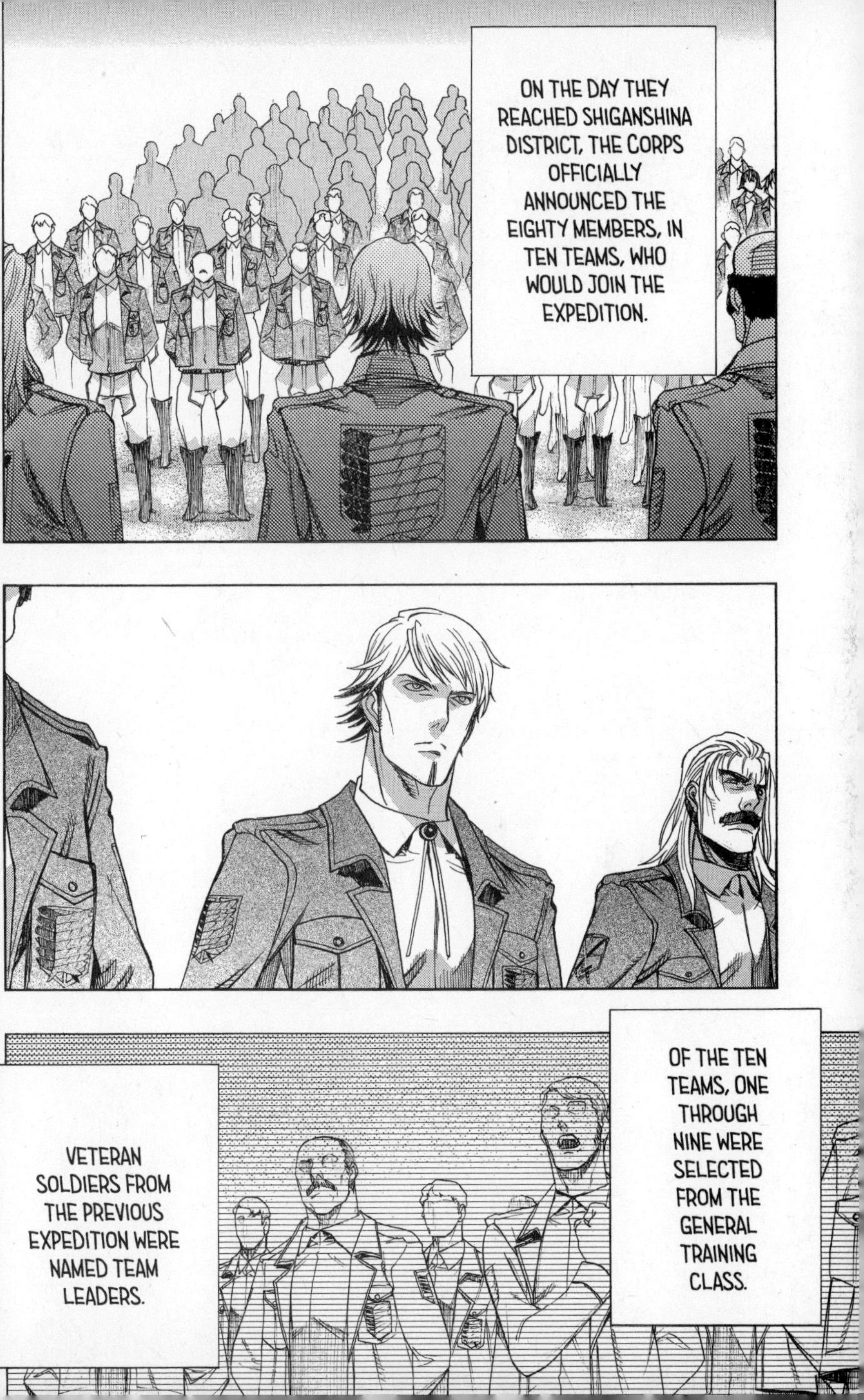
ON THE DAY THEY REACHED SHIGANSHINA DISTRICT, THE CORPS OFFICIALLY ANNOUNCED THE EIGHTY MEMBERS, IN TEN TEAMS, WHO WOULD JOIN THE EXPEDITION.
OF THE TEN TEAMS, ONE THROUGH NINE WERE SELECTED FROM THE GENERAL TRAINING CLASS.
VETERAN SOLDIERS FROM THE PREVIOUS EXPEDITION WERE NAMED TEAM LEADERS.

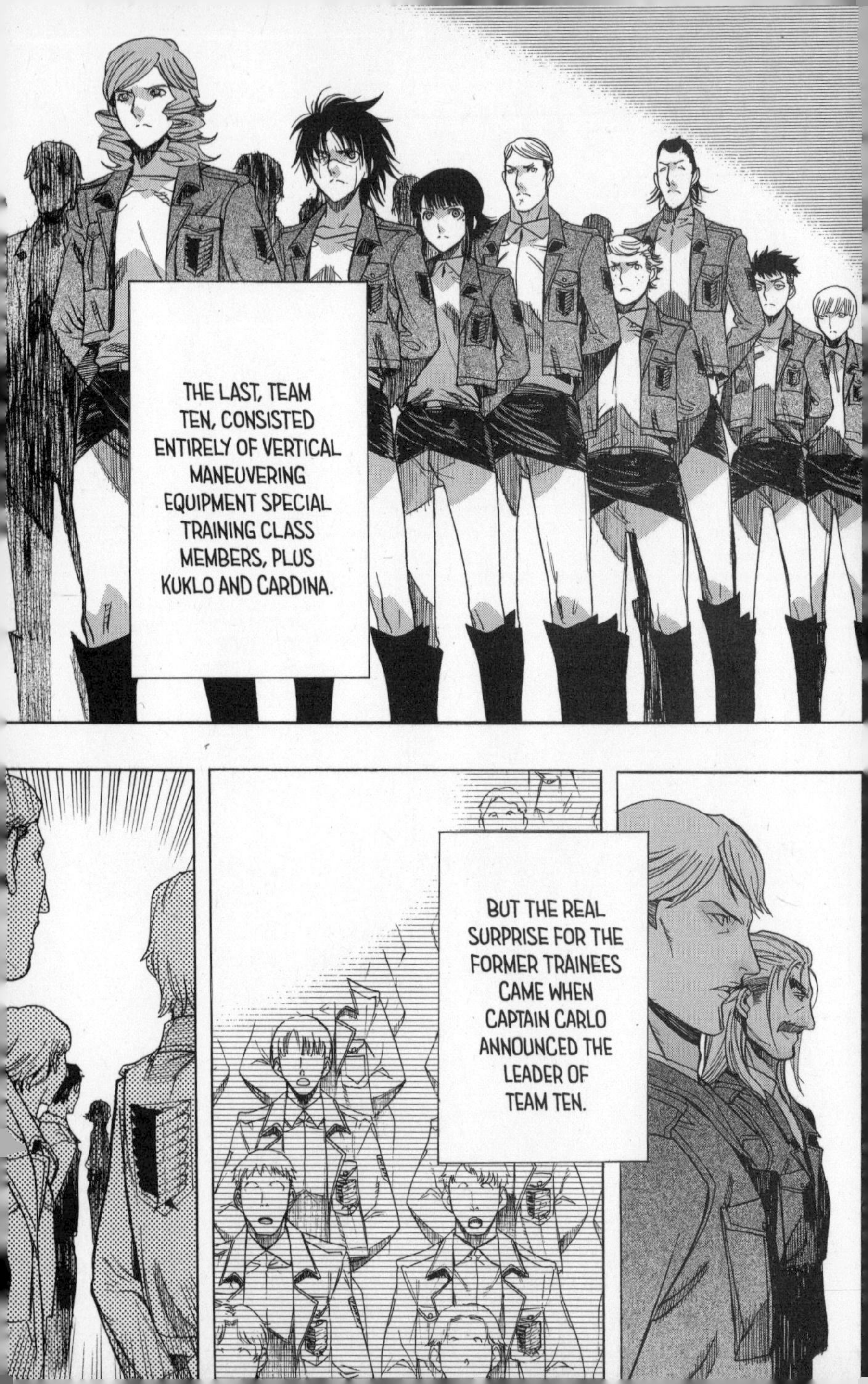
THE LAST, TEAM TEN, CONSISTED ENTIRELY OF VERTICAL MANEUVERING EQUIPMENT SPECIAL TRAINING CLASS MEMBERS, PLUS KUKLO AND CARDINA.
BUT THE REAL SURPRISE FOR THE FORMER TRAINEES CAME WHEN CAPTAIN CARLO ANNOUNCED THE LEADER OF TEAM TEN.

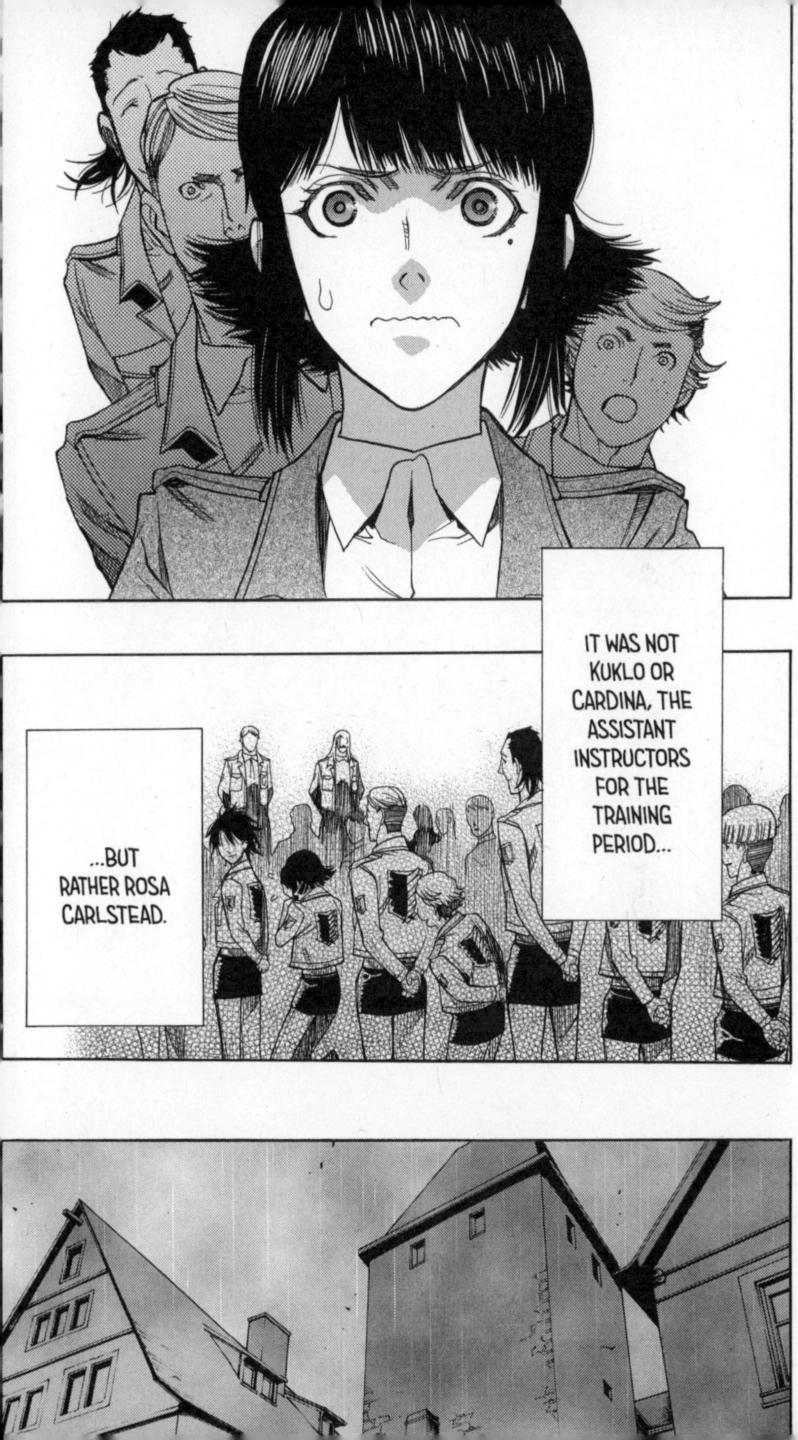
IT WAS NOT KUKLO OR CARDINA, THE ASSISTANT INSTRUCTORS FOR THE TRAINING PERIOD...
...BUT RATHER ROSA CARLSTEAD.

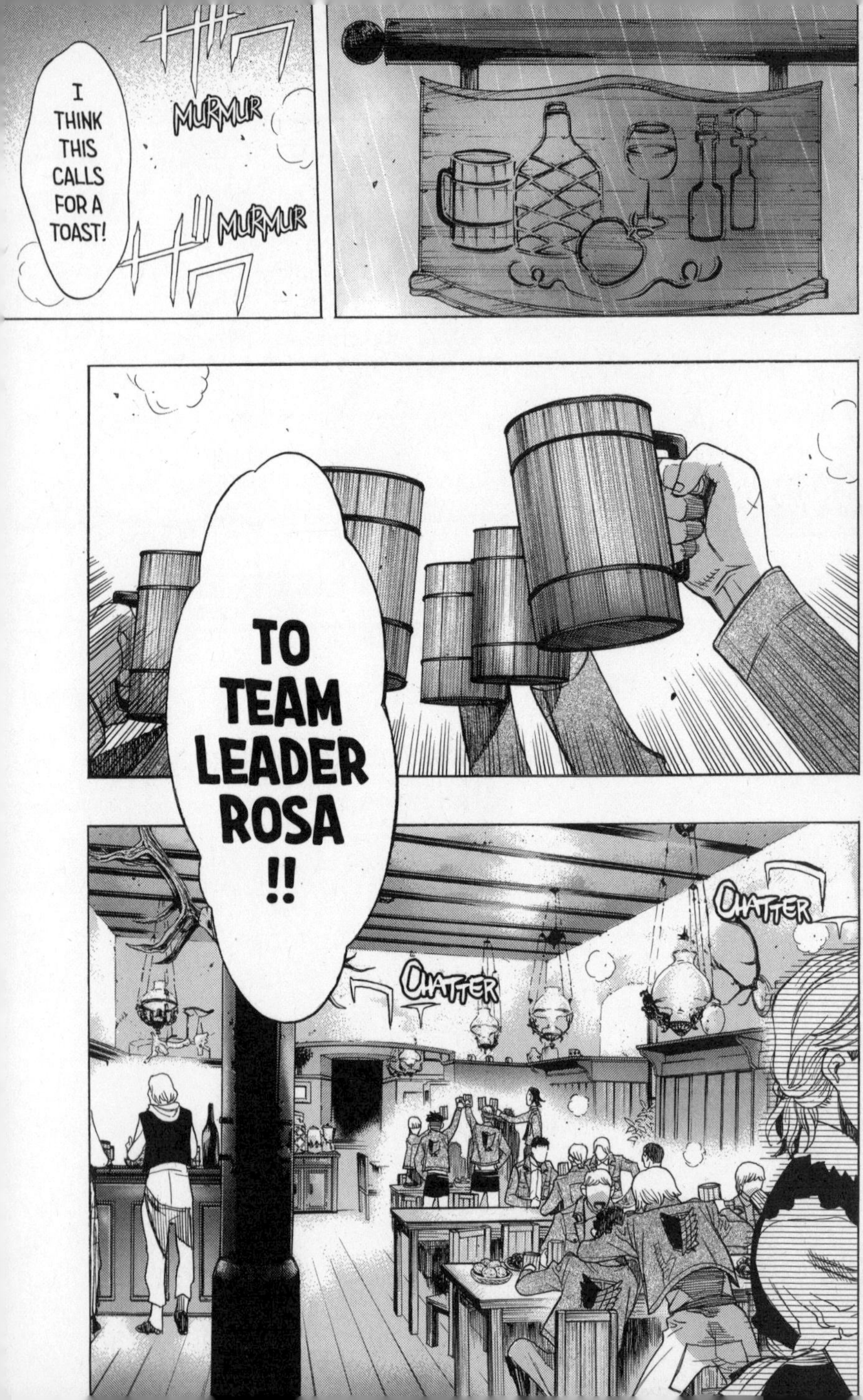
MURMUR
MURMUR
I THINK THIS CALLS FOR A TOAST!
TO TEAM LEADER ROSA !!
CHATTER
CHATTER

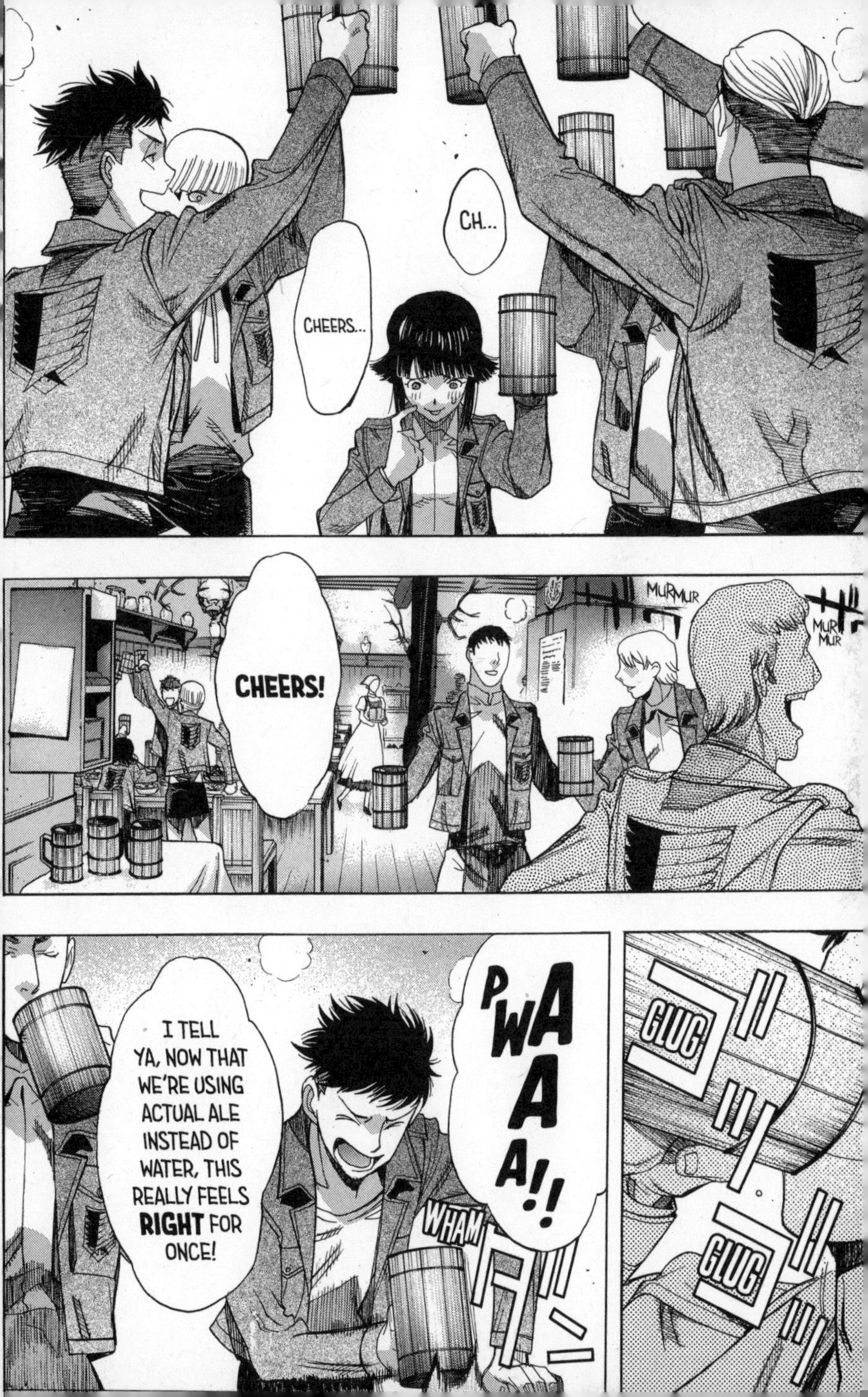
CH...
CHEERS...
MURMUR
MUR MUR
CHEERS!
GLUG
GLUG
PWAAAA!!
WHAM
I TELL YA, NOW THAT WE'RE USING ACTUAL ALE INSTEAD OF WATER, THIS REALLY FEELS RIGHT FOR ONCE!

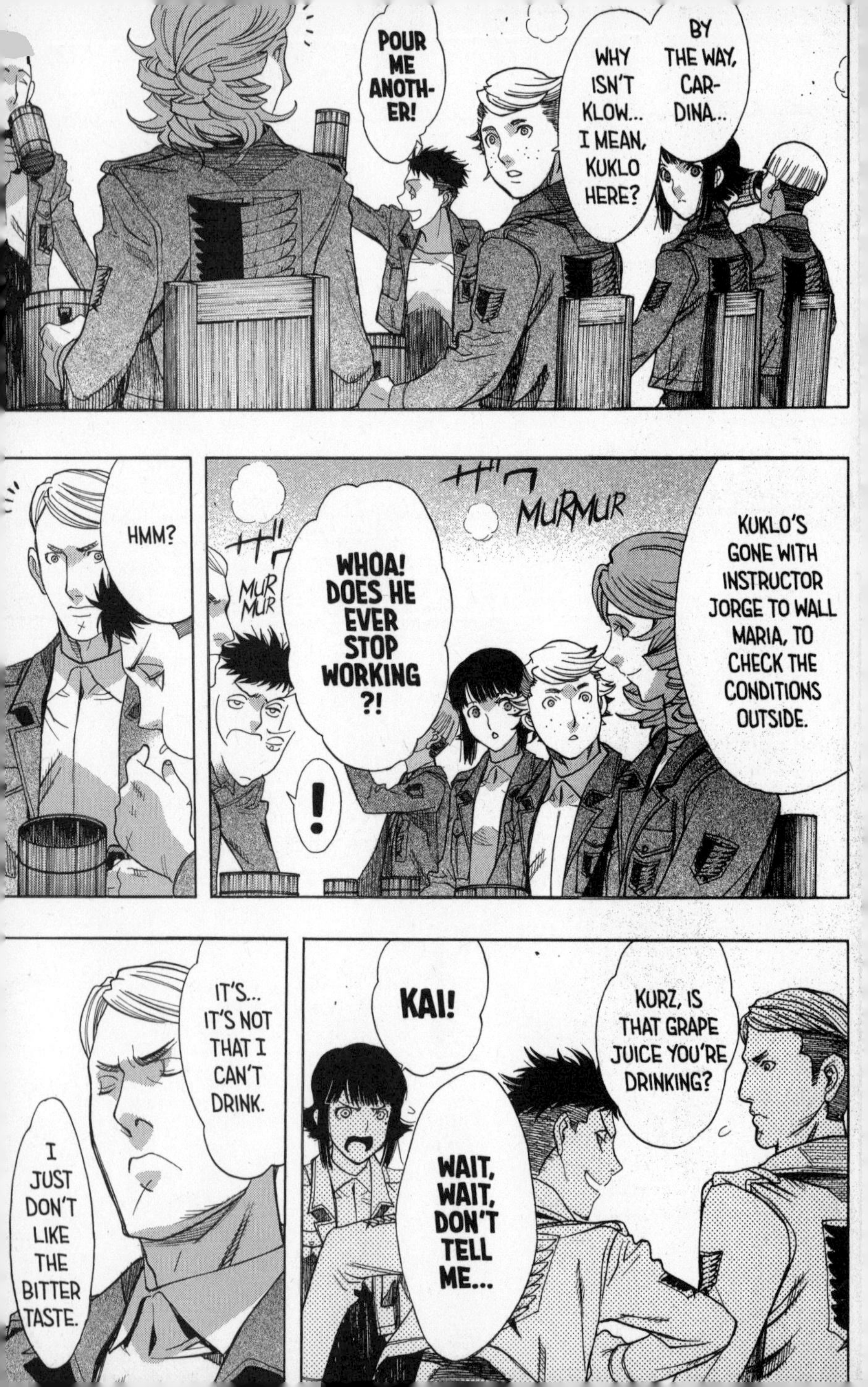
BY THE WAY, CARDINA...
WHY ISN'T KLOW... I MEAN, KUKLO HERE?
POUR ME ANOTHER!
KUKLO'S GONE WITH INSTRUCTOR JORGE TO WALL MARIA, TO CHECK THE CONDITIONS OUTSIDE.
MURMUR
WHOA! DOES HE EVER STOP WORKING?!
MUR MUR
!
HMM?
KURZ, IS THAT GRAPE JUICE YOU'RE DRINKING?
KAI!
WAIT, WAIT, DON'T TELL ME...
IT'S... IT'S NOT THAT I CAN'T DRINK.
I JUST DON'T LIKE THE BITTER TASTE.

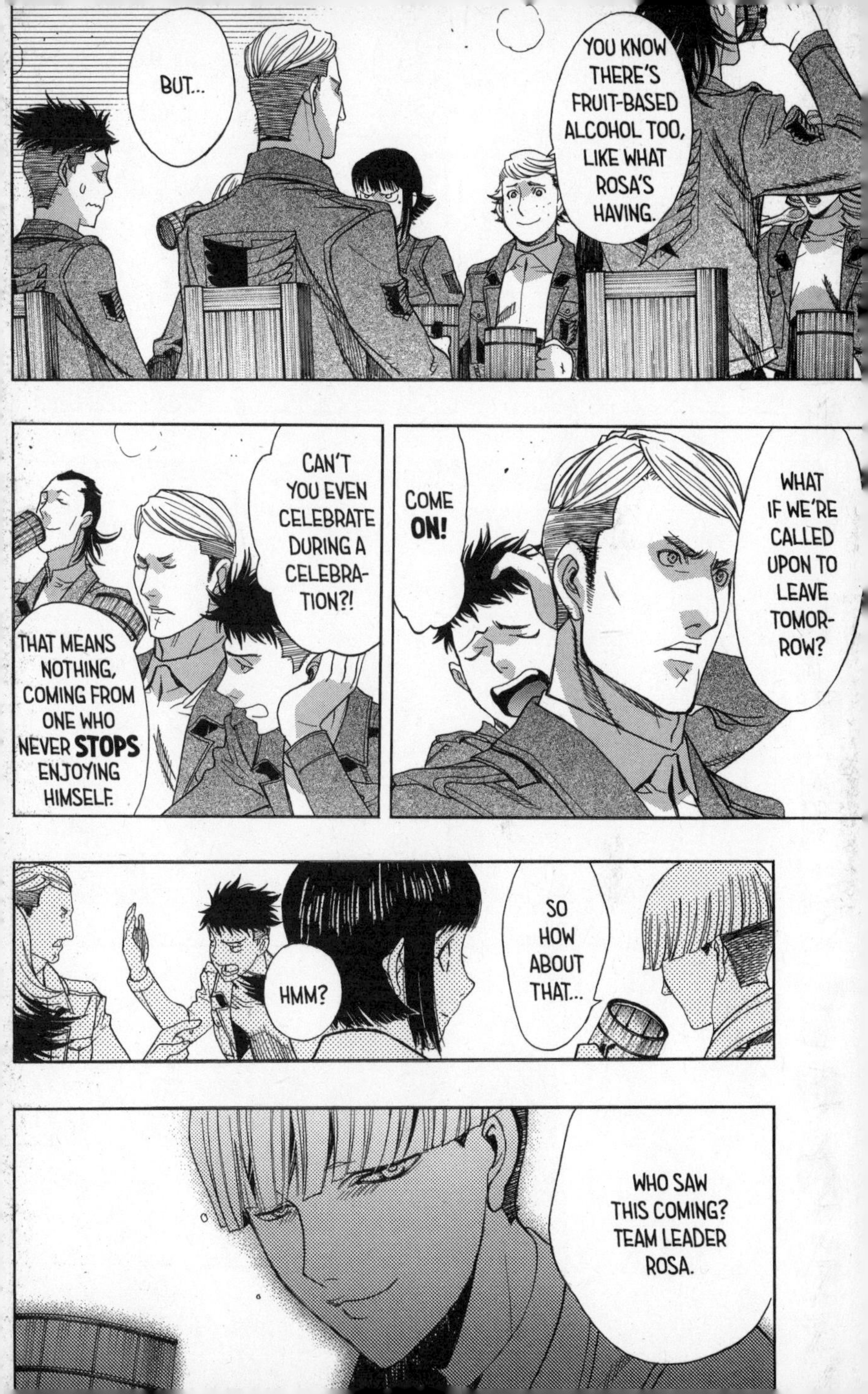
YOU KNOW THERE'S FRUIT-BASED ALCOHOL TOO, LIKE WHAT ROSA'S HAVING.
BUT...
WHAT IF WE'RE CALLED UPON TO LEAVE TOMORROW?
COME ON!
CAN'T YOU EVEN CELEBRATE DURING A CELEBRATION?!
THAT MEANS NOTHING, COMING FROM ONE WHO NEVER STOPS ENJOYING HIMSELF.
SO HOW ABOUT THAT...
HMM?
WHO SAW THIS COMING? TEAM LEADER ROSA.

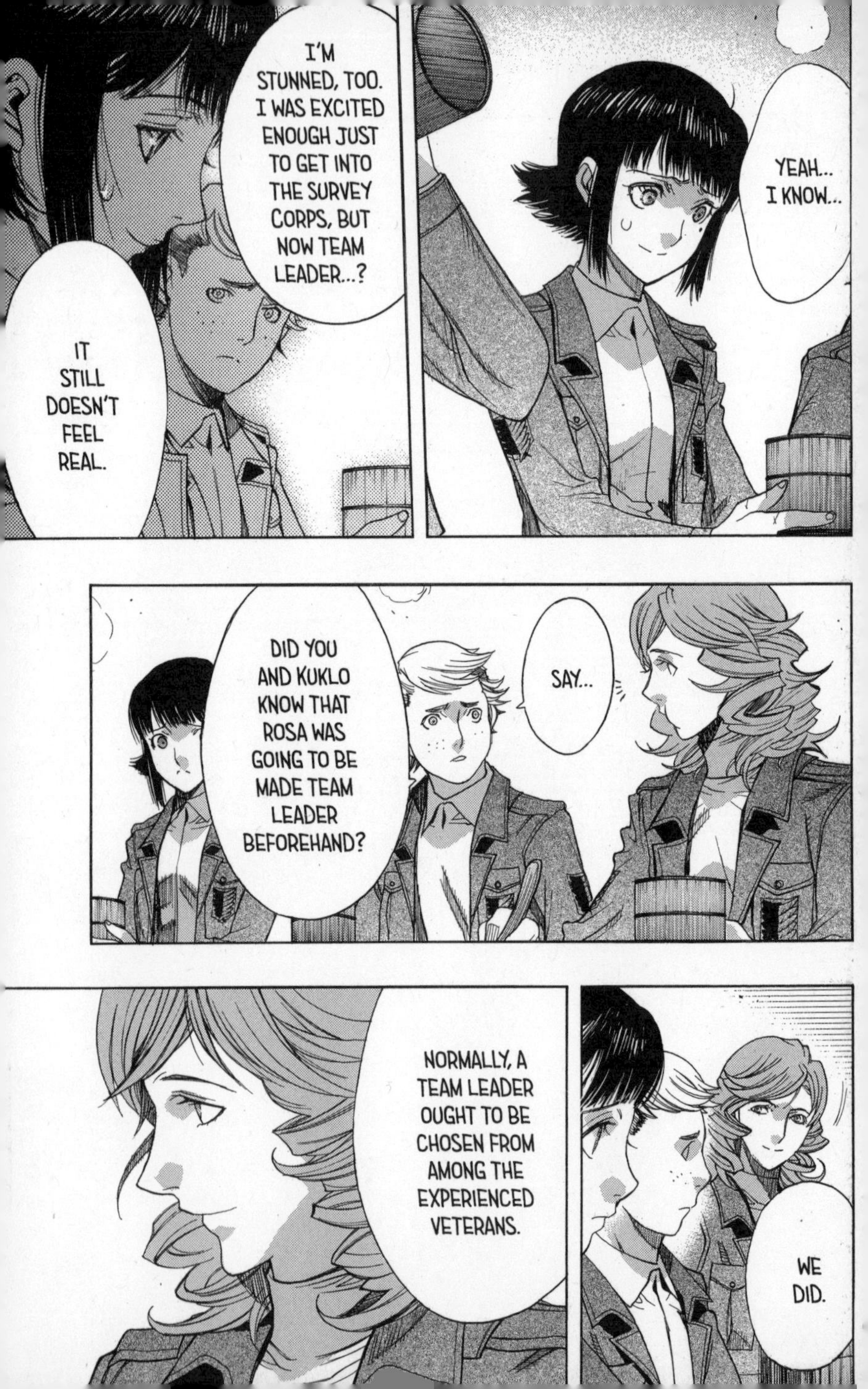
YEAH... I KNOW...
I'M STUNNED, TOO. I WAS EXCITED ENOUGH JUST TO GET INTO THE SURVEY CORPS, BUT NOW TEAM LEADER...?
IT STILL DOESN'T FEEL REAL.
SAY...
DID YOU AND KUKLO KNOW THAT ROSA WAS GOING TO BE MADE TEAM LEADER BEFOREHAND?
WE DID.
NORMALLY, A TEAM LEADER OUGHT TO BE CHOSEN FROM AMONG THE EXPERIENCED VETERANS.

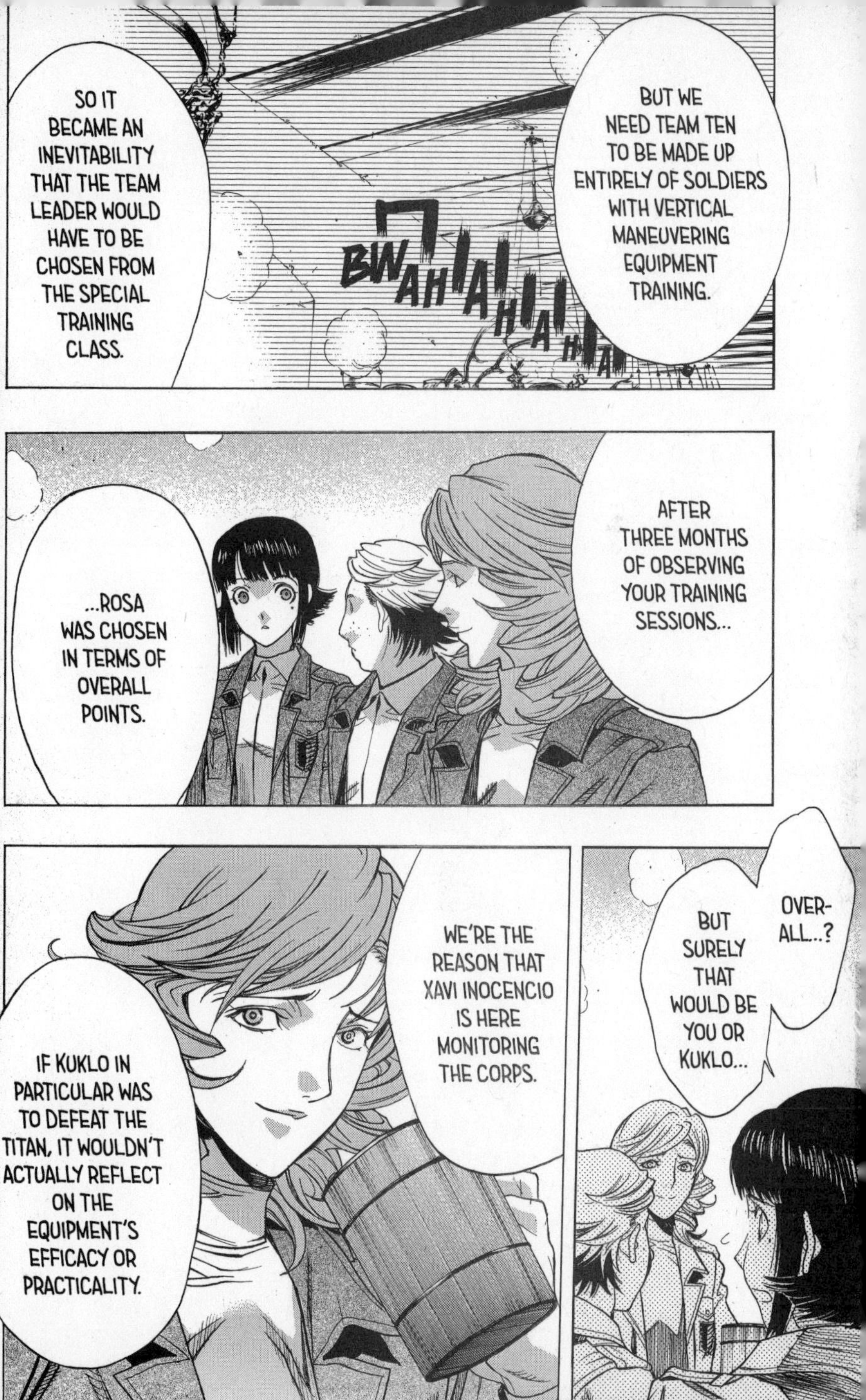
BUT WE NEED TEAM TEN TO BE MADE UP ENTIRELY OF SOLDIERS WITH VERTICAL MANEUVERING EQUIPMENT TRAINING.
BWAHAHAHAHA
SO IT BECAME AN INEVITABILITY THAT THE TEAM LEADER WOULD HAVE TO BE CHOSEN FROM THE SPECIAL TRAINING CLASS.
AFTER THREE MONTHS OF OBSERVING YOUR TRAINING SESSIONS...
...ROSA WAS CHOSEN IN TERMS OF OVERALL POINTS.
OVER-ALL...?
BUT SURELY THAT WOULD BE YOU OR KUKLO...
WE'RE THE REASON THAT XAVI INOCENCIO IS HERE MONITORING THE CORPS.
IF KUKLO IN PARTICULAR WAS TO DEFEAT THE TITAN, IT WOULDN'T ACTUALLY REFLECT ON THE EQUIPMENT'S EFFICACY OR PRACTICALITY.

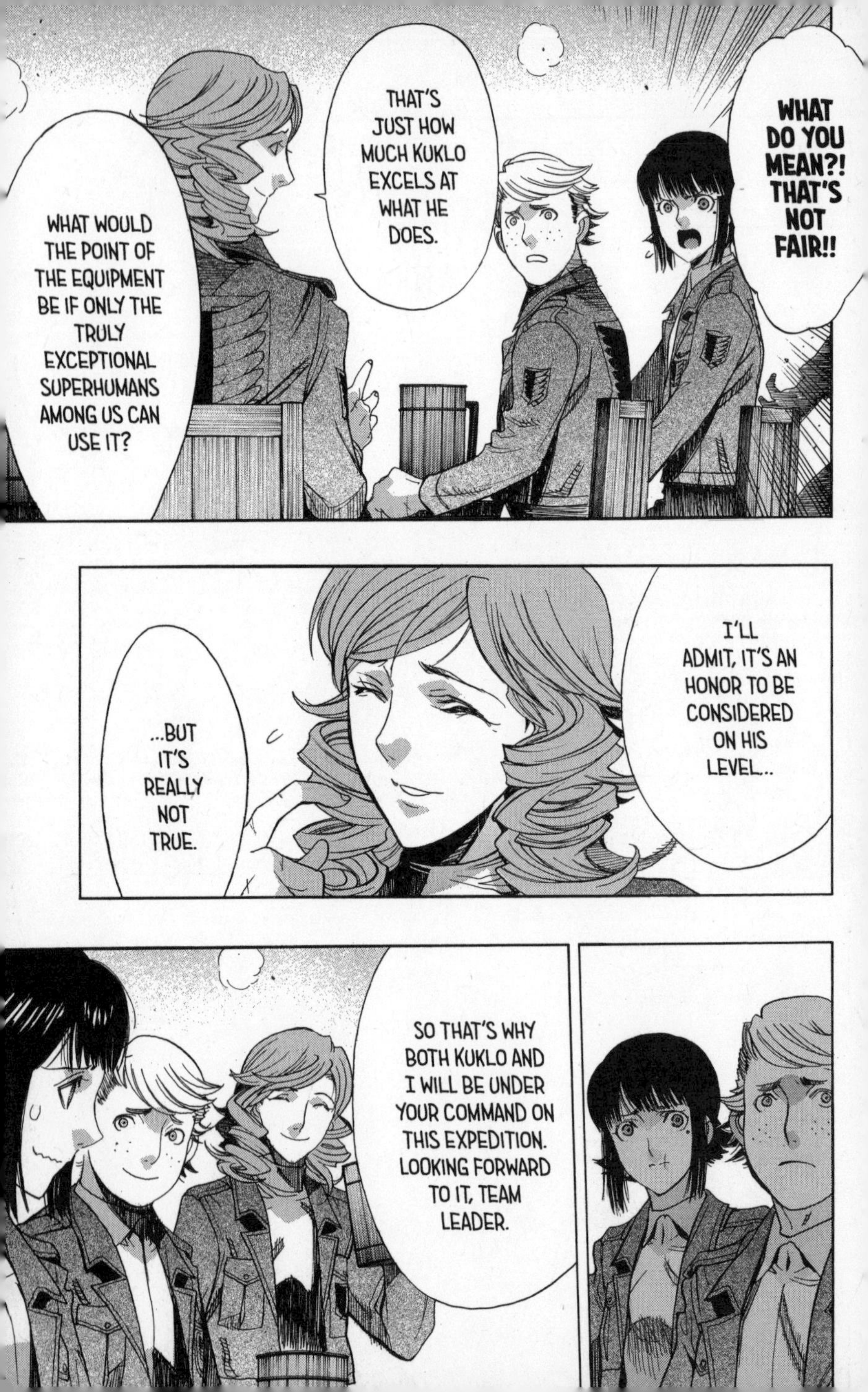
WHAT DO YOU MEAN?! THAT'S NOT FAIR!!
THAT'S JUST HOW MUCH KUKLO EXCELS AT WHAT HE DOES.
WHAT WOULD THE POINT OF THE EQUIPMENT BE IF ONLY THE TRULY EXCEPTIONAL SUPERHUMANS AMONG US CAN USE IT?
I'LL ADMIT, IT'S AN HONOR TO BE CONSIDERED ON HIS LEVEL...
...BUT IT'S REALLY NOT TRUE.
SO THAT'S WHY BOTH KUKLO AND I WILL BE UNDER YOUR COMMAND ON THIS EXPEDITION. LOOKING FORWARD TO IT, TEAM LEADER.

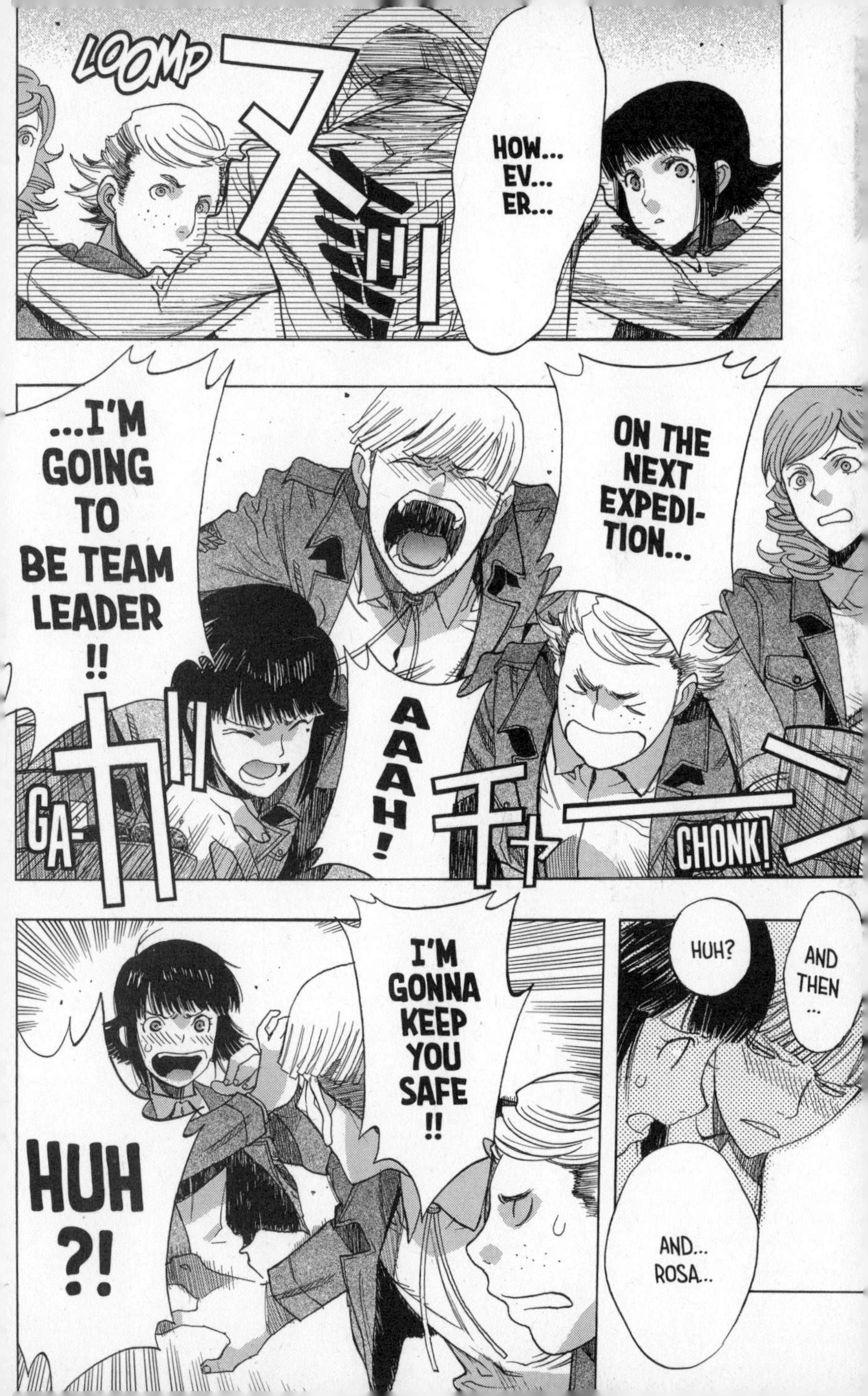
HOW... EV... ER...
LOOMP
ON THE NEXT EXPEDITION...
...I'M GOING TO BE TEAM LEADER!!
CHONK!
AAAH!
GA-
AND THEN ...
HUH?
AND... ROSA...
I'M GONNA KEEP YOU SAFE!!
HUH?!

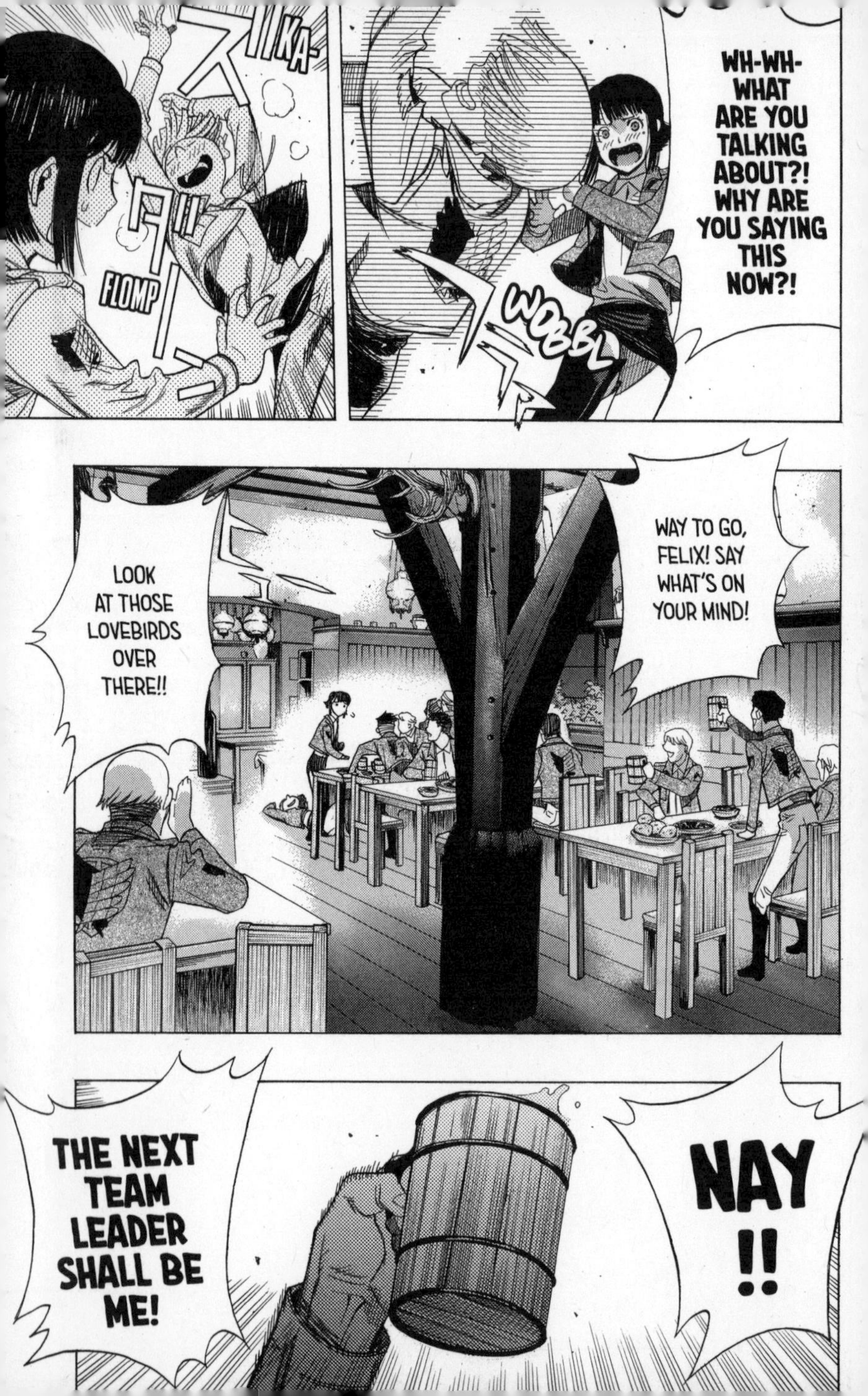
WH-WH-WHAT ARE YOU TALKING ABOUT?! WHY ARE YOU SAYING THIS NOW?!
WOBBL
KA-
FLOMP
WAY TO GO, FELIX! SAY WHAT'S ON YOUR MIND!
LOOK AT THOSE LOVEBIRDS OVER THERE!!
NAY!!
THE NEXT TEAM LEADER SHALL BE ME!

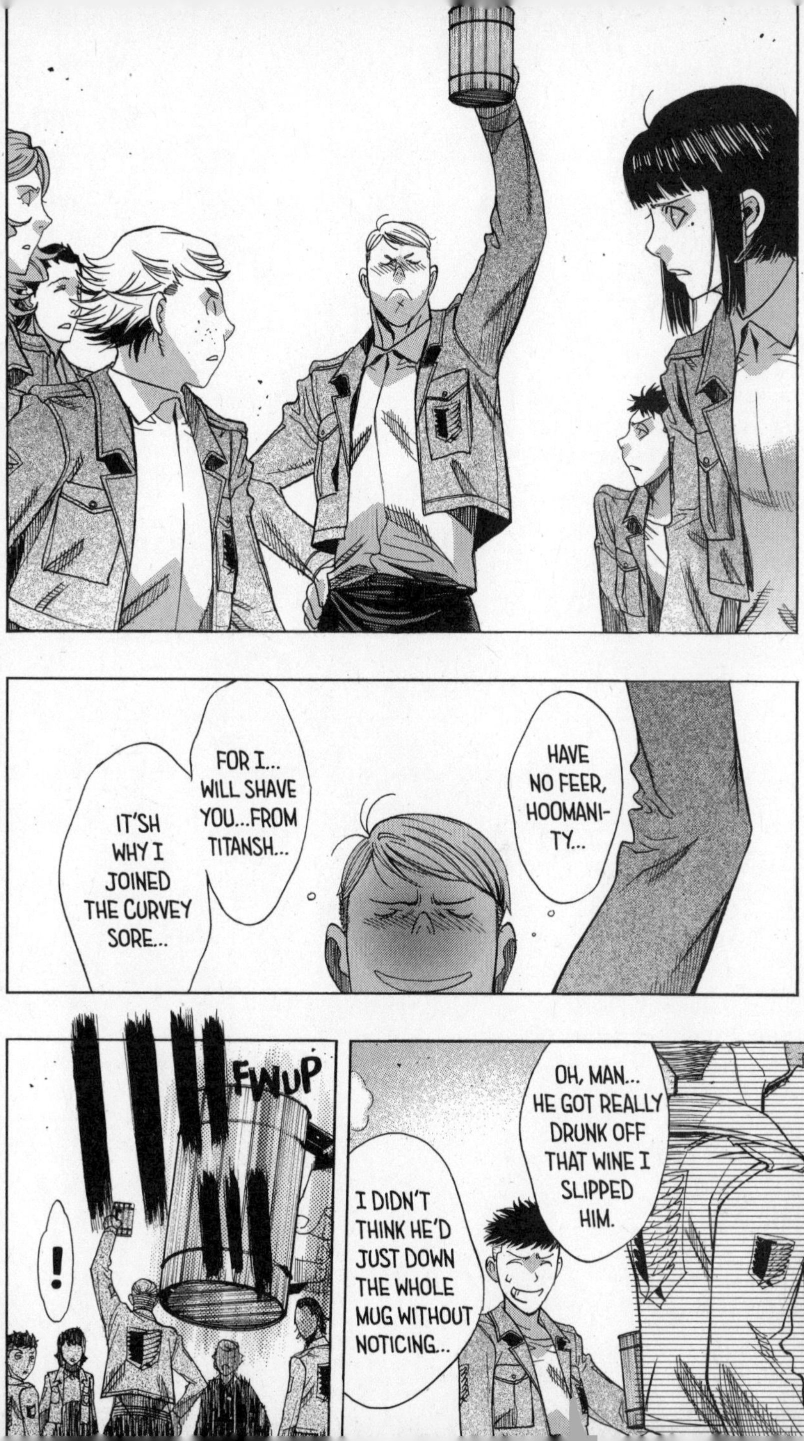
HAVE NO FEER, HOOMANI-TY...
FOR I... WILL SHAVE YOU...FROM TITANSH...
IT'SH WHY I JOINED THE CURVEY SORE...
OH, MAN... HE GOT REALLY DRUNK OFF THAT WINE I SLIPPED HIM.
I DIDN'T THINK HE'D JUST DOWN THE WHOLE MUG WITHOUT NOTICING...
FWUP
!

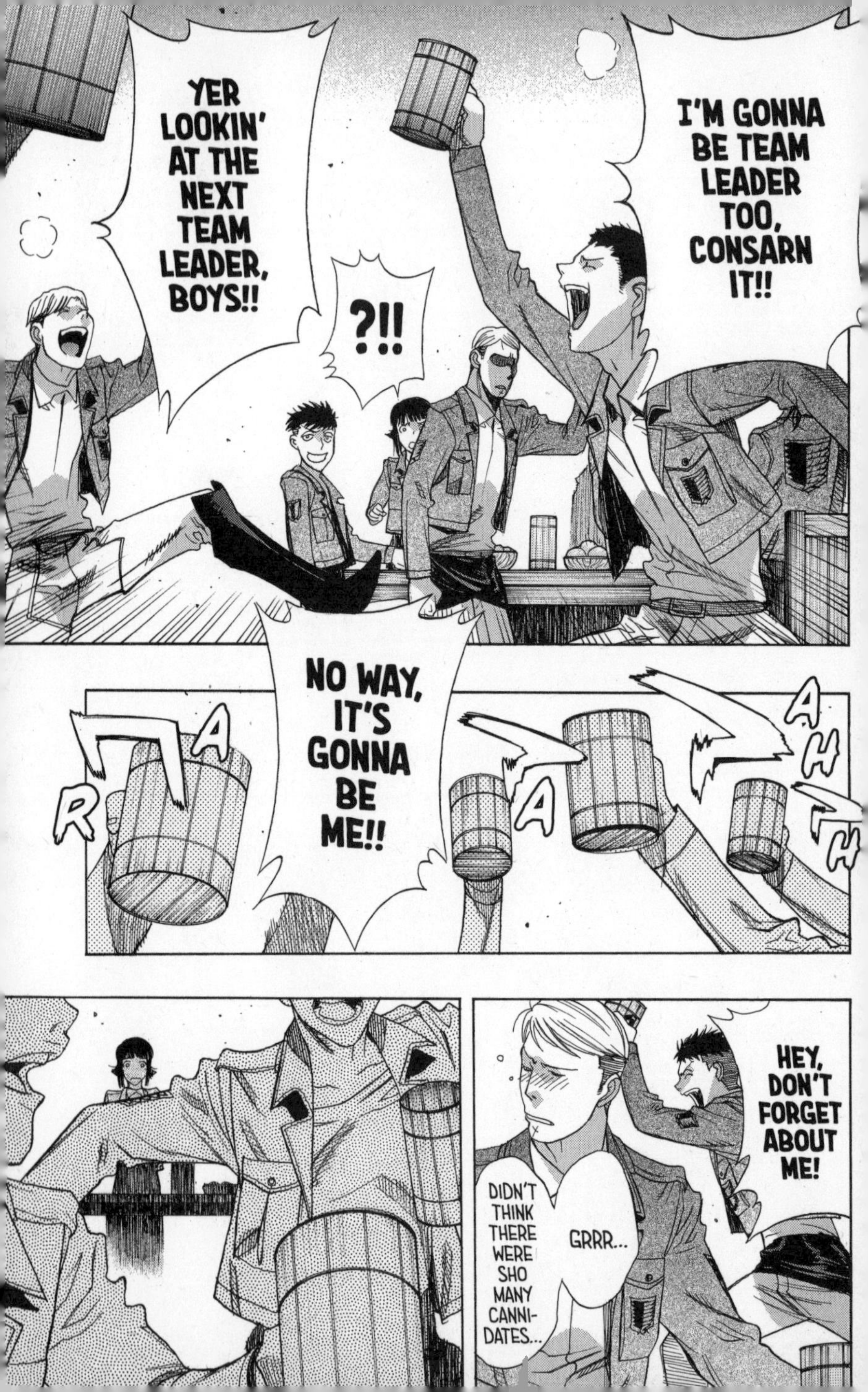

I'M GONNA BE TEAM LEADER TOO, CONSARN IT!!
YER LOOKIN' AT THE NEXT TEAM LEADER, BOYS!!
?!!
AHH
A
NO WAY, IT'S GONNA BE ME!!
A
R
HEY, DON'T FORGET ABOUT ME!
GRRR...
DIDN'T THINK THERE WERE SHO MANY CANNI-DATES...

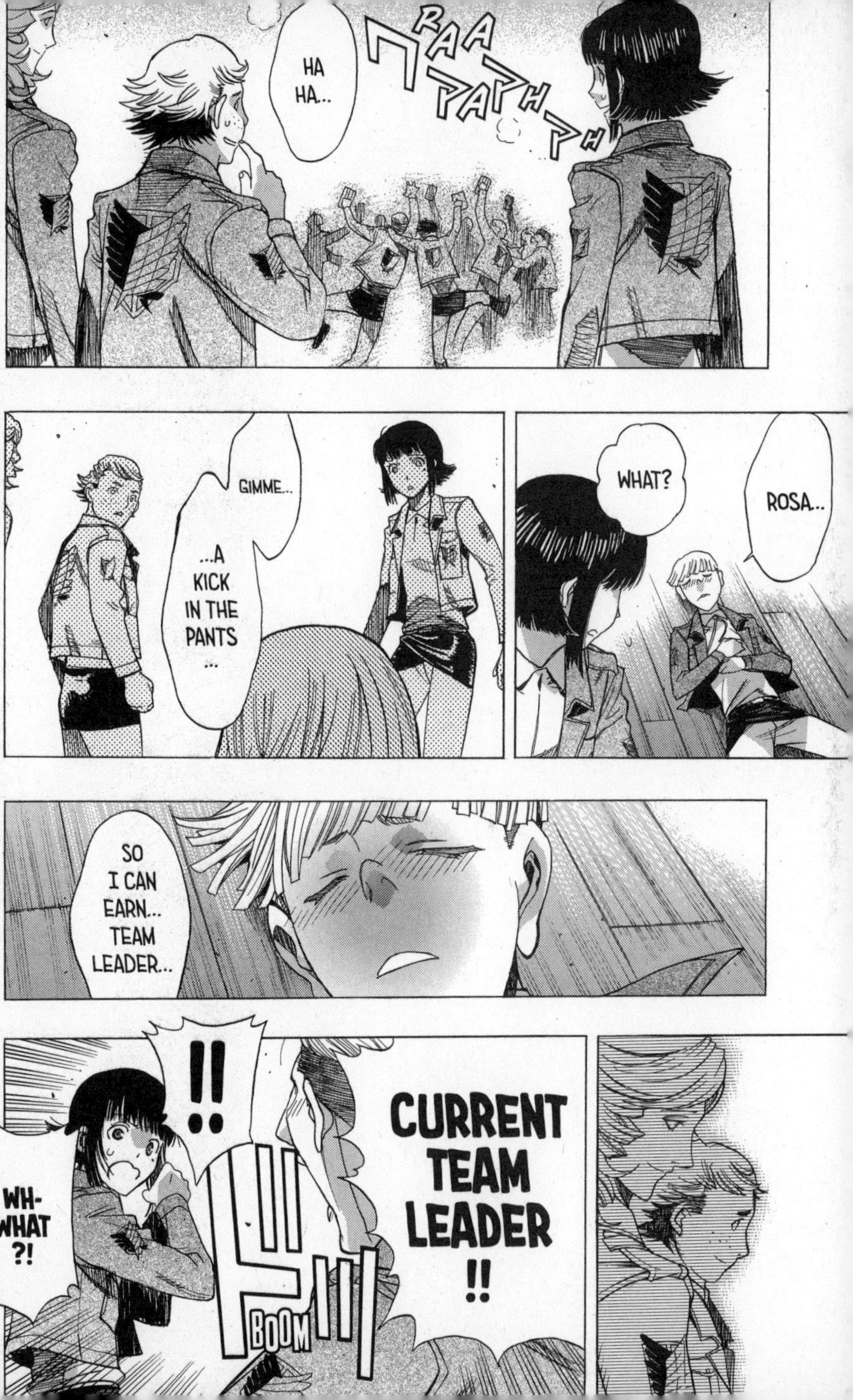
RAA PAHH
HA HA...
ROSA...
WHAT?
GIMME...
...A KICK IN THE PANTS...
SO I CAN EARN... TEAM LEADER...
CURRENT TEAM LEADER !!
!!
BOOM
WH-WHAT ?!

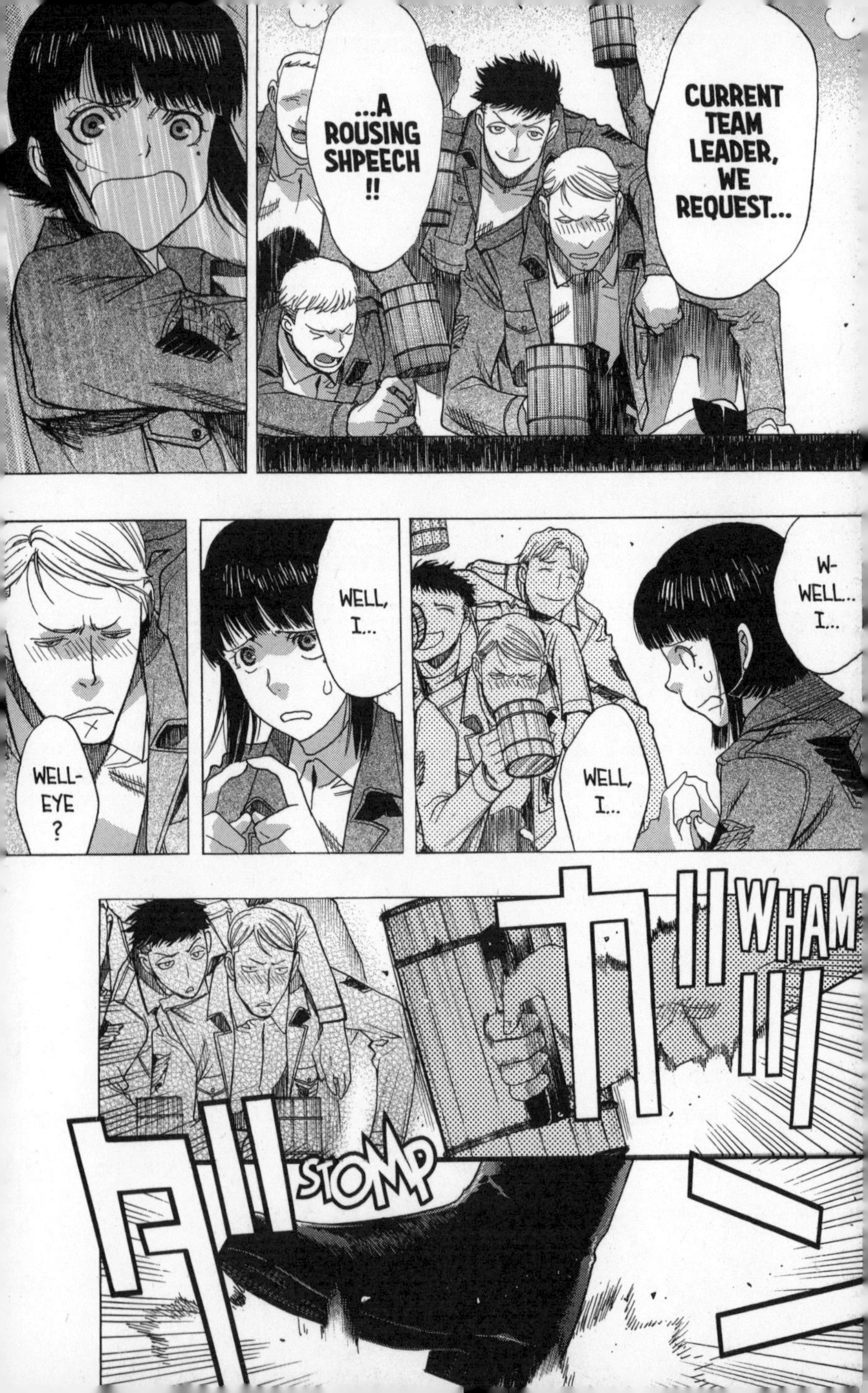
CURRENT TEAM LEADER, WE REQUEST...
...A ROUSING SHPEECH!!
W-WELL... I...
WELL, I...
WELL, I...
WELL-EYE?
WHAM
STOMP

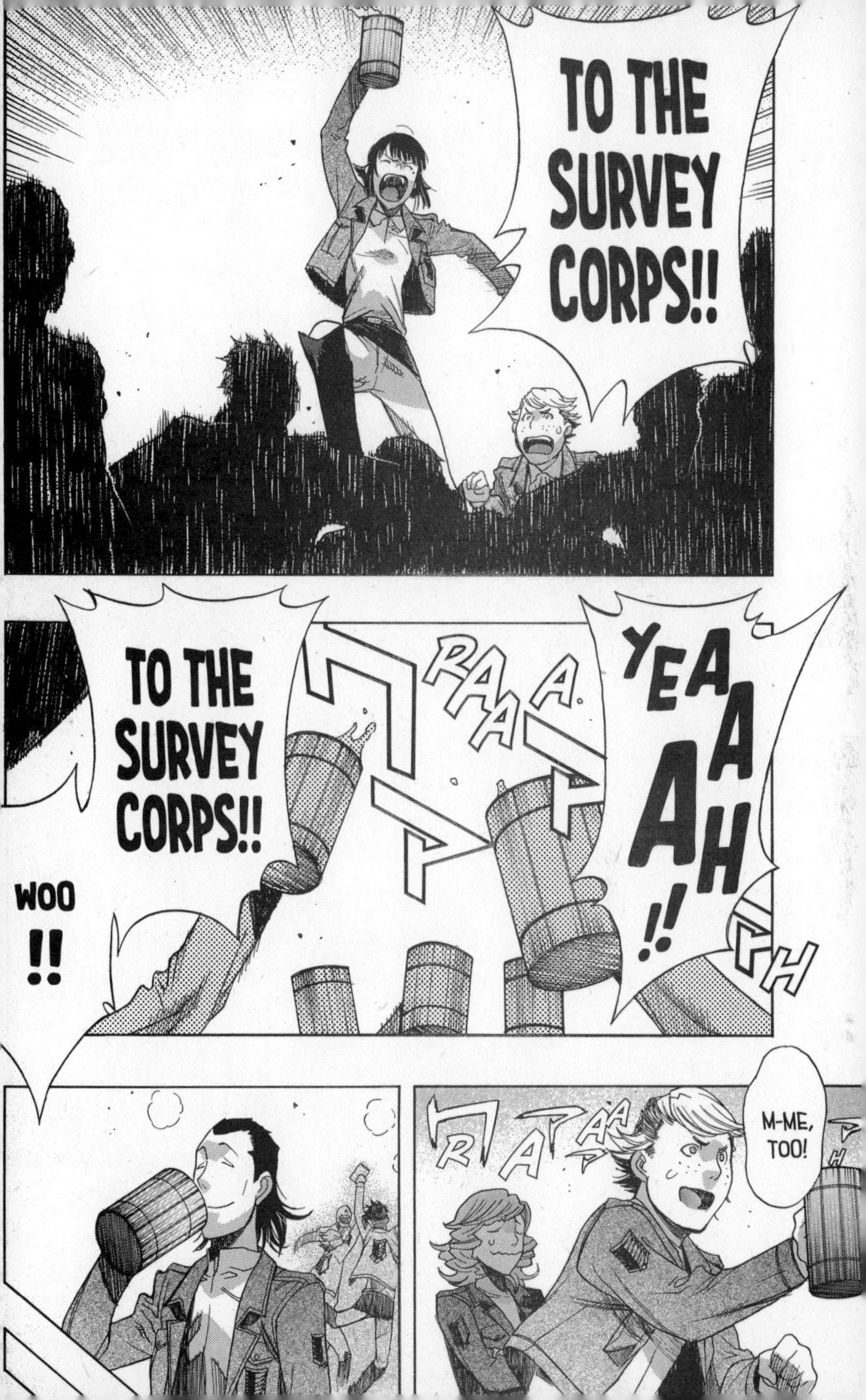
TO THE SURVEY CORPS!!
YEAAAAH!!
RAAAA
TO THE SURVEY CORPS!!
WOO!!
M-ME, TOO!
RATAAA

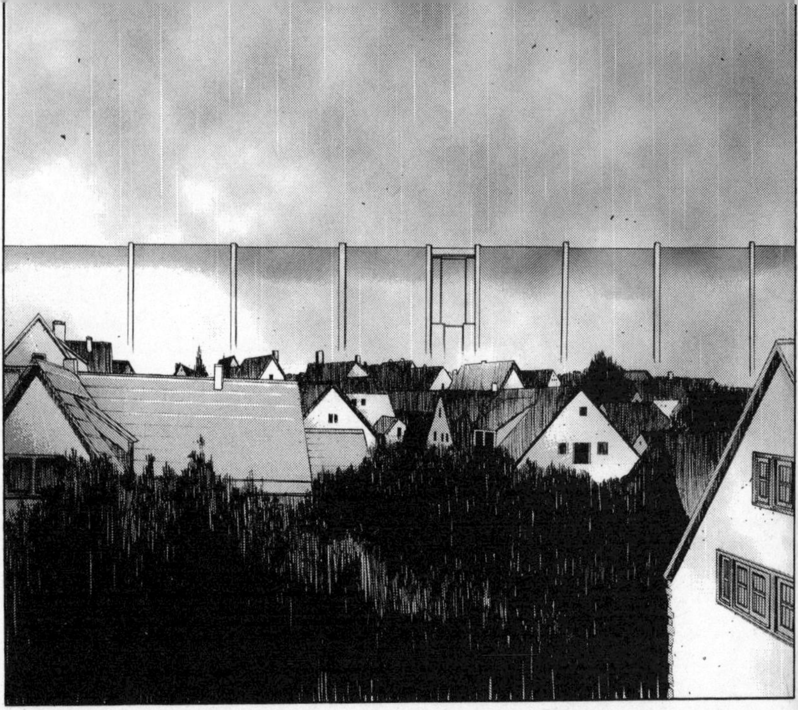

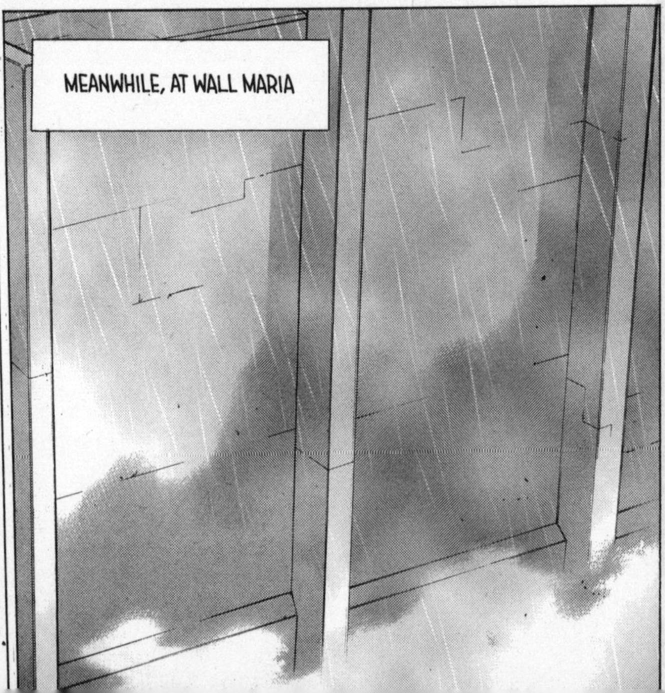
MEANWHILE, AT WALL MARIA

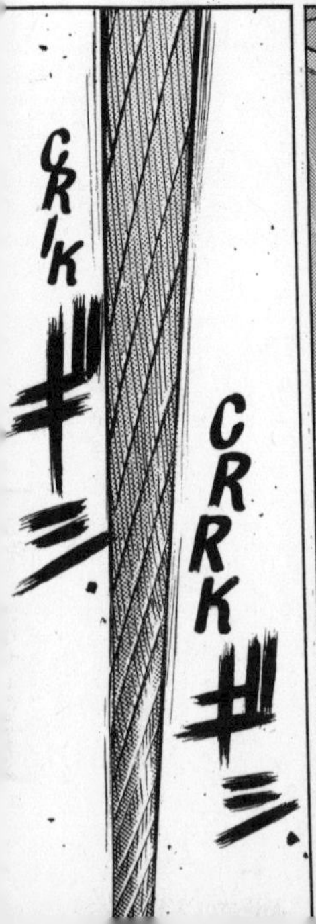
CRIK
CRRK

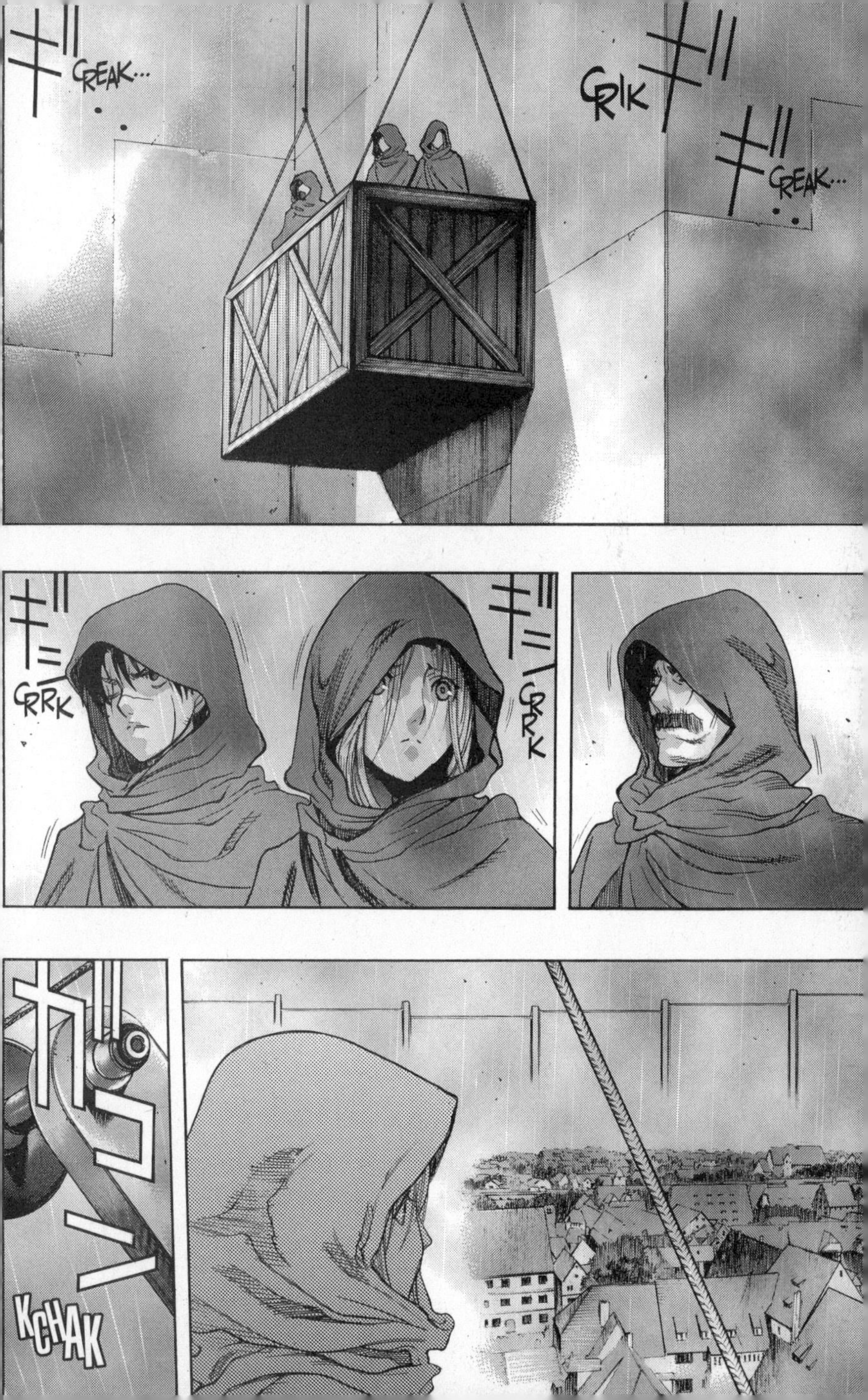
CRIK
CREAK...
CREAK...
CRRK
CRRK
KCHAK

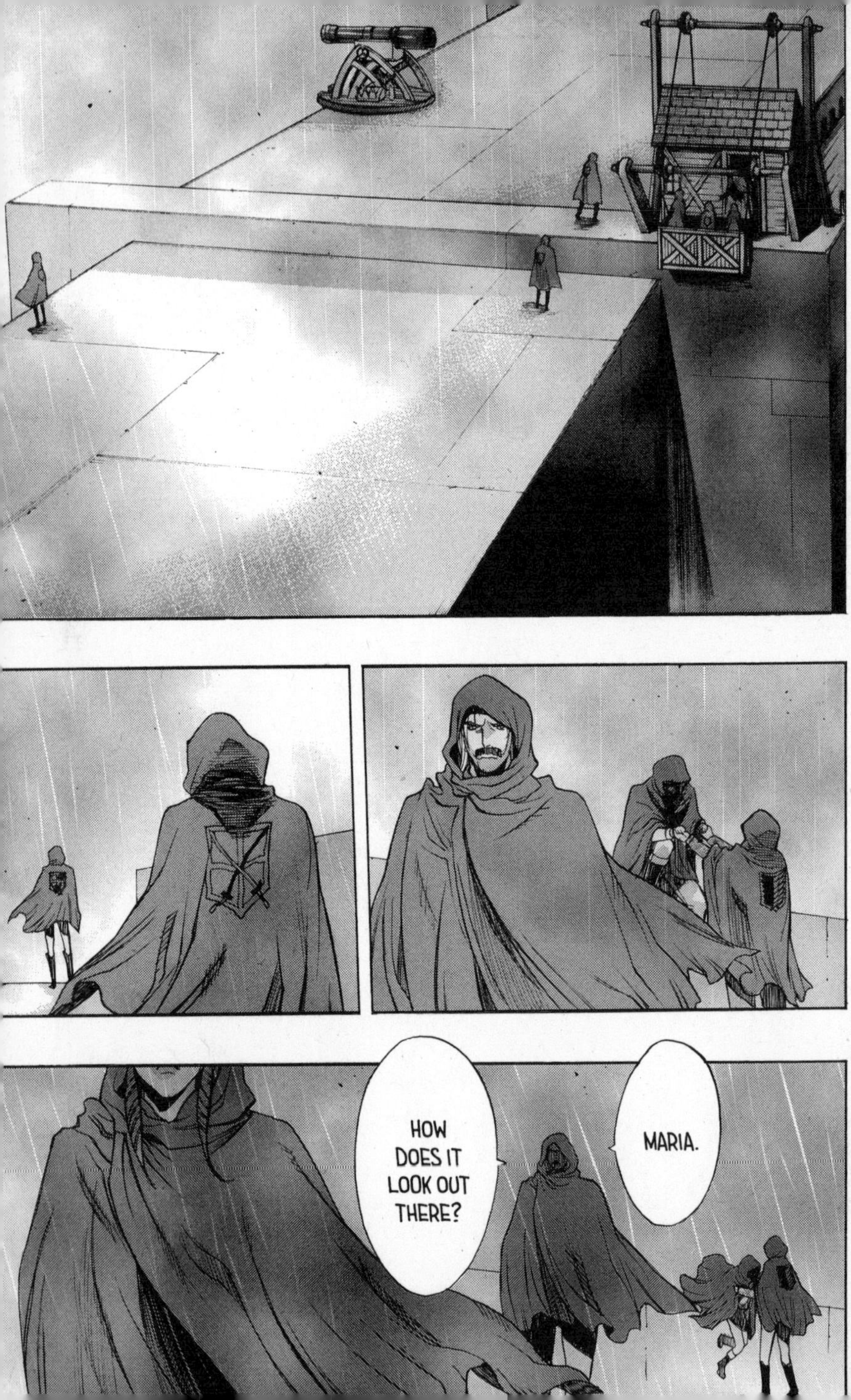
MARIA.
HOW DOES IT LOOK OUT THERE?

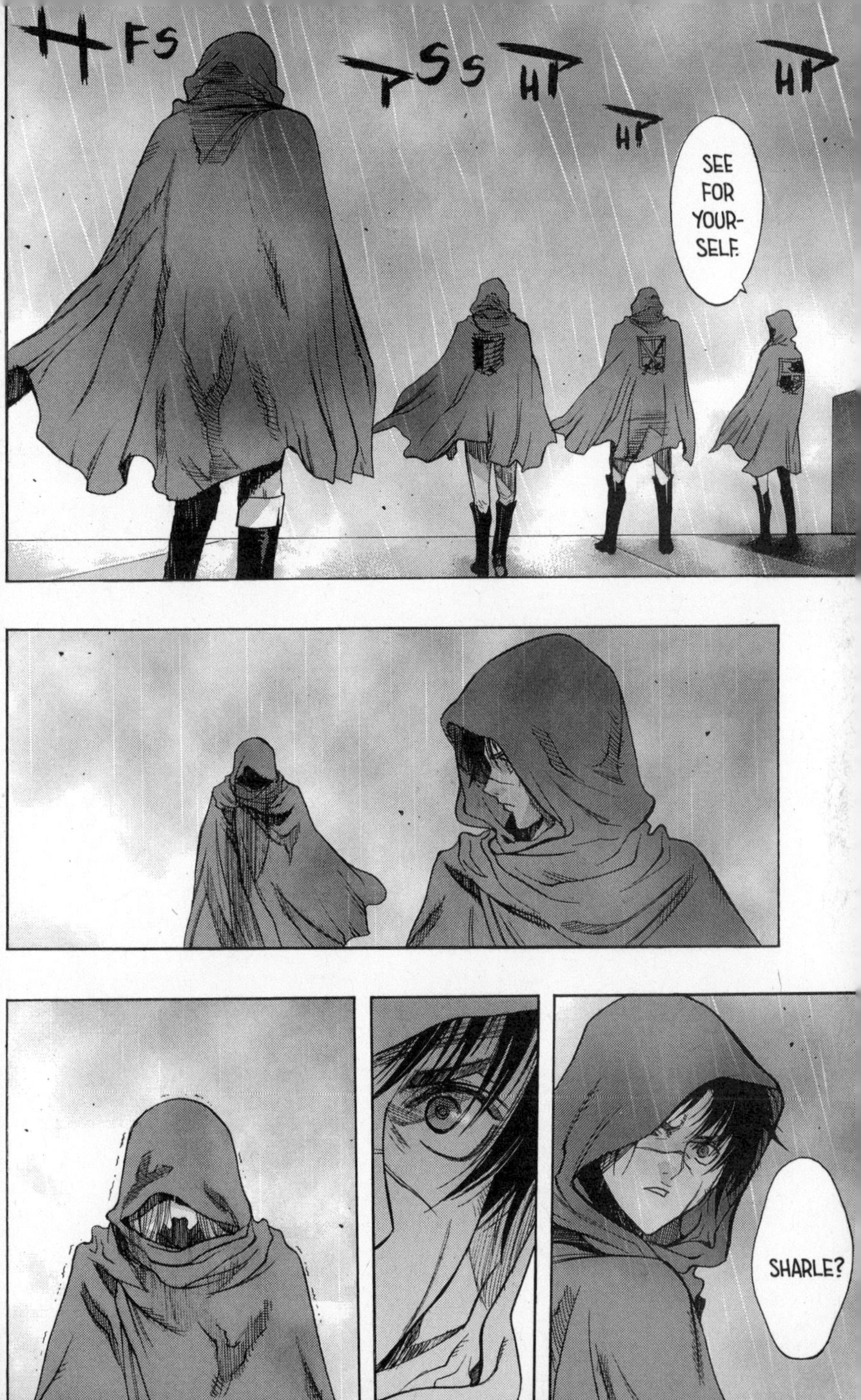
HP
HP
SEE FOR YOUR-SELF.
PSS HP
HFS
SHARLE?

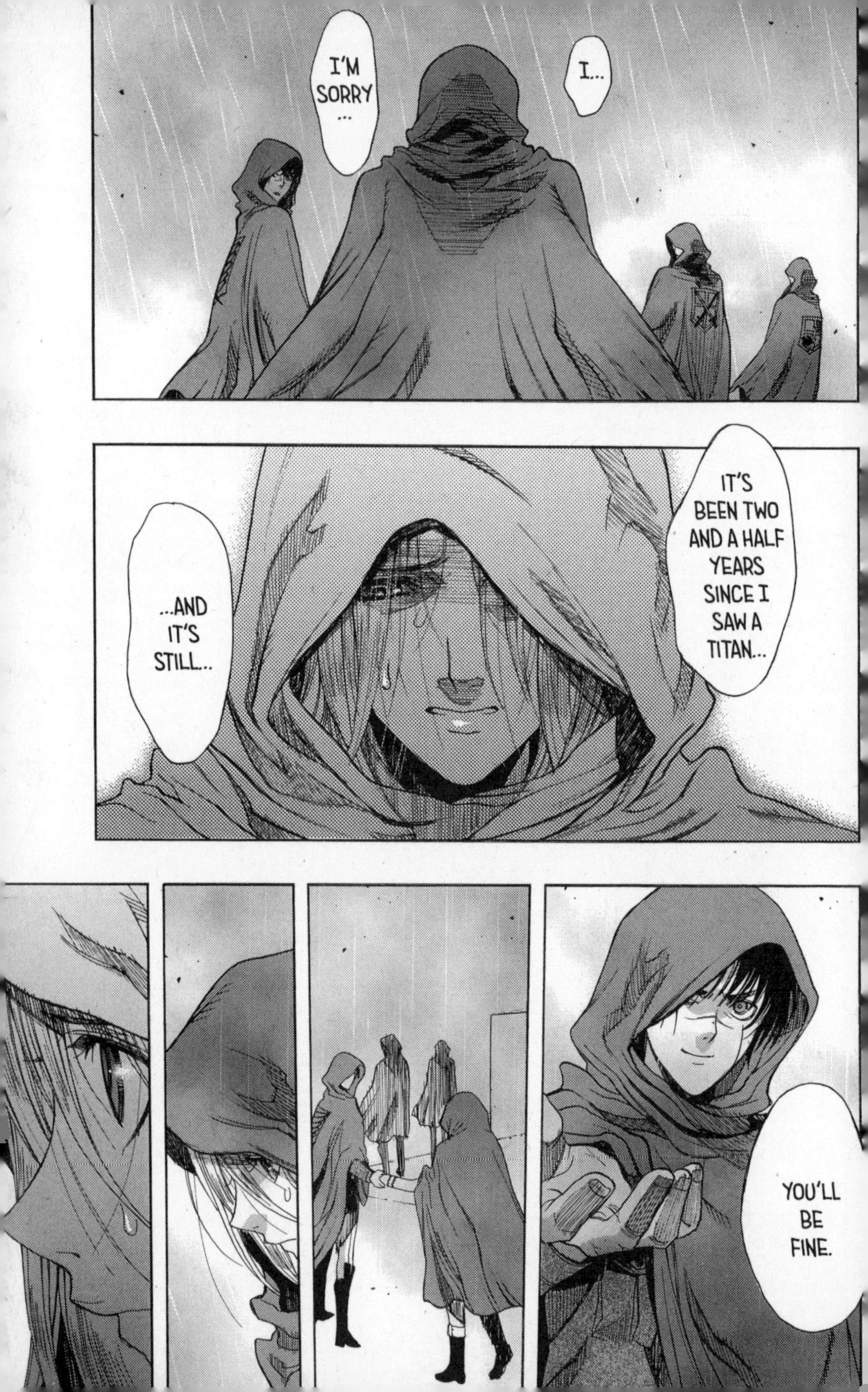
I...
I'M SORRY ...
IT'S BEEN TWO AND A HALF YEARS SINCE I SAW A TITAN...
...AND IT'S STILL...
YOU'LL BE FINE.

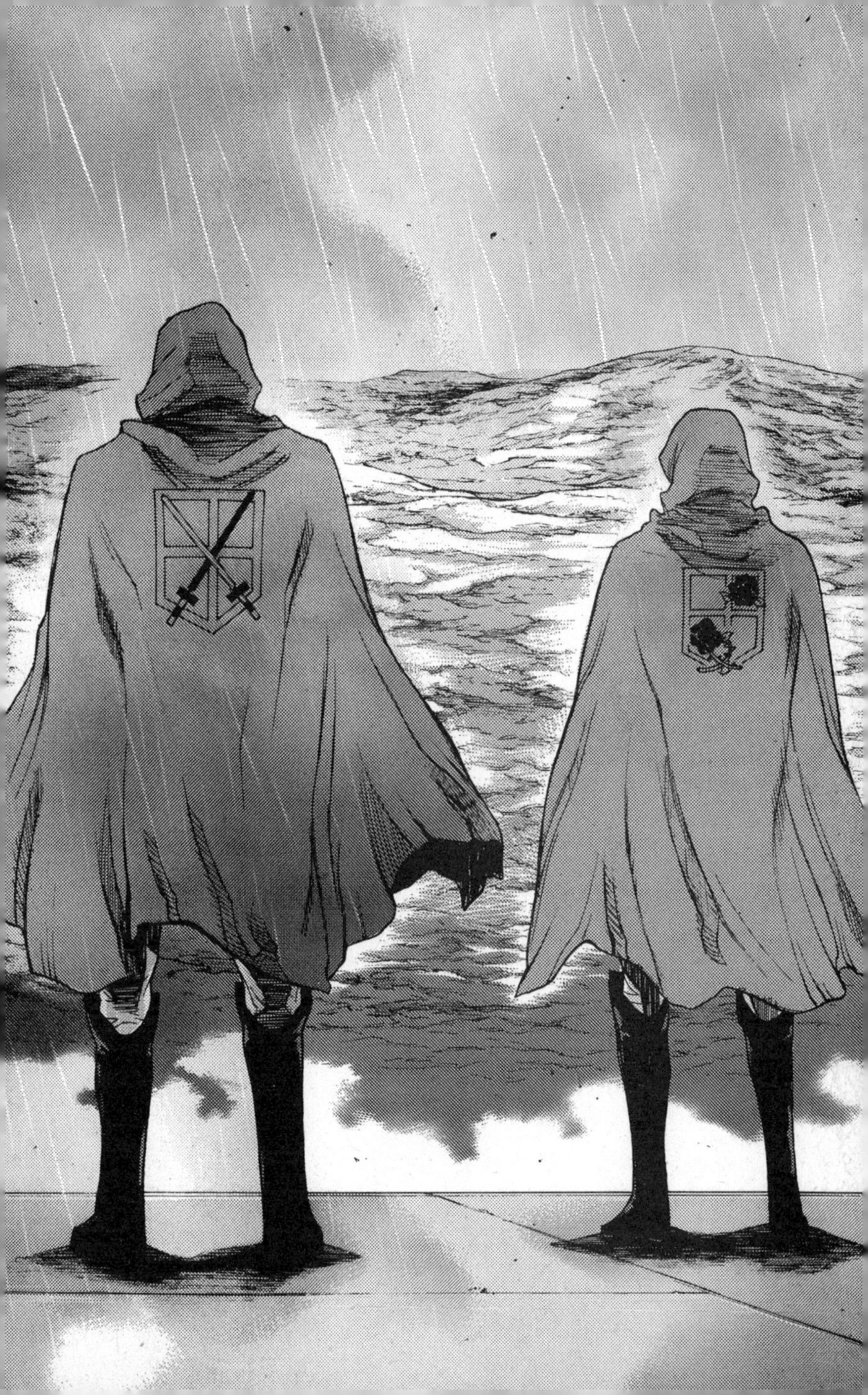

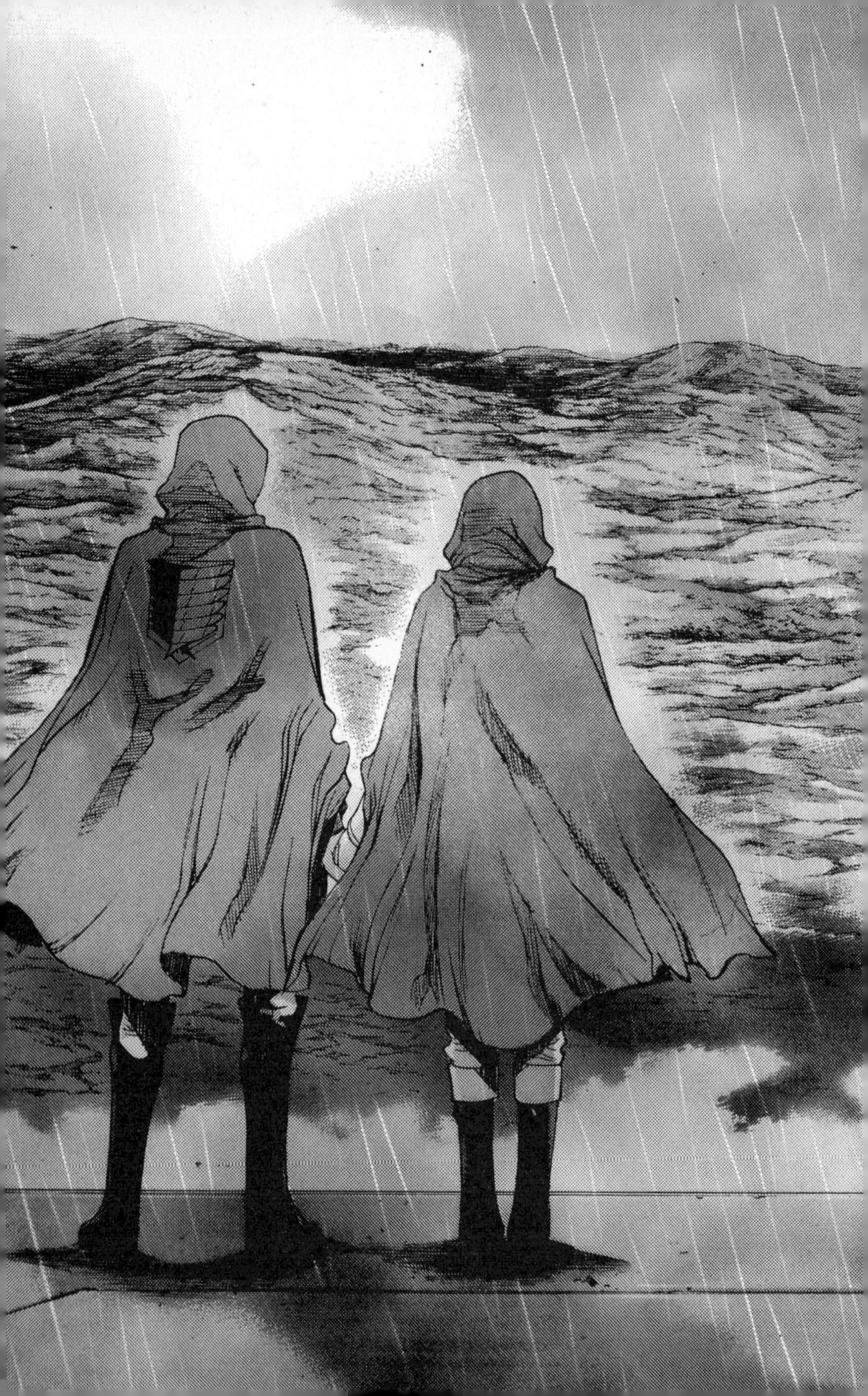

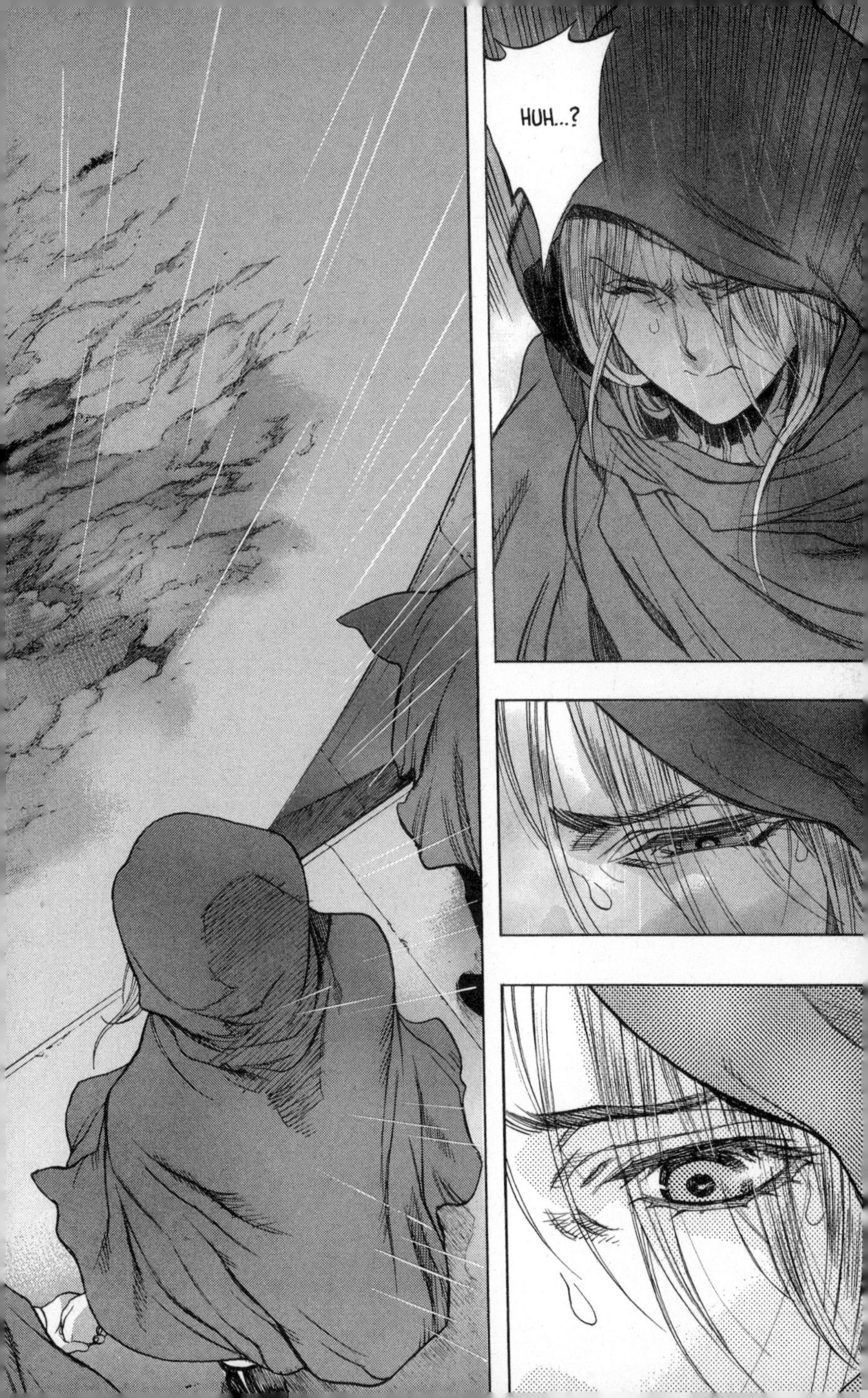
HUH...?

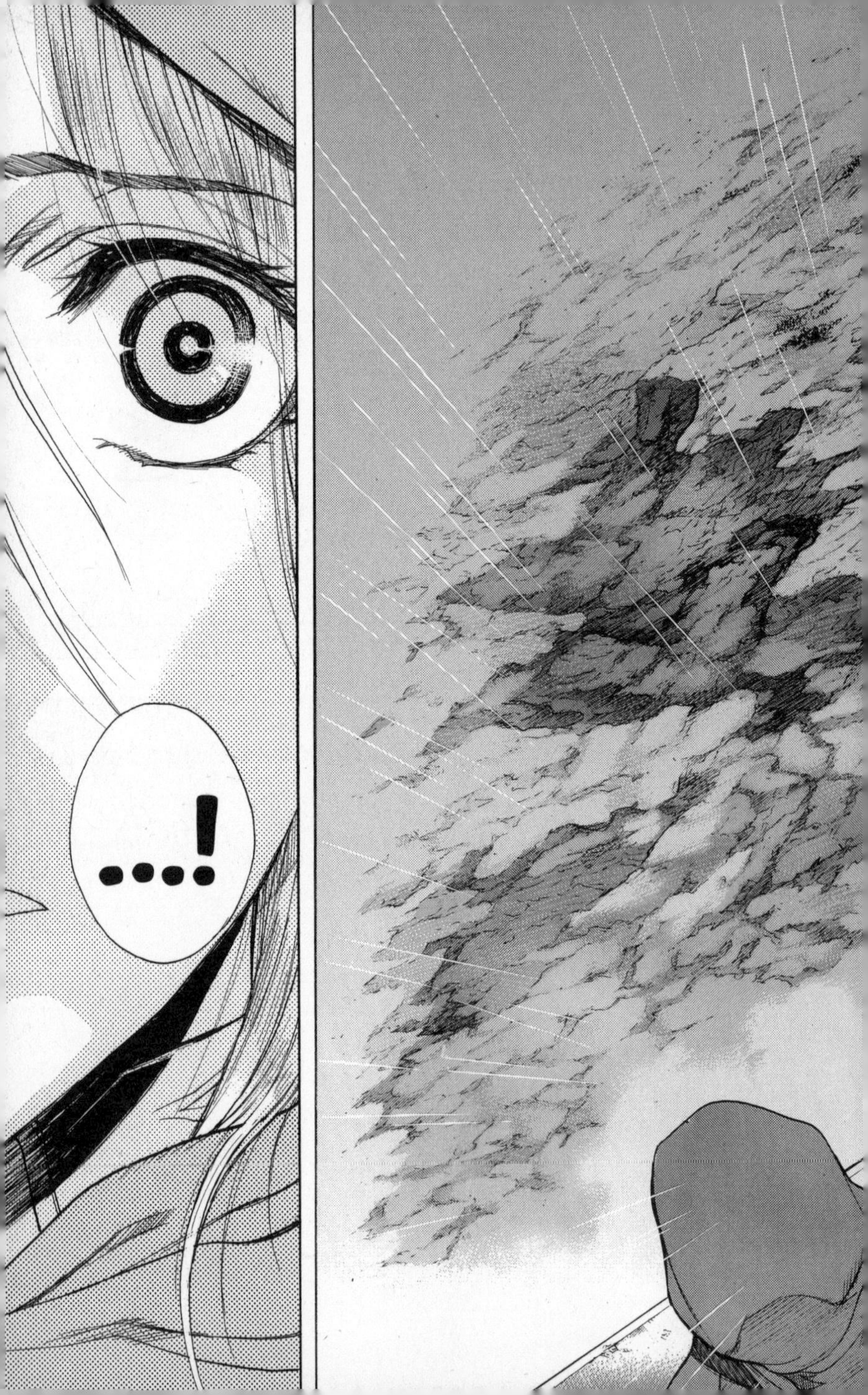
...!

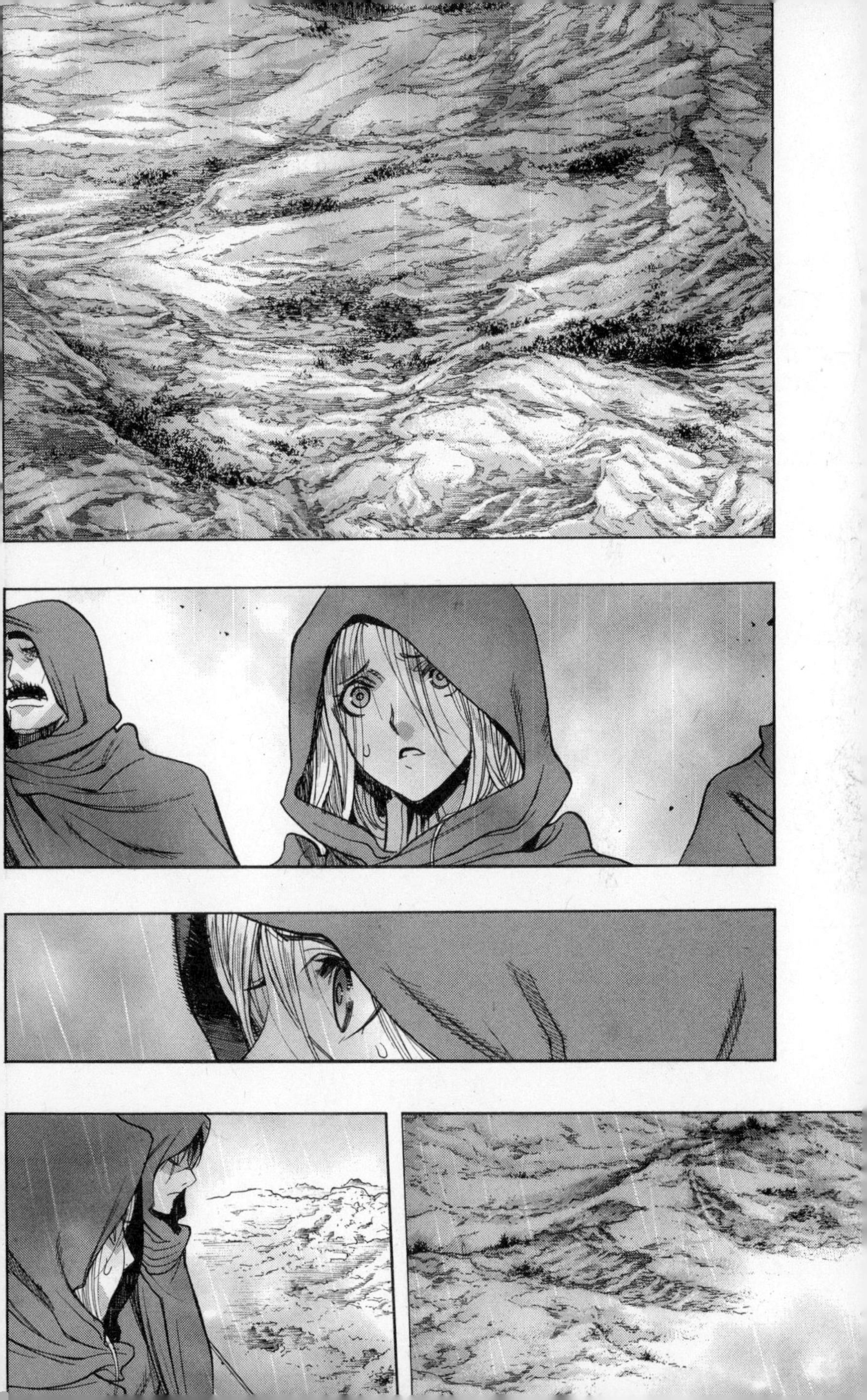

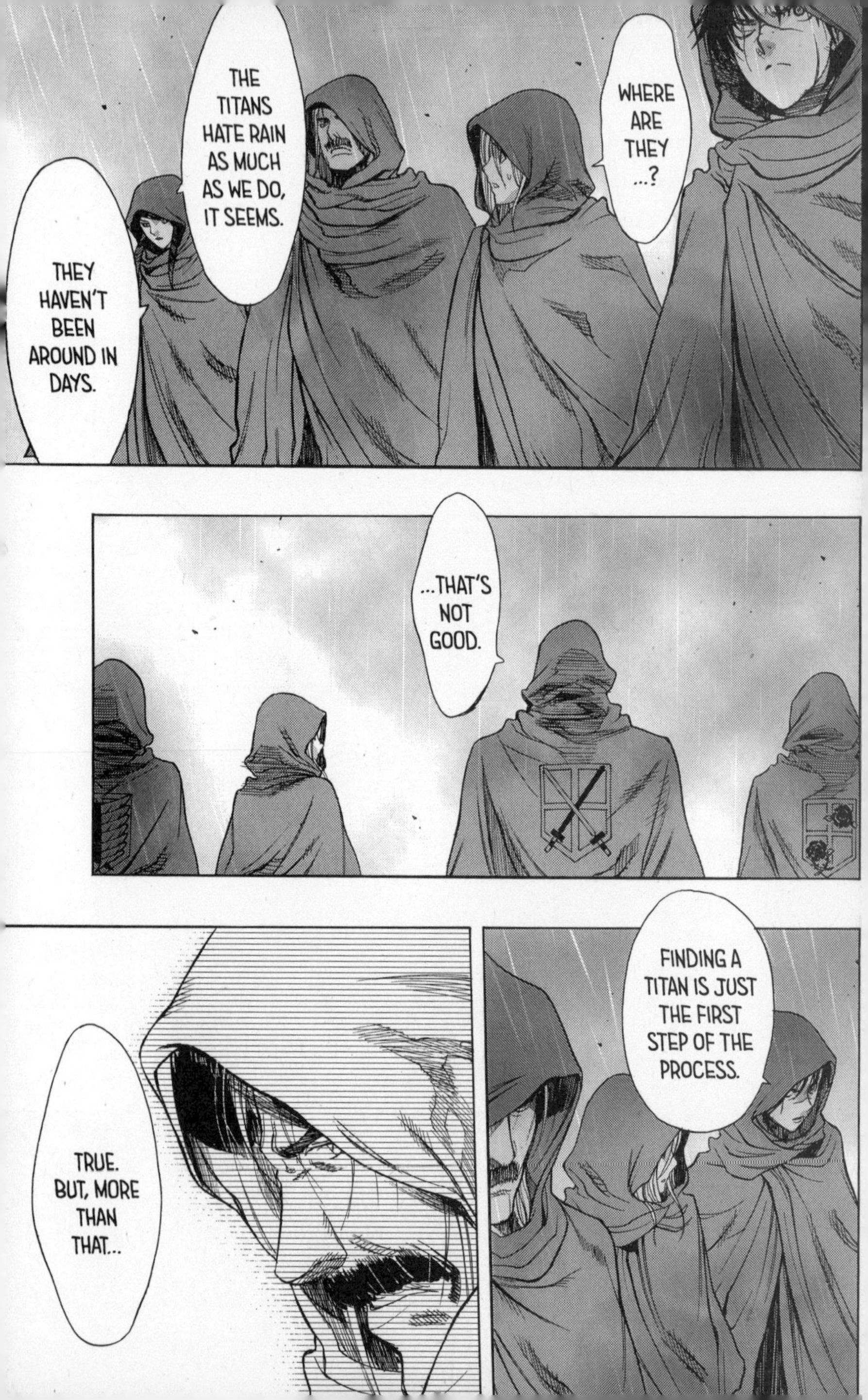
WHERE ARE THEY ...?
THE TITANS HATE RAIN AS MUCH AS WE DO, IT SEEMS.
THEY HAVEN'T BEEN AROUND IN DAYS.
...THAT'S NOT GOOD.
FINDING A TITAN IS JUST THE FIRST STEP OF THE PROCESS.
TRUE. BUT, MORE THAN THAT...

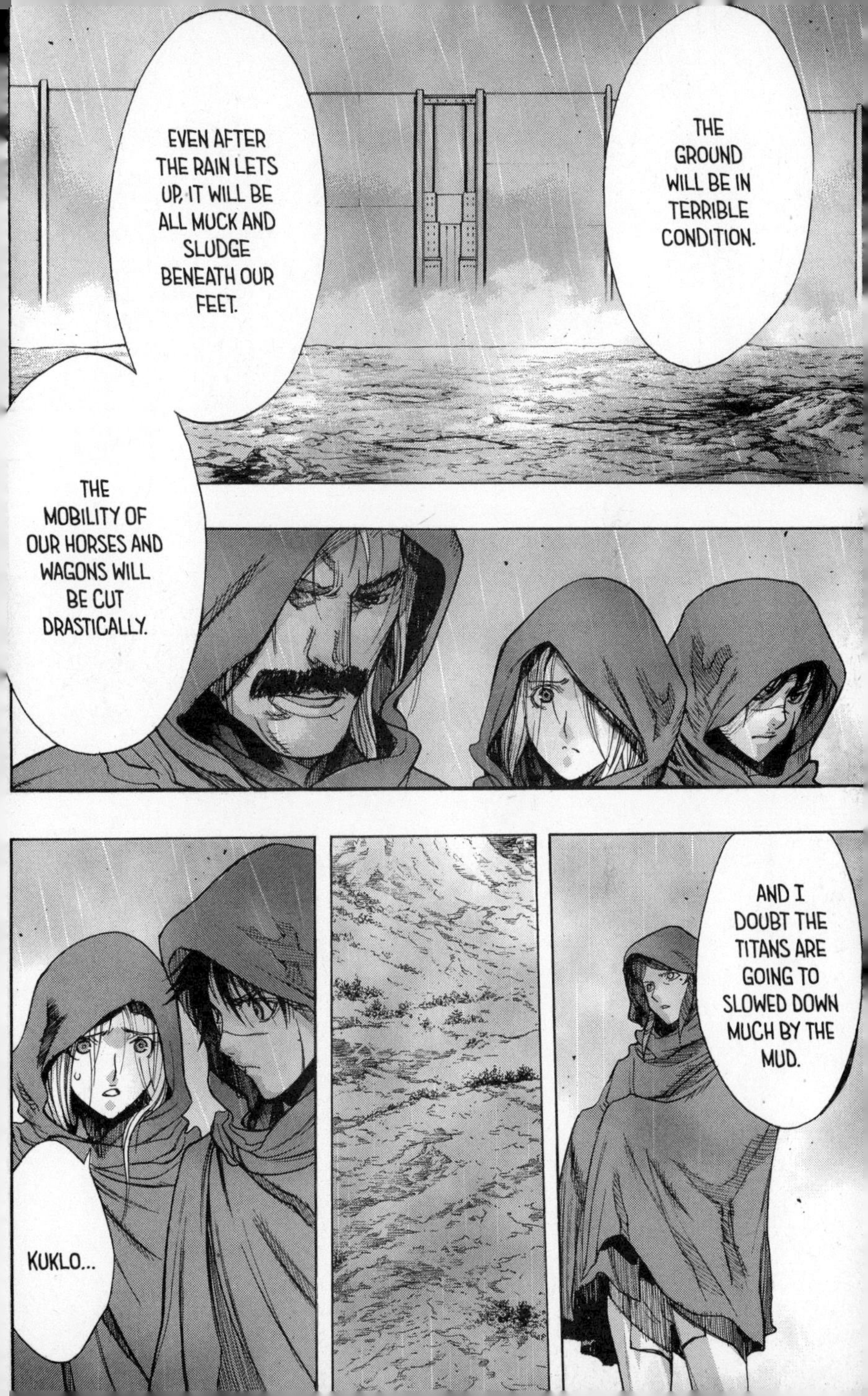
THE GROUND WILL BE IN TERRIBLE CONDITION.
EVEN AFTER THE RAIN LETS UP, IT WILL BE ALL MUCK AND SLUDGE BENEATH OUR FEET.
THE MOBILITY OF OUR HORSES AND WAGONS WILL BE CUT DRASTICALLY.
AND I DOUBT THE TITANS ARE GOING TO SLOWED DOWN MUCH BY THE MUD.
KUKLO...

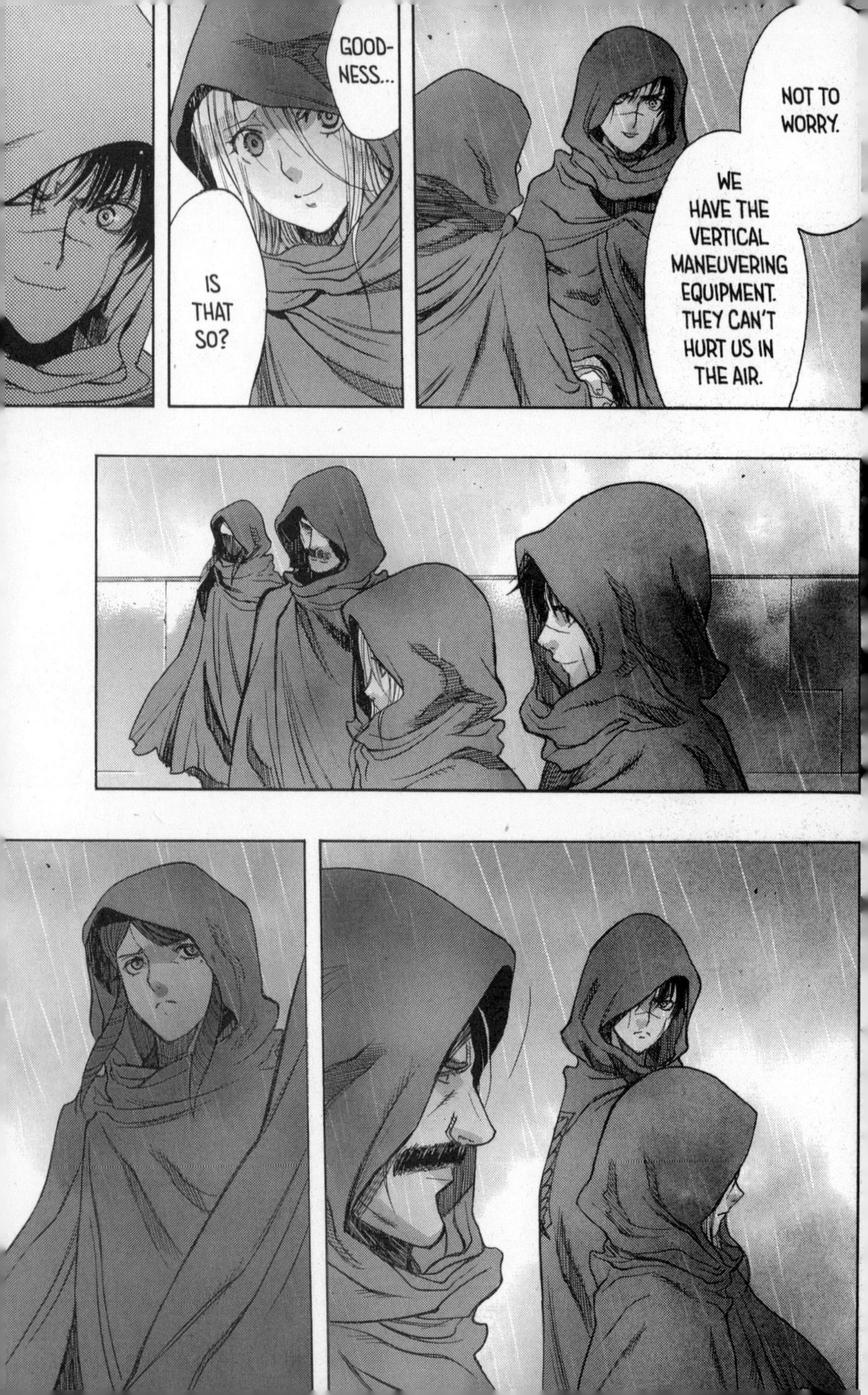
NOT TO WORRY.
WE HAVE THE VERTICAL MANEUVERING EQUIPMENT. THEY CAN'T HURT US IN THE AIR.
GOOD-NESS...
IS THAT SO?

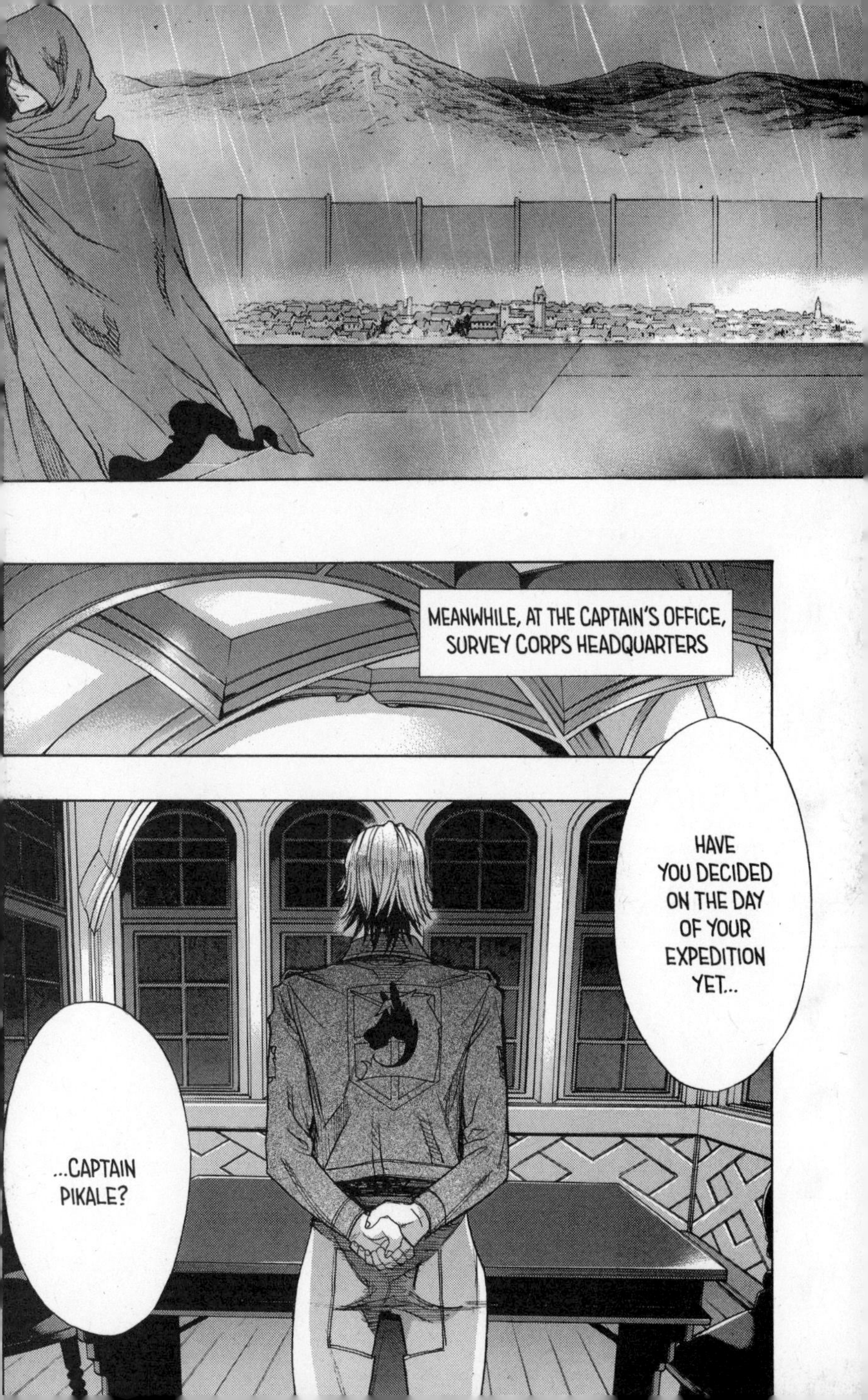
MEANWHILE, AT THE CAPTAIN'S OFFICE, SURVEY CORPS HEADQUARTERS
HAVE YOU DECIDED ON THE DAY OF YOUR EXPEDITION YET...
...CAPTAIN PIKALE?

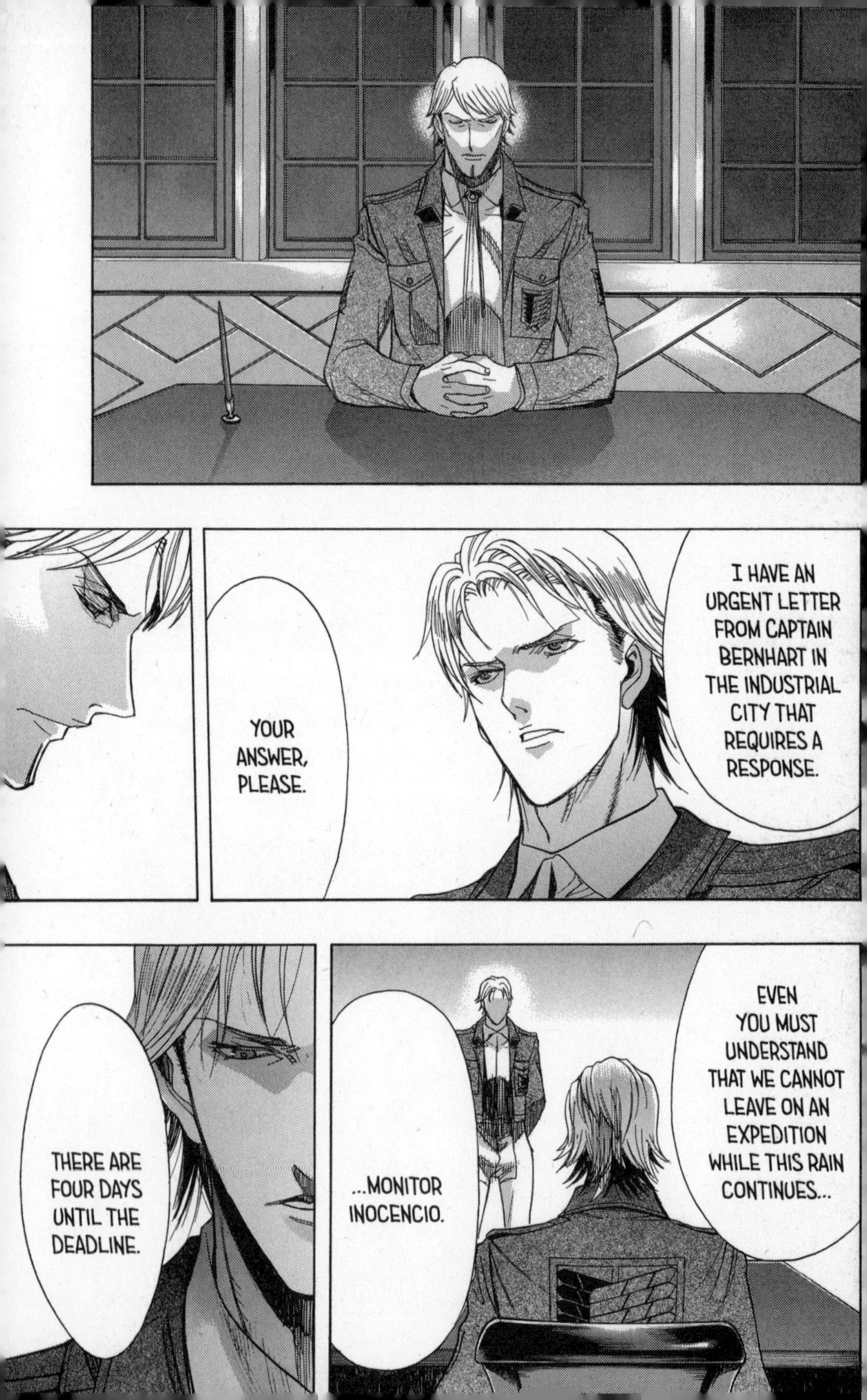
I HAVE AN URGENT LETTER FROM CAPTAIN BERNHART IN THE INDUSTRIAL CITY THAT REQUIRES A RESPONSE.
YOUR ANSWER, PLEASE.
EVEN YOU MUST UNDERSTAND THAT WE CANNOT LEAVE ON AN EXPEDITION WHILE THIS RAIN CONTINUES...
...MONITOR INOCENCIO.
THERE ARE FOUR DAYS UNTIL THE DEADLINE.

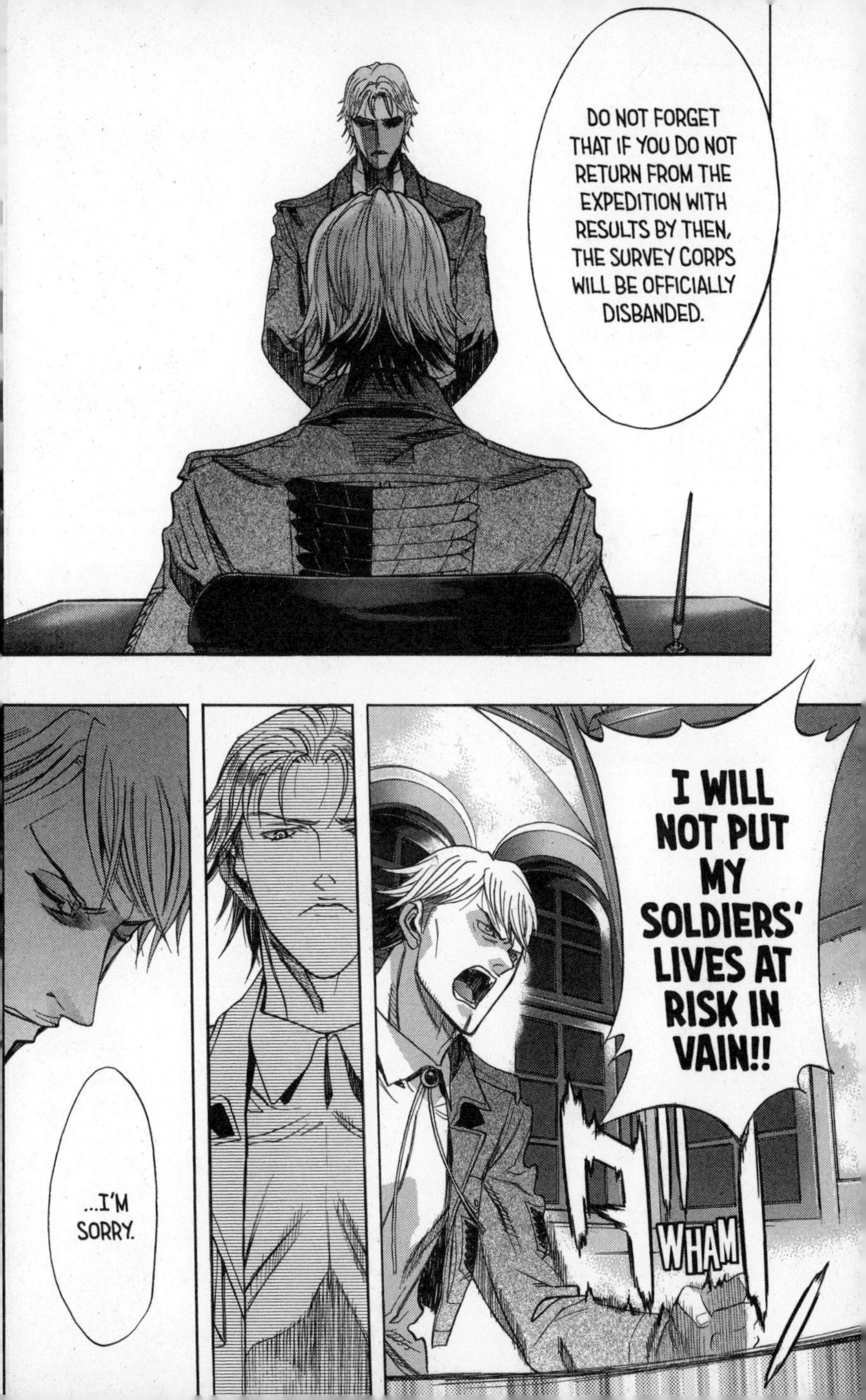
DO NOT FORGET THAT IF YOU DO NOT RETURN FROM THE EXPEDITION WITH RESULTS BY THEN, THE SURVEY CORPS WILL BE OFFICIALLY DISBANDED.
I WILL NOT PUT MY SOLDIERS' LIVES AT RISK IN VAIN!!
WHAM
...I'M SORRY.

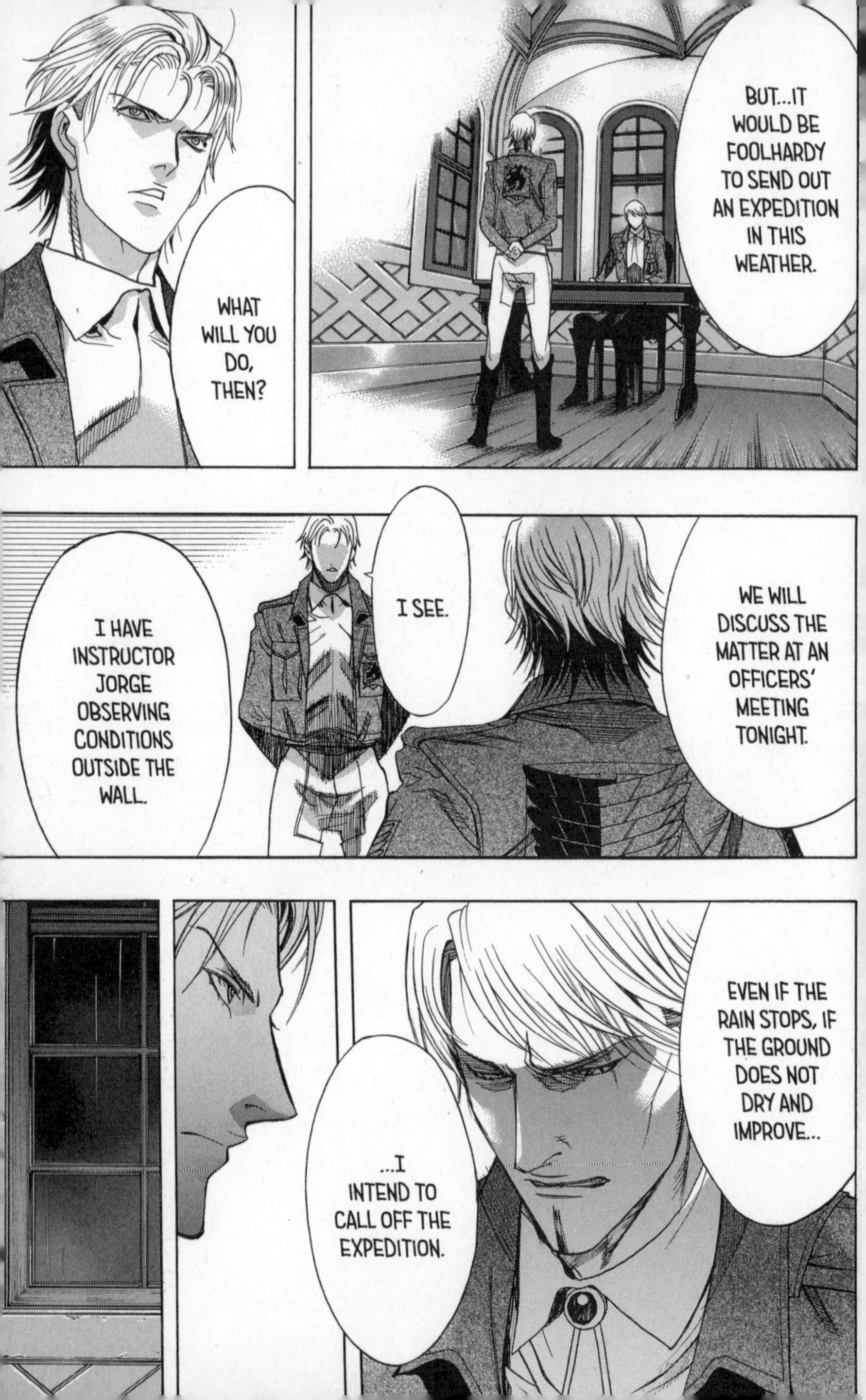
BUT...IT WOULD BE FOOLHARDY TO SEND OUT AN EXPEDITION IN THIS WEATHER.
WHAT WILL YOU DO, THEN?
WE WILL DISCUSS THE MATTER AT AN OFFICERS' MEETING TONIGHT.
I SEE.
I HAVE INSTRUCTOR JORGE OBSERVING CONDITIONS OUTSIDE THE WALL.
EVEN IF THE RAIN STOPS, IF THE GROUND DOES NOT DRY AND IMPROVE...
...I INTEND TO CALL OFF THE EXPEDITION.

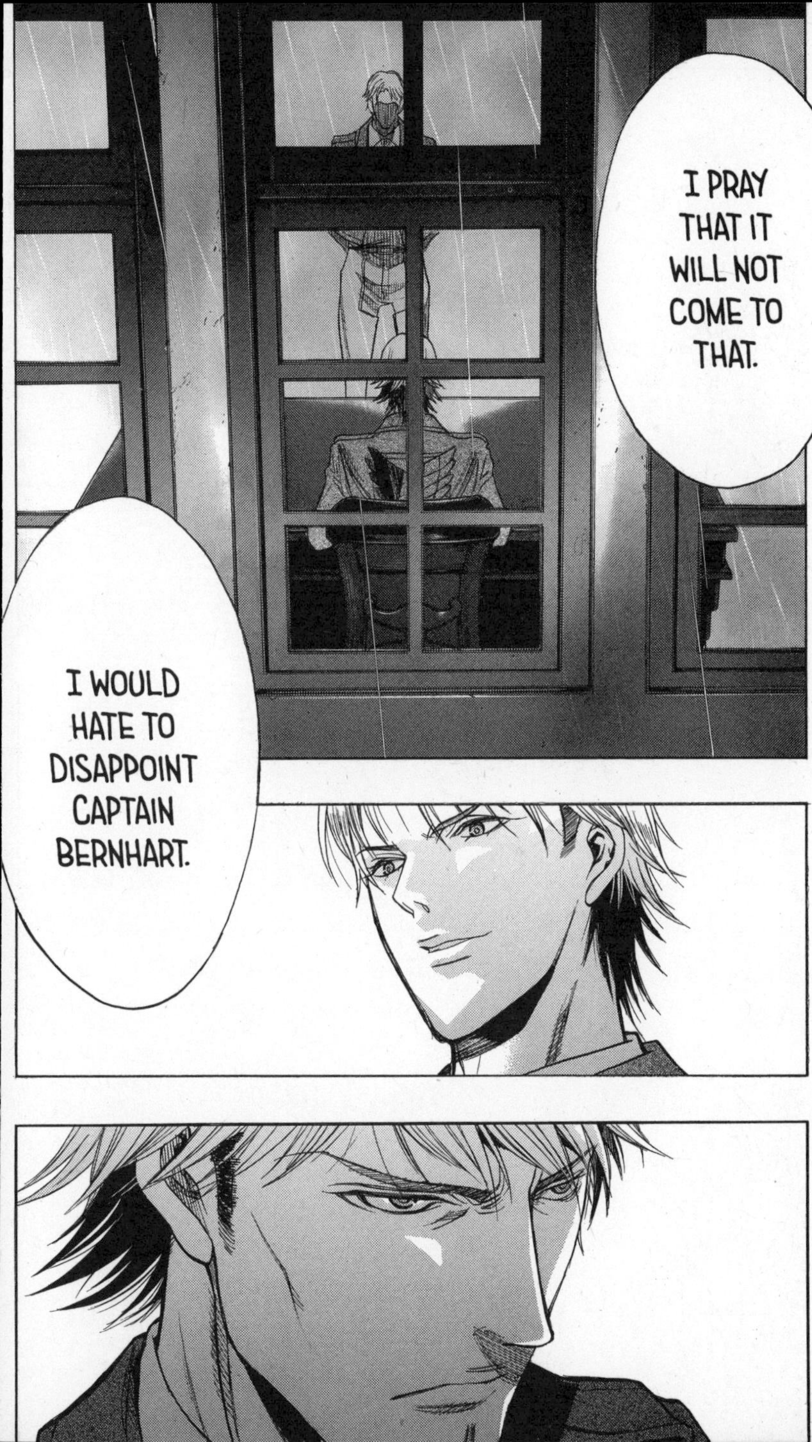
I PRAY THAT IT WILL NOT COME TO THAT.
I WOULD HATE TO DISAPPOINT CAPTAIN BERNHART.

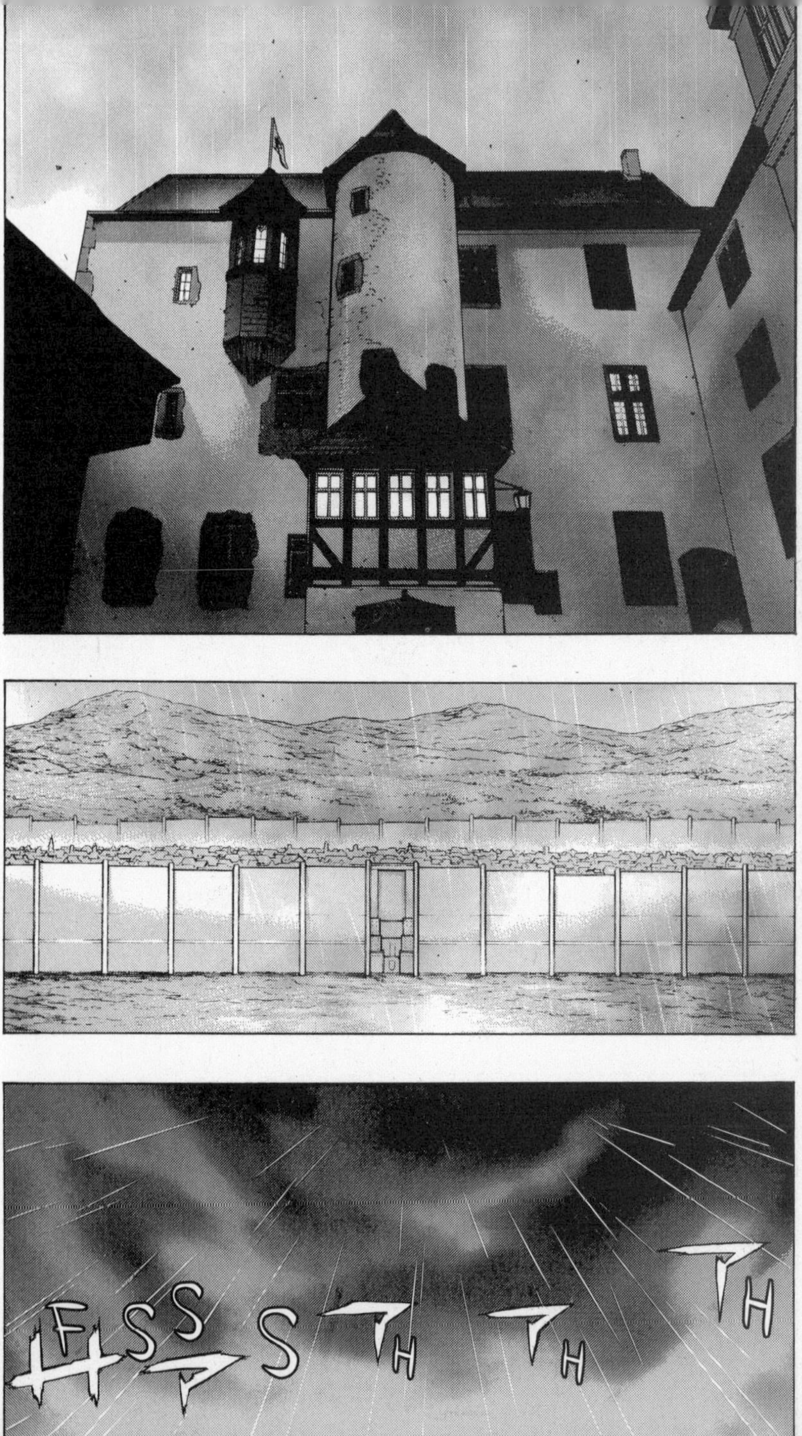
FSSS

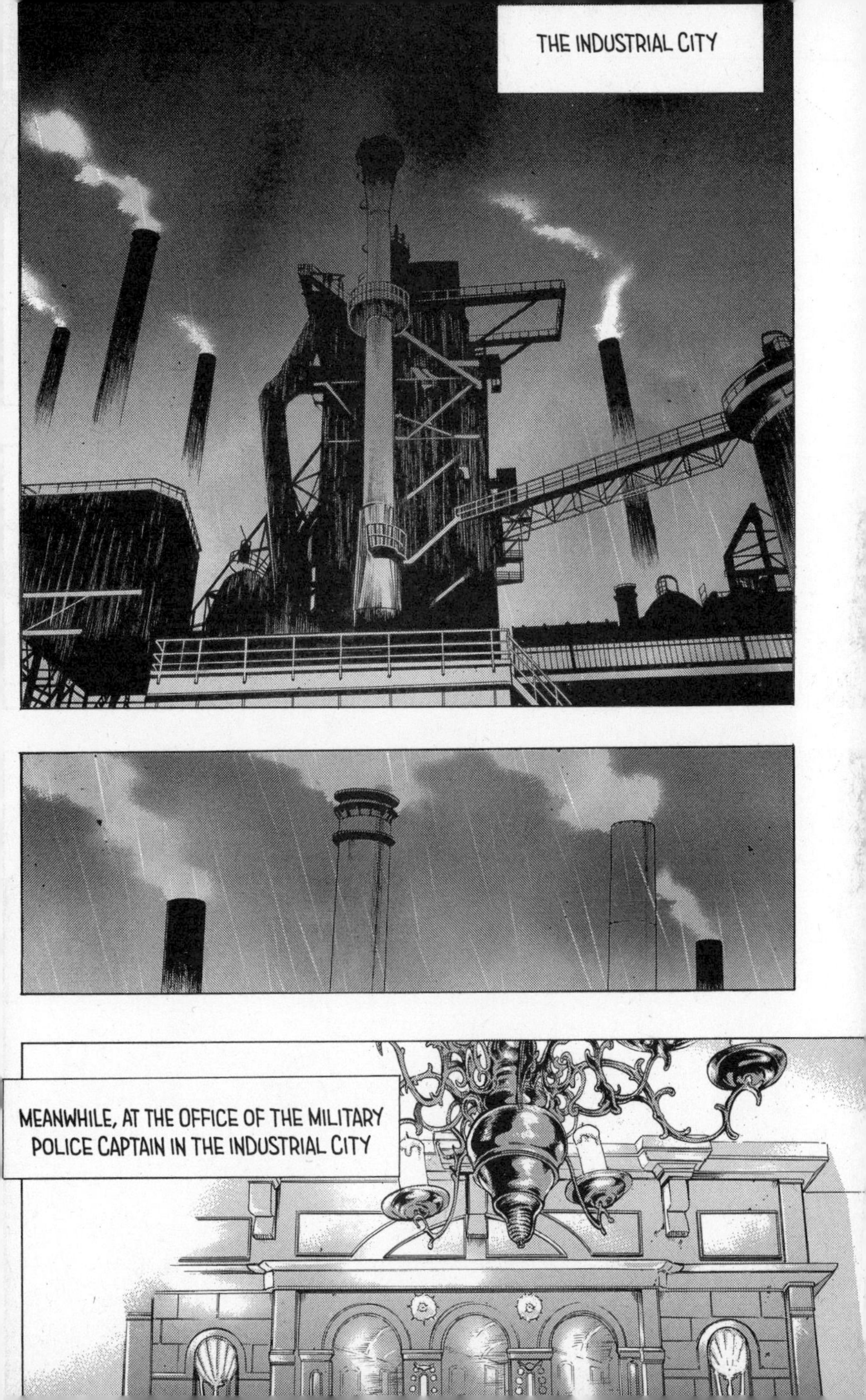
THE INDUSTRIAL CITY
MEANWHILE, AT THE OFFICE OF THE MILITARY POLICE CAPTAIN IN THE INDUSTRIAL CITY

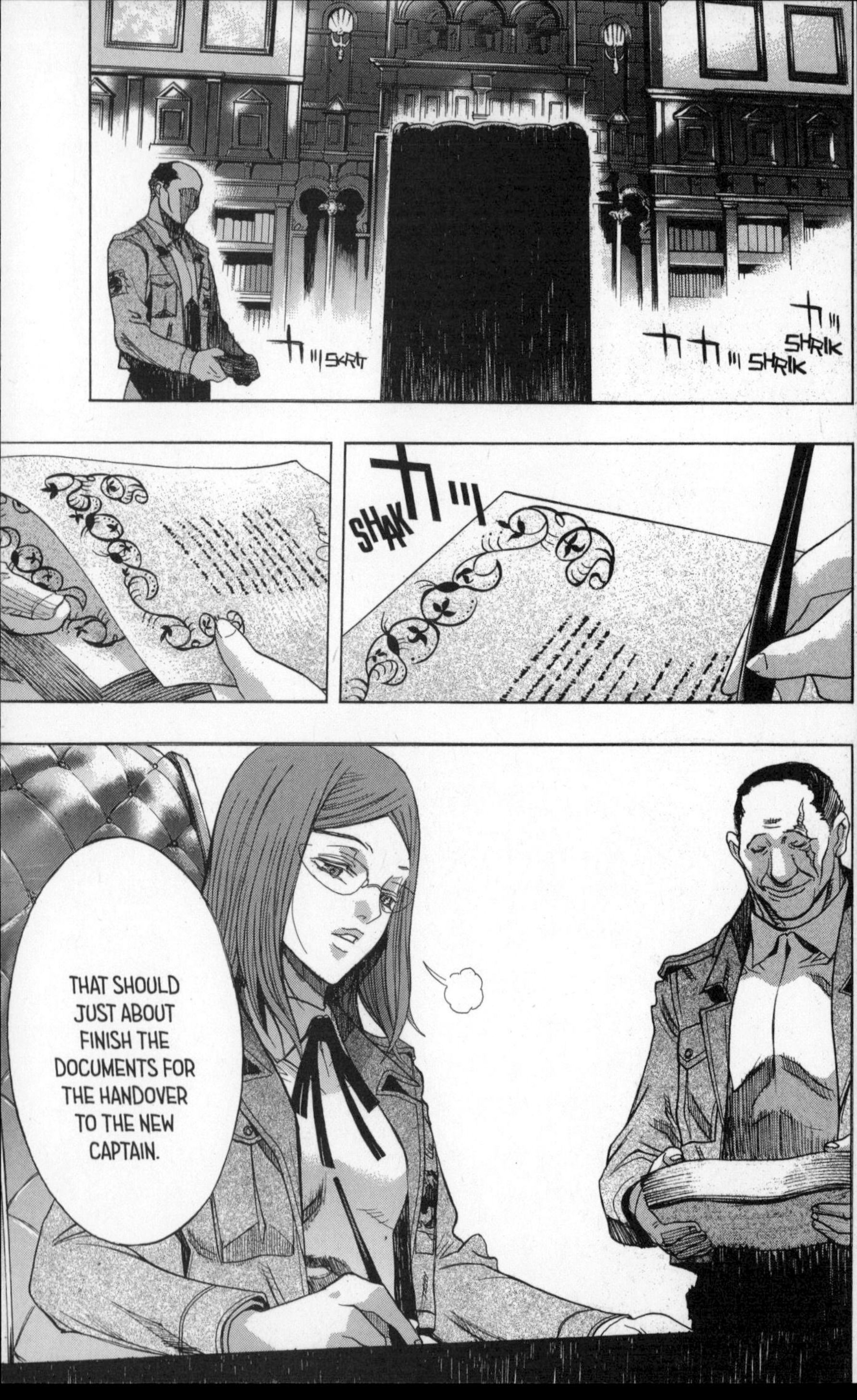
SHRIK
SHRIK
SKRIT
SHAK
THAT SHOULD JUST ABOUT FINISH THE DOCUMENTS FOR THE HANDOVER TO THE NEW CAPTAIN.

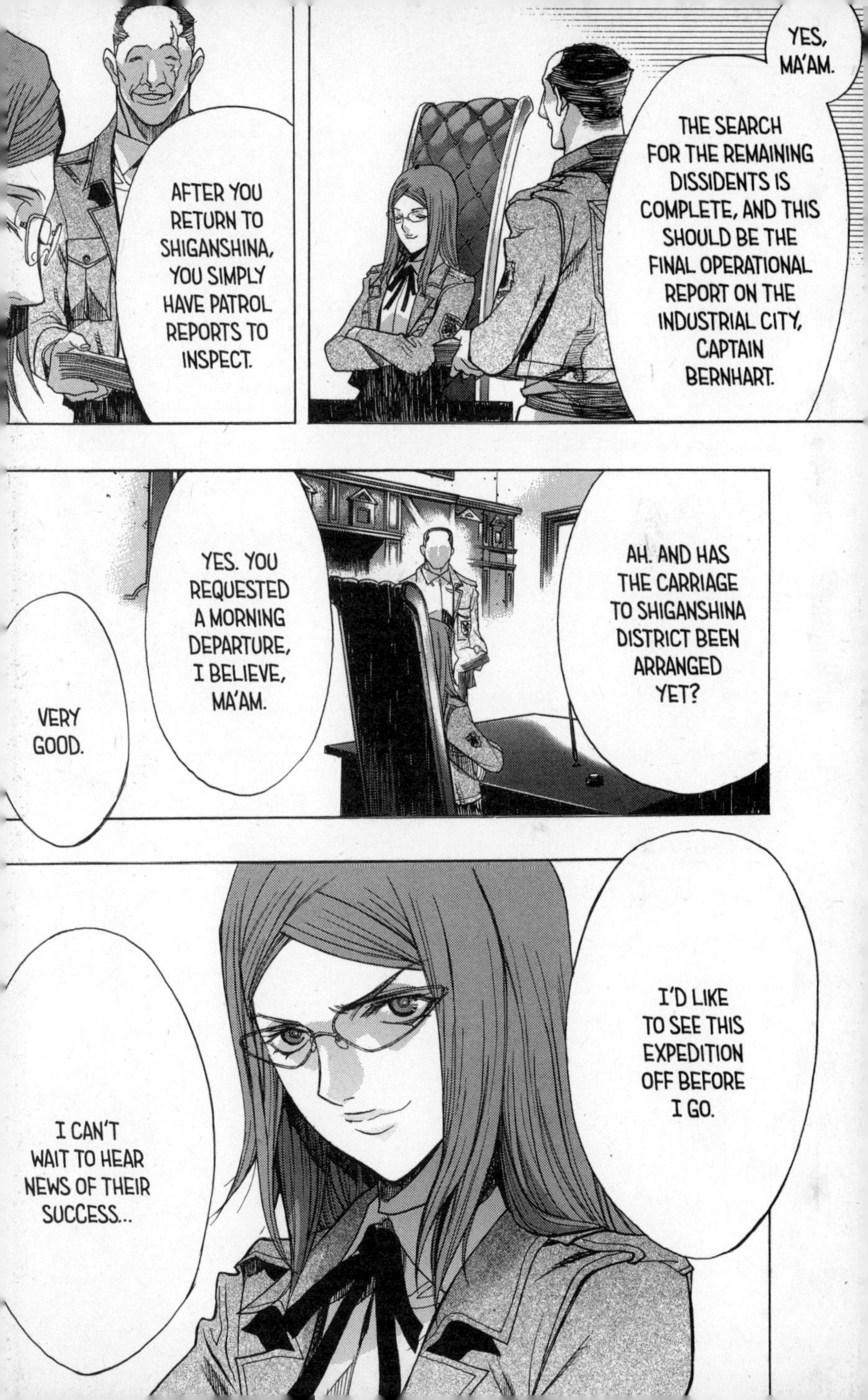
YES, MA'AM.
THE SEARCH FOR THE REMAINING DISSIDENTS IS COMPLETE, AND THIS SHOULD BE THE FINAL OPERATIONAL REPORT ON THE INDUSTRIAL CITY, CAPTAIN BERNHART.
AFTER YOU RETURN TO SHIGANSHINA, YOU SIMPLY HAVE PATROL REPORTS TO INSPECT.
AH. AND HAS THE CARRIAGE TO SHIGANSHINA DISTRICT BEEN ARRANGED YET?
YES. YOU REQUESTED A MORNING DEPARTURE, I BELIEVE, MA'AM.
VERY GOOD.
I'D LIKE TO SEE THIS EXPEDITION OFF BEFORE I GO.
I CAN'T WAIT TO HEAR NEWS OF THEIR SUCCESS...

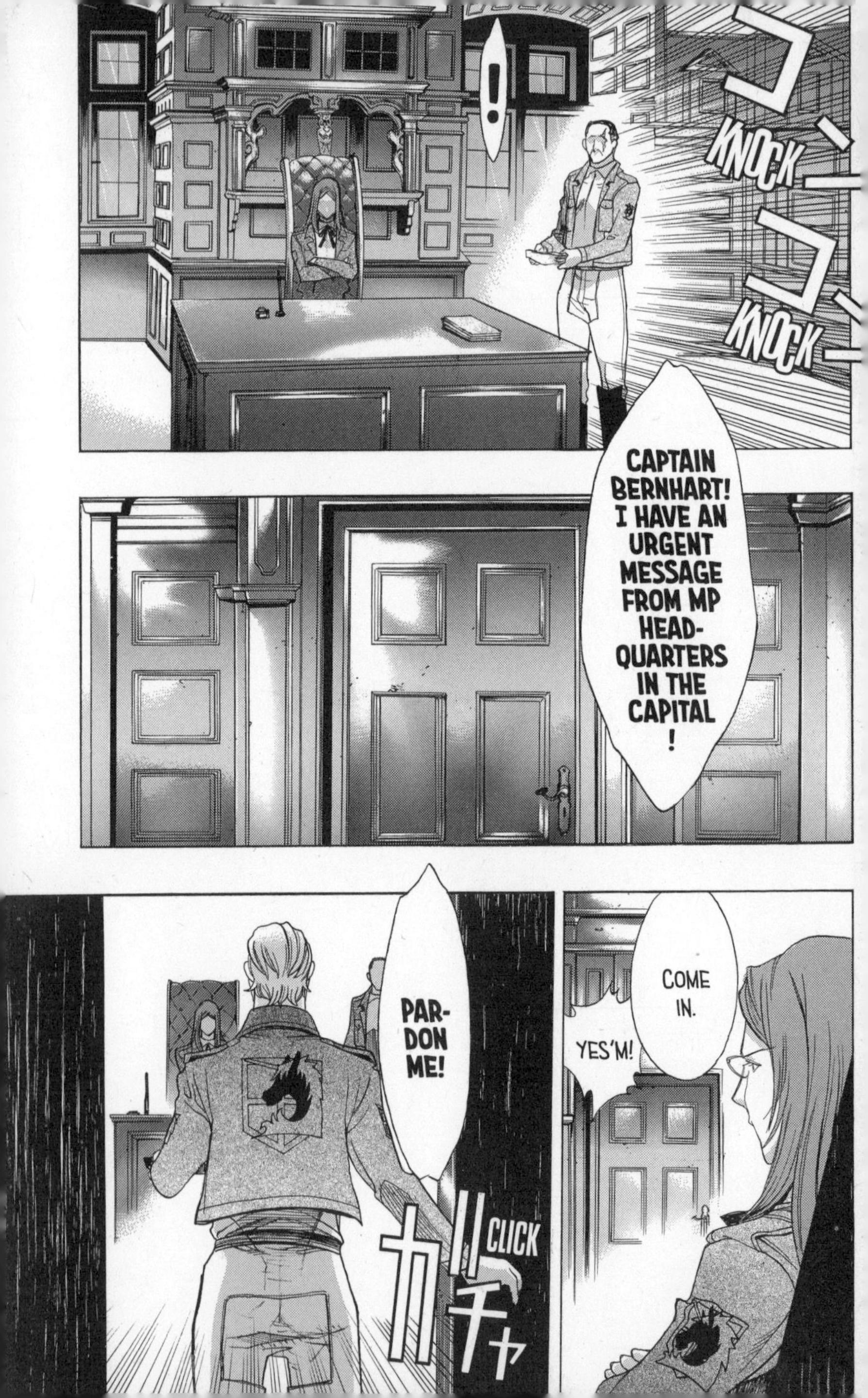
KNOCK
KNOCK
!
CAPTAIN BERNHART! I HAVE AN URGENT MESSAGE FROM MP HEAD-QUARTERS IN THE CAPITAL!
COME IN.
YES'M!
PAR-DON ME!
CLICK

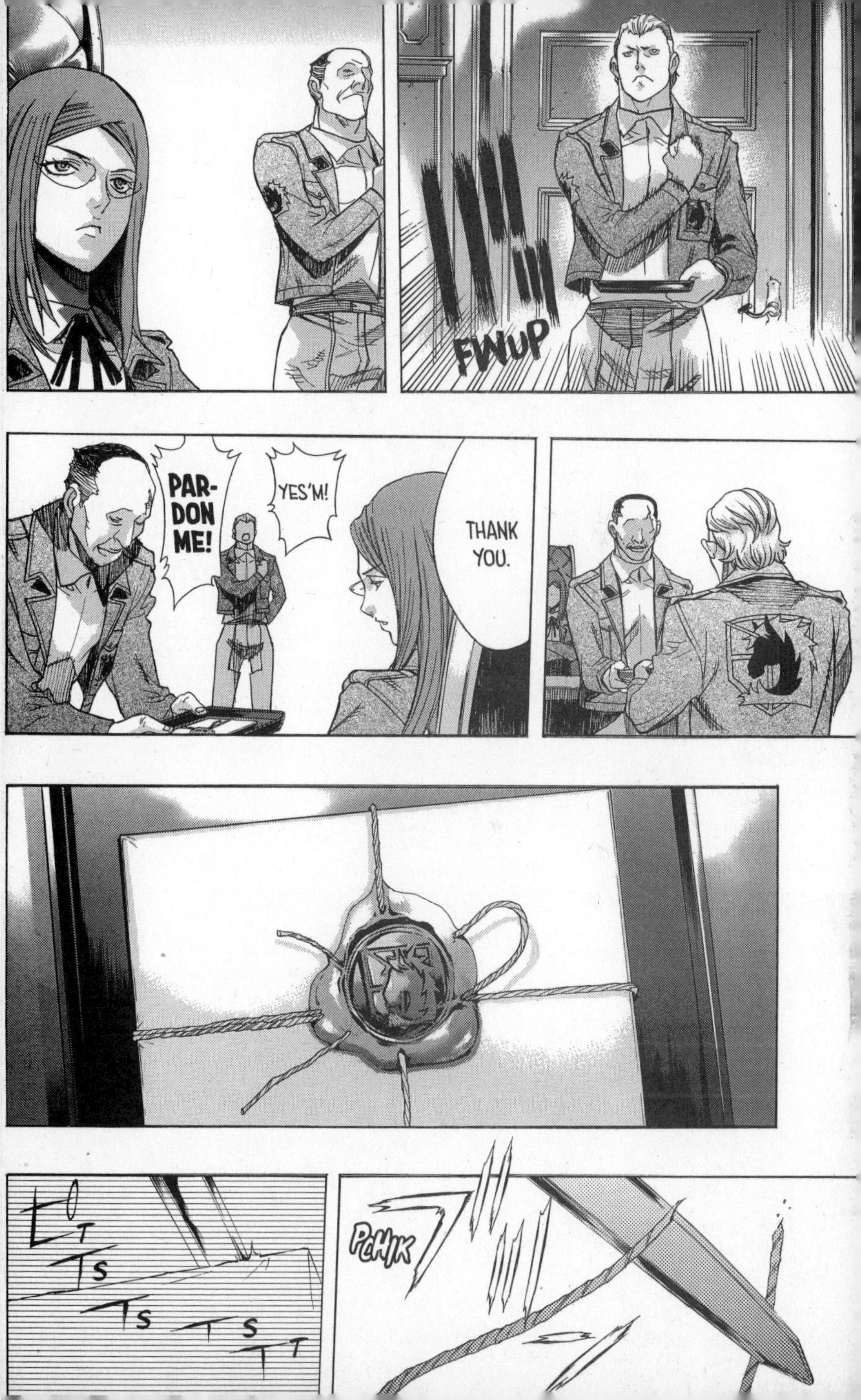
FWUP
THANK YOU.
YES'M!
PAR-DON ME!
PCHIK

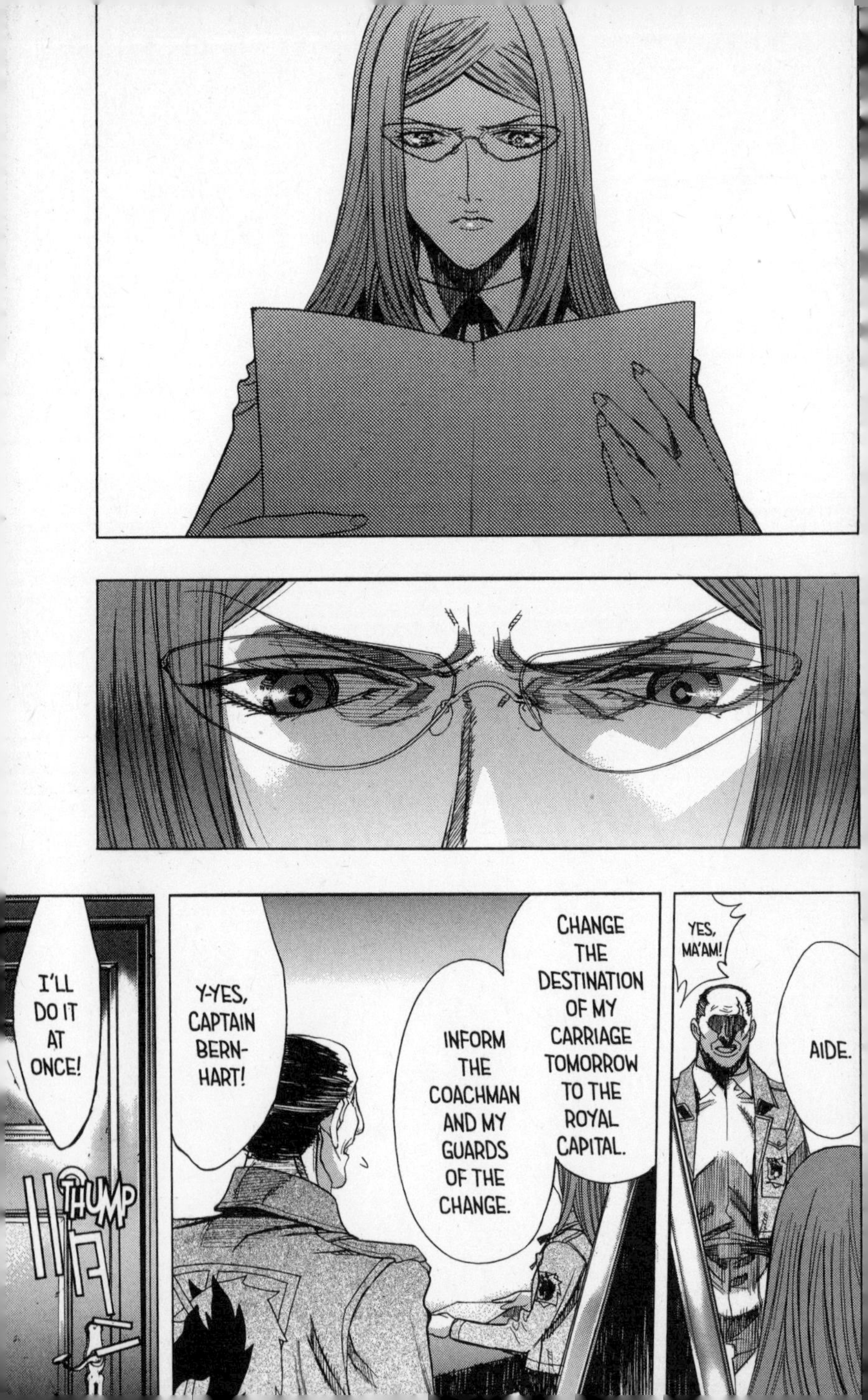
AIDE.
YES, MA'AM!
CHANGE THE DESTINATION OF MY CARRIAGE TOMORROW TO THE ROYAL CAPITAL.
INFORM THE COACHMAN AND MY GUARDS OF THE CHANGE.
Y-YES, CAPTAIN BERN-HART!
I'LL DO IT AT ONCE!
THUMP

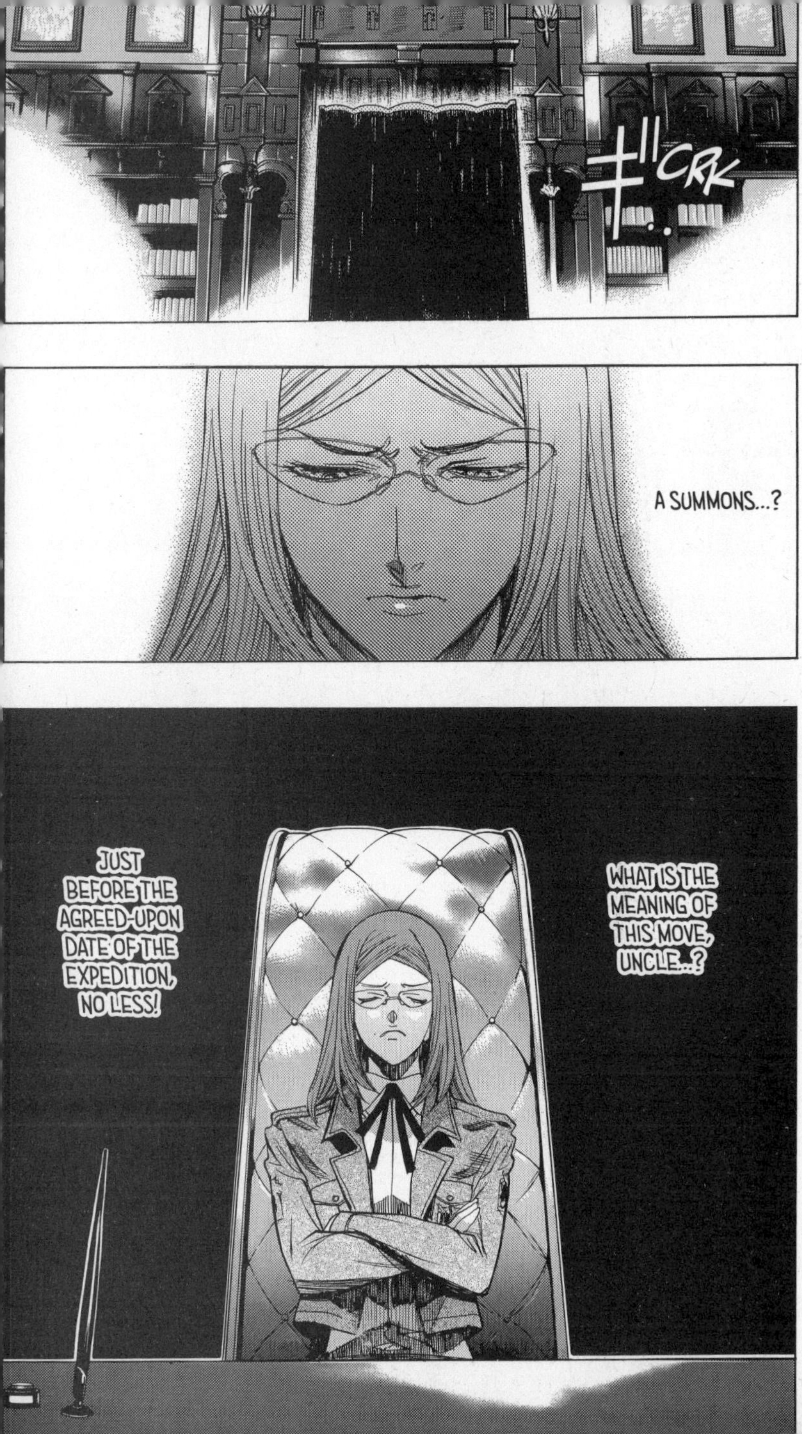
CRK
A SUMMONS...?
WHAT IS THE MEANING OF THIS MOVE, UNCLE...?
JUST BEFORE THE AGREED-UPON DATE OF THE EXPEDITION, NO LESS!

**Chapter 57: Before the Expedition · End**

ATTACK on TITAN
BEFORE THE FALL

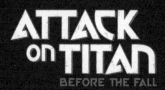

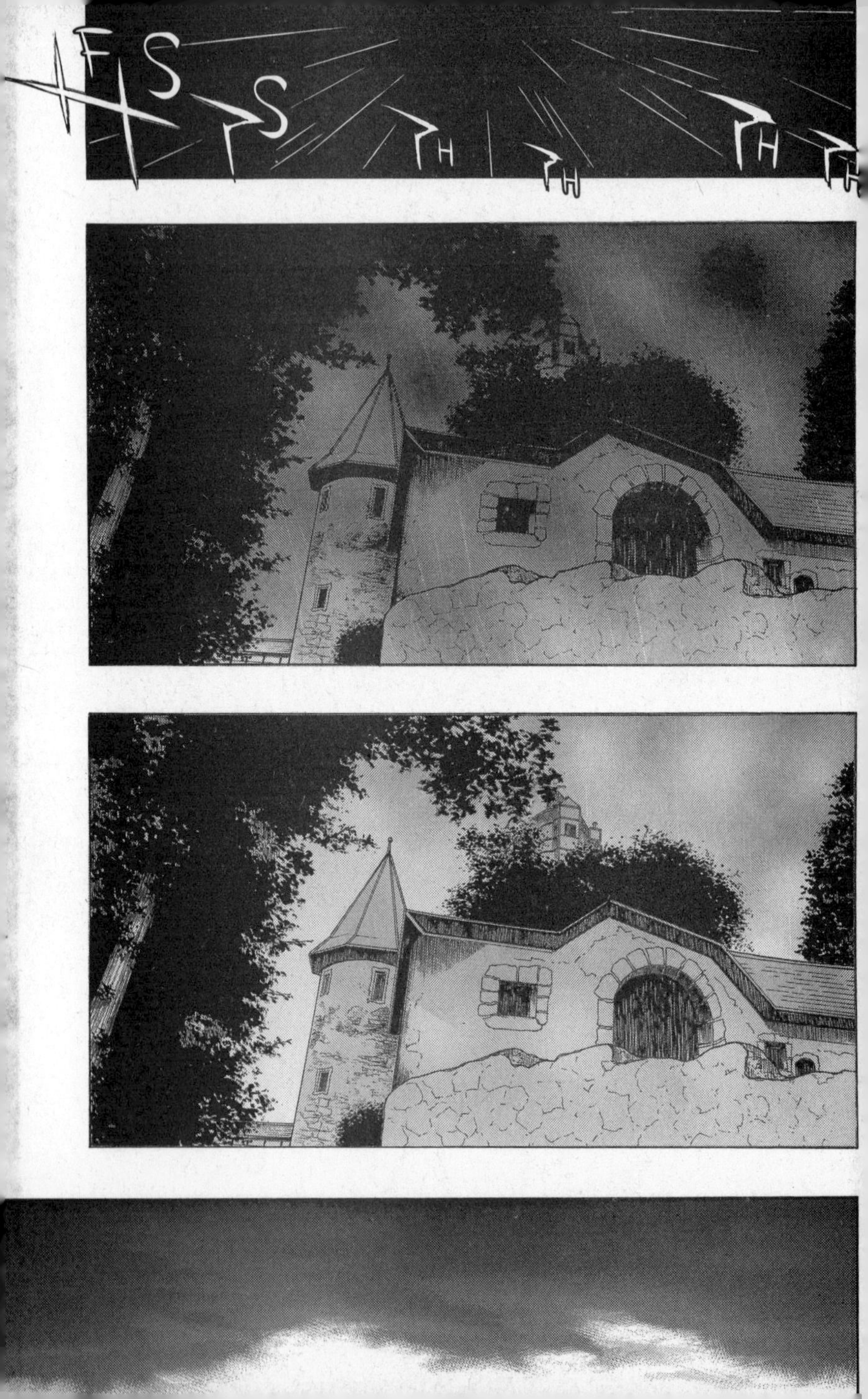

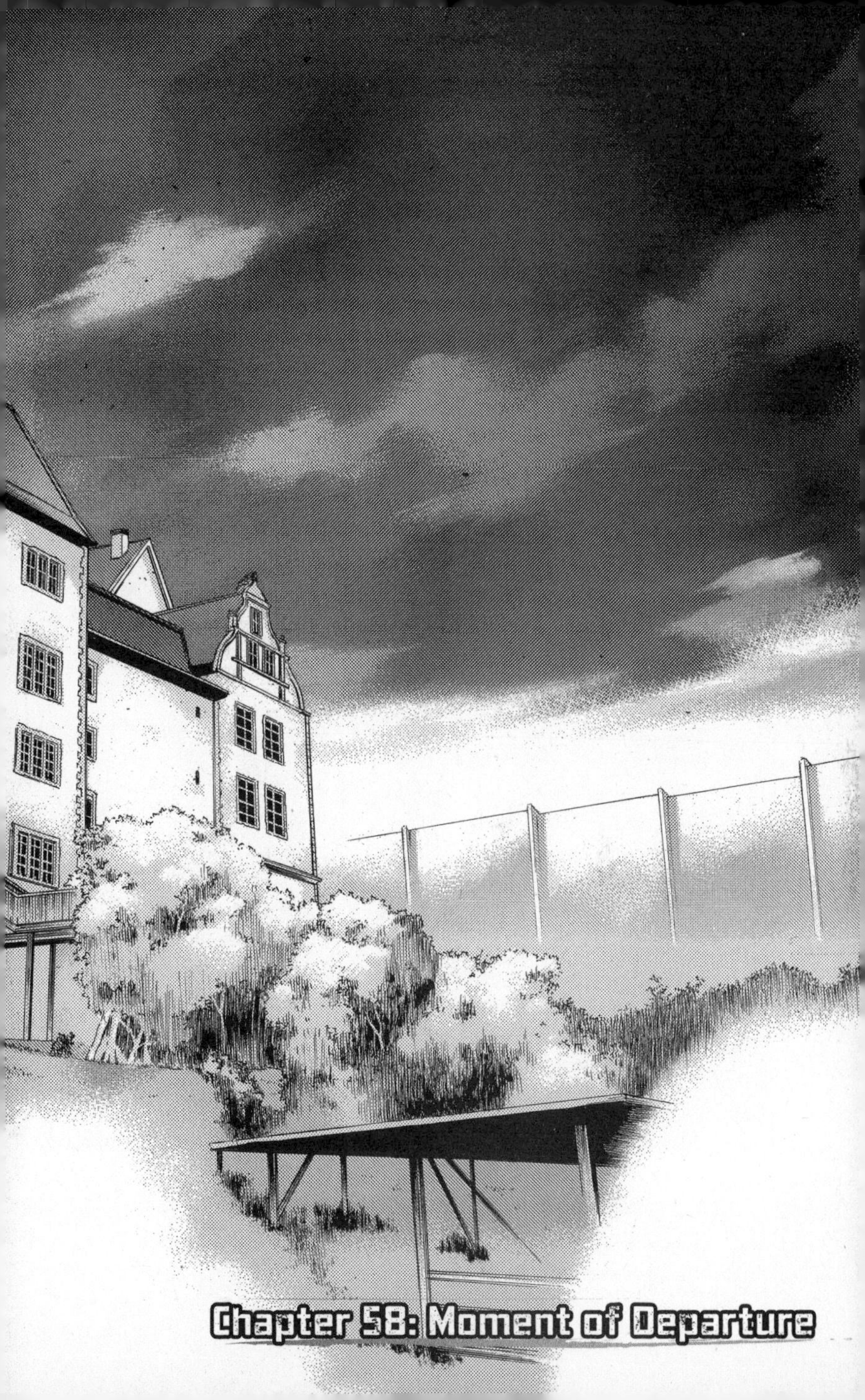
Chapter 58: Moment of Departure

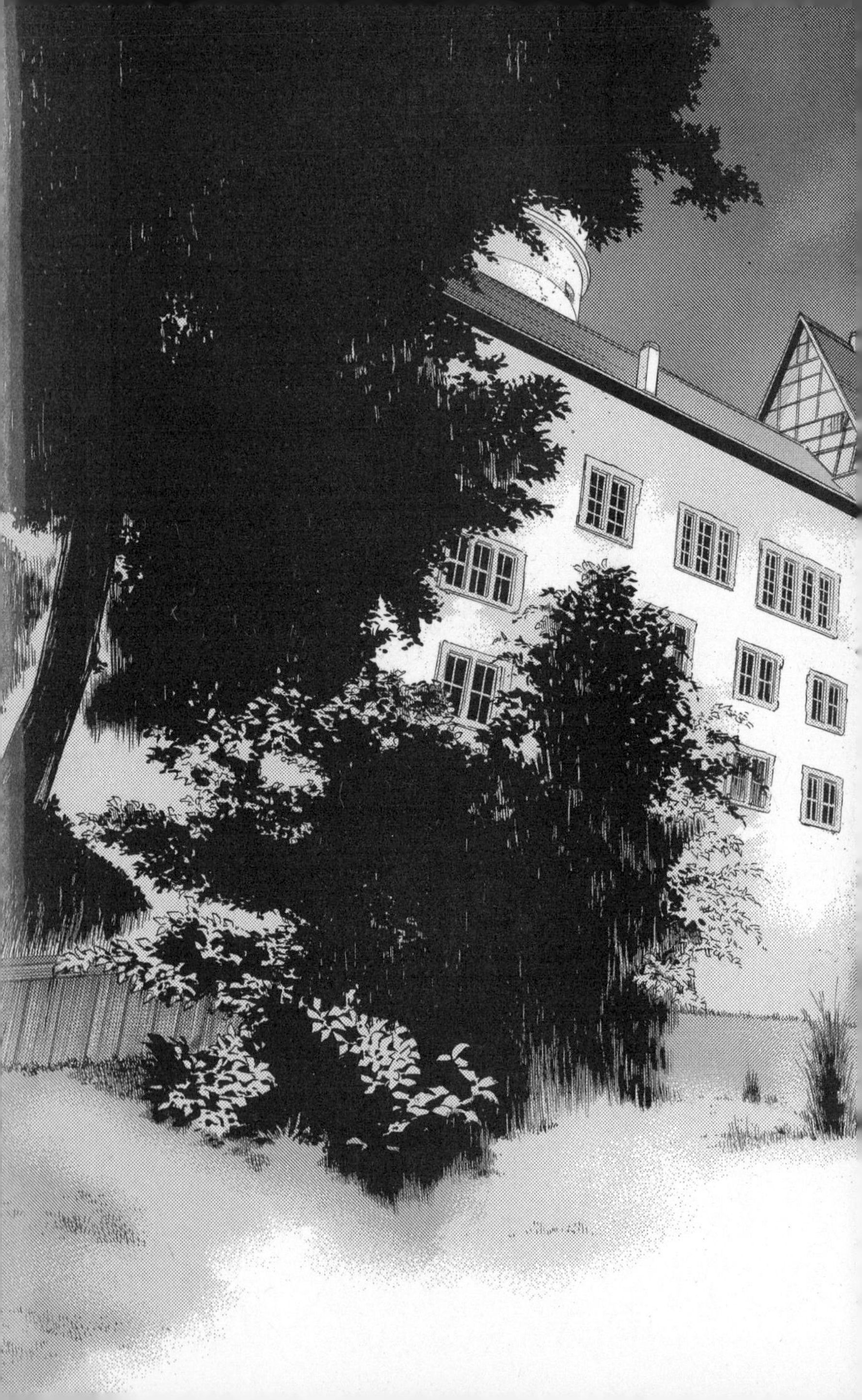

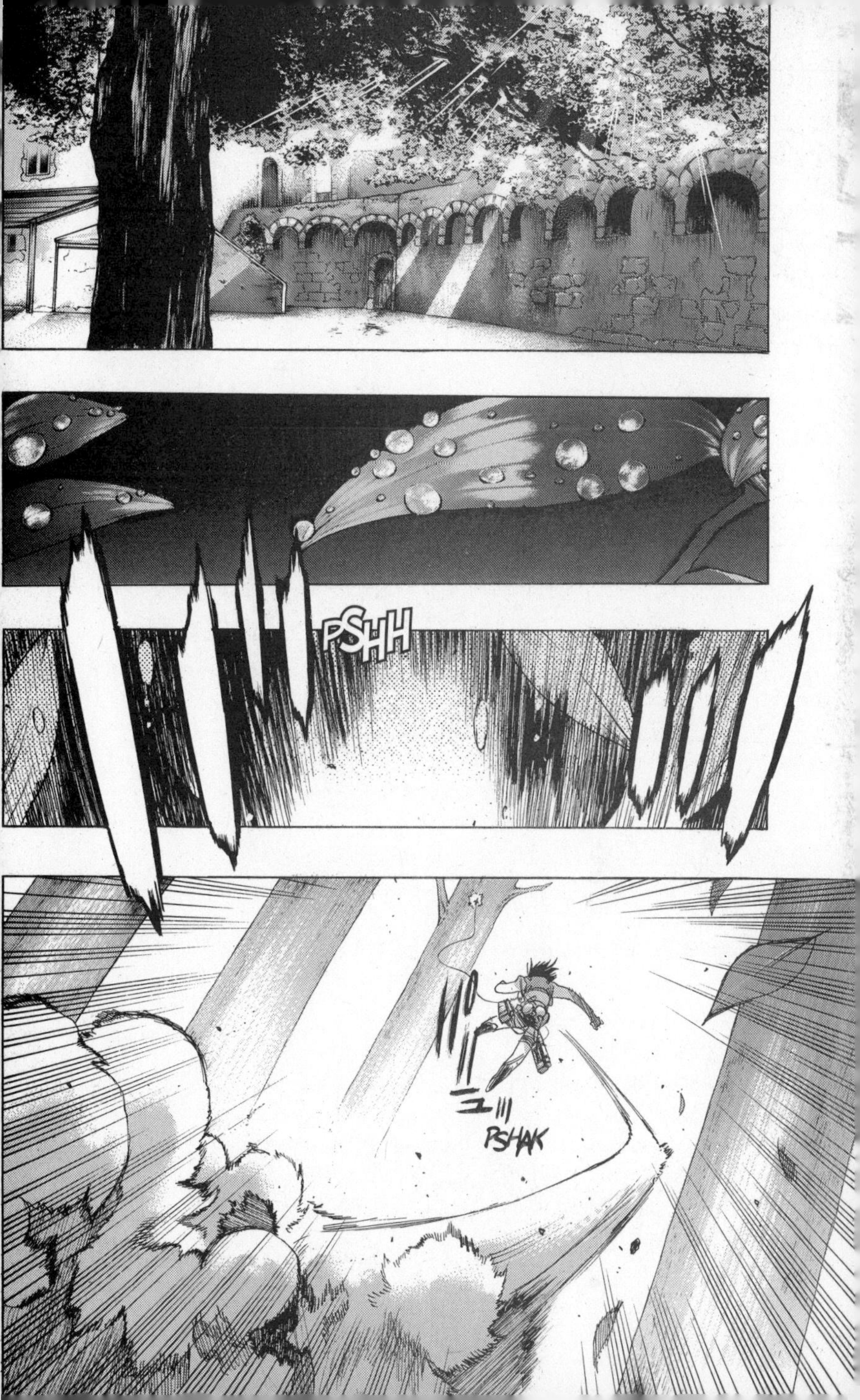
PSHH
PSHAK

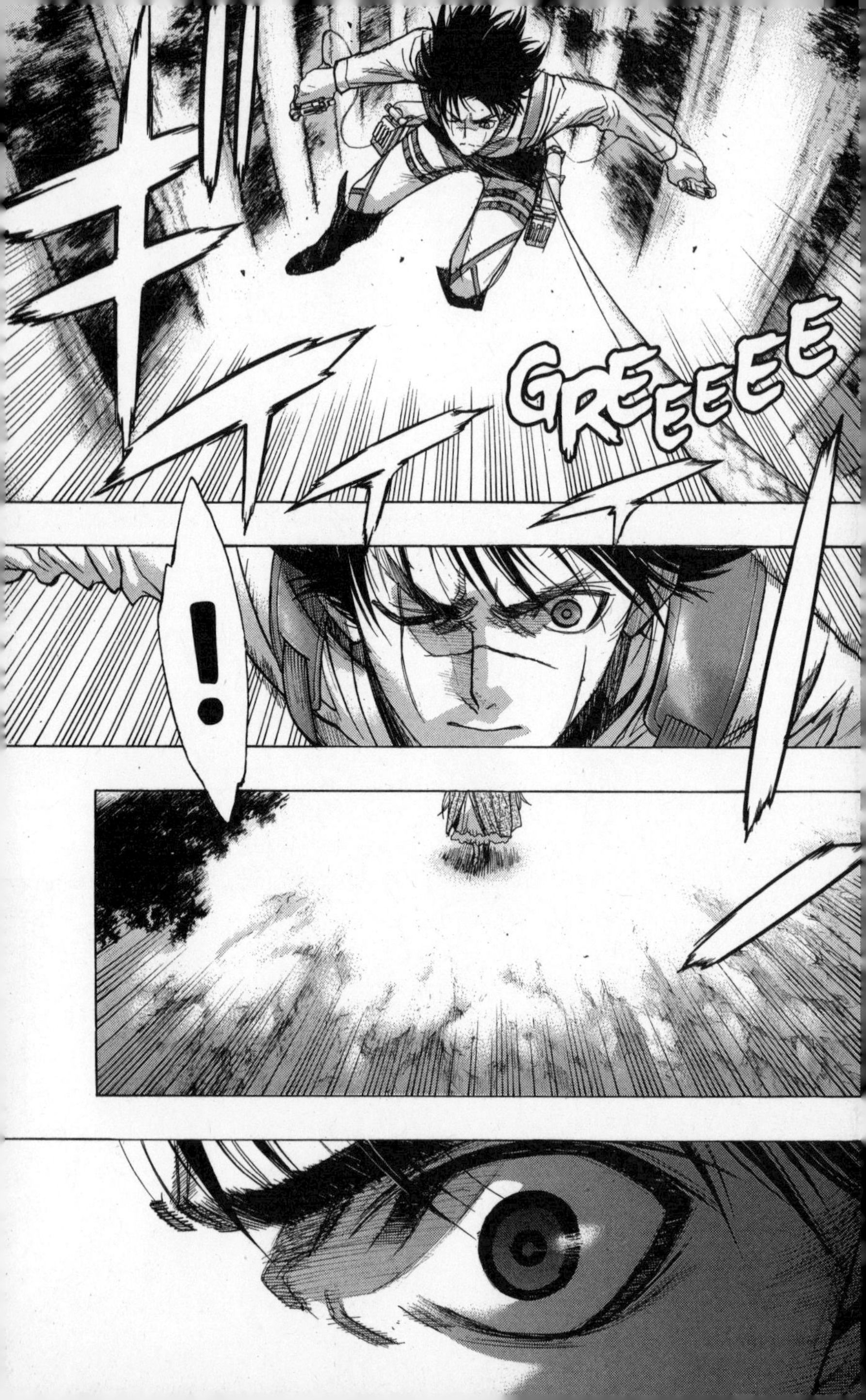
GREEEEEE
!

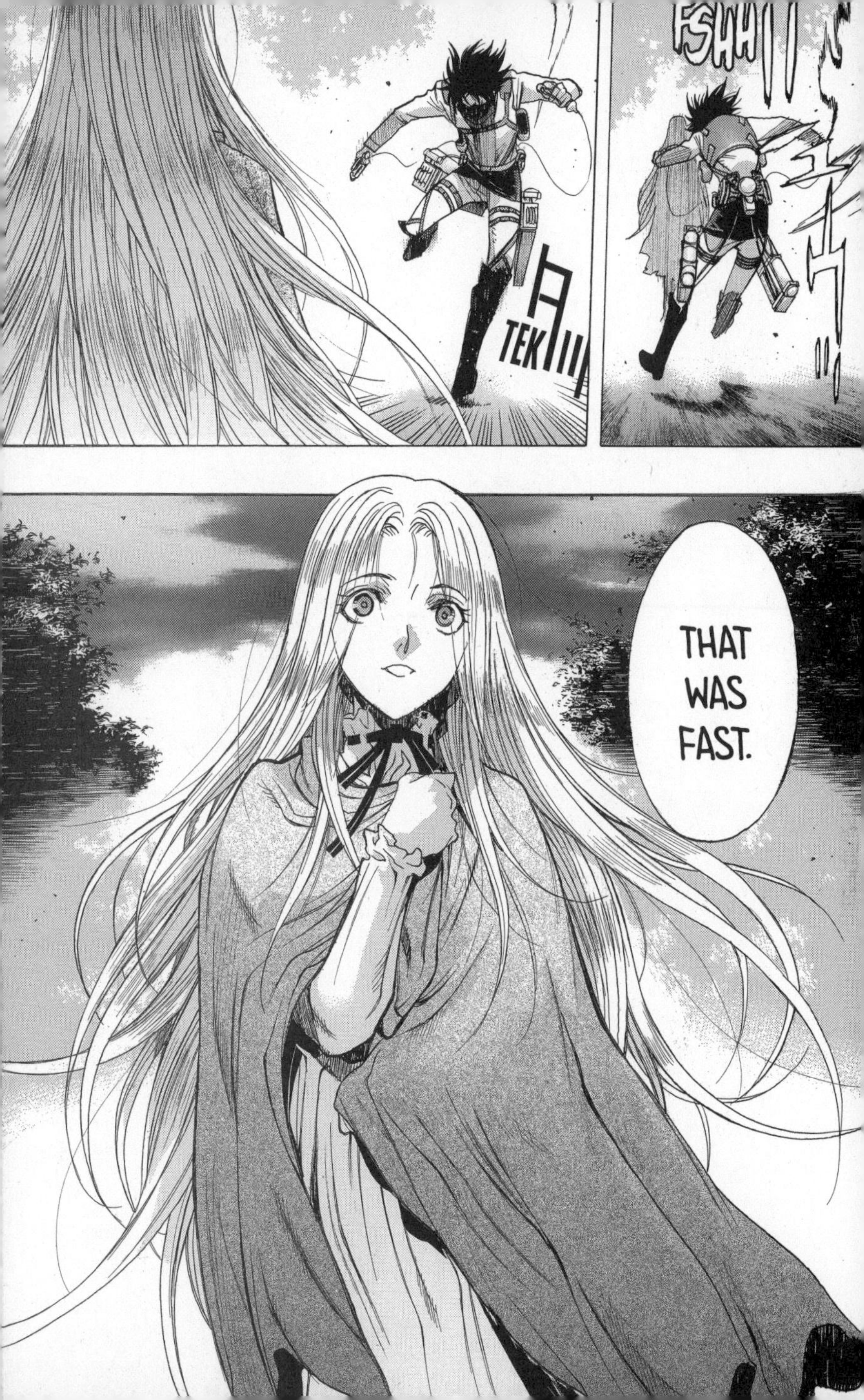
FSHH
TEK
THAT WAS FAST.

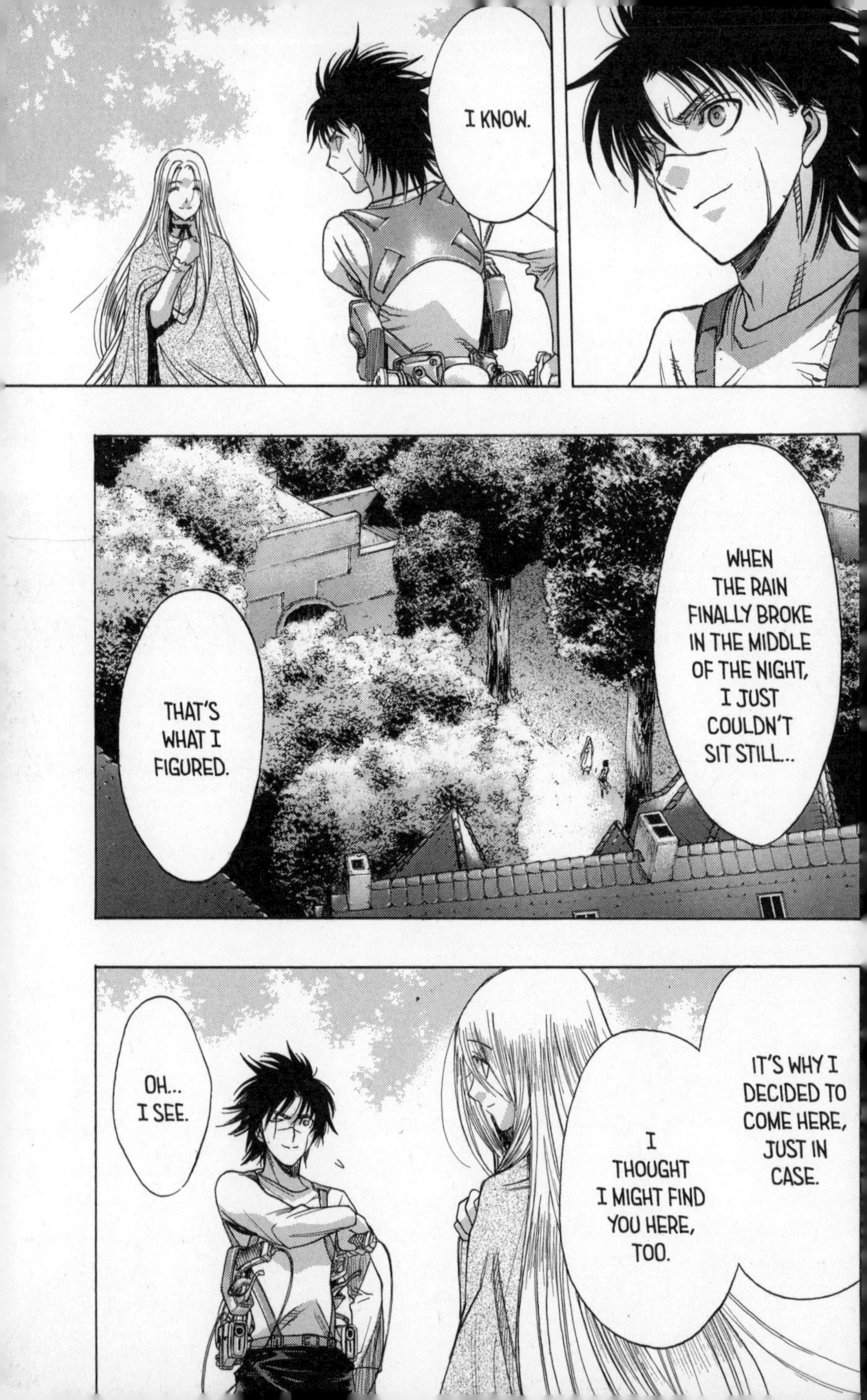
I KNOW.
WHEN THE RAIN FINALLY BROKE IN THE MIDDLE OF THE NIGHT, I JUST COULDN'T SIT STILL...
THAT'S WHAT I FIGURED.
IT'S WHY I DECIDED TO COME HERE, JUST IN CASE.
I THOUGHT I MIGHT FIND YOU HERE, TOO.
OH... I SEE.

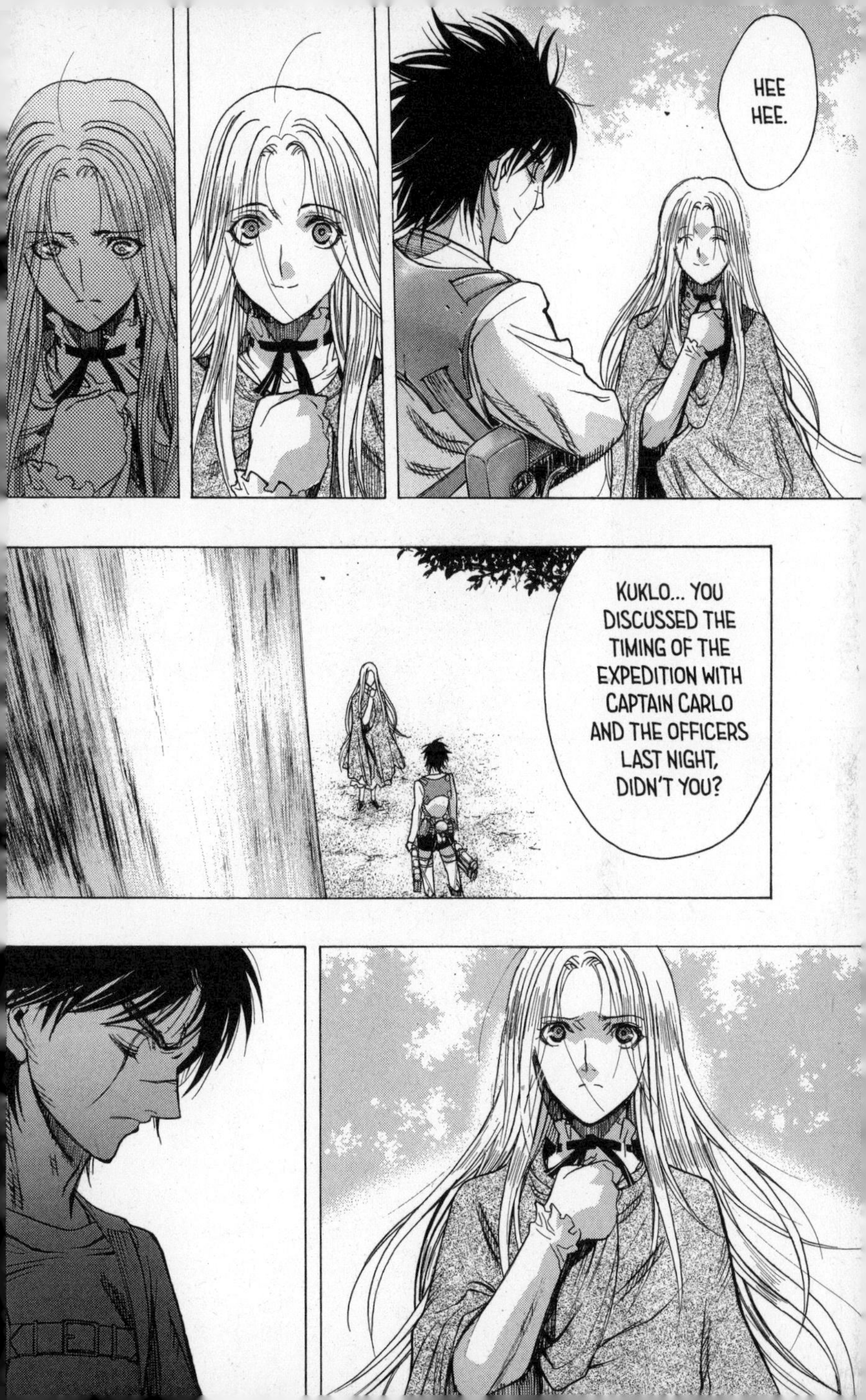
HEE HEE.
KUKLO... YOU DISCUSSED THE TIMING OF THE EXPEDITION WITH CAPTAIN CARLO AND THE OFFICERS LAST NIGHT, DIDN'T YOU?

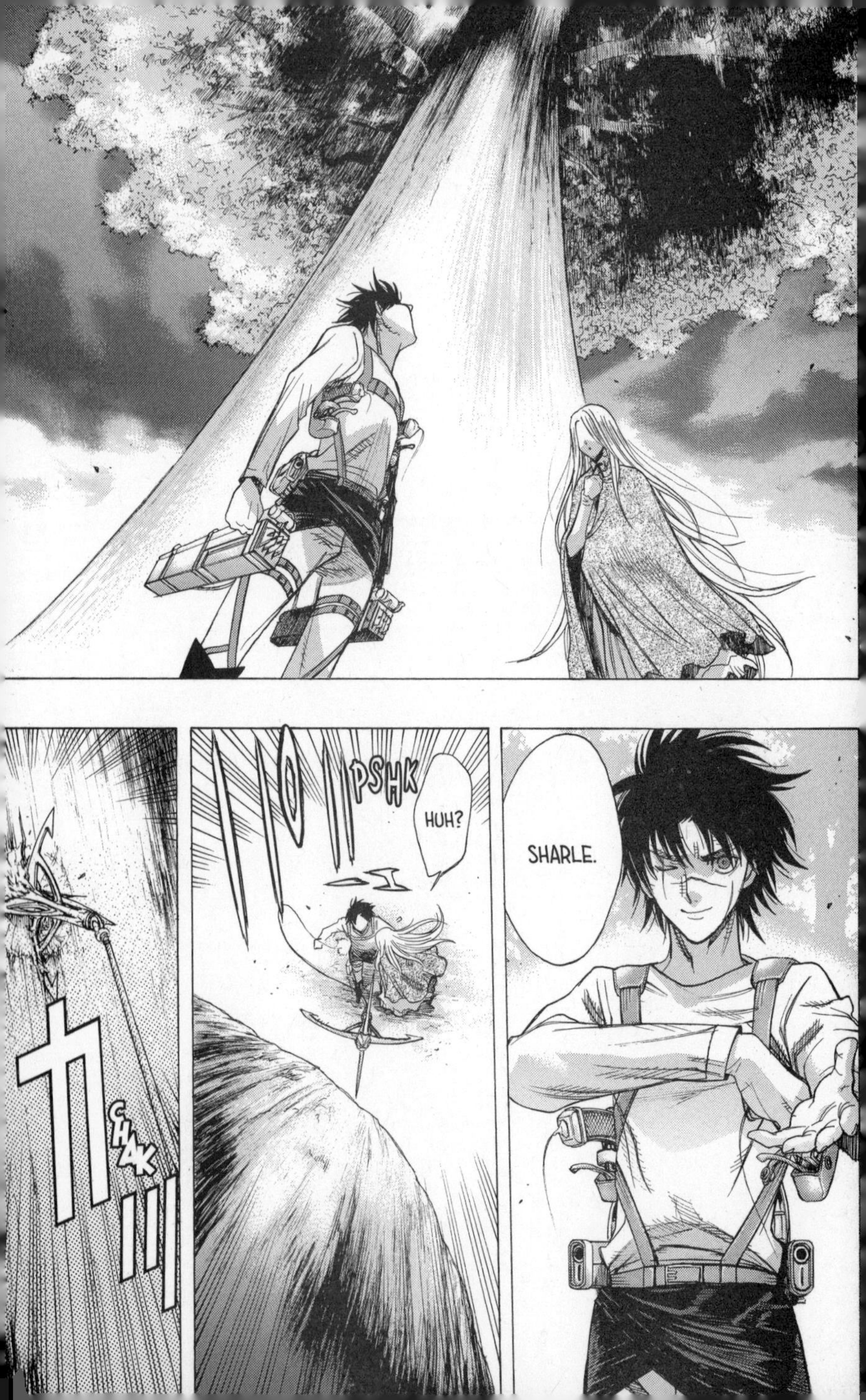
SHARLE.
PSHK
HUH?
CHAK

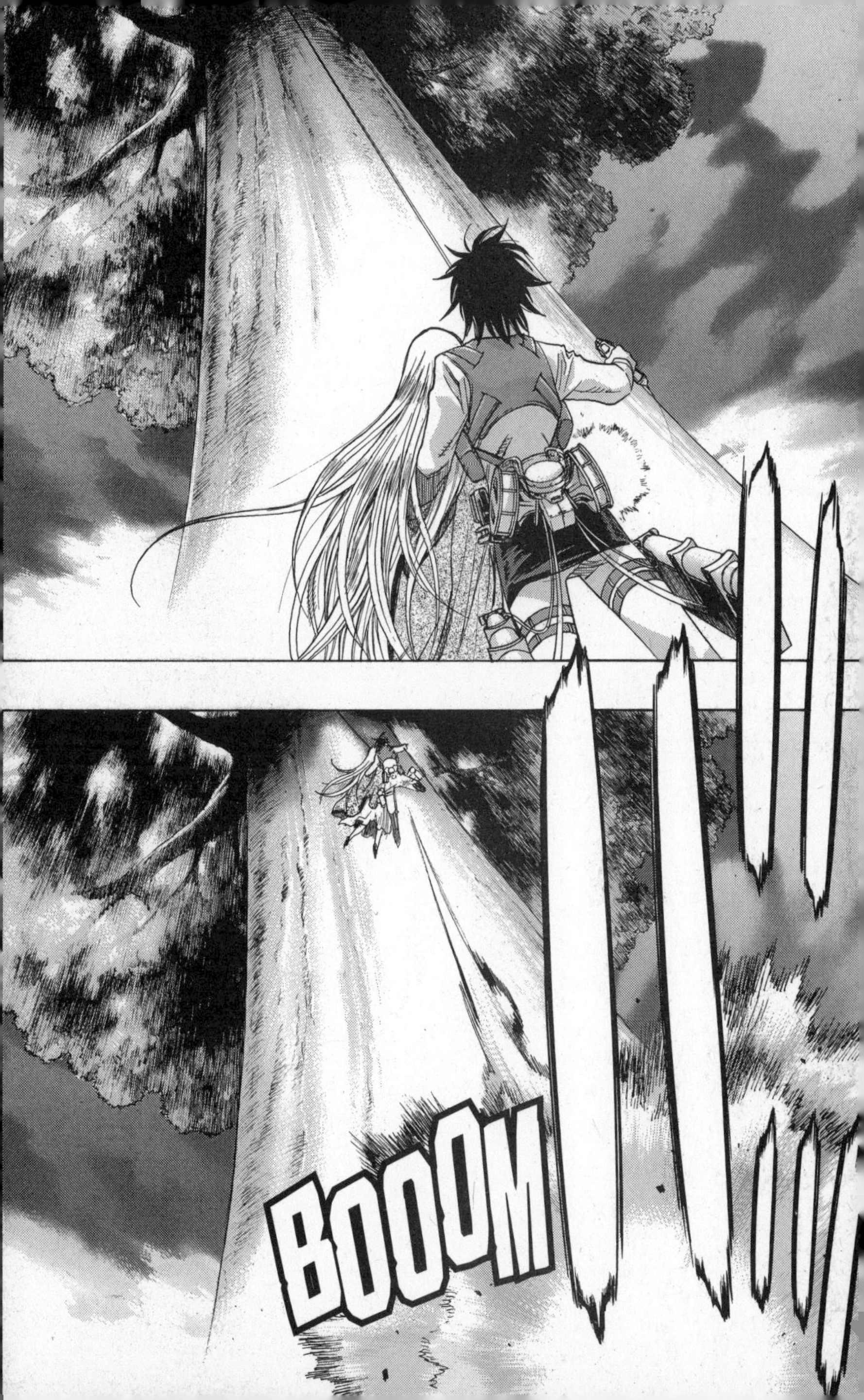
BOOOM

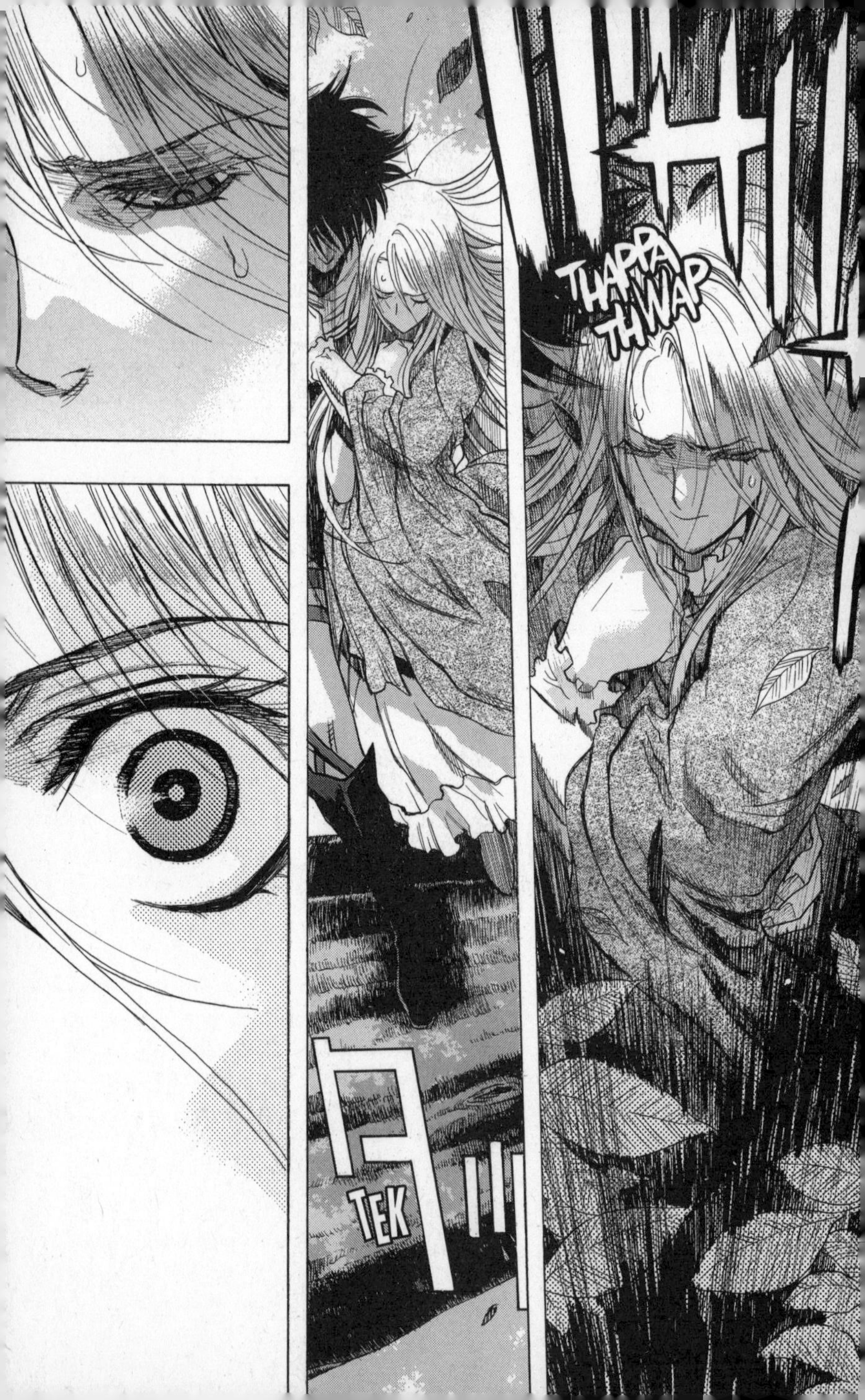
THAPPA THWAP
TEK

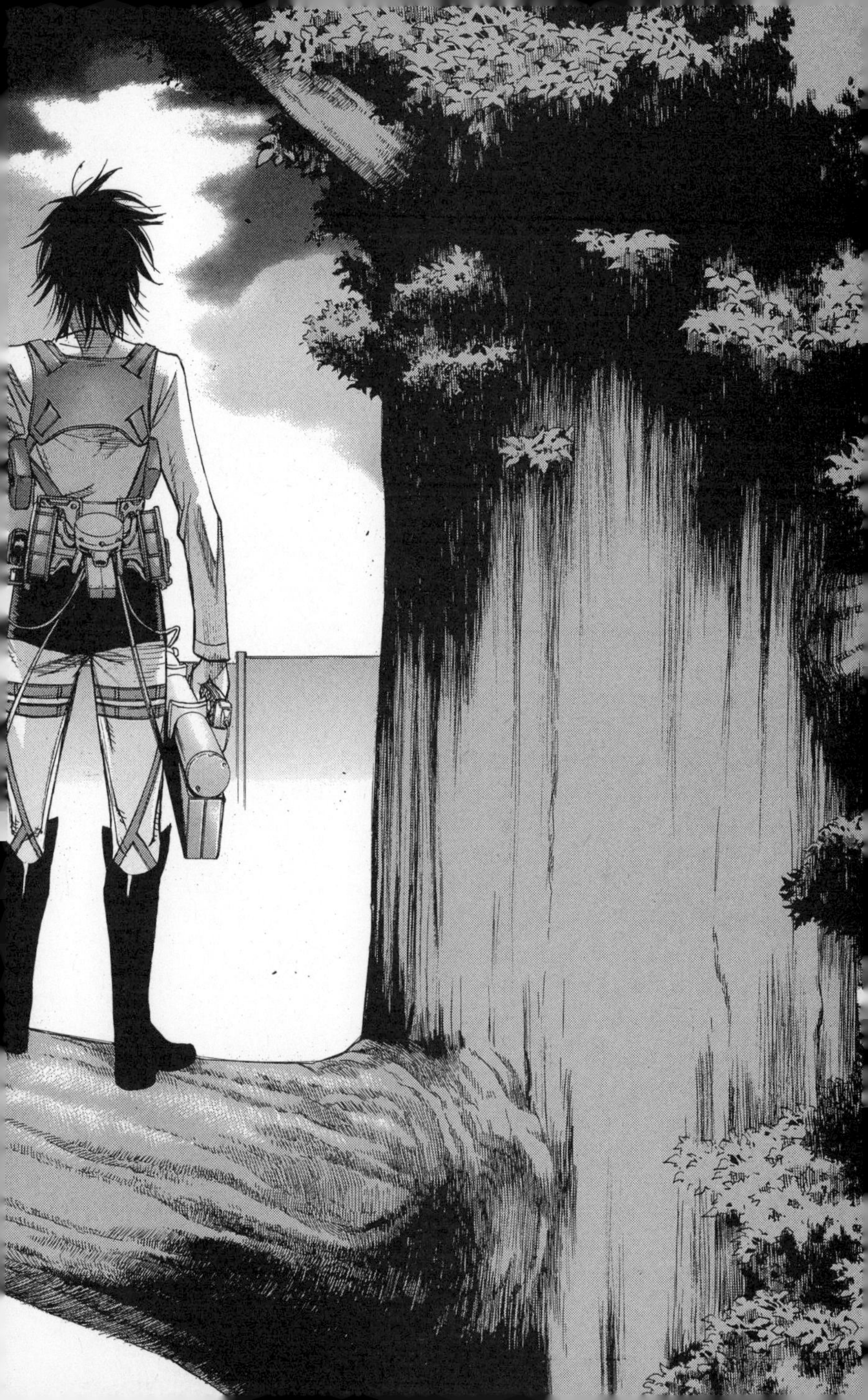

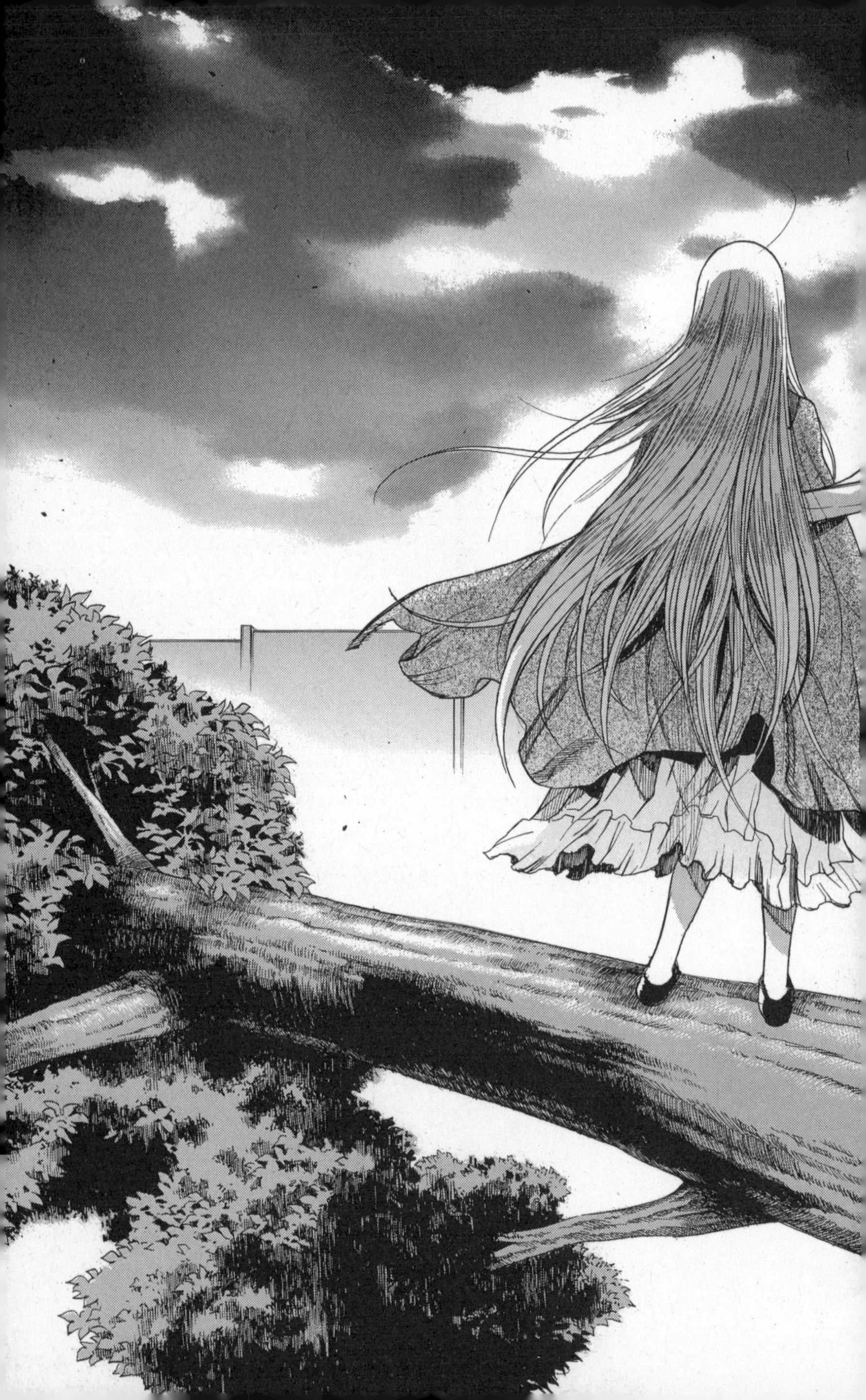

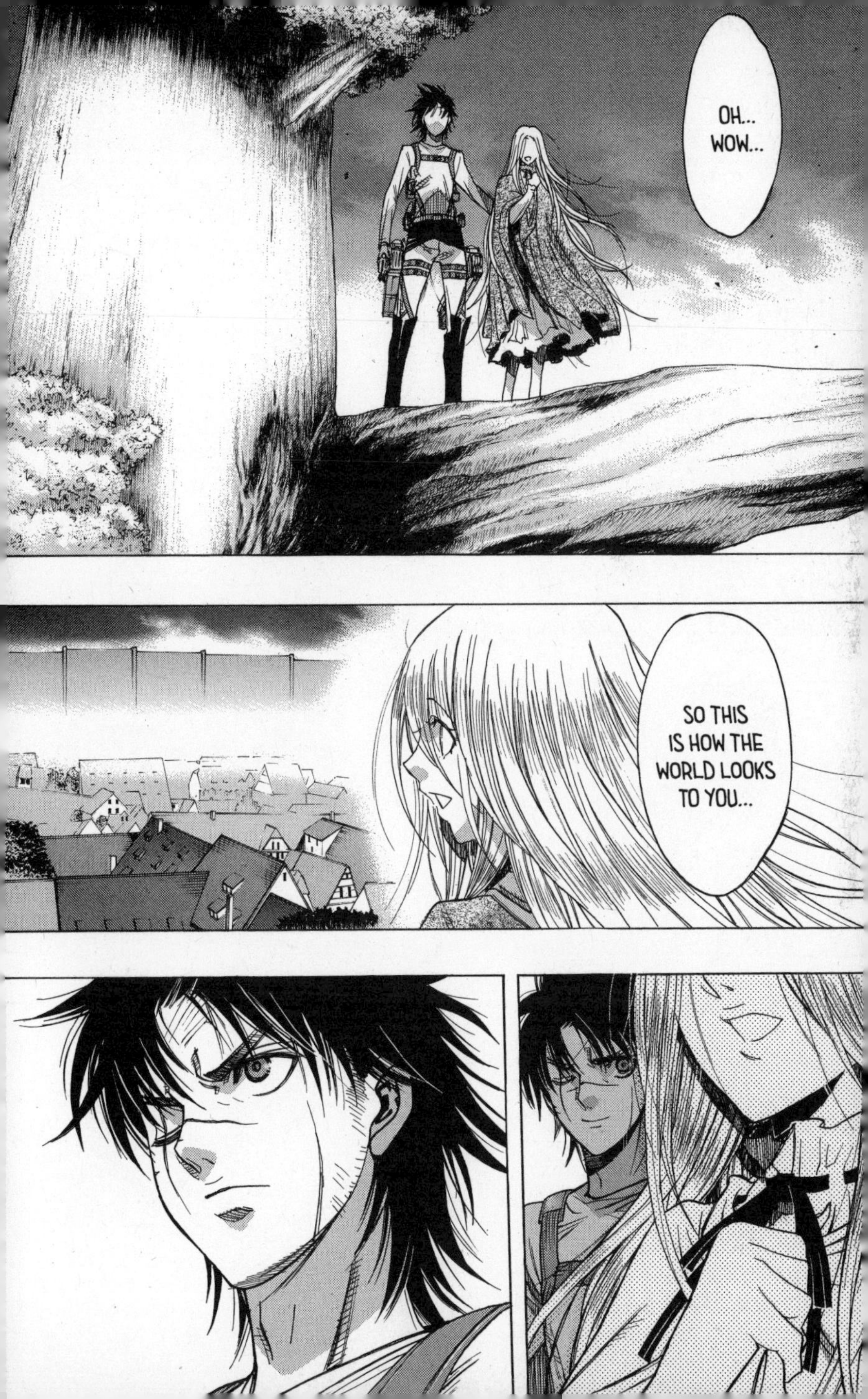
OH... WOW...
SO THIS IS HOW THE WORLD LOOKS TO YOU...

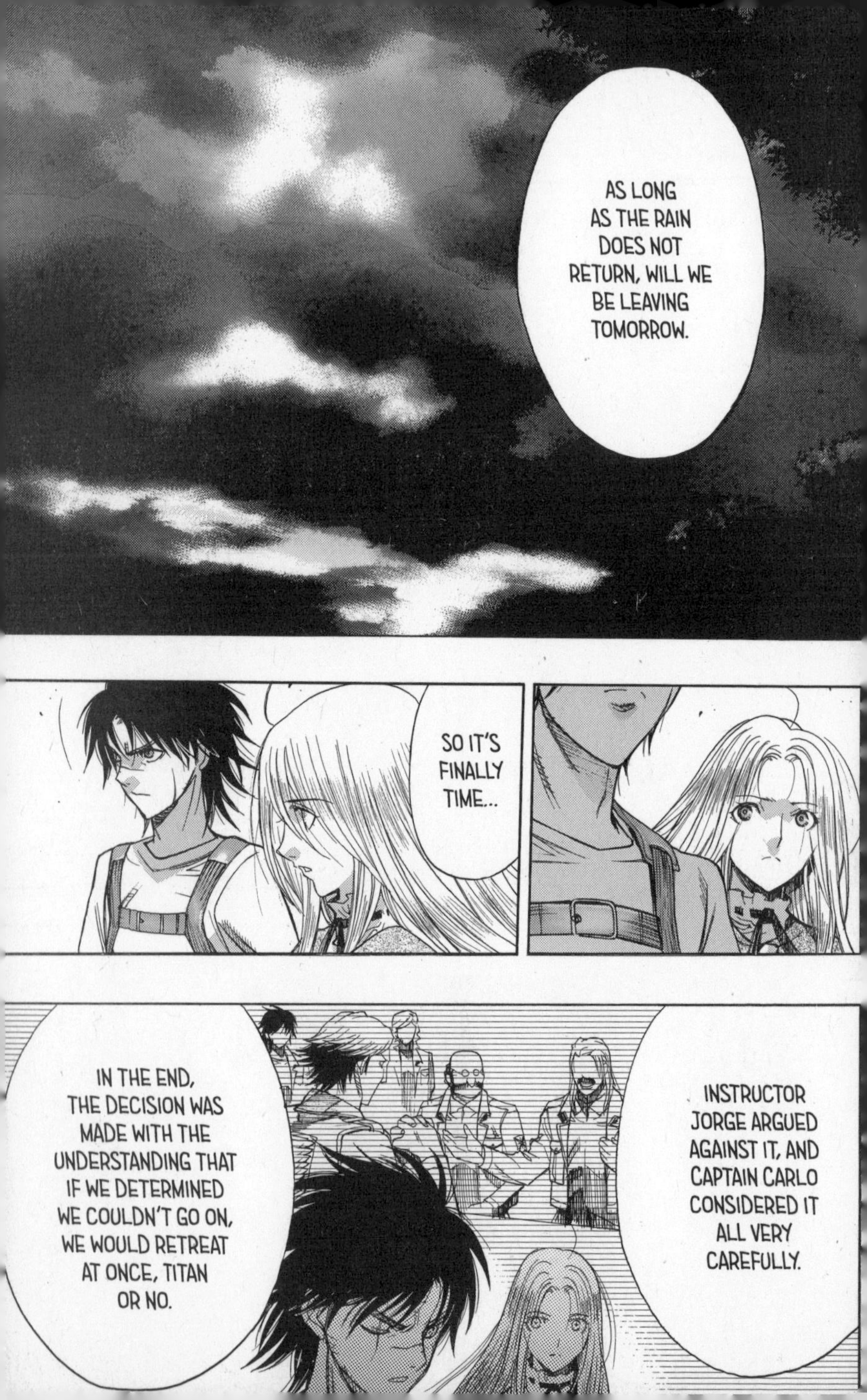
AS LONG AS THE RAIN DOES NOT RETURN, WILL WE BE LEAVING TOMORROW.
SO IT'S FINALLY TIME...
INSTRUCTOR JORGE ARGUED AGAINST IT, AND CAPTAIN CARLO CONSIDERED IT ALL VERY CAREFULLY.
IN THE END, THE DECISION WAS MADE WITH THE UNDERSTANDING THAT IF WE DETERMINED WE COULDN'T GO ON, WE WOULD RETREAT AT ONCE, TITAN OR NO.

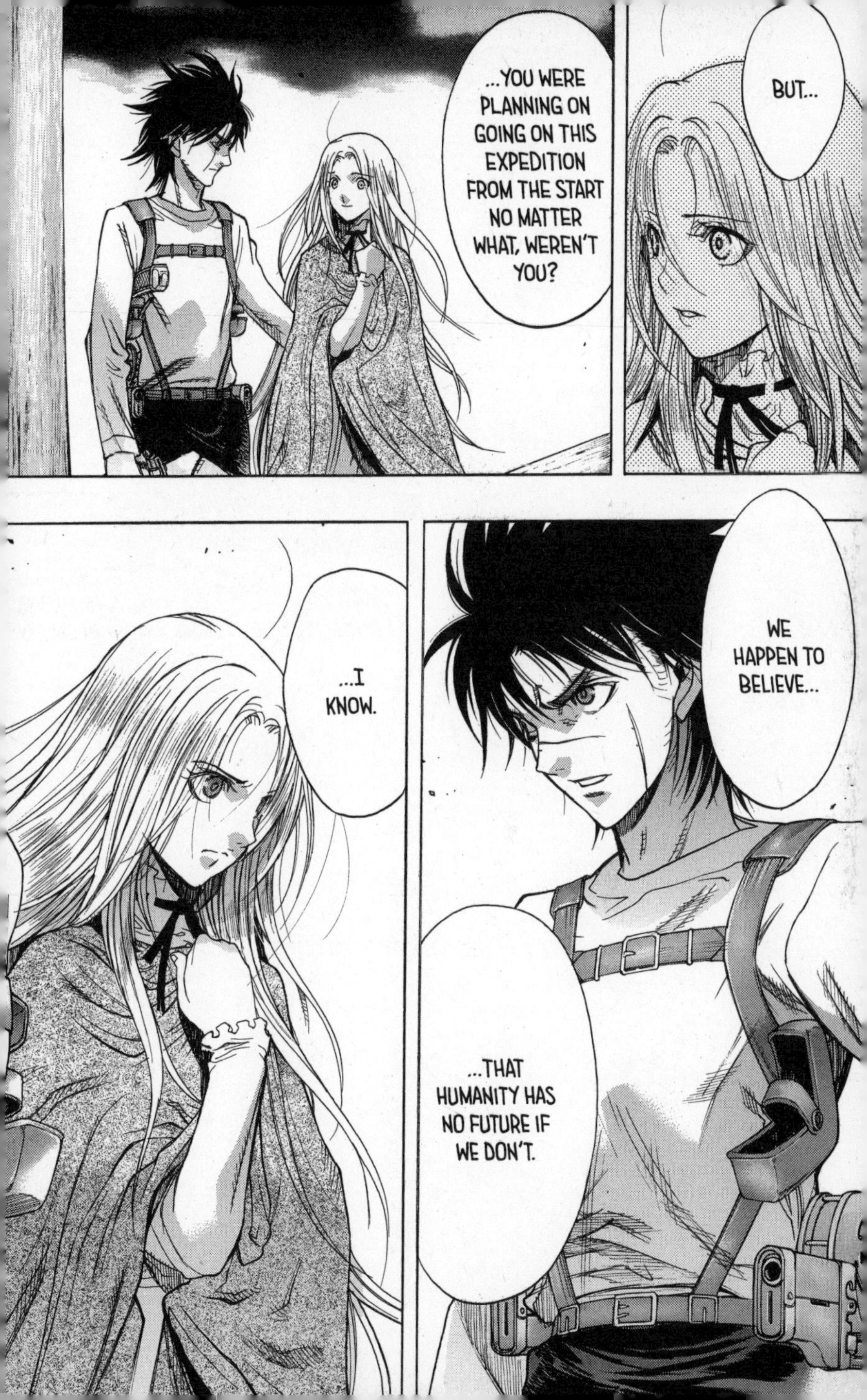
BUT...
...YOU WERE PLANNING ON GOING ON THIS EXPEDITION FROM THE START NO MATTER WHAT, WEREN'T YOU?
WE HAPPEN TO BELIEVE...
...THAT HUMANITY HAS NO FUTURE IF WE DON'T.
...I KNOW.

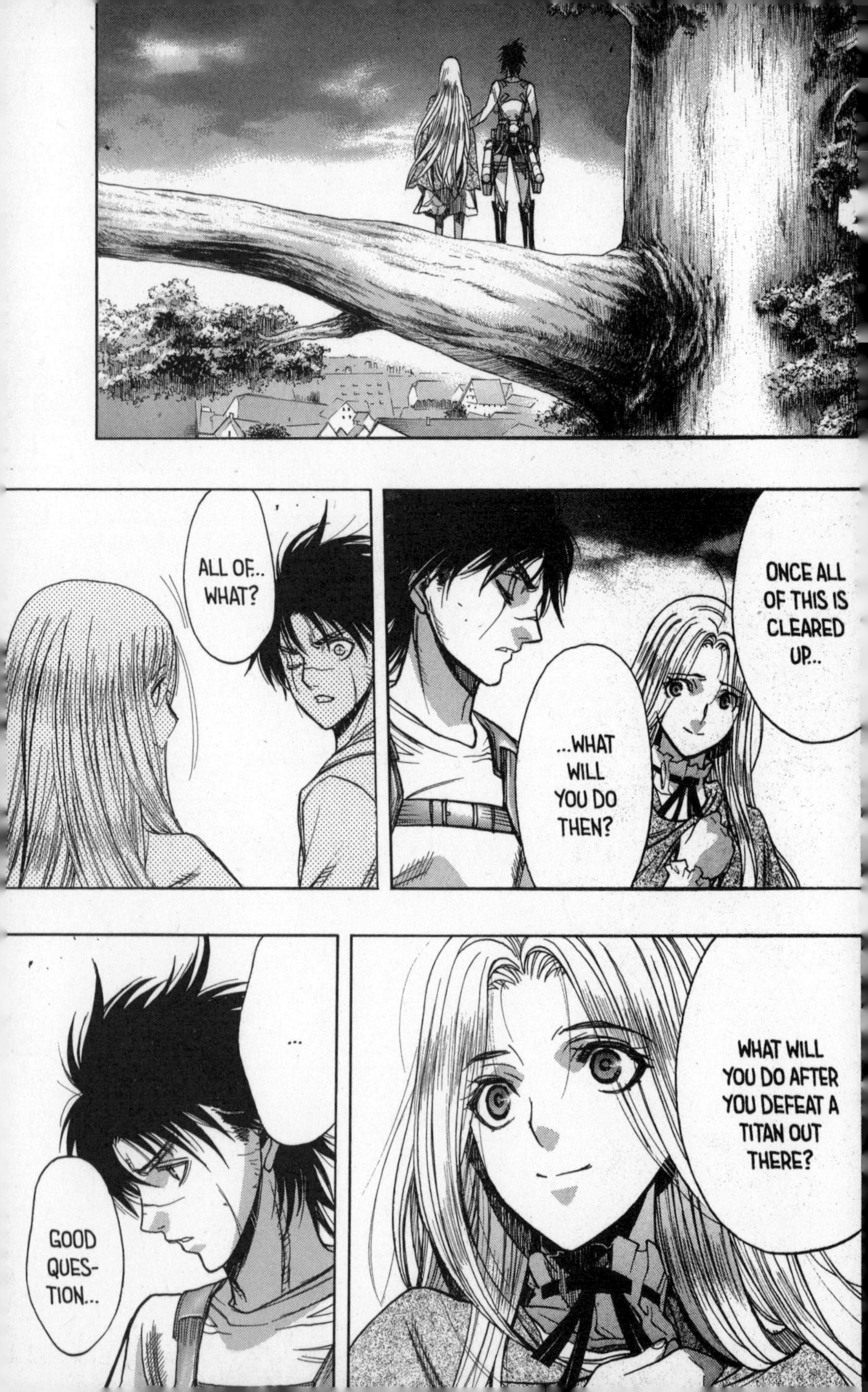
ONCE ALL OF THIS IS CLEARED UP...
...WHAT WILL YOU DO THEN?
ALL OF... WHAT?
WHAT WILL YOU DO AFTER YOU DEFEAT A TITAN OUT THERE?
...
GOOD QUES-TION...

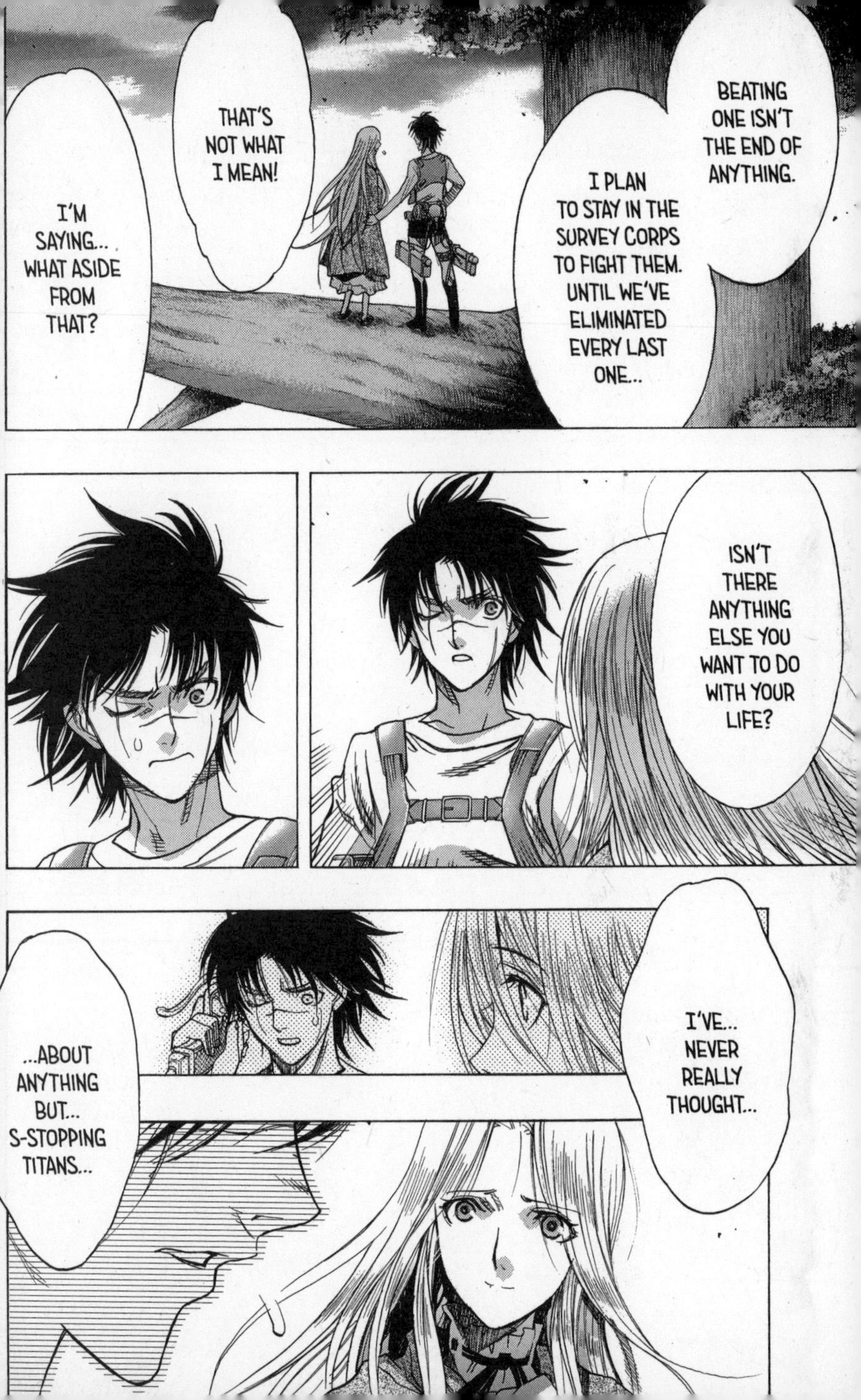
BEATING ONE ISN'T THE END OF ANYTHING.
I PLAN TO STAY IN THE SURVEY CORPS TO FIGHT THEM. UNTIL WE'VE ELIMINATED EVERY LAST ONE...
THAT'S NOT WHAT I MEAN!
I'M SAYING... WHAT ASIDE FROM THAT?
ISN'T THERE ANYTHING ELSE YOU WANT TO DO WITH YOUR LIFE?
I'VE... NEVER REALLY THOUGHT...
...ABOUT ANYTHING BUT... S-STOPPING TITANS...

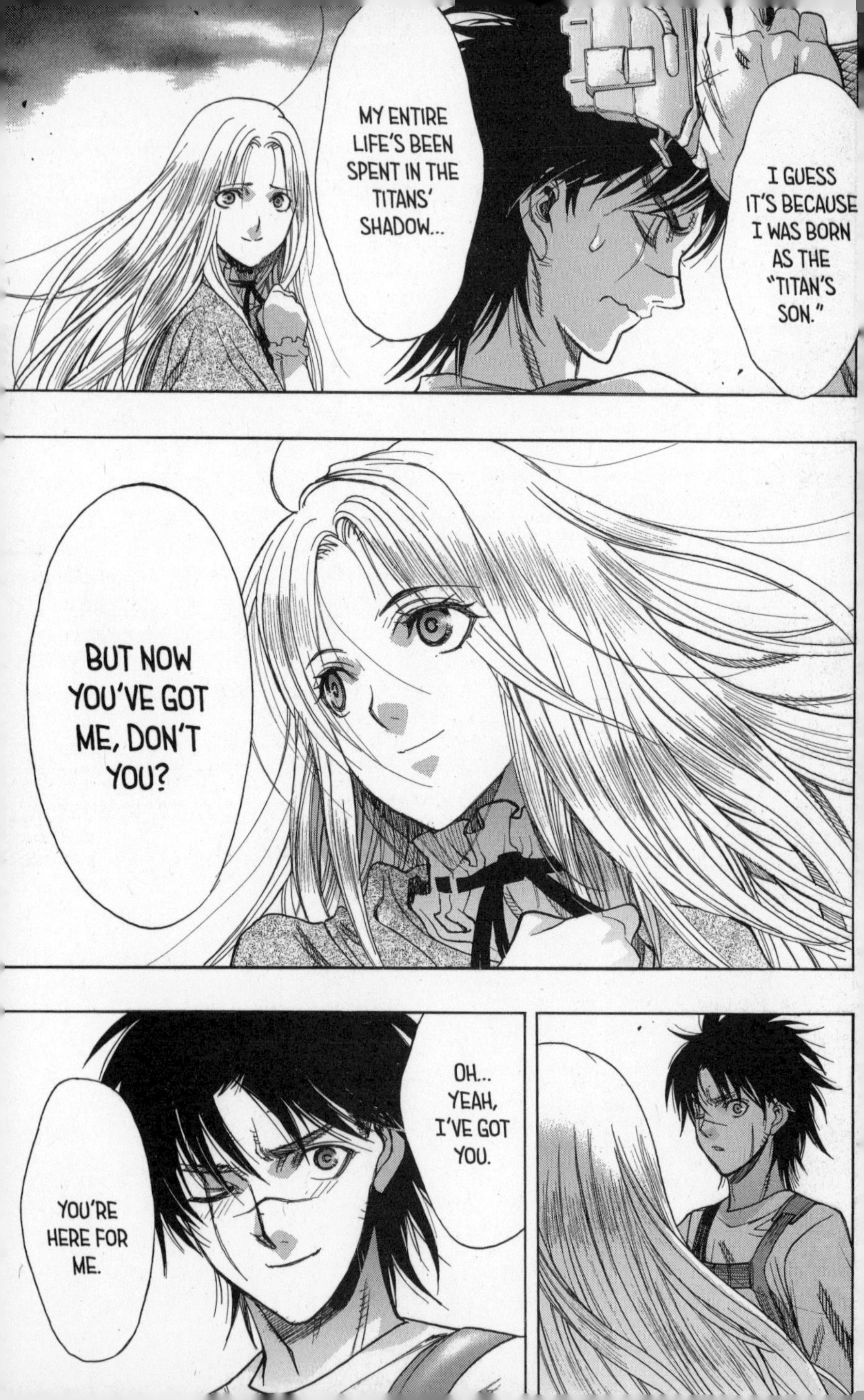
I GUESS IT'S BECAUSE I WAS BORN AS THE "TITAN'S SON."
MY ENTIRE LIFE'S BEEN SPENT IN THE TITANS' SHADOW...
BUT NOW YOU'VE GOT ME, DON'T YOU?
OH... YEAH, I'VE GOT YOU.
YOU'RE HERE FOR ME.

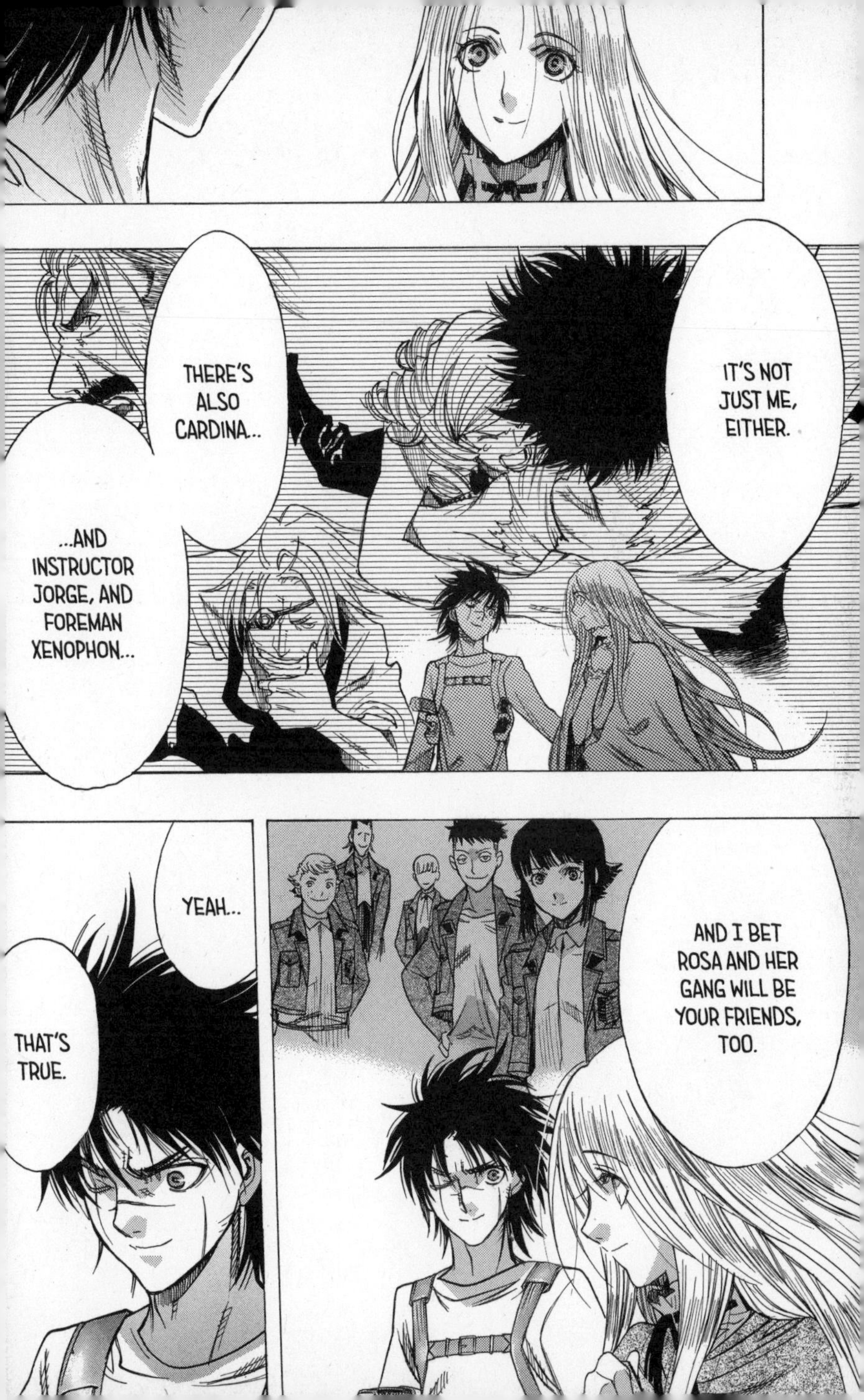
IT'S NOT JUST ME, EITHER.
THERE'S ALSO CARDINA...
...AND INSTRUCTOR JORGE, AND FOREMAN XENOPHON...
AND I BET ROSA AND HER GANG WILL BE YOUR FRIENDS, TOO.
YEAH...
THAT'S TRUE.

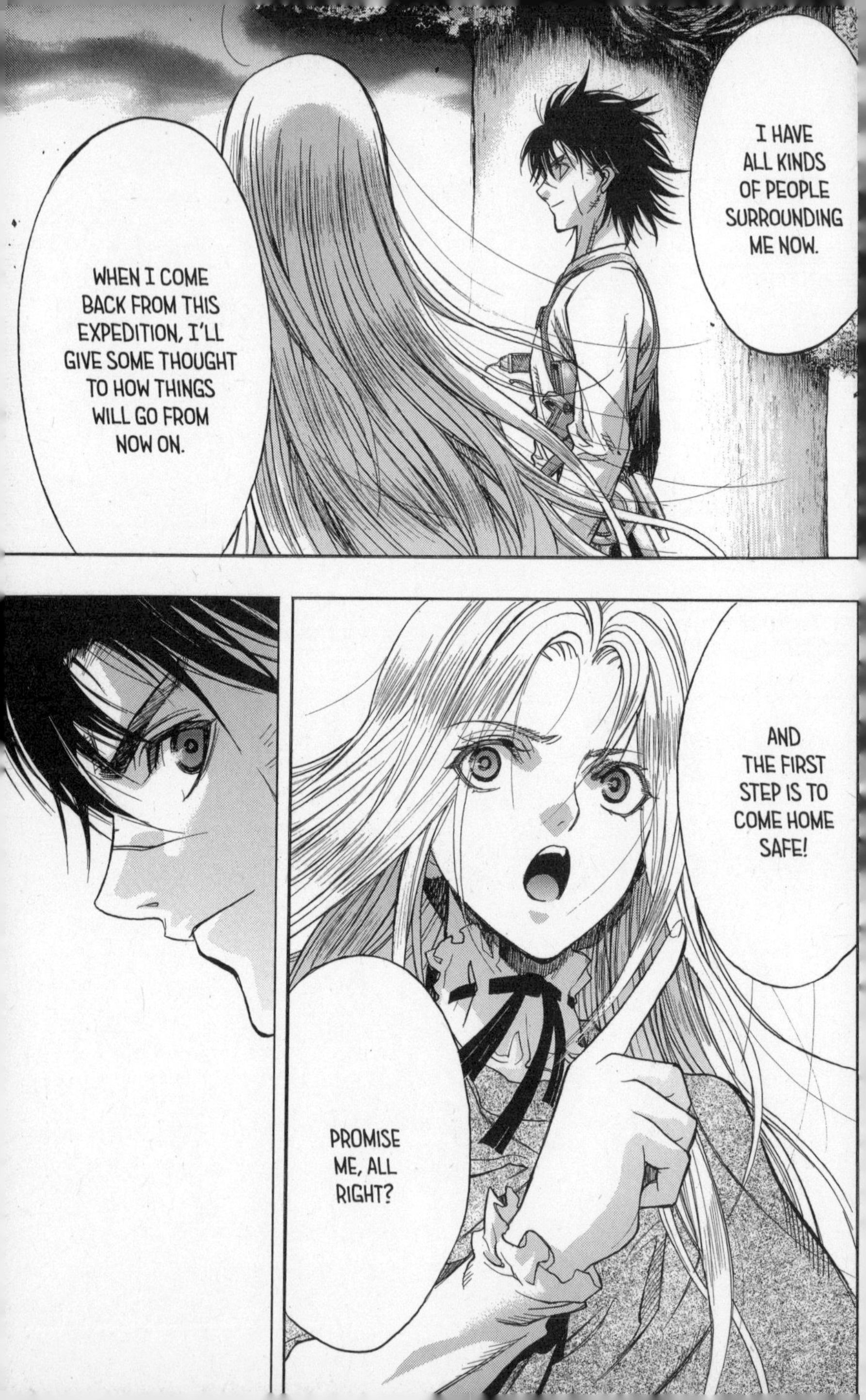
I HAVE ALL KINDS OF PEOPLE SURROUNDING ME NOW.
WHEN I COME BACK FROM THIS EXPEDITION, I'LL GIVE SOME THOUGHT TO HOW THINGS WILL GO FROM NOW ON.
AND THE FIRST STEP IS TO COME HOME SAFE!
PROMISE ME, ALL RIGHT?

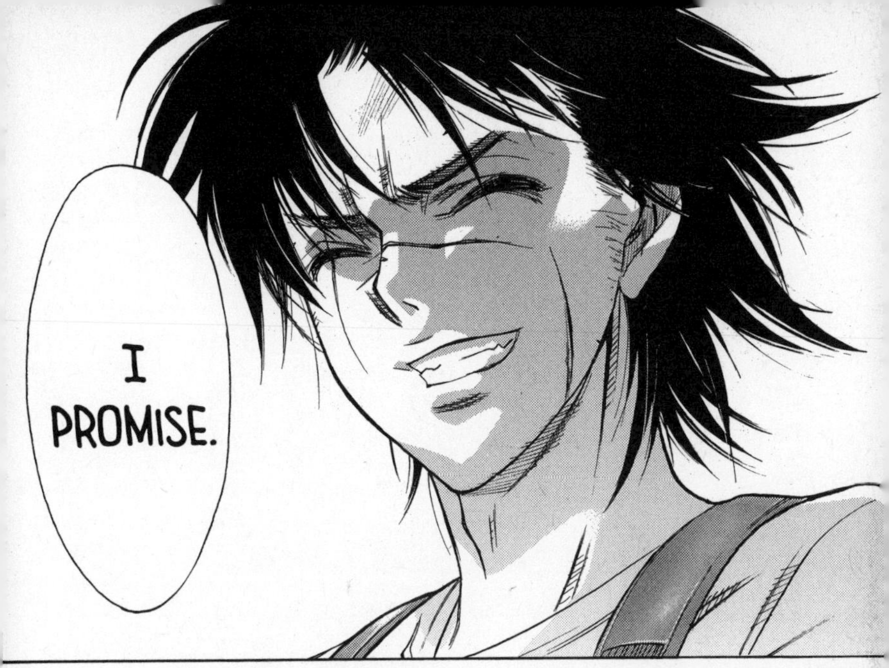
I PROMISE.
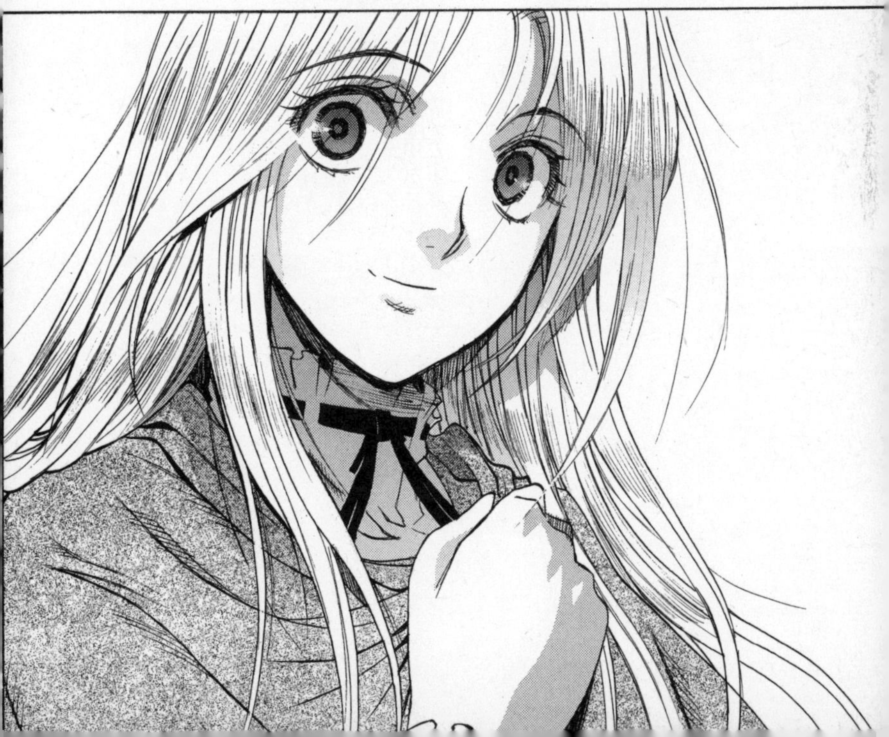

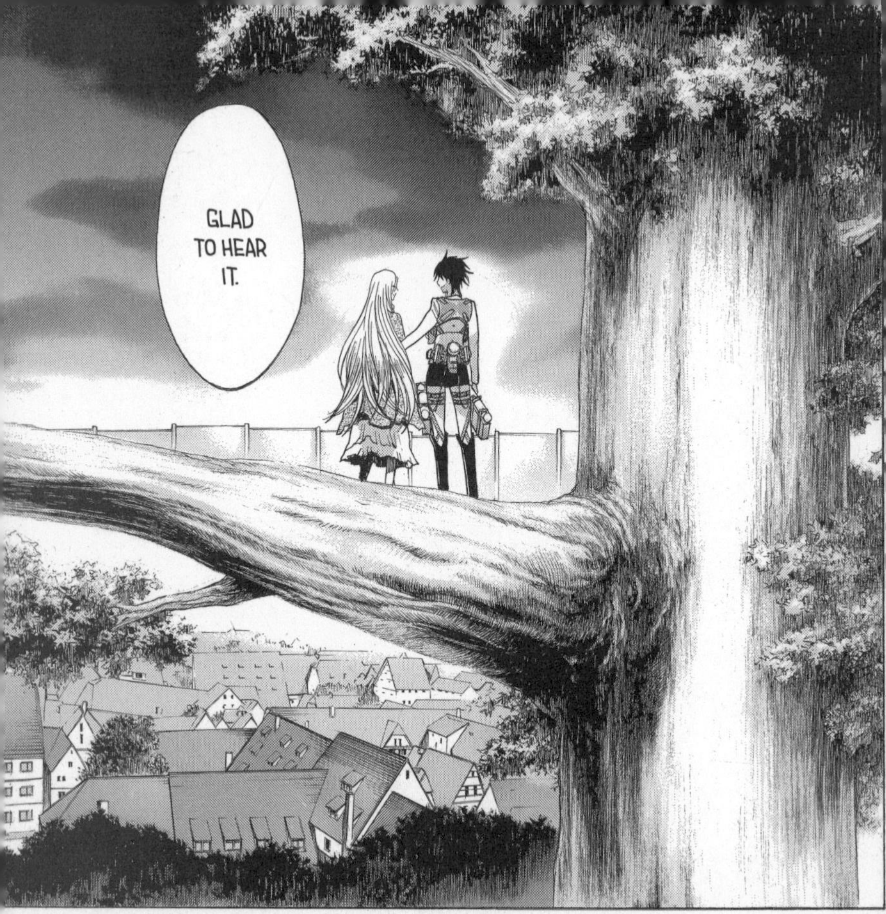
GLAD TO HEAR IT.

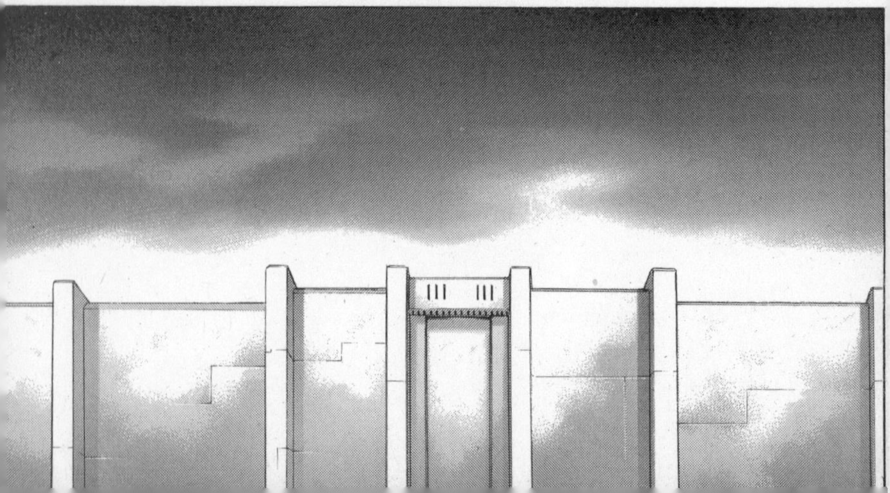

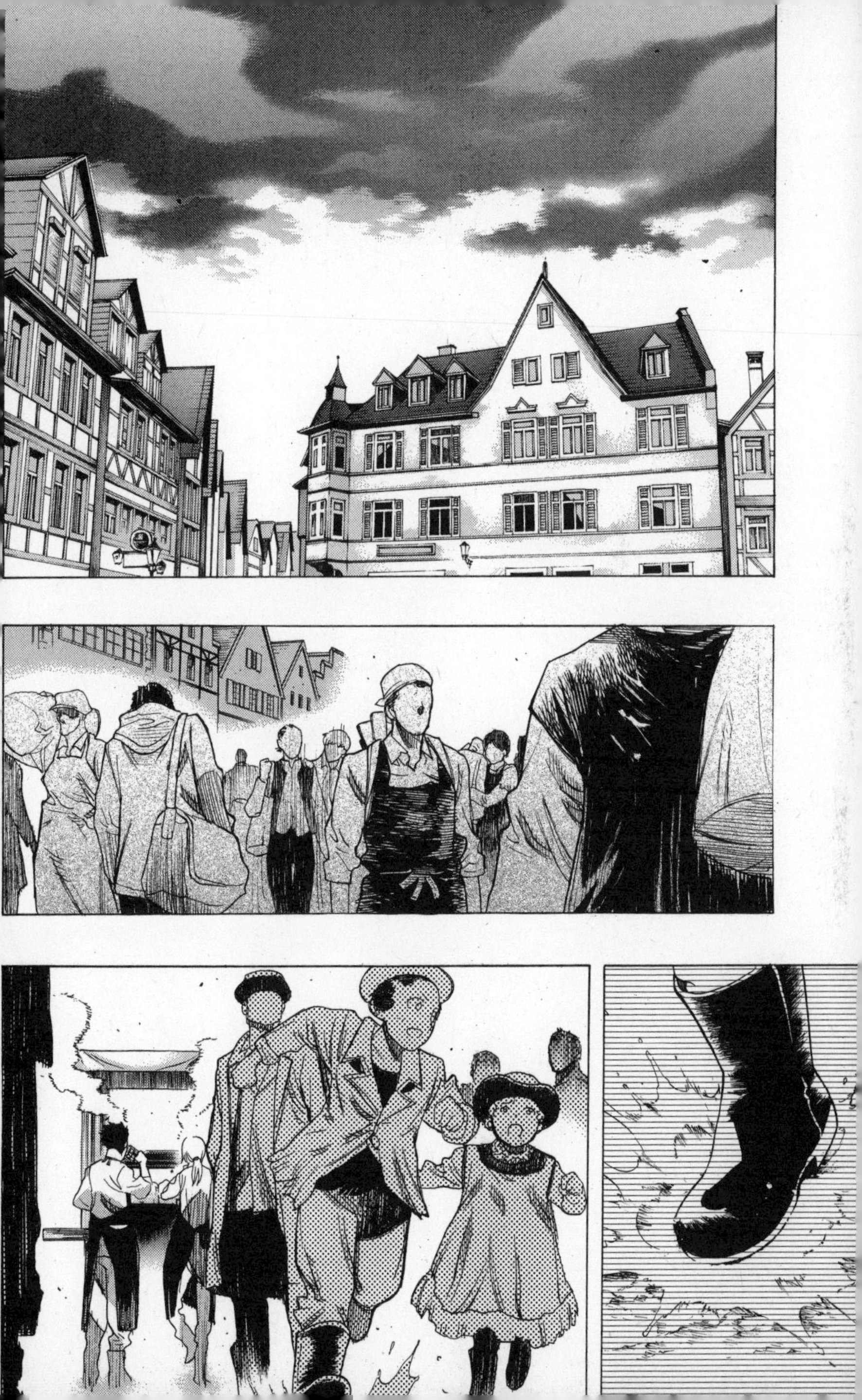

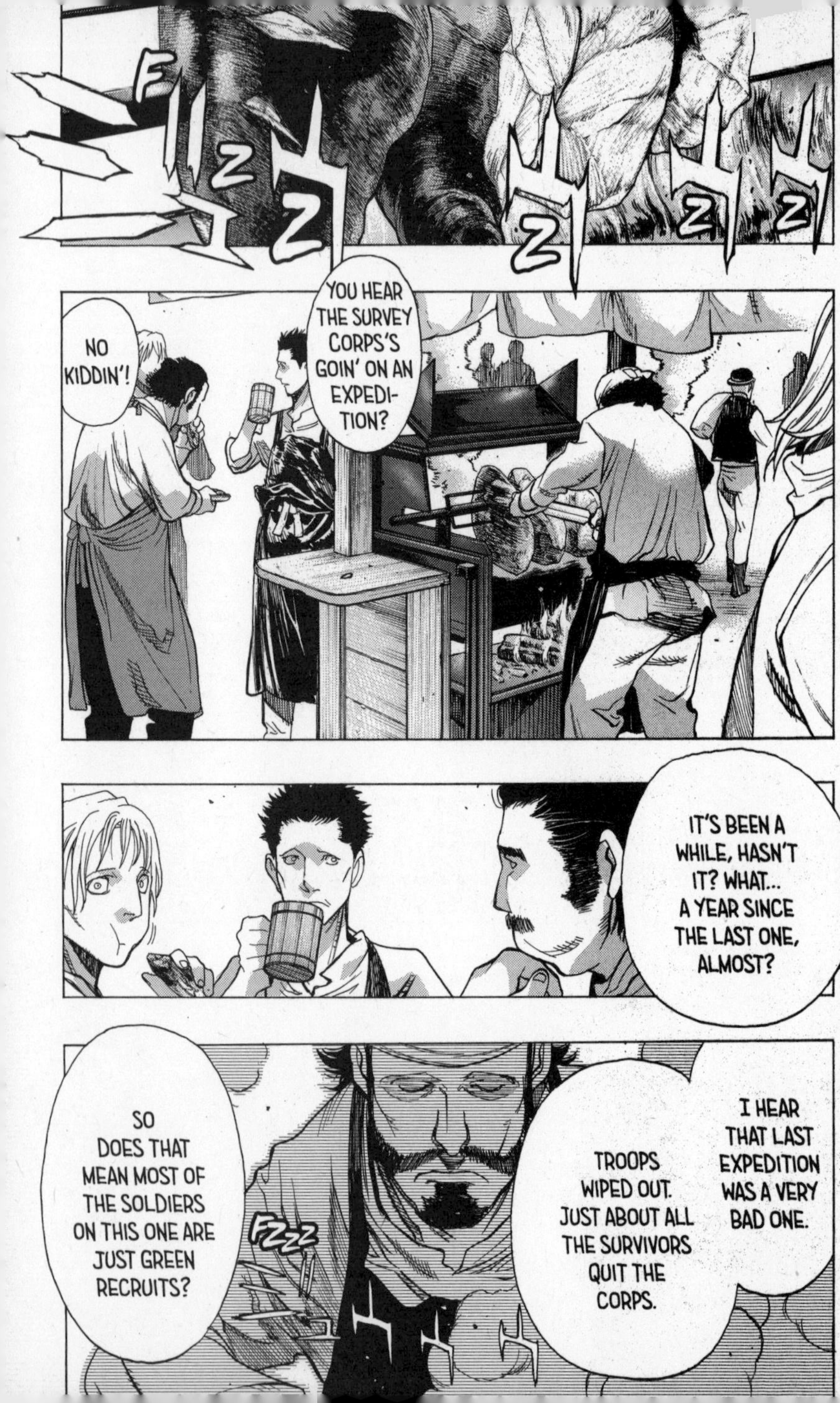
ZZZ
FIZZ
YOU HEAR THE SURVEY CORPS'S GOIN' ON AN EXPEDITION?
NO KIDDIN'!
IT'S BEEN A WHILE, HASN'T IT? WHAT... A YEAR SINCE THE LAST ONE, ALMOST?
I HEAR THAT LAST EXPEDITION WAS A VERY BAD ONE.
TROOPS WIPED OUT. JUST ABOUT ALL THE SURVIVORS QUIT THE CORPS.
SO DOES THAT MEAN MOST OF THE SOLDIERS ON THIS ONE ARE JUST GREEN RECRUITS?
FZZZ

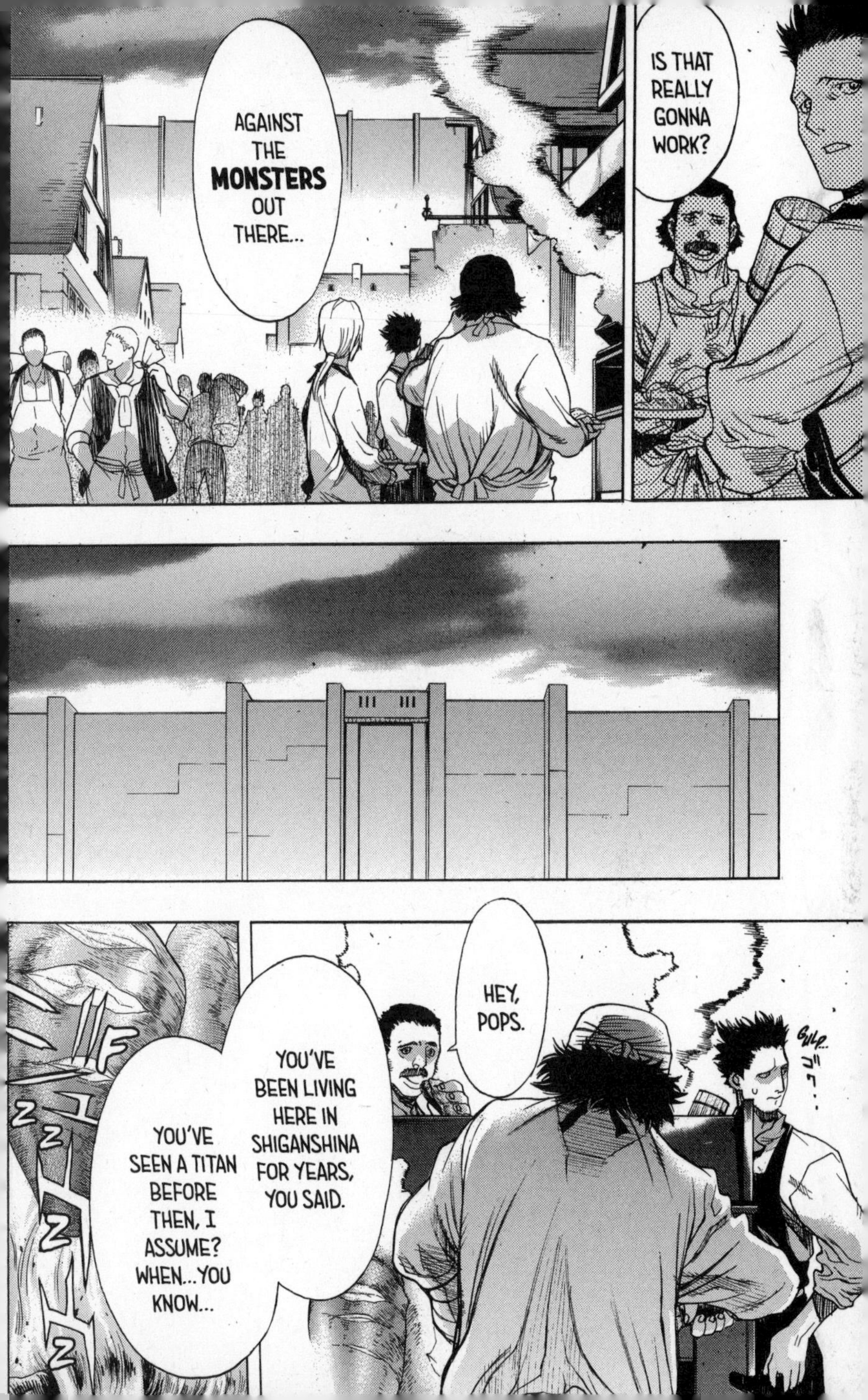
IS THAT REALLY GONNA WORK?
AGAINST THE **MONSTERS** OUT THERE...
HEY, POPS.
GULP...
YOU'VE BEEN LIVING HERE IN SHIGANSHINA FOR YEARS, YOU SAID.
YOU'VE SEEN A TITAN BEFORE THEN, I ASSUME? WHEN...YOU KNOW...

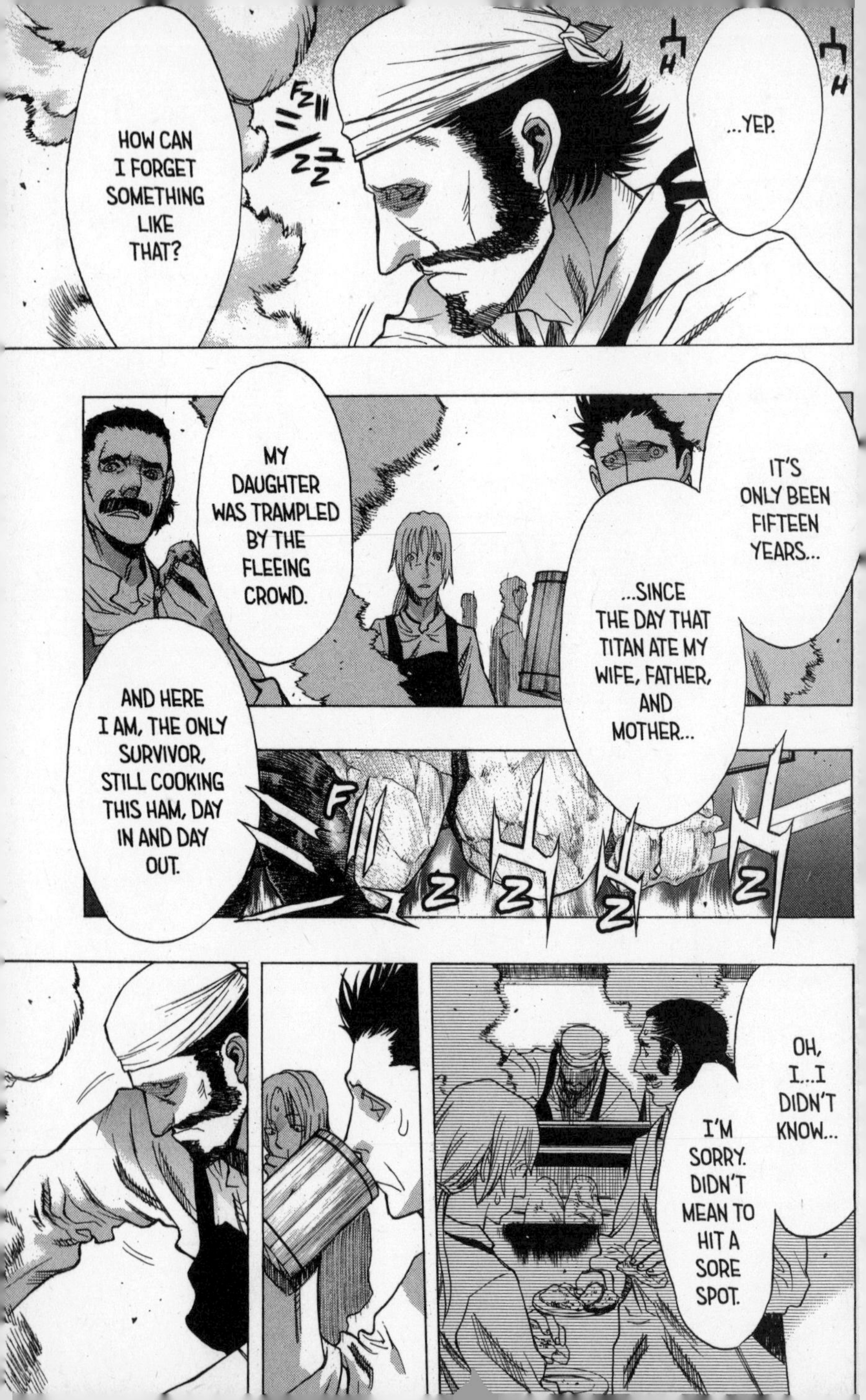
HN
HN
...YEP.
FZZZ
HOW CAN I FORGET SOMETHING LIKE THAT?
IT'S ONLY BEEN FIFTEEN YEARS...
...SINCE THE DAY THAT TITAN ATE MY WIFE, FATHER, AND MOTHER...
MY DAUGHTER WAS TRAMPLED BY THE FLEEING CROWD.
HZZZ
AND HERE I AM, THE ONLY SURVIVOR, STILL COOKING THIS HAM, DAY IN AND DAY OUT.
FIZZ
OH, I...I DIDN'T KNOW...
I'M SORRY. DIDN'T MEAN TO HIT A SORE SPOT.

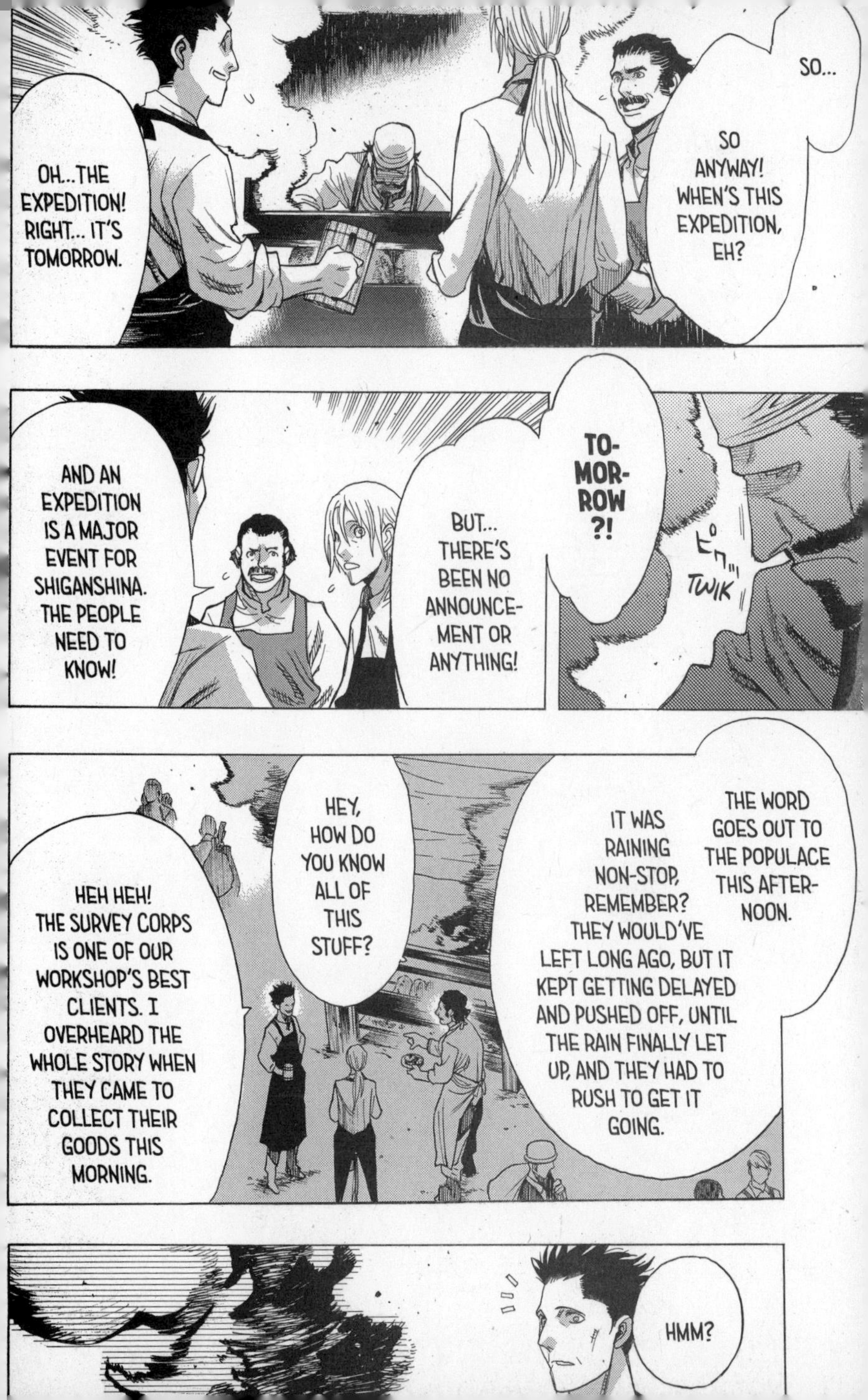
SO...
SO ANYWAY! WHEN'S THIS EXPEDITION, EH?
OH...THE EXPEDITION! RIGHT... IT'S TOMORROW.
TO-MOR-ROW?!
TWIK
BUT... THERE'S BEEN NO ANNOUNCE-MENT OR ANYTHING!
AND AN EXPEDITION IS A MAJOR EVENT FOR SHIGANSHINA. THE PEOPLE NEED TO KNOW!
THE WORD GOES OUT TO THE POPULACE THIS AFTER-NOON.
IT WAS RAINING NON-STOP, REMEMBER? THEY WOULD'VE LEFT LONG AGO, BUT IT KEPT GETTING DELAYED AND PUSHED OFF, UNTIL THE RAIN FINALLY LET UP, AND THEY HAD TO RUSH TO GET IT GOING.
HEY, HOW DO YOU KNOW ALL OF THIS STUFF?
HEH HEH! THE SURVEY CORPS IS ONE OF OUR WORKSHOP'S BEST CLIENTS. I OVERHEARD THE WHOLE STORY WHEN THEY CAME TO COLLECT THEIR GOODS THIS MORNING.
HMM?

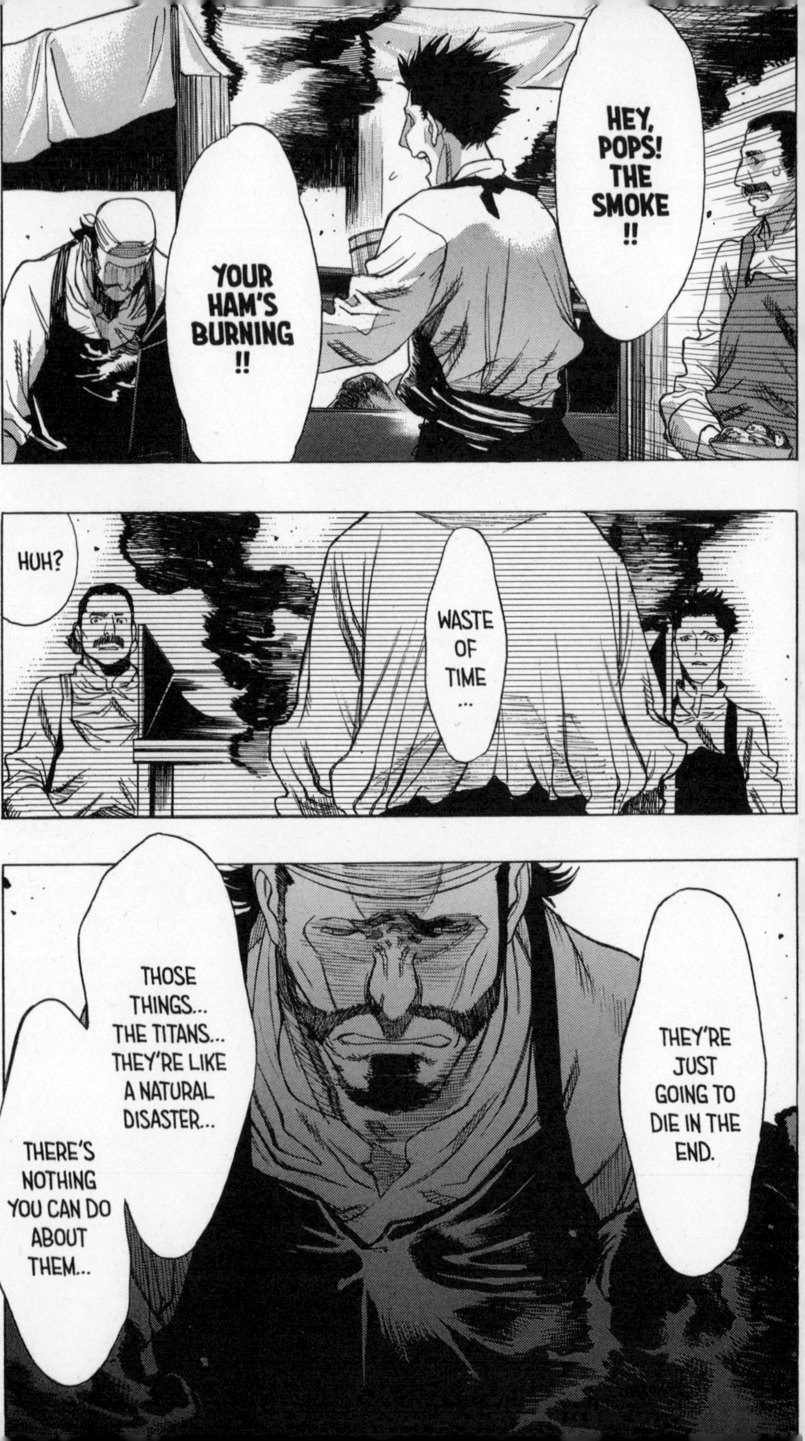
HEY, POPS! THE SMOKE !!
YOUR HAM'S BURNING !!
WASTE OF TIME ...
HUH?
THEY'RE JUST GOING TO DIE IN THE END.
THOSE THINGS... THE TITANS... THEY'RE LIKE A NATURAL DISASTER...
THERE'S NOTHING YOU CAN DO ABOUT THEM...

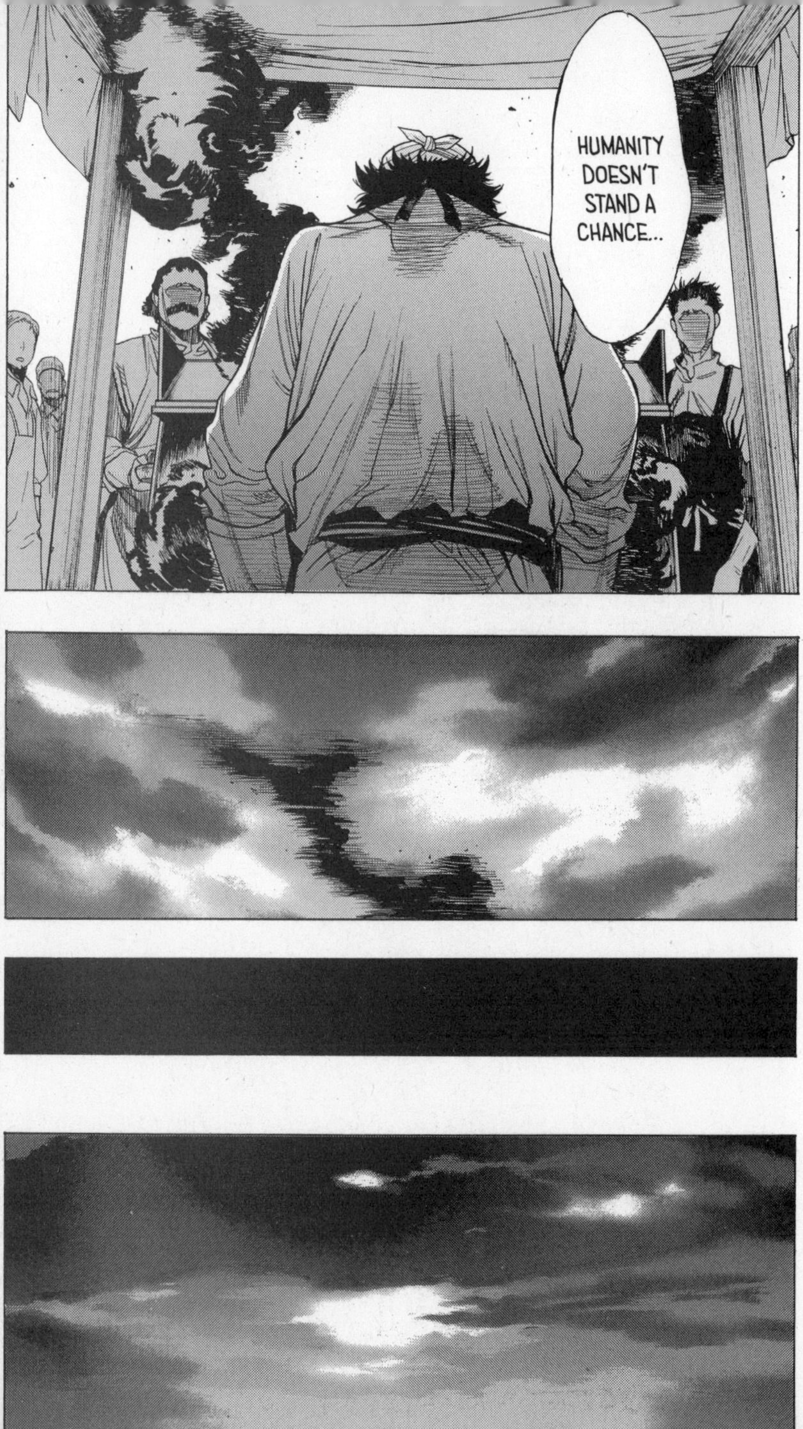
HUMANITY DOESN'T STAND A CHANCE...

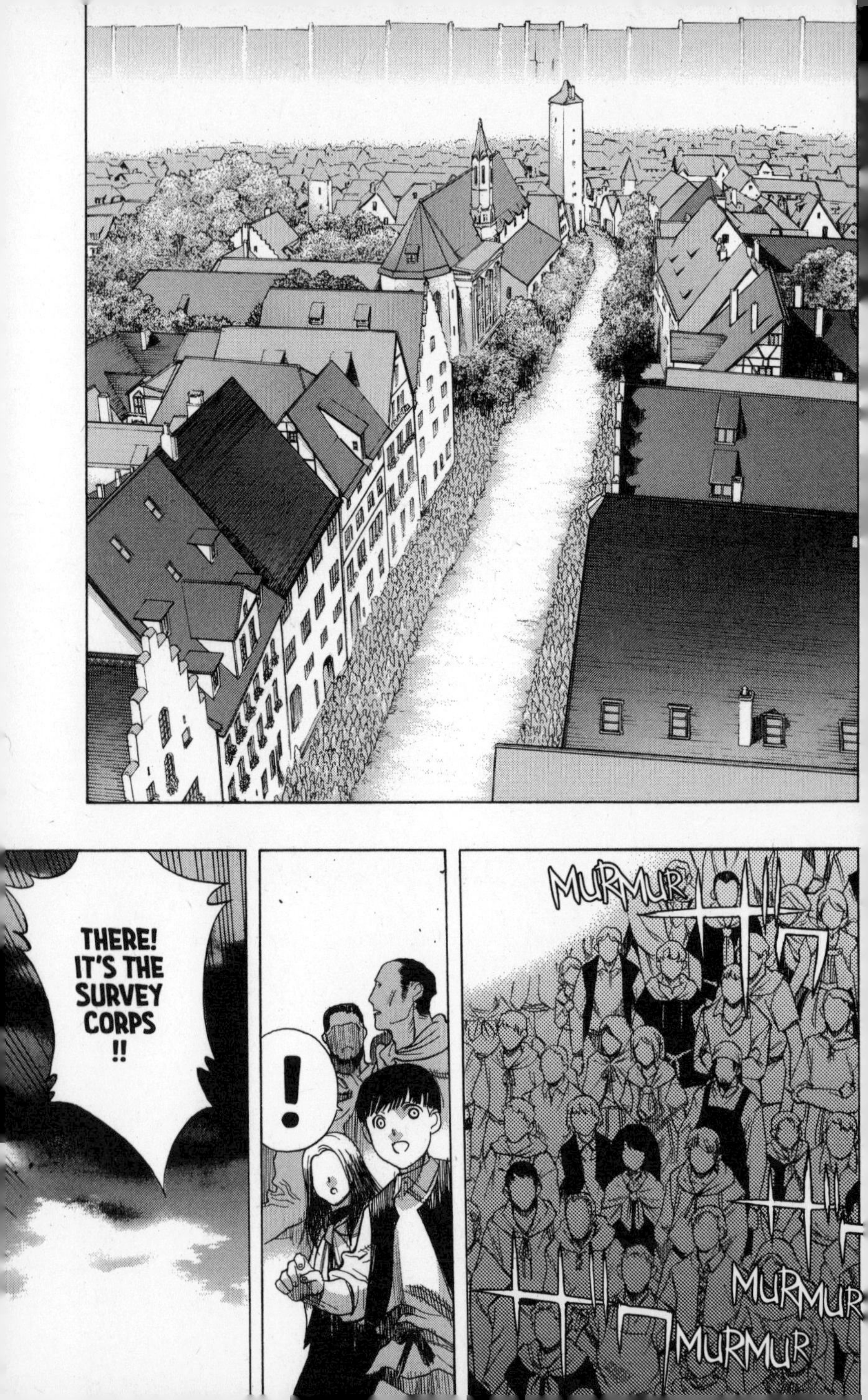
MURMUR
MURMUR
MURMUR
!
THERE! IT'S THE SURVEY CORPS !!

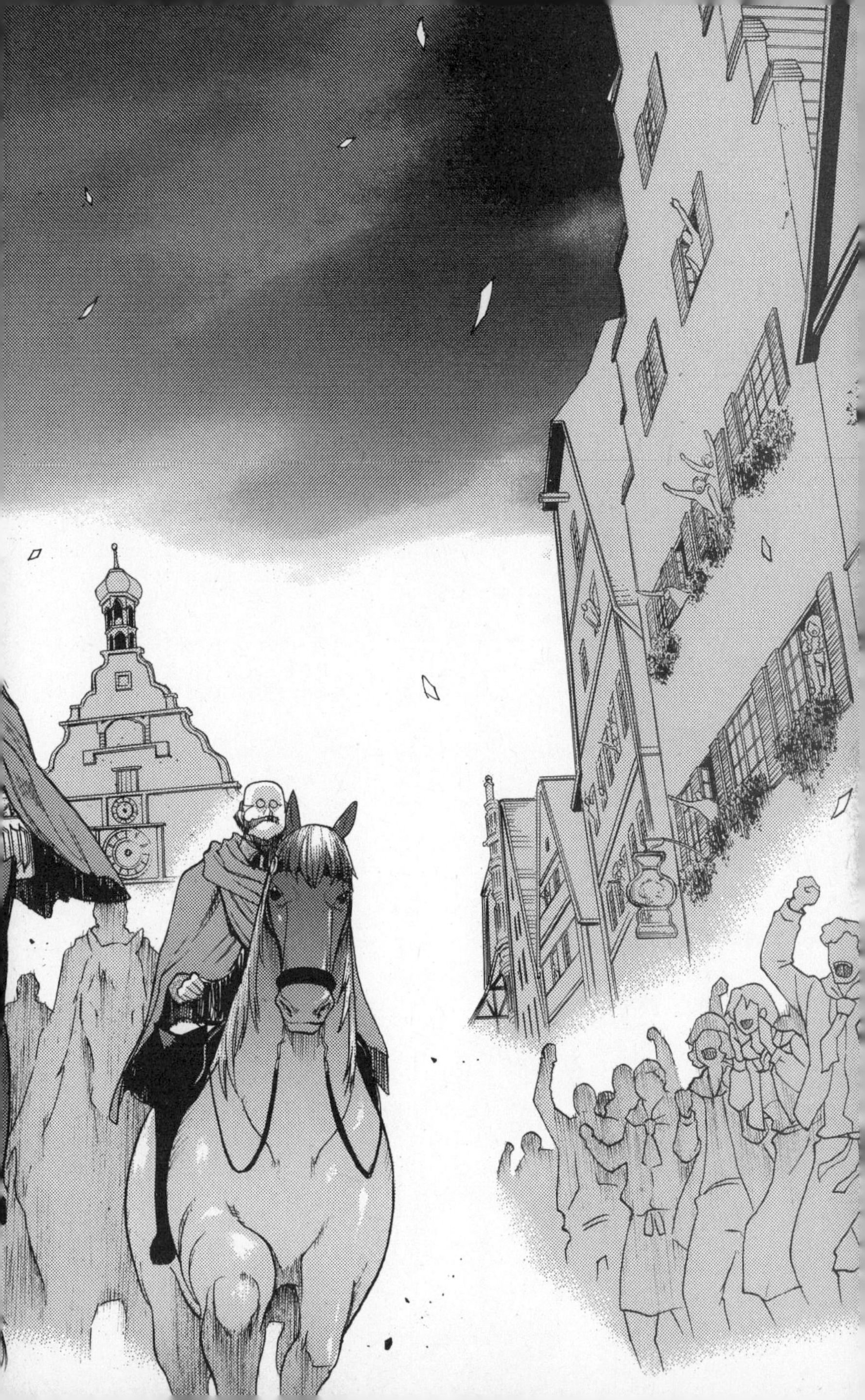

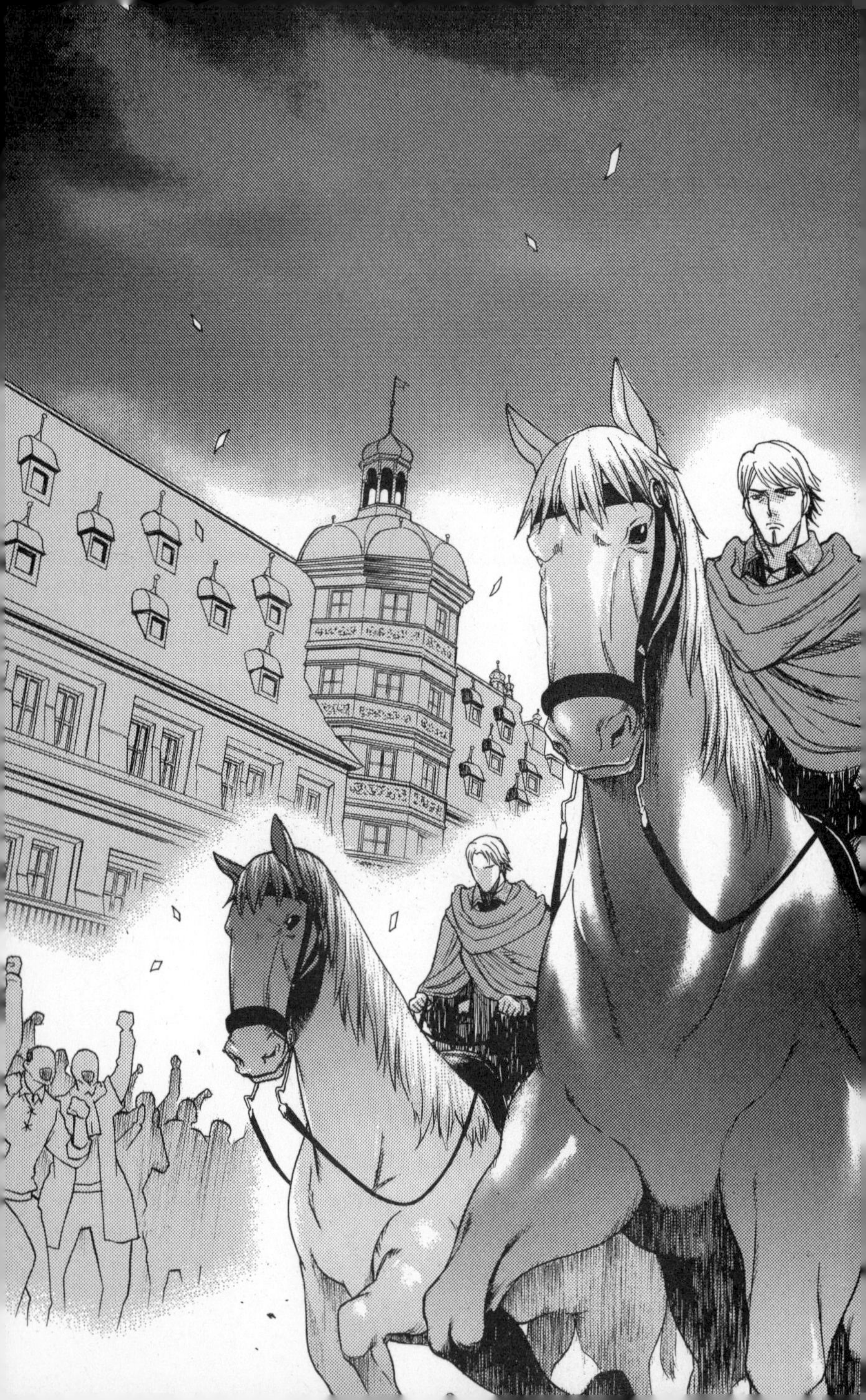

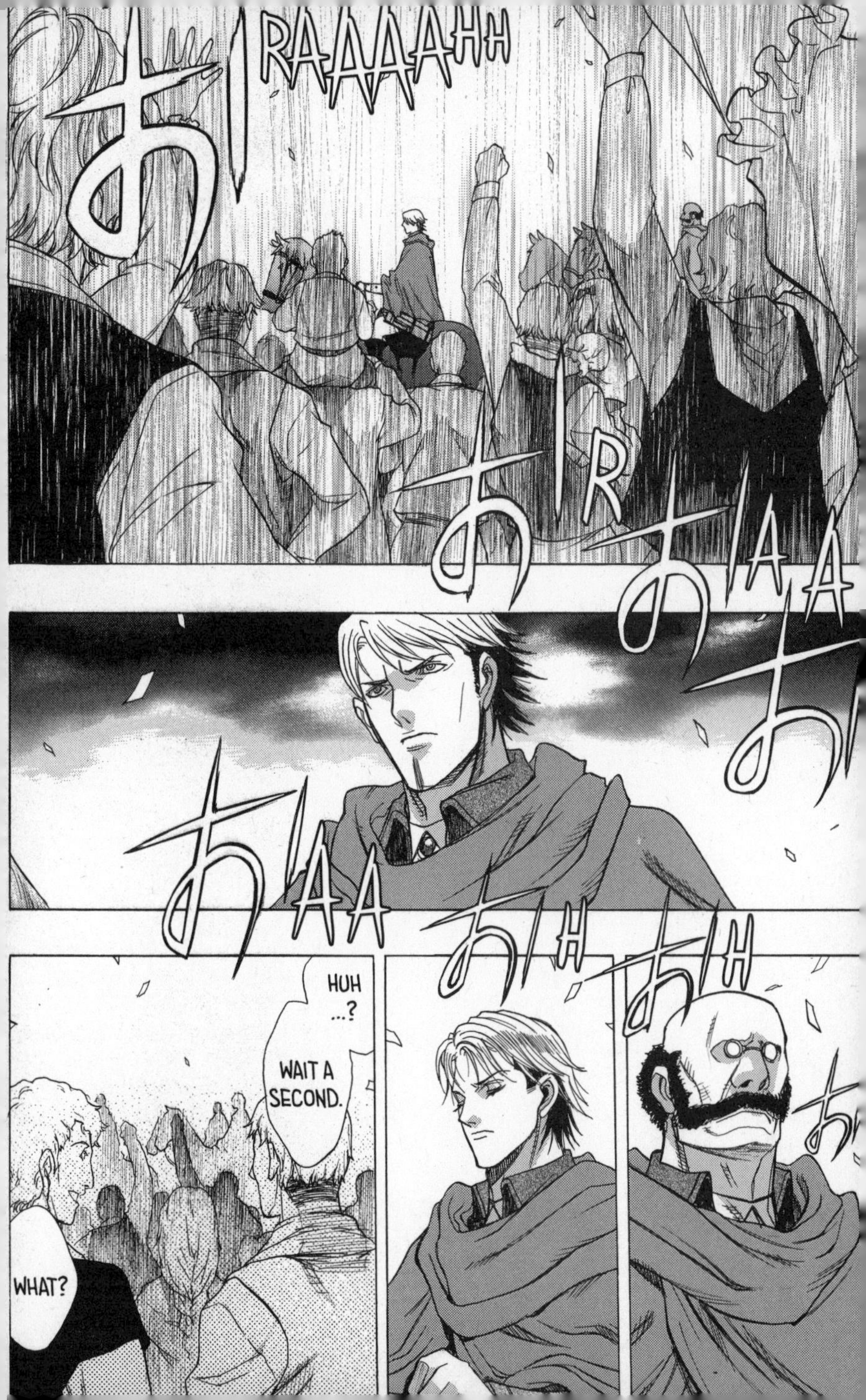

RAAAAAHH
R
AA
A
AA
H
H
HUH ...? WAIT A SECOND.
WHAT?

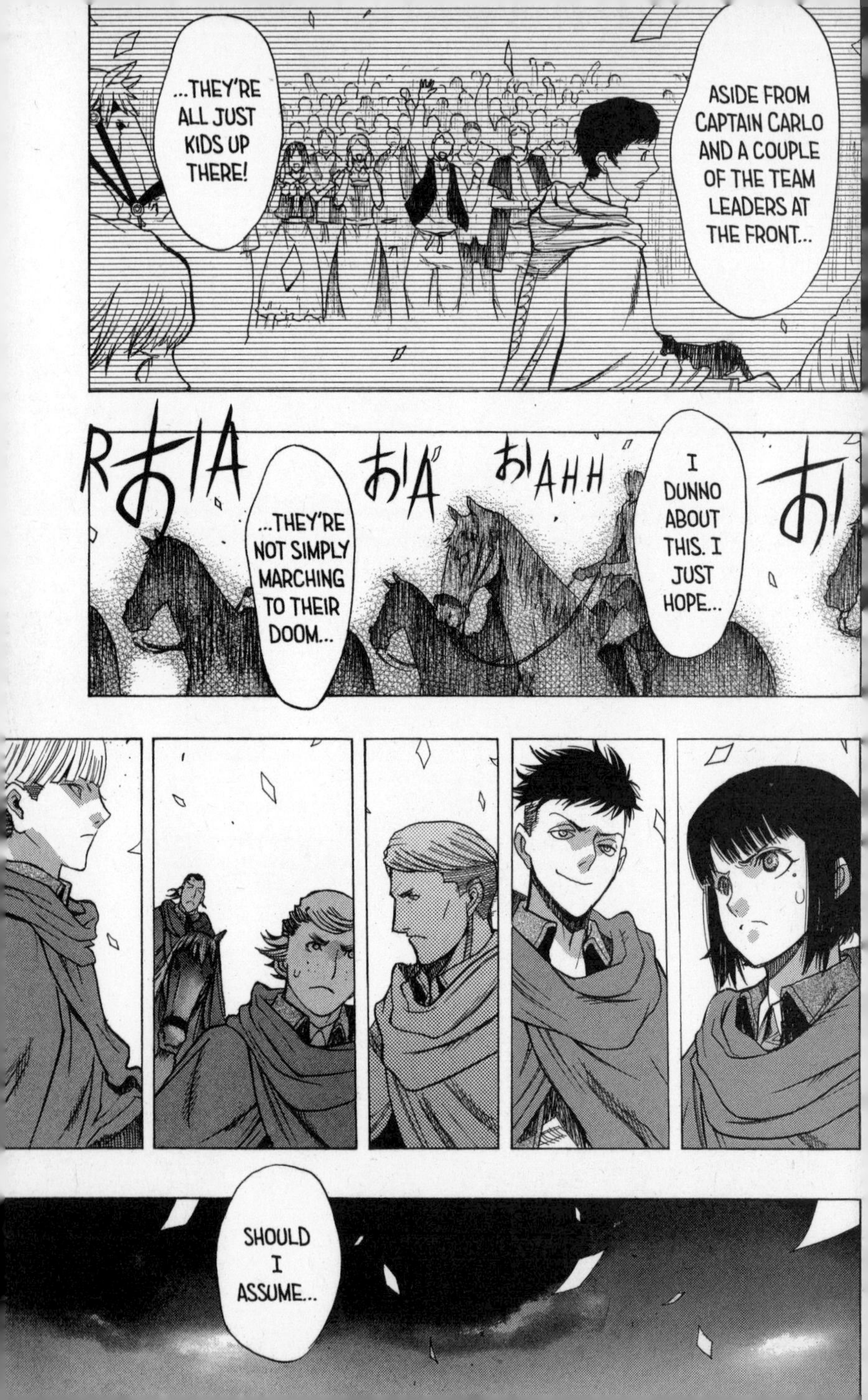
ASIDE FROM CAPTAIN CARLO AND A COUPLE OF THE TEAM LEADERS AT THE FRONT...
...THEY'RE ALL JUST KIDS UP THERE!
I DUNNO ABOUT THIS. I JUST HOPE...
おAHH
おA
...THEY'RE NOT SIMPLY MARCHING TO THEIR DOOM...
RおA
SHOULD I ASSUME...

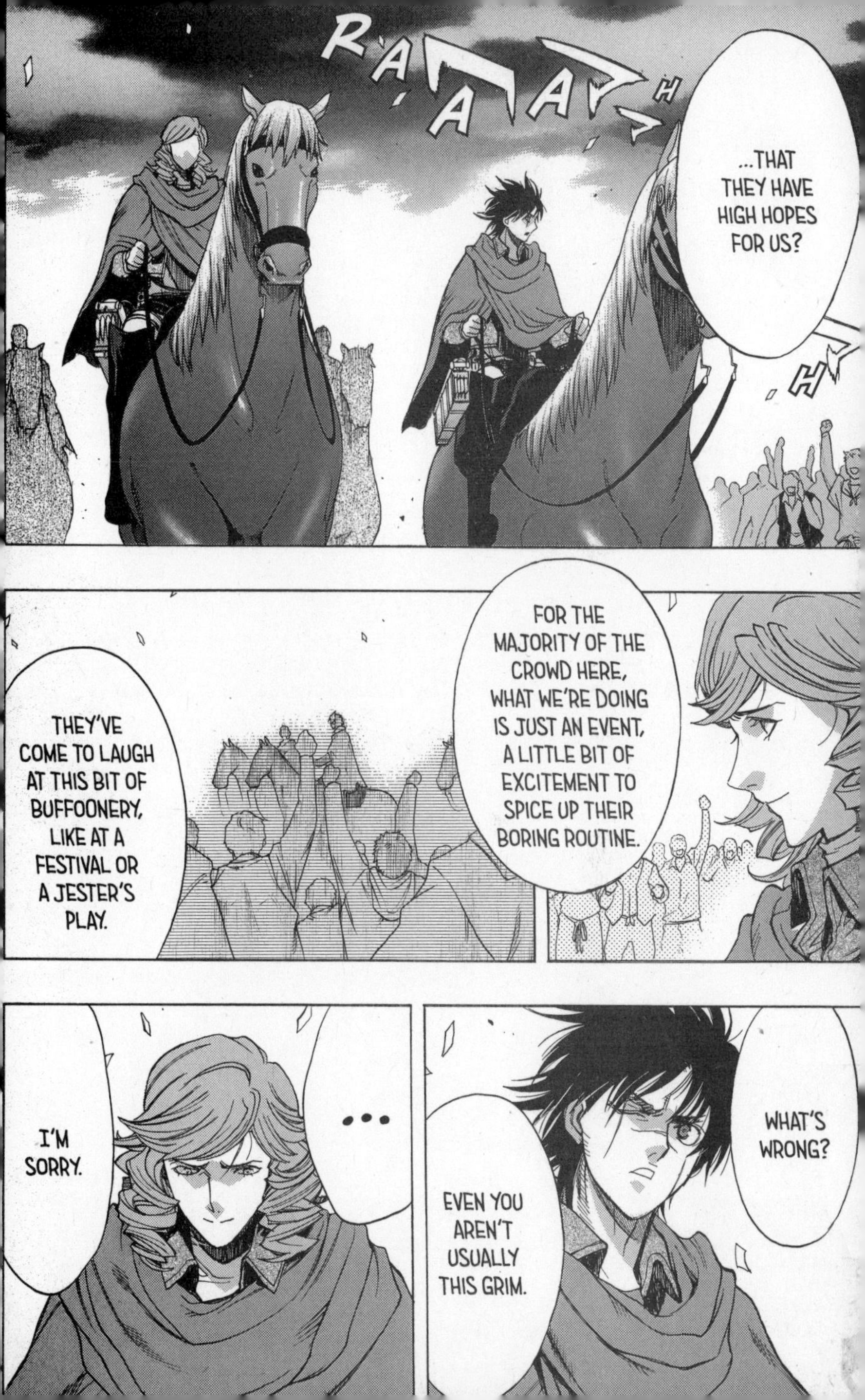
RAAAAAH
...THAT THEY HAVE HIGH HOPES FOR US?
H
FOR THE MAJORITY OF THE CROWD HERE, WHAT WE'RE DOING IS JUST AN EVENT, A LITTLE BIT OF EXCITEMENT TO SPICE UP THEIR BORING ROUTINE.
THEY'VE COME TO LAUGH AT THIS BIT OF BUFFOONERY, LIKE AT A FESTIVAL OR A JESTER'S PLAY.
WHAT'S WRONG?
EVEN YOU AREN'T USUALLY THIS GRIM.
...
I'M SORRY.

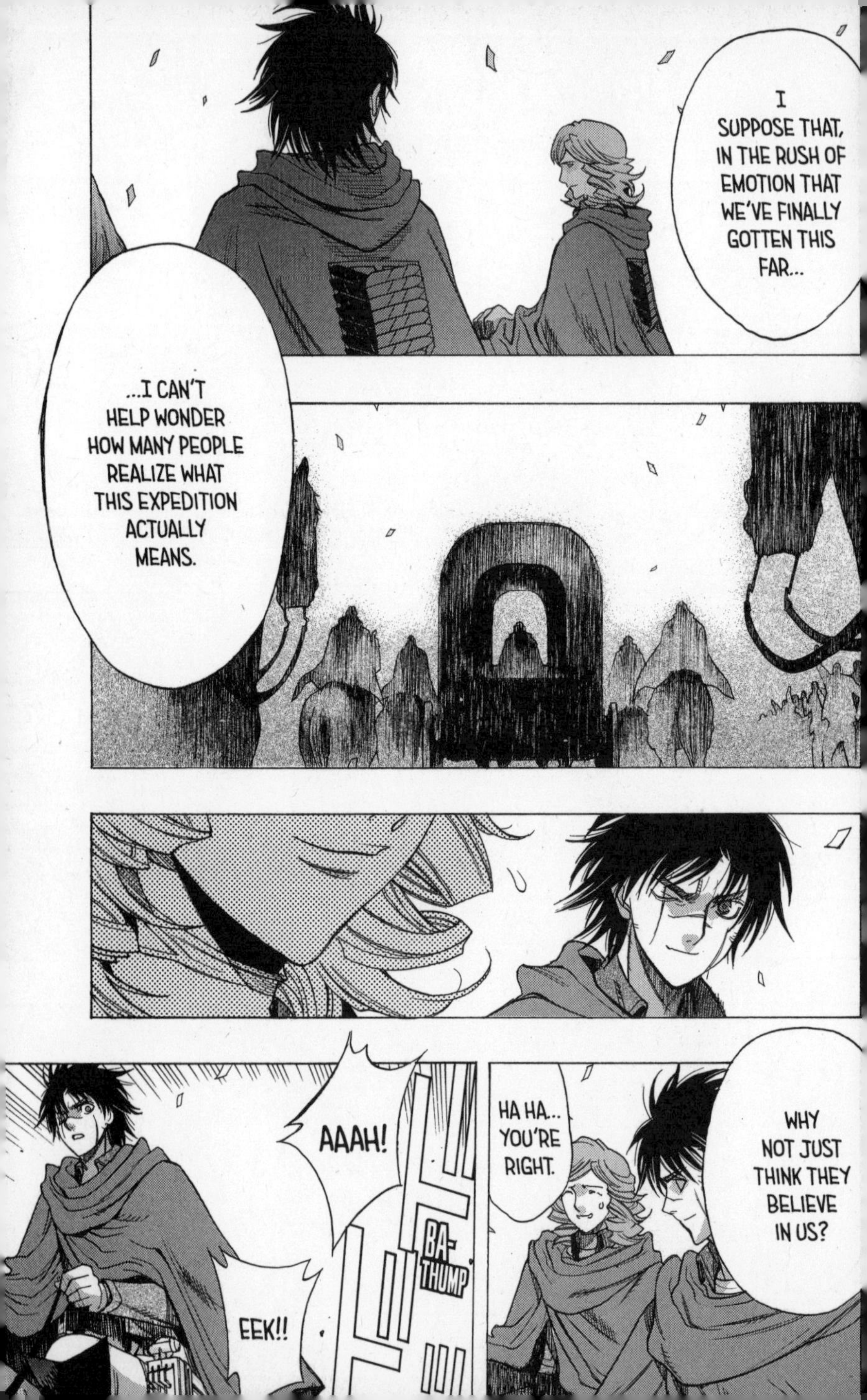
I SUPPOSE THAT, IN THE RUSH OF EMOTION THAT WE'VE FINALLY GOTTEN THIS FAR...
...I CAN'T HELP WONDER HOW MANY PEOPLE REALIZE WHAT THIS EXPEDITION ACTUALLY MEANS.
WHY NOT JUST THINK THEY BELIEVE IN US?
HA HA... YOU'RE RIGHT.
AAAH!
BA-THUMP
EEK!!

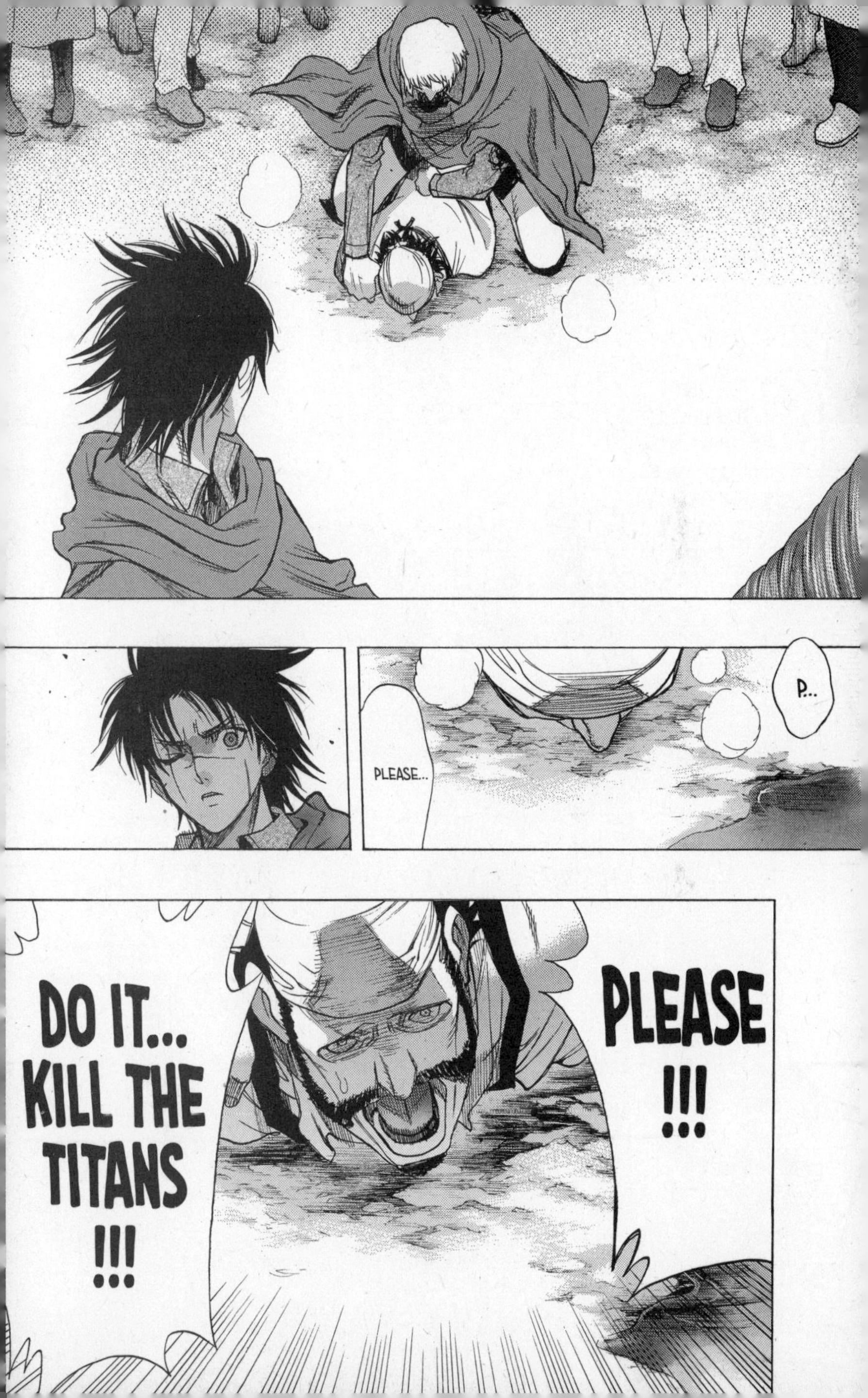
P...
PLEASE...
PLEASE !!!
DO IT... KILL THE TITANS !!!

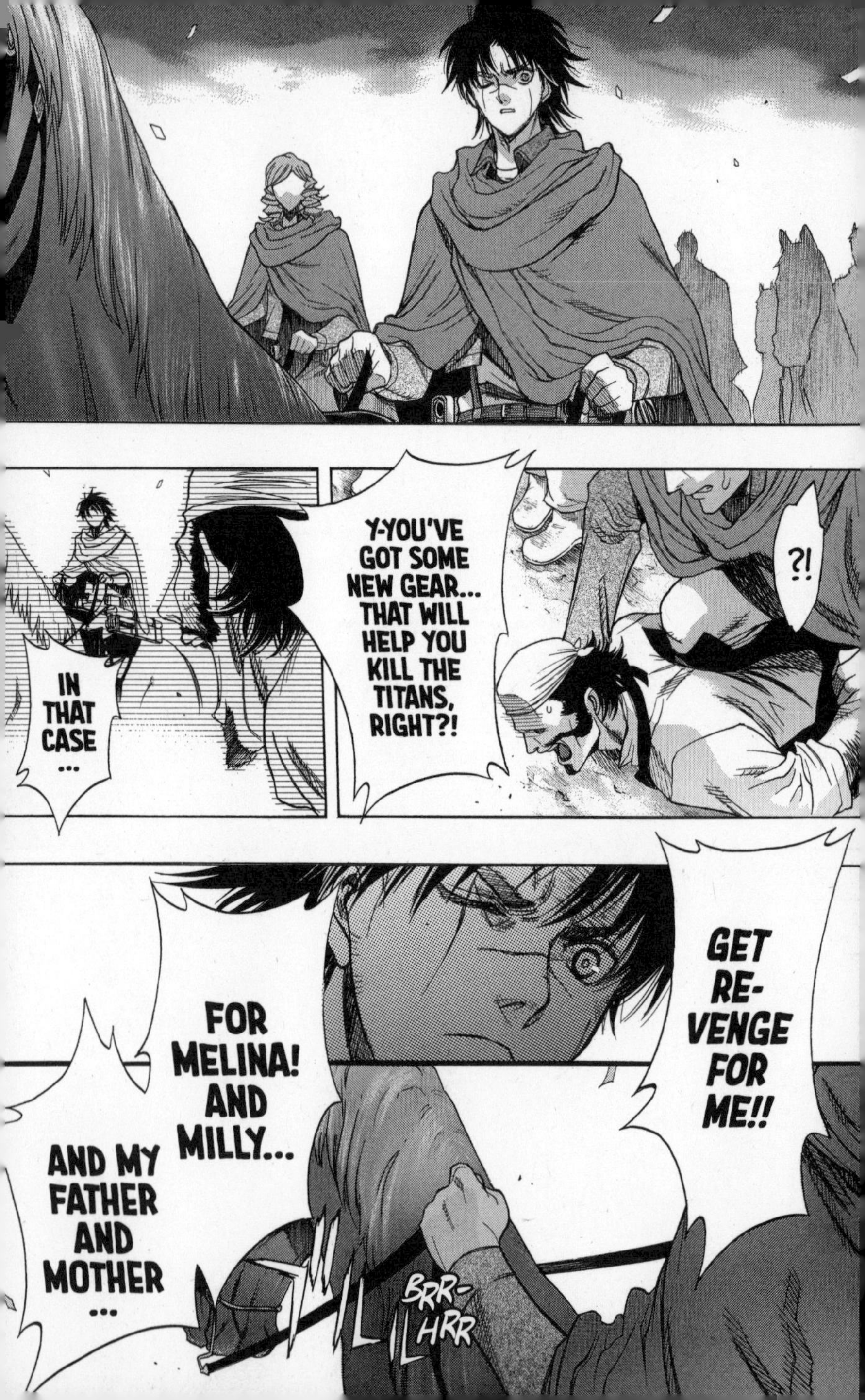
?!
Y-YOU'VE GOT SOME NEW GEAR... THAT WILL HELP YOU KILL THE TITANS, RIGHT?!
IN THAT CASE ...
GET RE-VENGE FOR ME!!
FOR MELINA! AND MILLY...
AND MY FATHER AND MOTHER ...
BRR-HRR

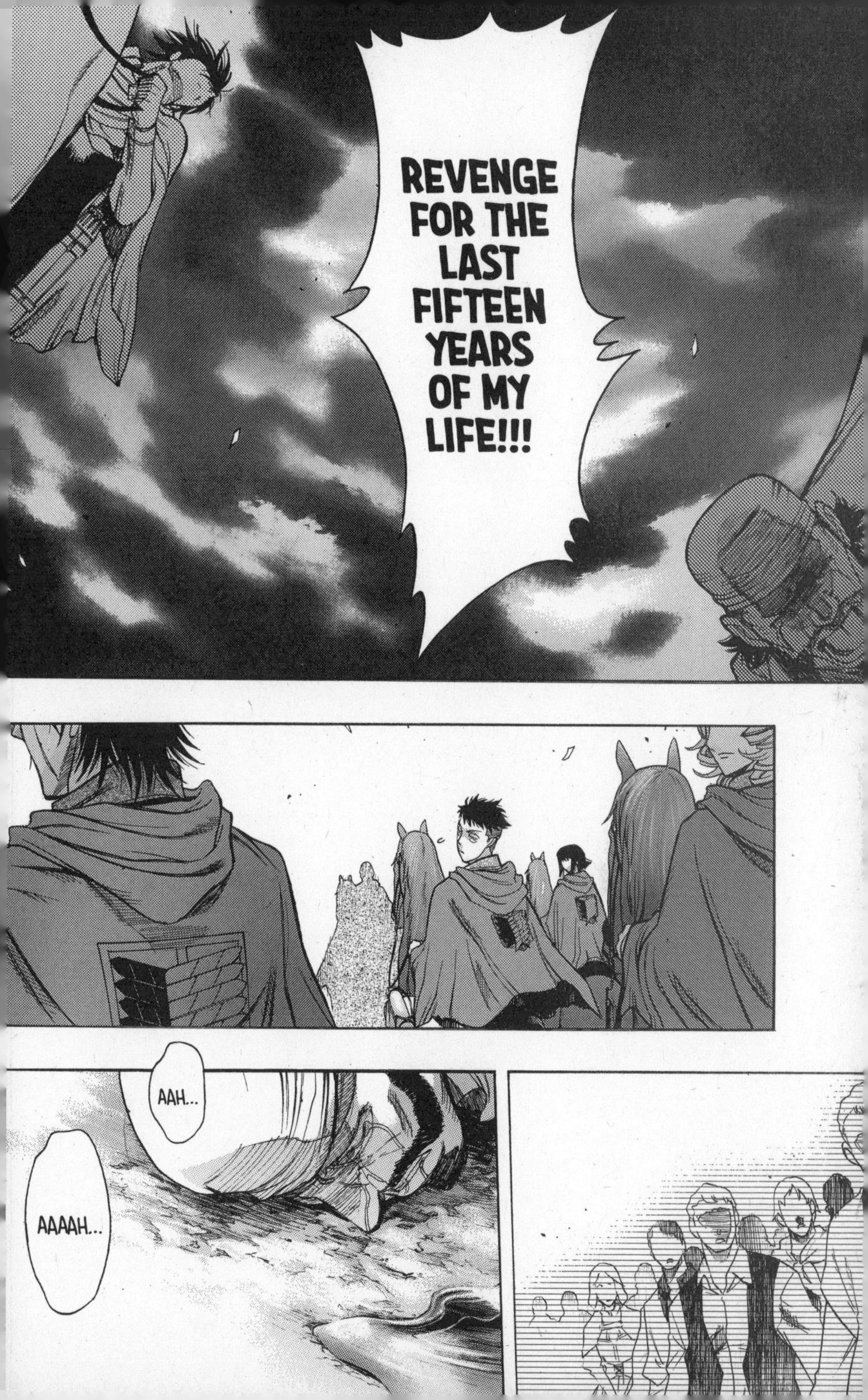
REVENGE FOR THE LAST FIFTEEN YEARS OF MY LIFE!!!
AAH...
AAAAH...

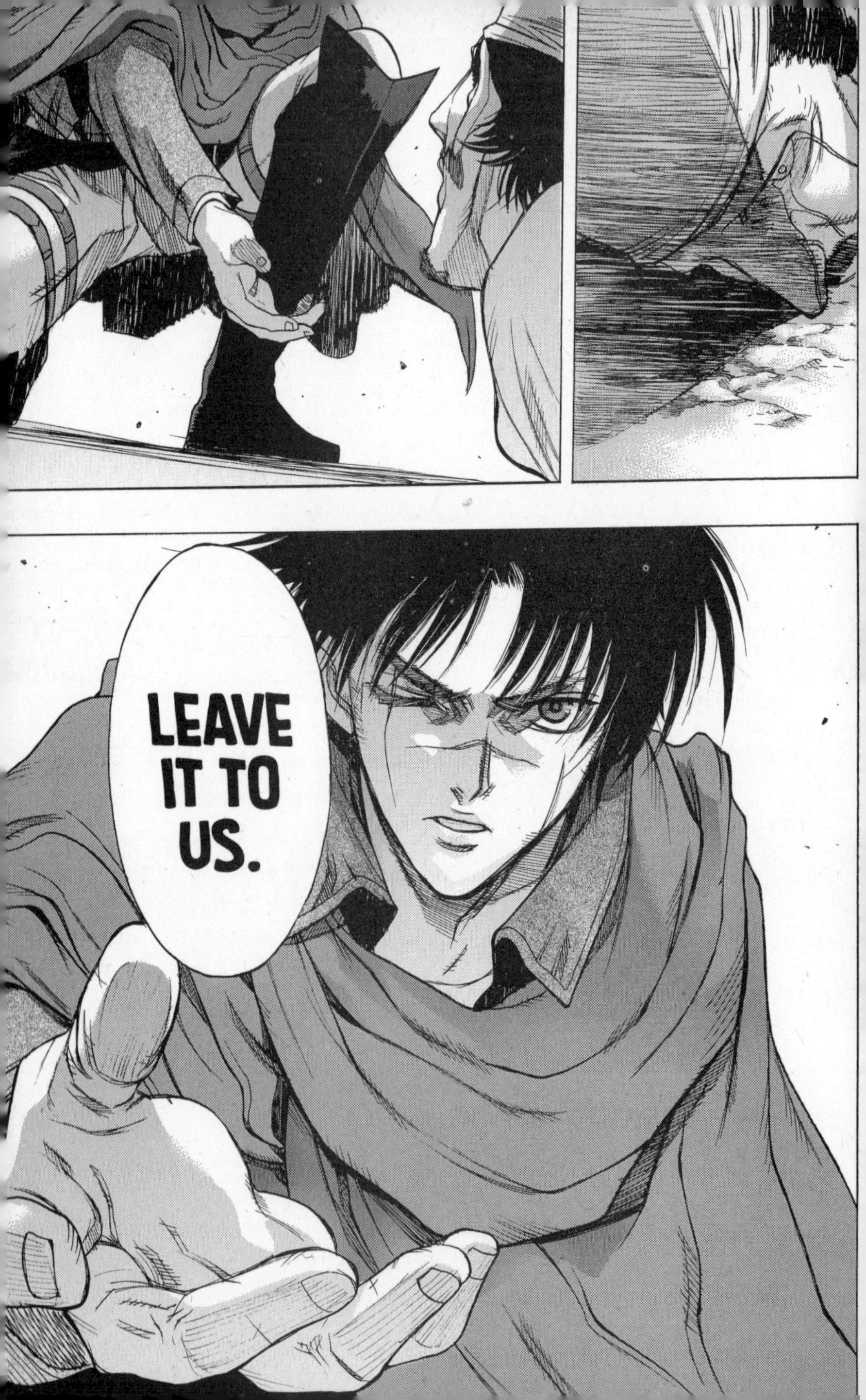
LEAVE IT TO US.

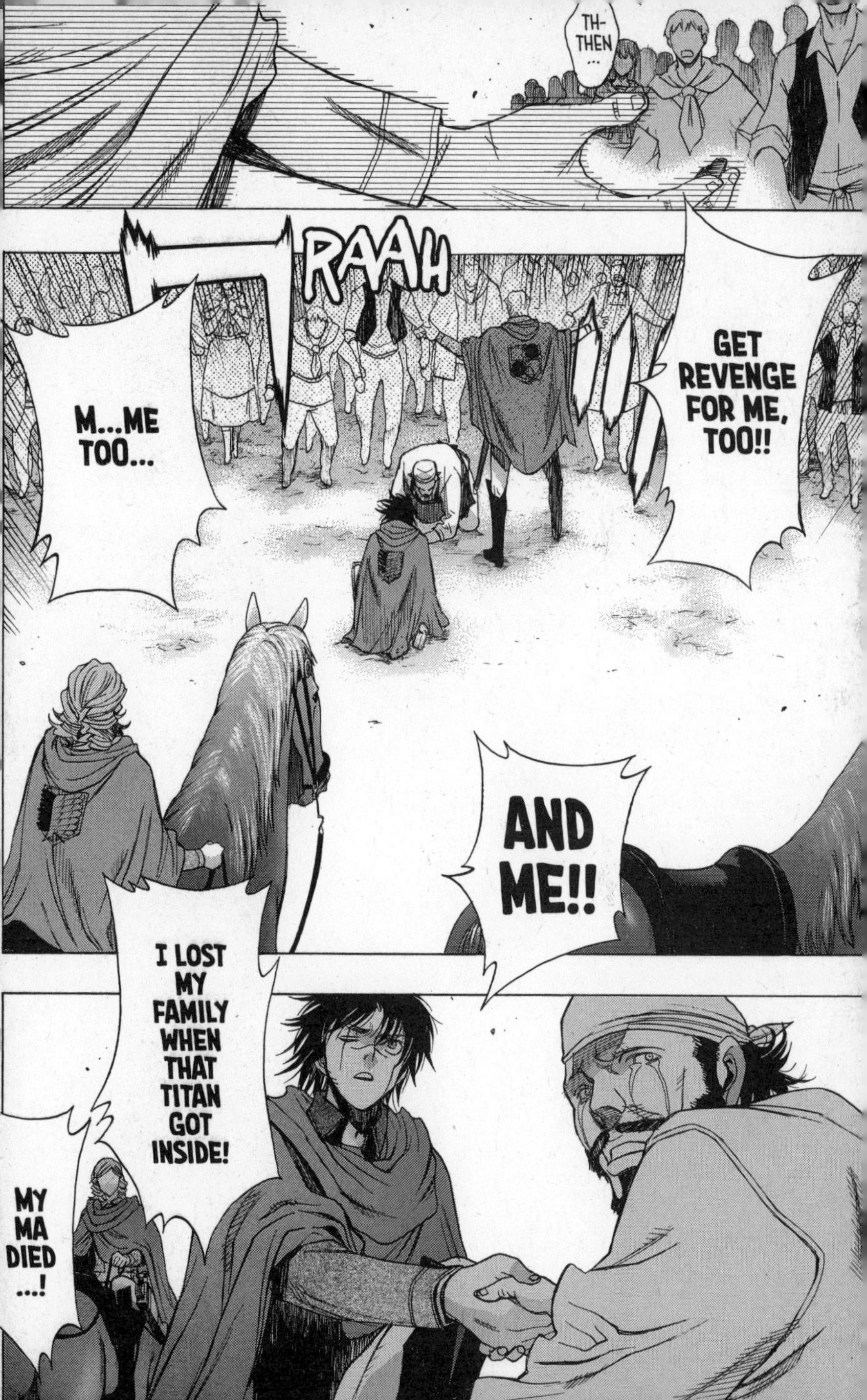
TH-THEN...
GET REVENGE FOR ME, TOO!!
RAAH
M...ME TOO...
AND ME!!
I LOST MY FAMILY WHEN THAT TITAN GOT INSIDE!
MY MA DIED...!

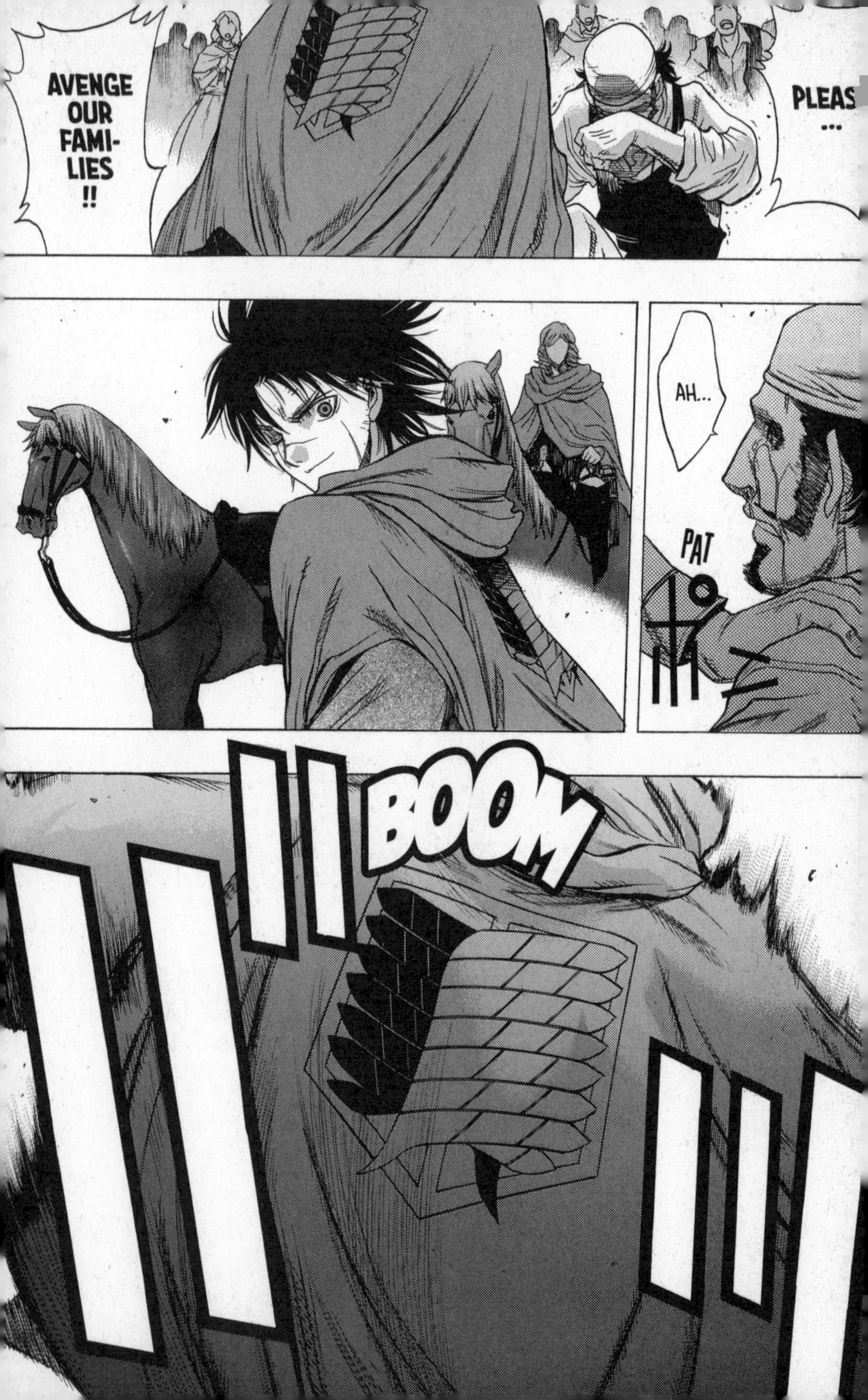
PLEAS ...
AVENGE OUR FAMI- LIES !!
AH...
PAT
BOOM

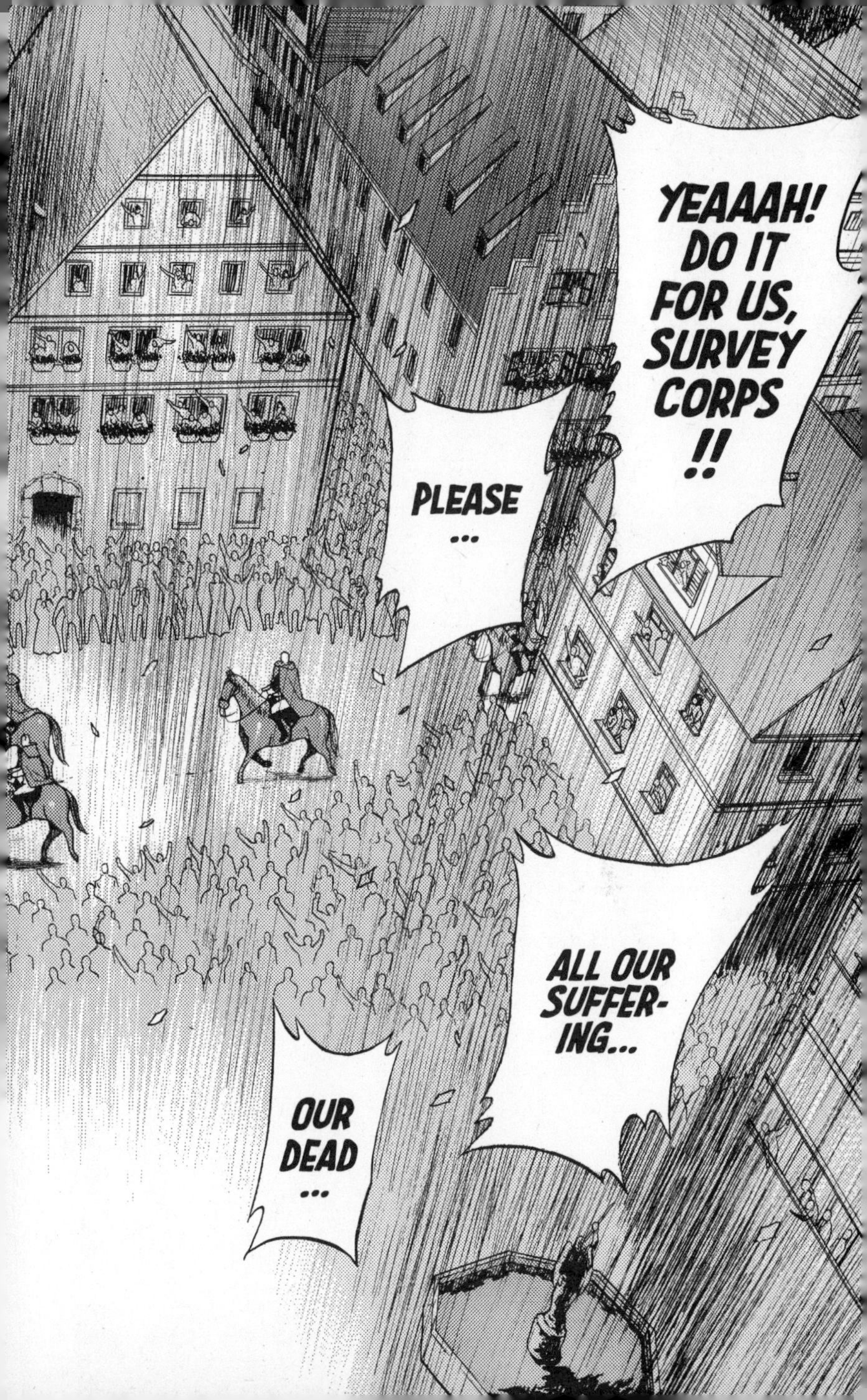
YEAAAH! DO IT FOR US, SURVEY CORPS !!
PLEASE ...
ALL OUR SUFFER-ING...
OUR DEAD ...

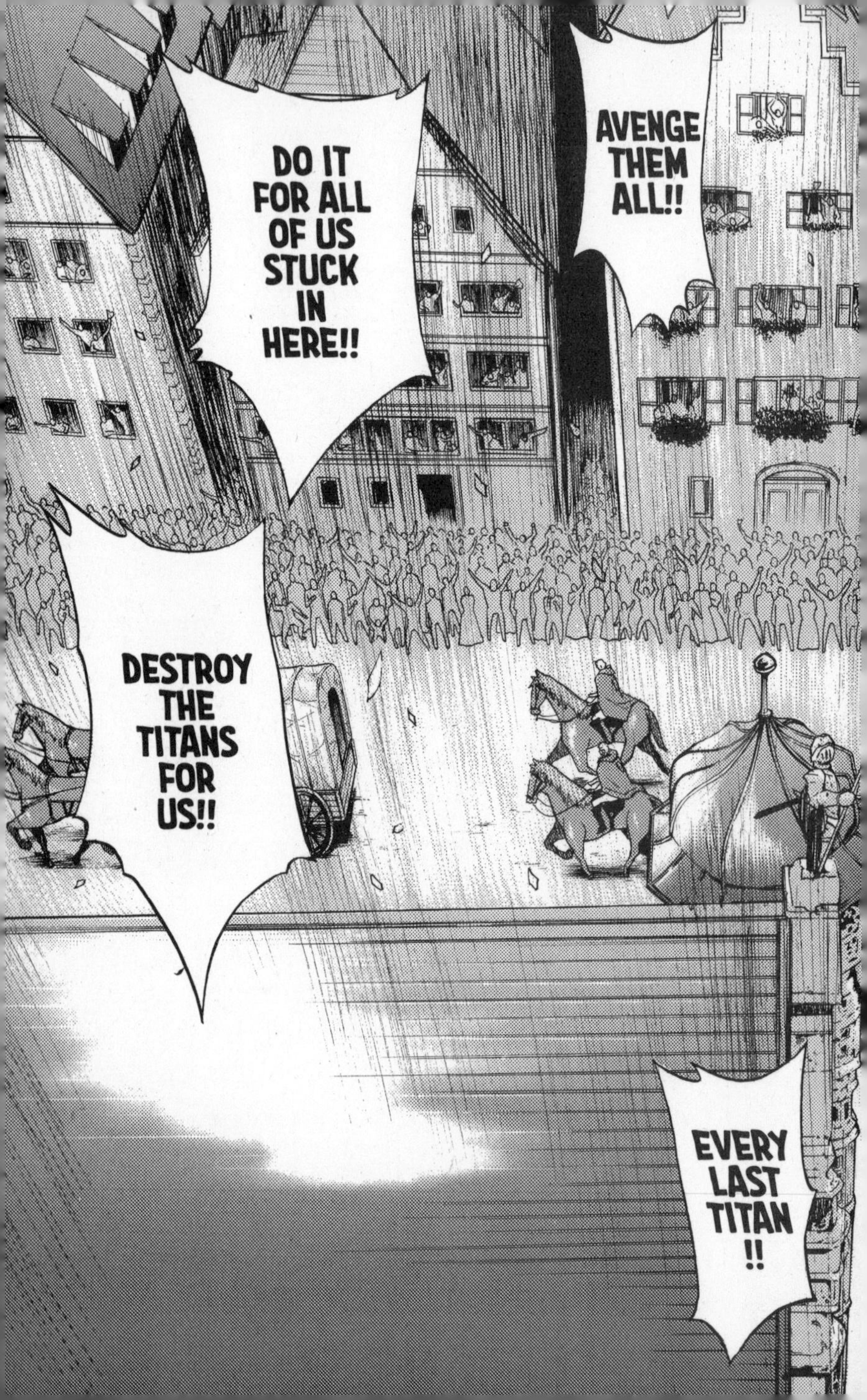
AVENGE THEM ALL!!
DO IT FOR ALL OF US STUCK IN HERE!!
DESTROY THE TITANS FOR US!!
EVERY LAST TITAN!!

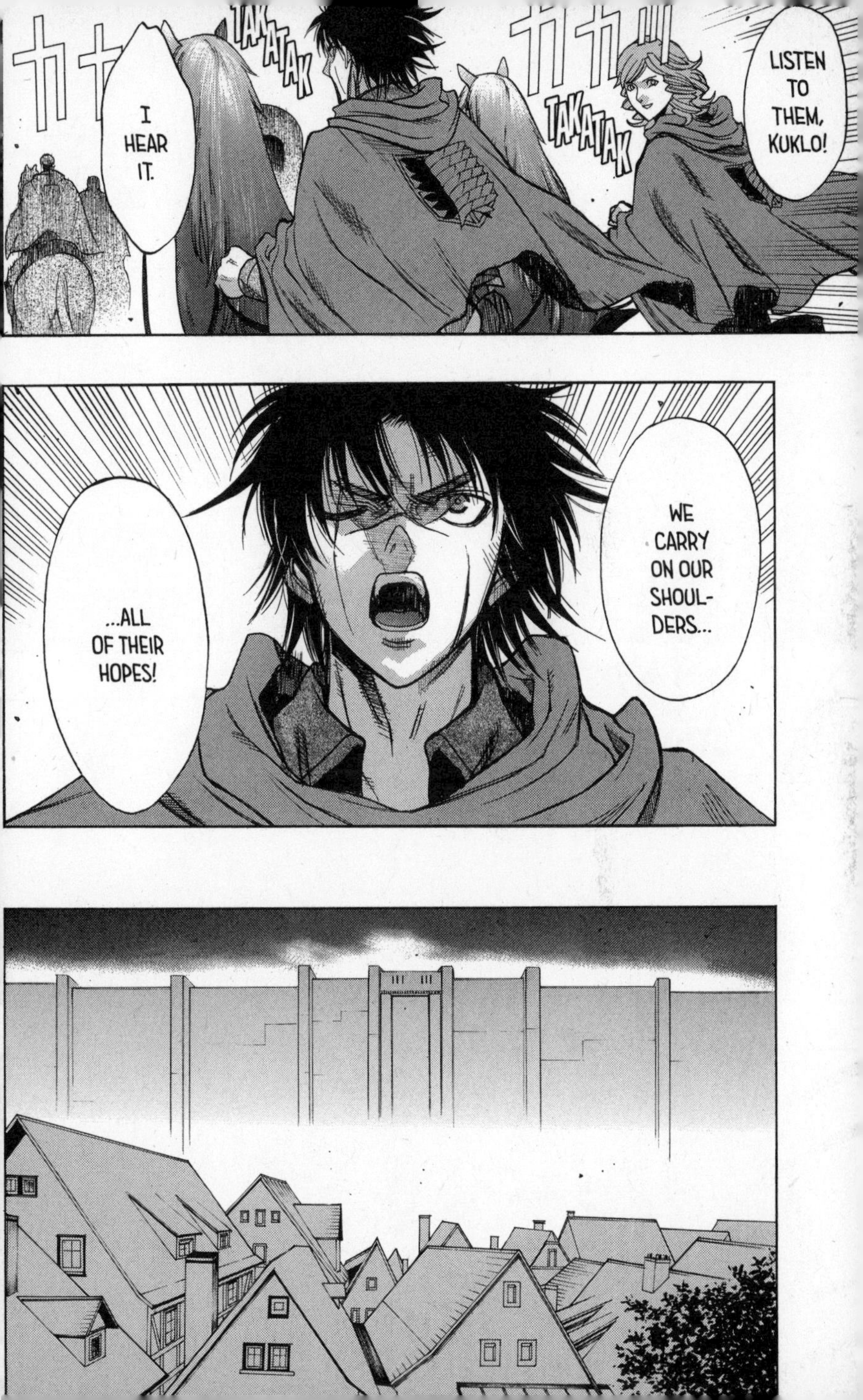

カカッ
LISTEN TO THEM, KUKLO!
TAKATAK
TAKATAK
カカ
I HEAR IT.
WE CARRY ON OUR SHOUL-DERS...
...ALL OF THEIR HOPES!

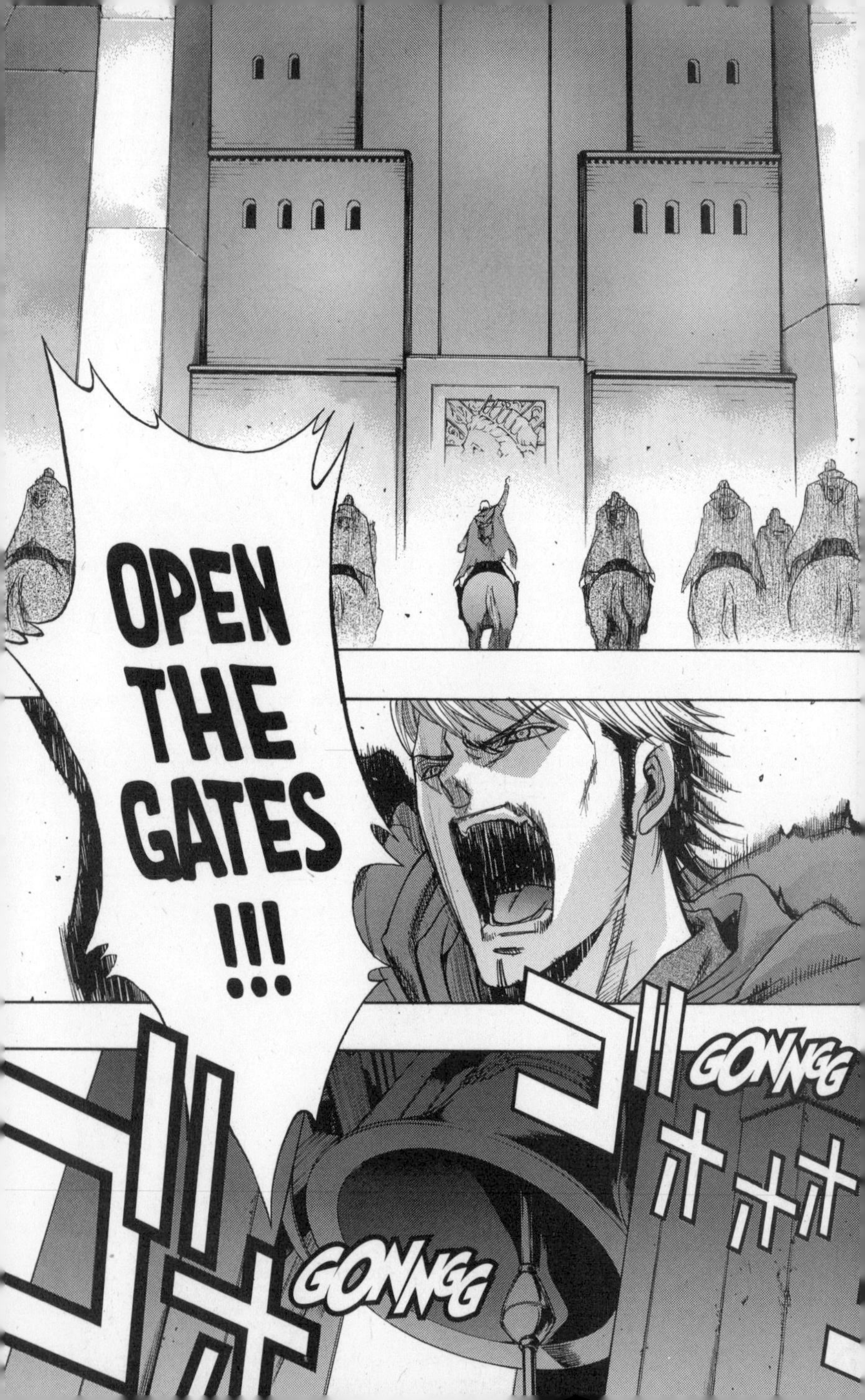
OPEN THE GATES!!!
GONNGG
GONNGG

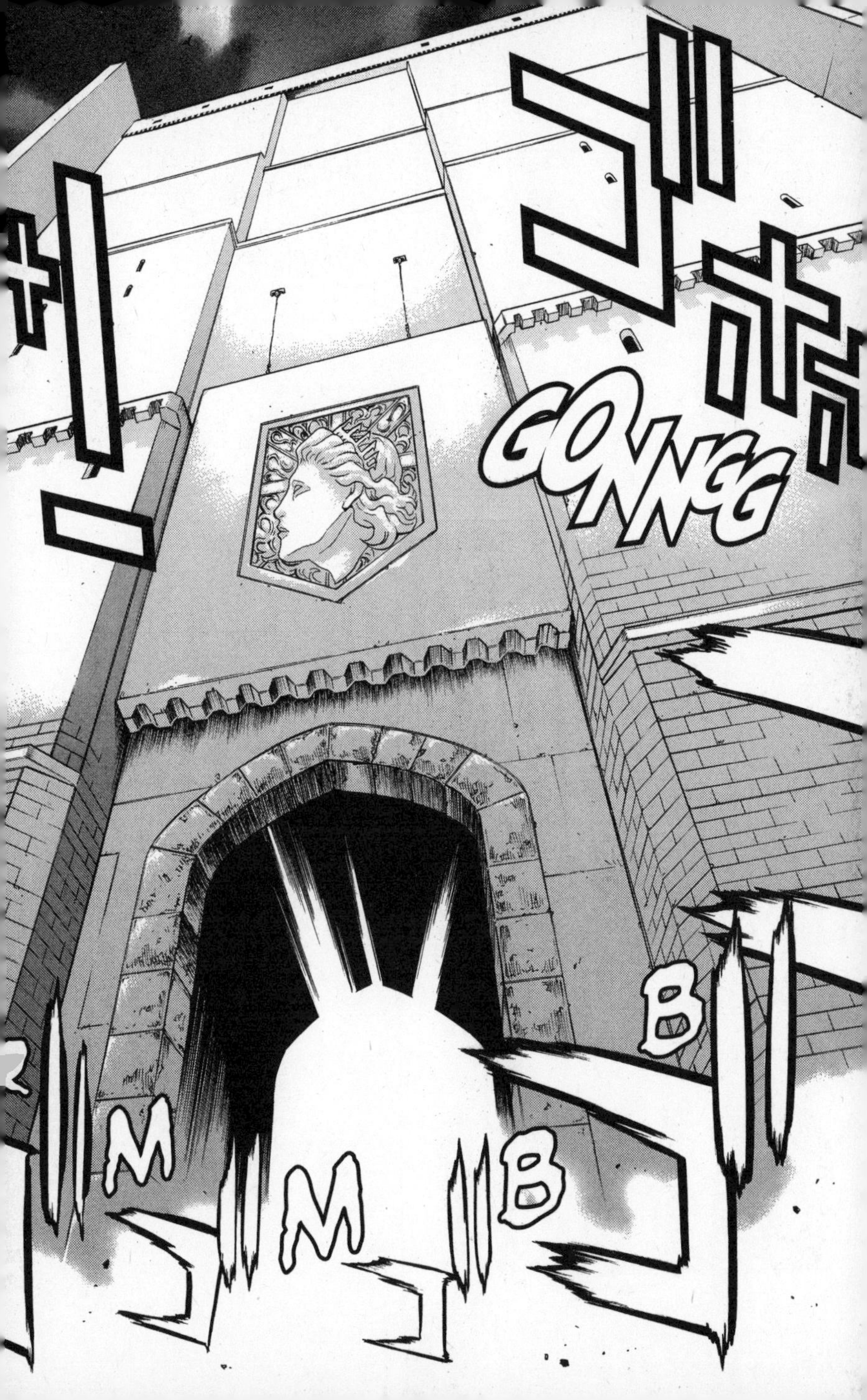
GONNGG
MMBB

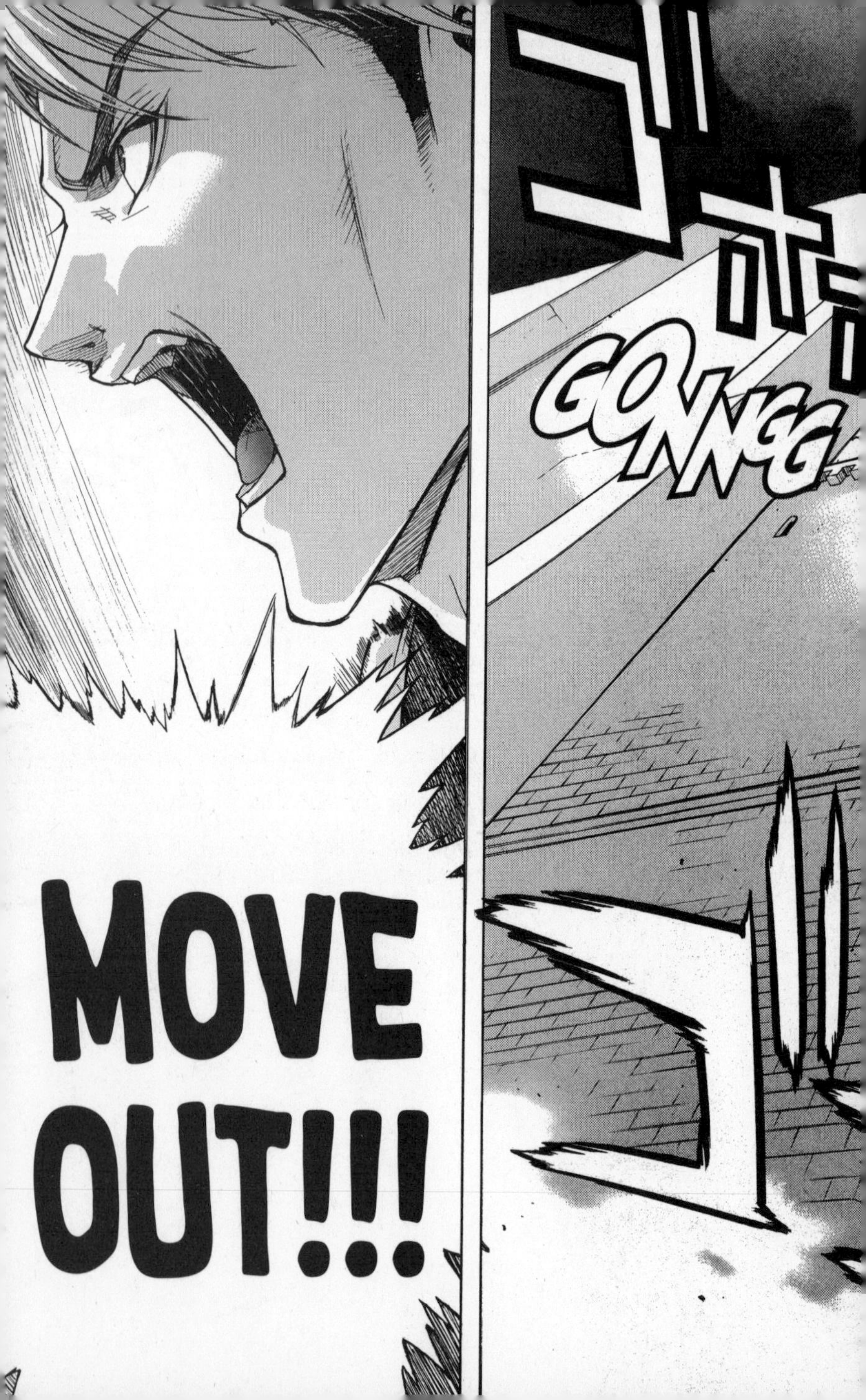
GONNG
MOVE OUT!!!

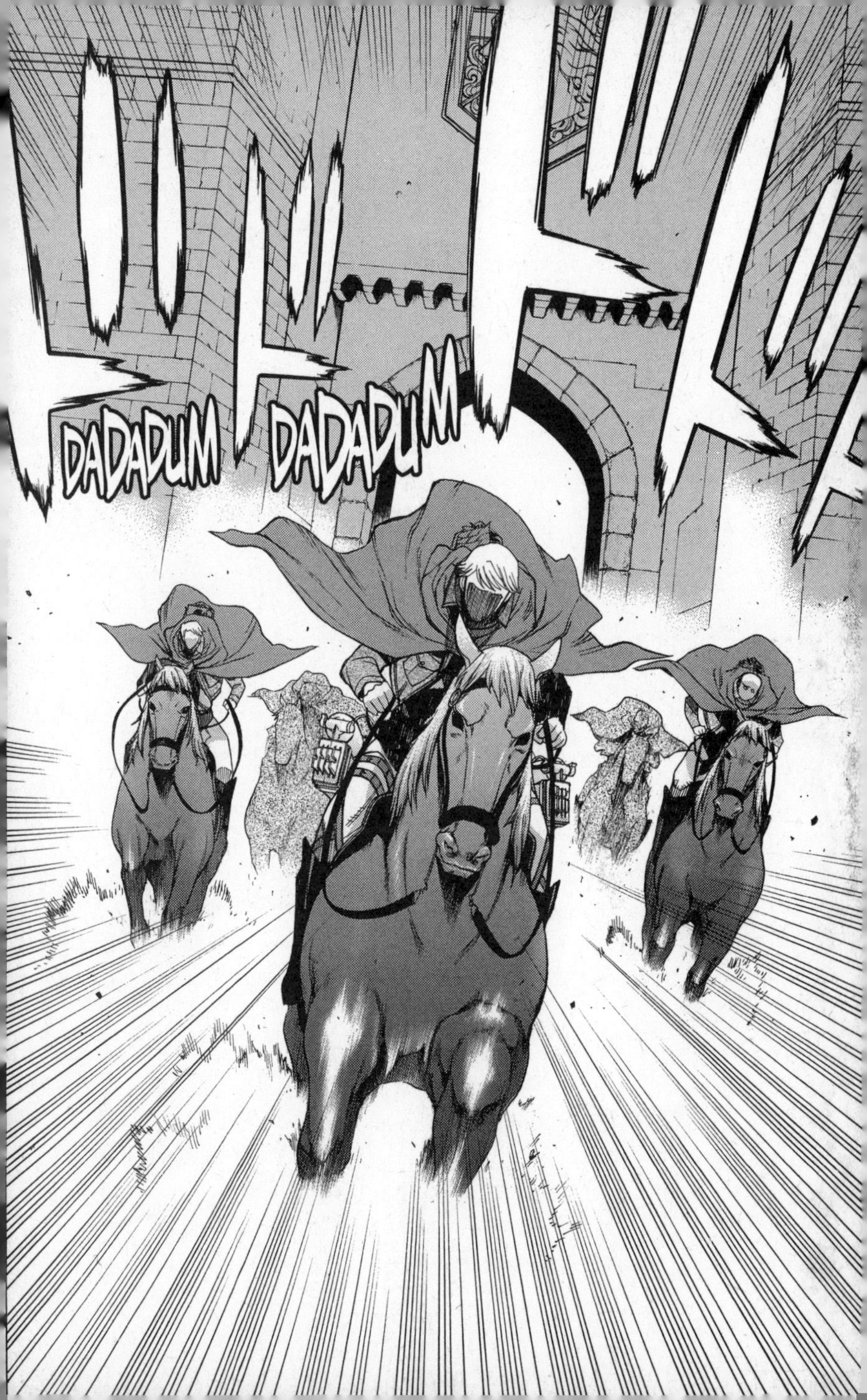
DADADUM DADADUM

# Chapter 58: Moment of Departure · End

ATTACK on TITAN

BEFORE THE FALL

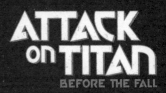

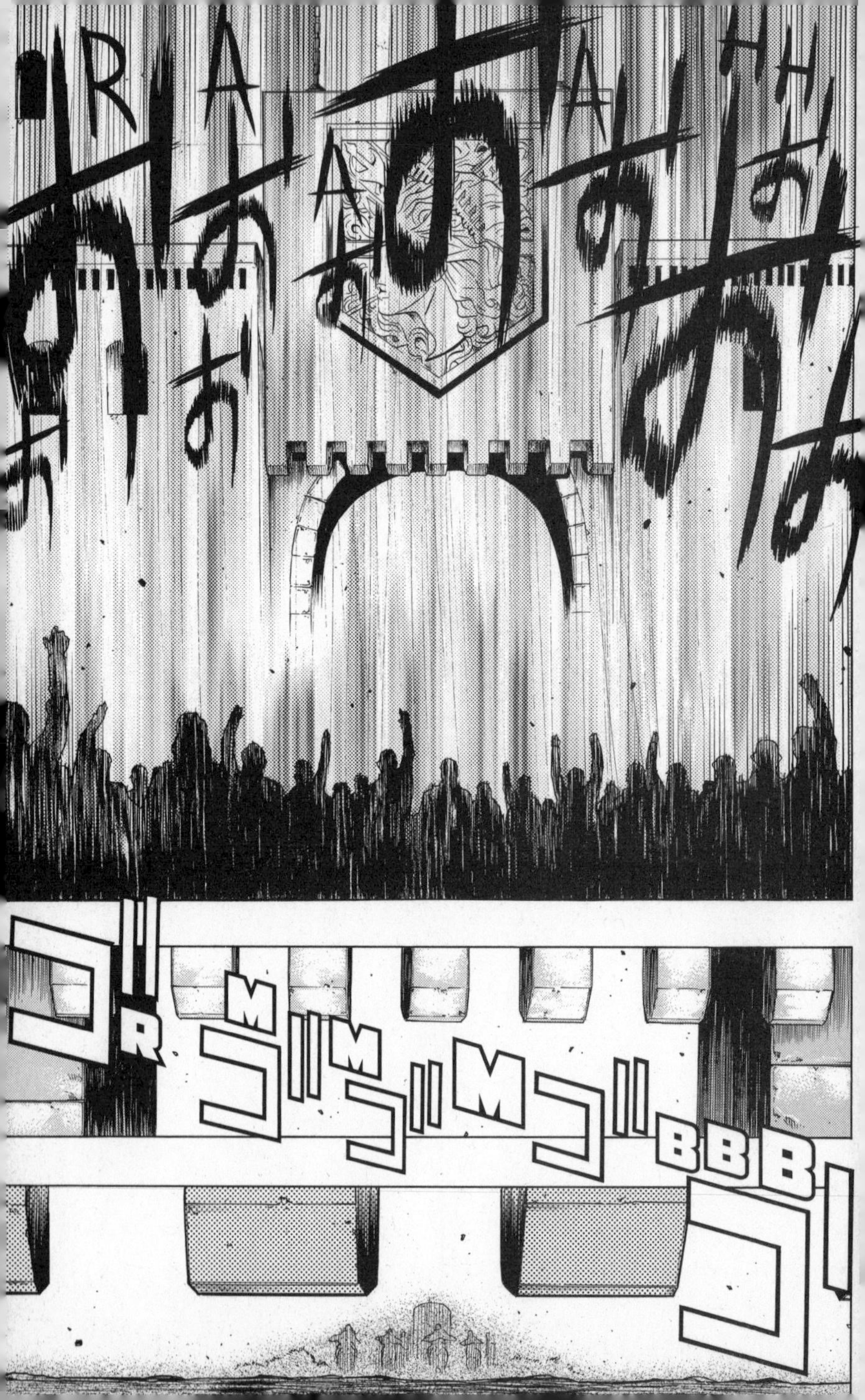
RAAAHH
RMMMBBB

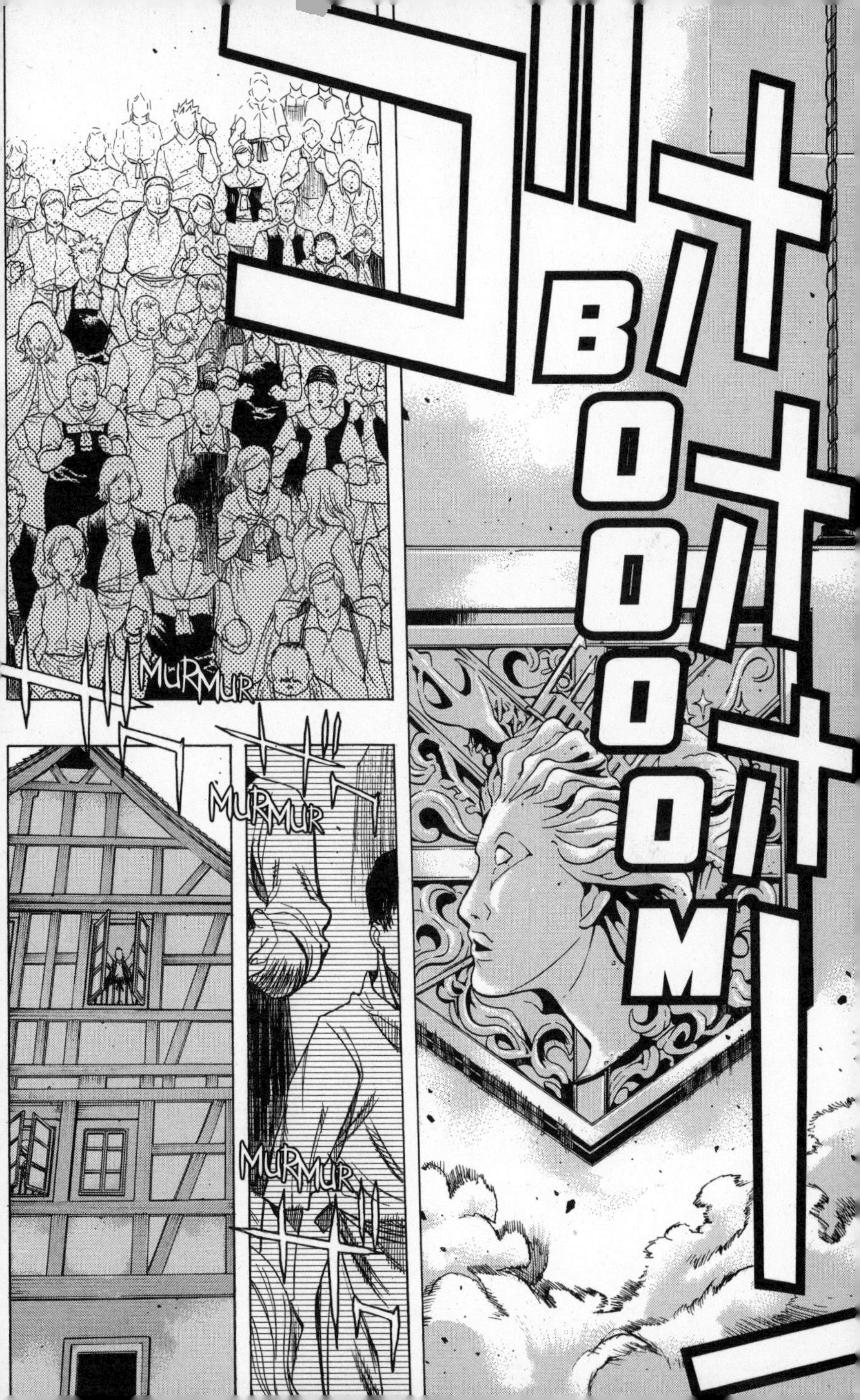
BOOOOM
MURMUR
MURMUR
MURMUR

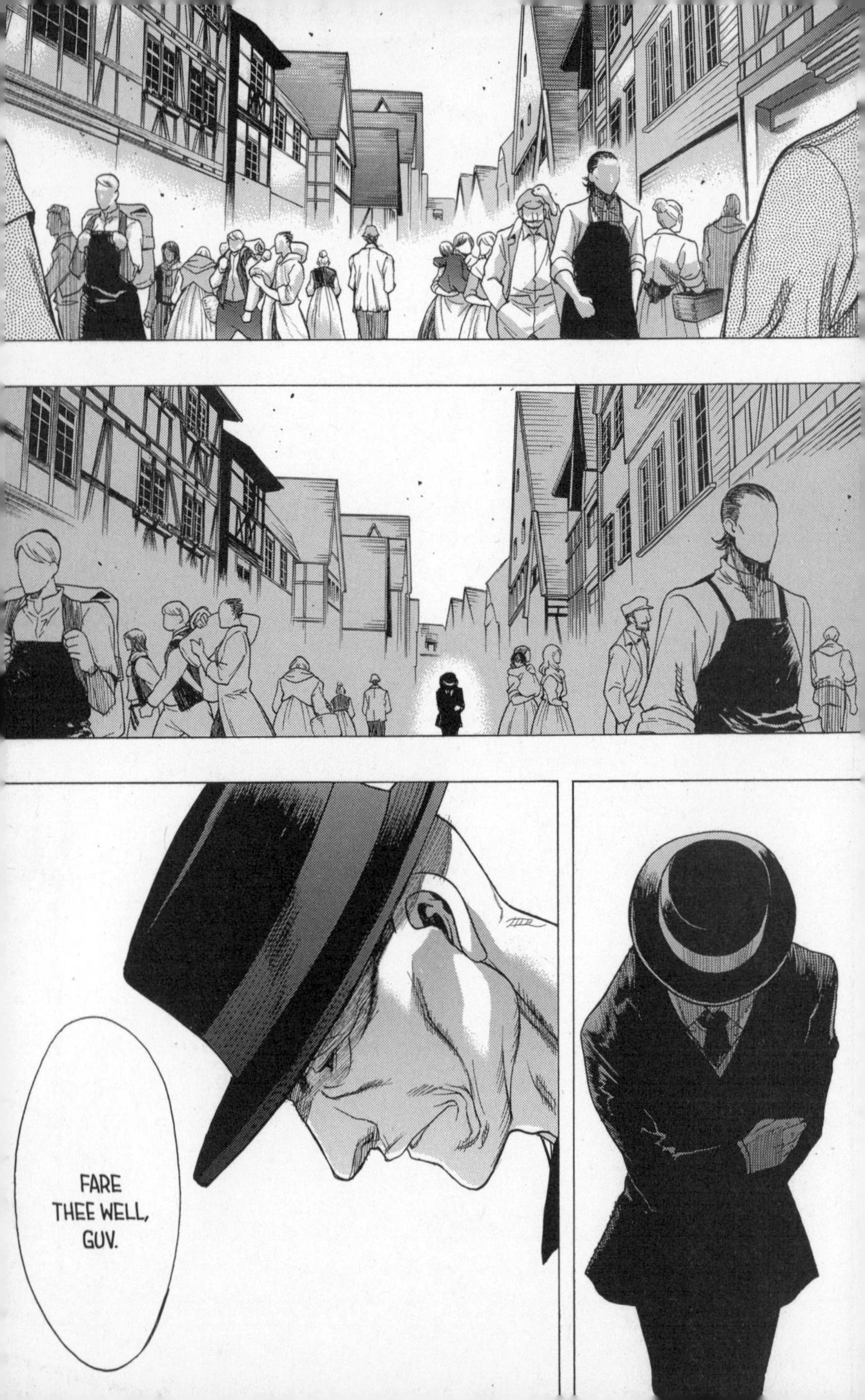
FARE THEE WELL, GUV.

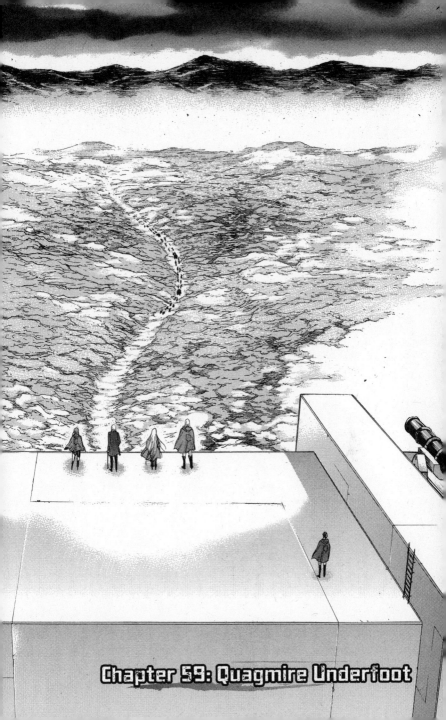

Chapter 59: Quagmire Underfoot

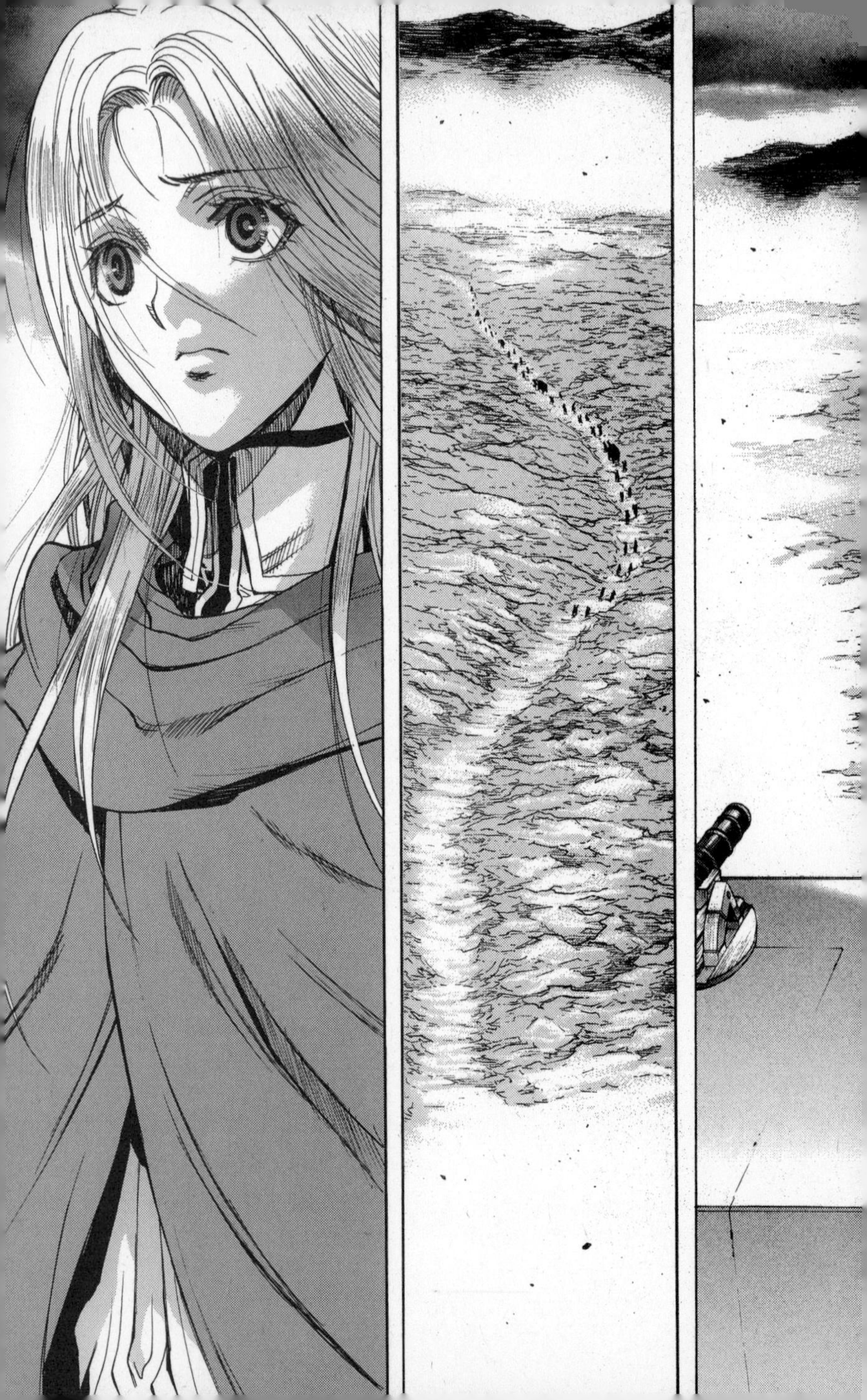

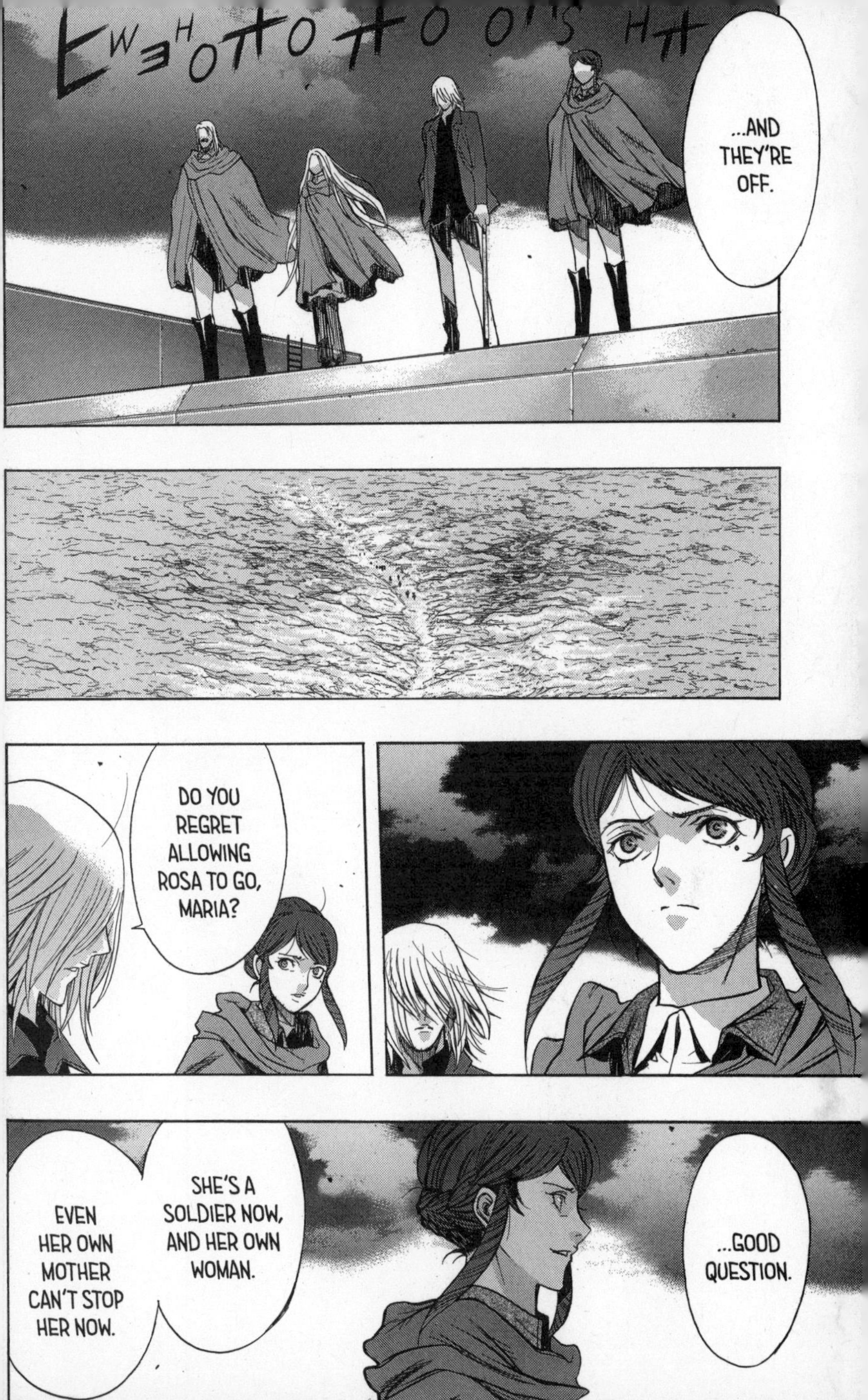
...AND THEY'RE OFF.
DO YOU REGRET ALLOWING ROSA TO GO, MARIA?
...GOOD QUESTION.
SHE'S A SOLDIER NOW, AND HER OWN WOMAN.
EVEN HER OWN MOTHER CAN'T STOP HER NOW.

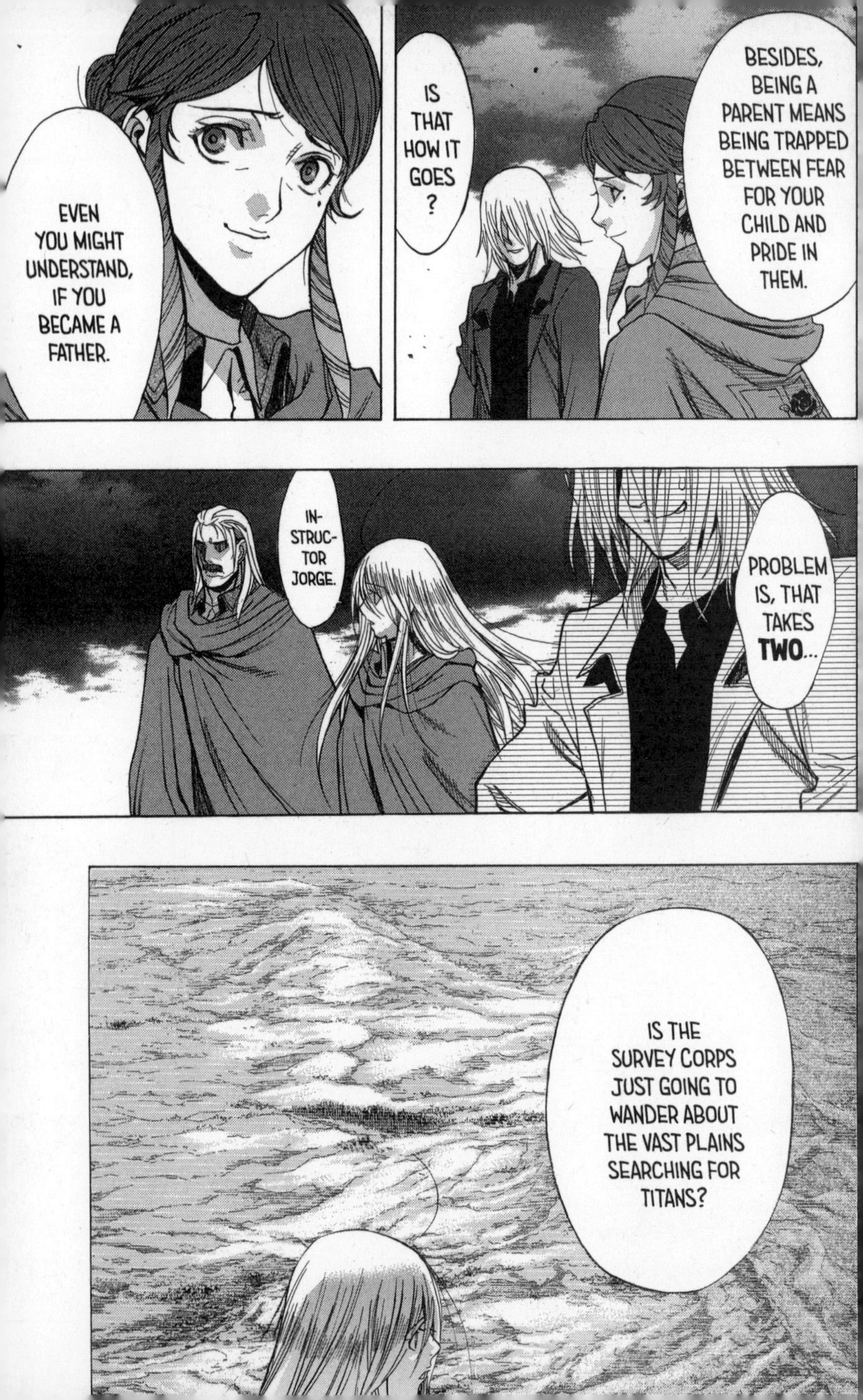
BESIDES, BEING A PARENT MEANS BEING TRAPPED BETWEEN FEAR FOR YOUR CHILD AND PRIDE IN THEM.
IS THAT HOW IT GOES?
EVEN YOU MIGHT UNDERSTAND, IF YOU BECAME A FATHER.
PROBLEM IS, THAT TAKES **TWO**...
IN-STRUC-TOR JORGE.
IS THE SURVEY CORPS JUST GOING TO WANDER ABOUT THE VAST PLAINS SEARCHING FOR TITANS?

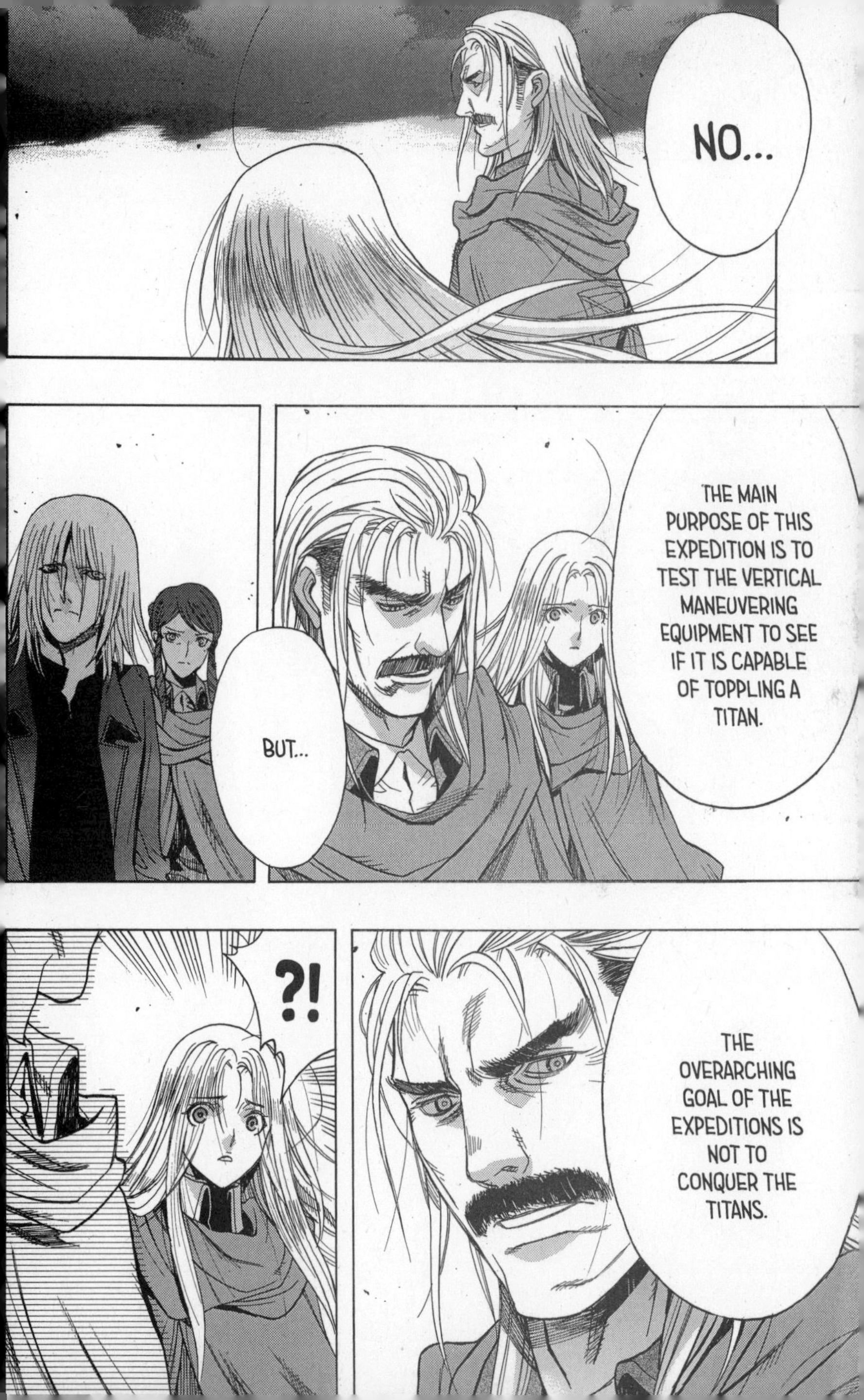
NO...
THE MAIN PURPOSE OF THIS EXPEDITION IS TO TEST THE VERTICAL MANEUVERING EQUIPMENT TO SEE IF IT IS CAPABLE OF TOPPLING A TITAN.
BUT...
THE OVERARCHING GOAL OF THE EXPEDITIONS IS NOT TO CONQUER THE TITANS.
?!

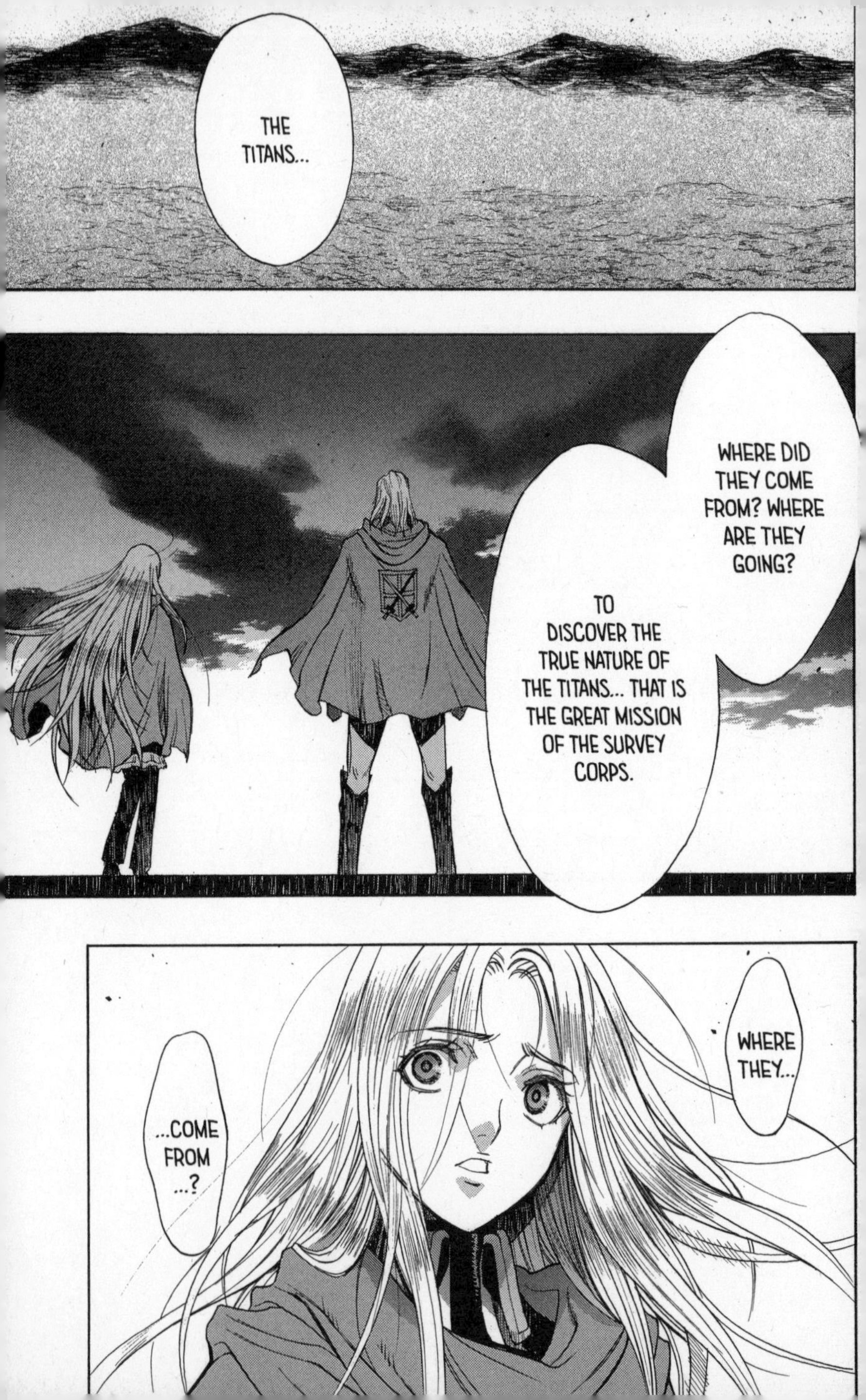
THE TITANS...
WHERE DID THEY COME FROM? WHERE ARE THEY GOING?
TO DISCOVER THE TRUE NATURE OF THE TITANS... THAT IS THE GREAT MISSION OF THE SURVEY CORPS.
WHERE THEY...
...COME FROM ...?

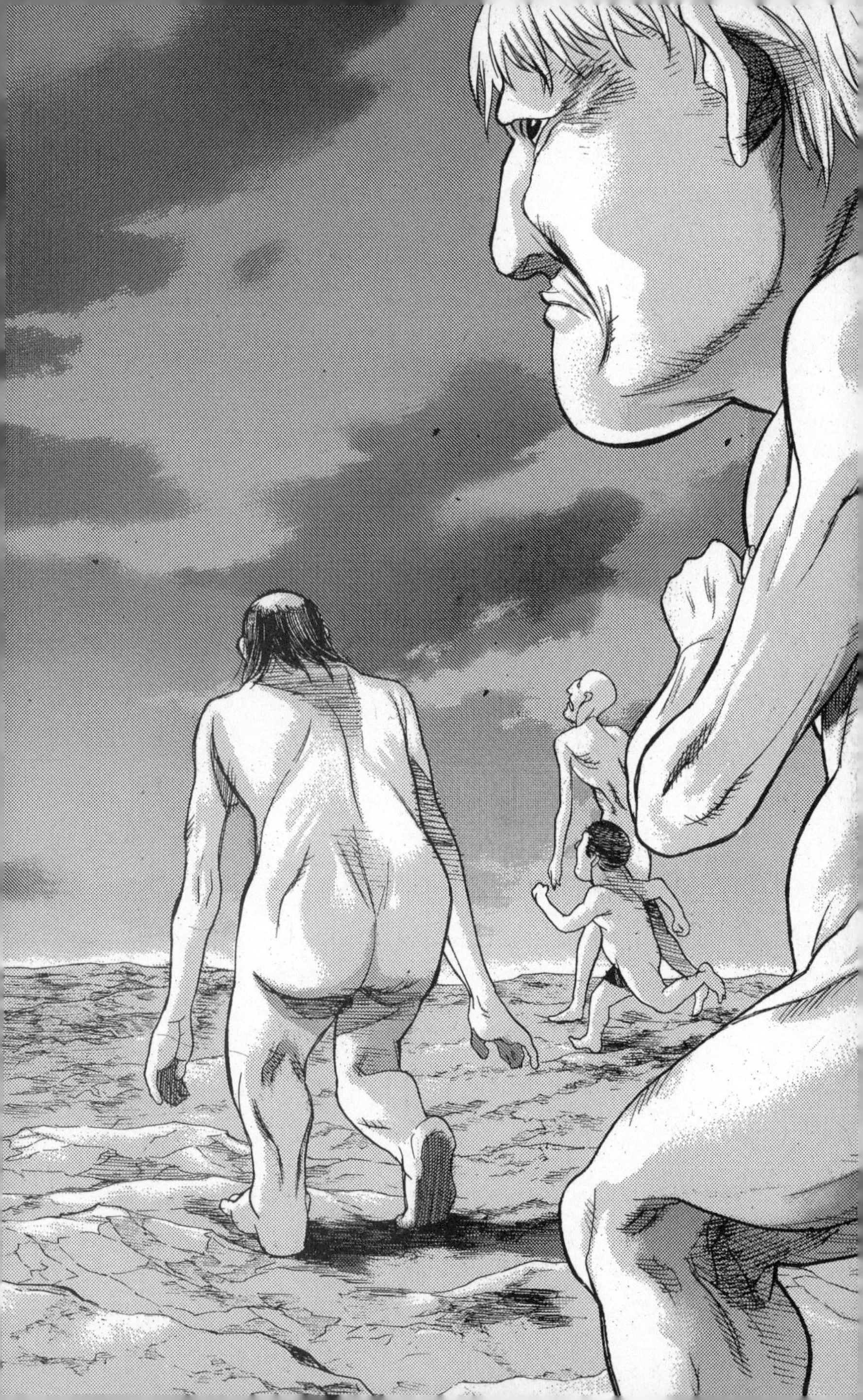

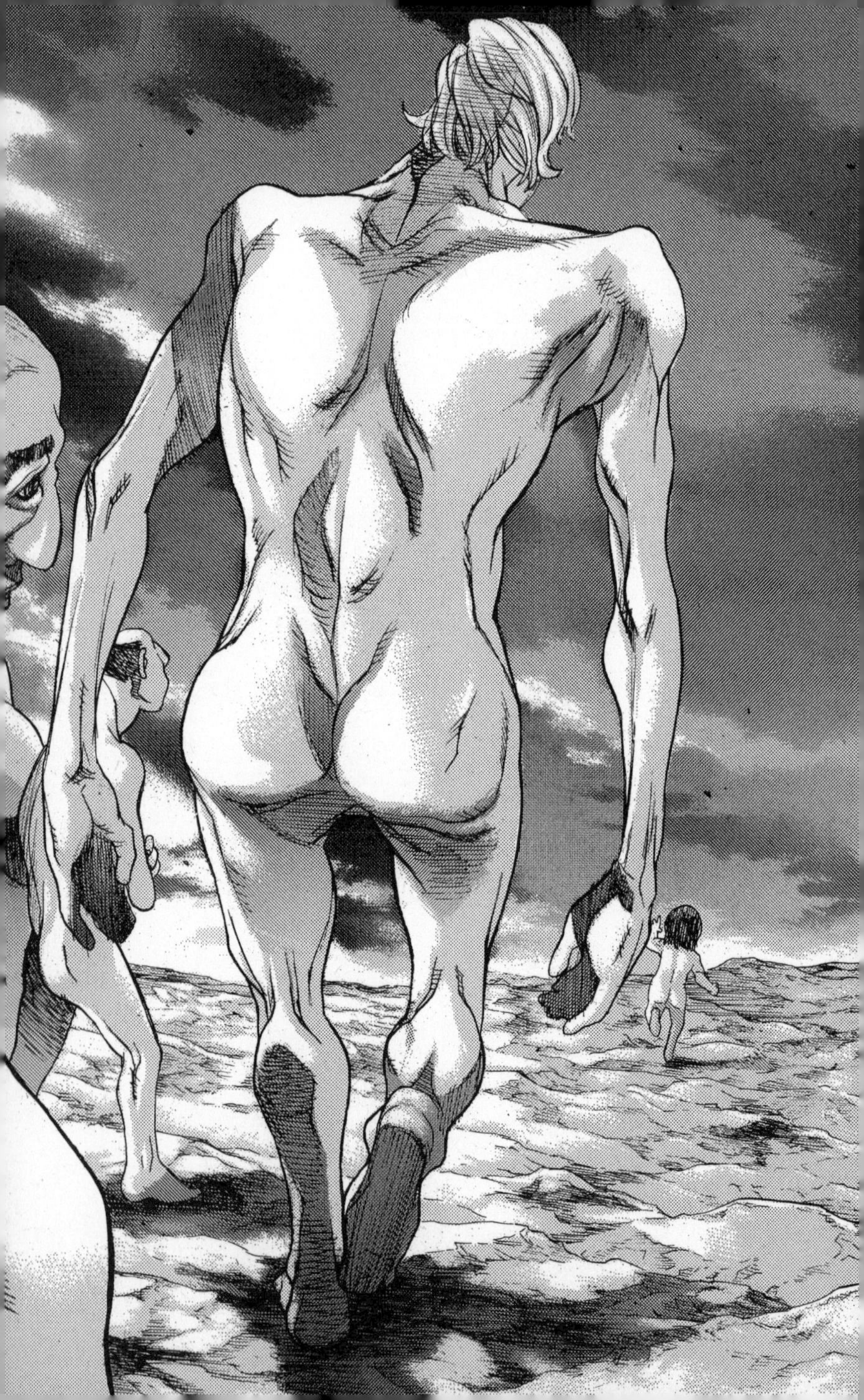

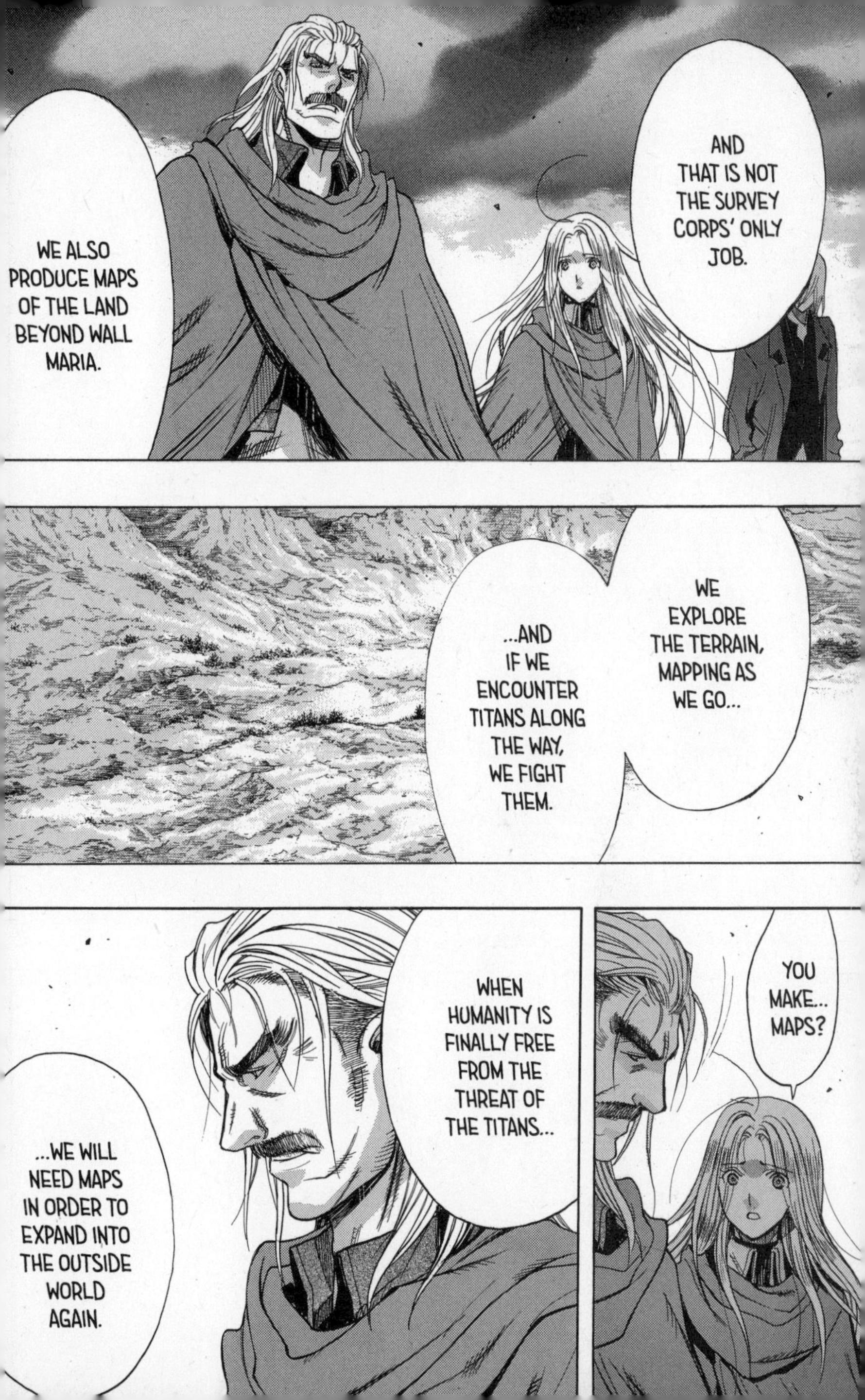
AND THAT IS NOT THE SURVEY CORPS' ONLY JOB.
WE ALSO PRODUCE MAPS OF THE LAND BEYOND WALL MARIA.
WE EXPLORE THE TERRAIN, MAPPING AS WE GO...
...AND IF WE ENCOUNTER TITANS ALONG THE WAY, WE FIGHT THEM.
YOU MAKE... MAPS?
WHEN HUMANITY IS FINALLY FREE FROM THE THREAT OF THE TITANS...
...WE WILL NEED MAPS IN ORDER TO EXPAND INTO THE OUTSIDE WORLD AGAIN.

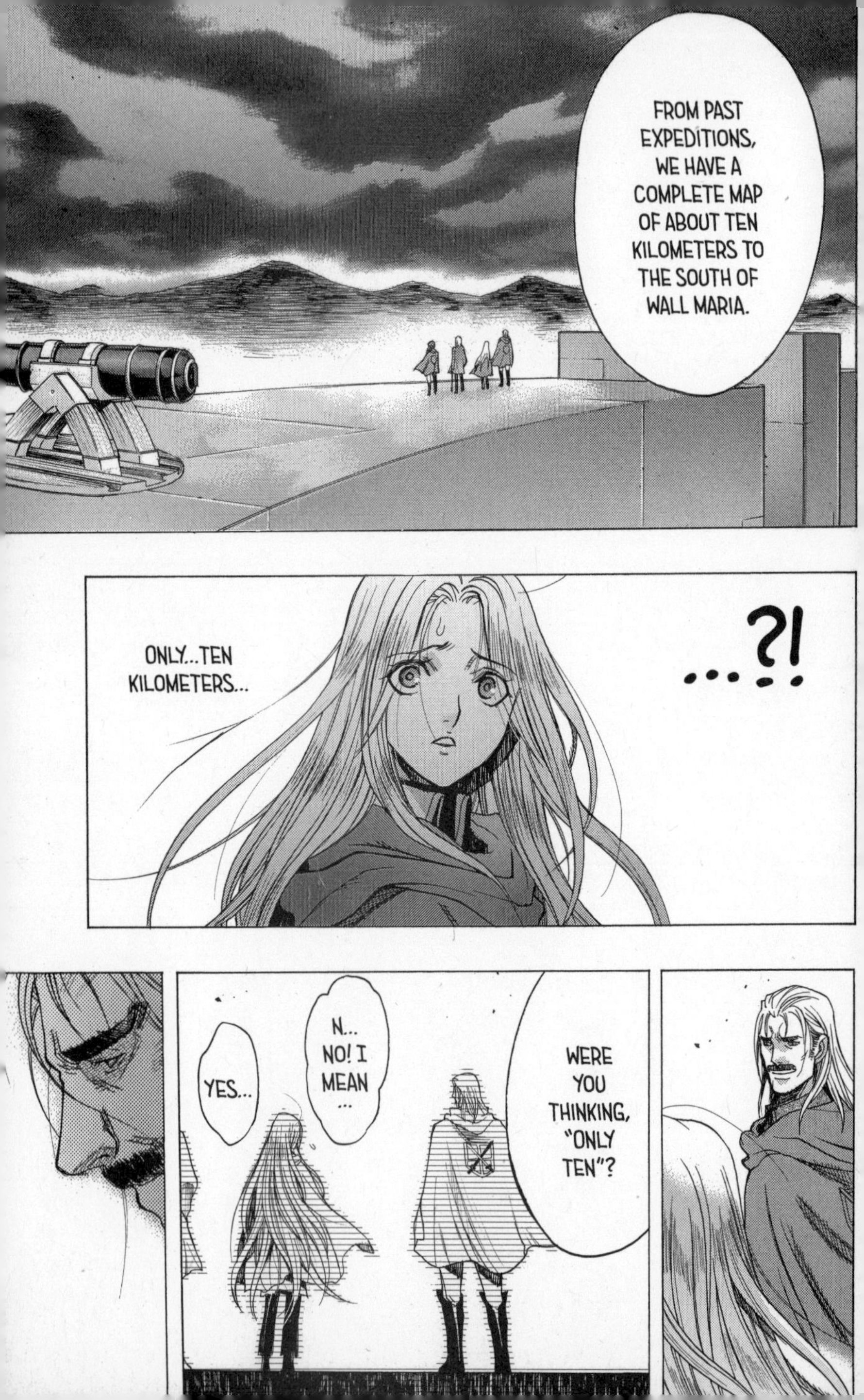
FROM PAST EXPEDITIONS, WE HAVE A COMPLETE MAP OF ABOUT TEN KILOMETERS TO THE SOUTH OF WALL MARIA.
...?!
ONLY...TEN KILOMETERS...
WERE YOU THINKING, "ONLY TEN"?
N... NO! I MEAN ...
YES...

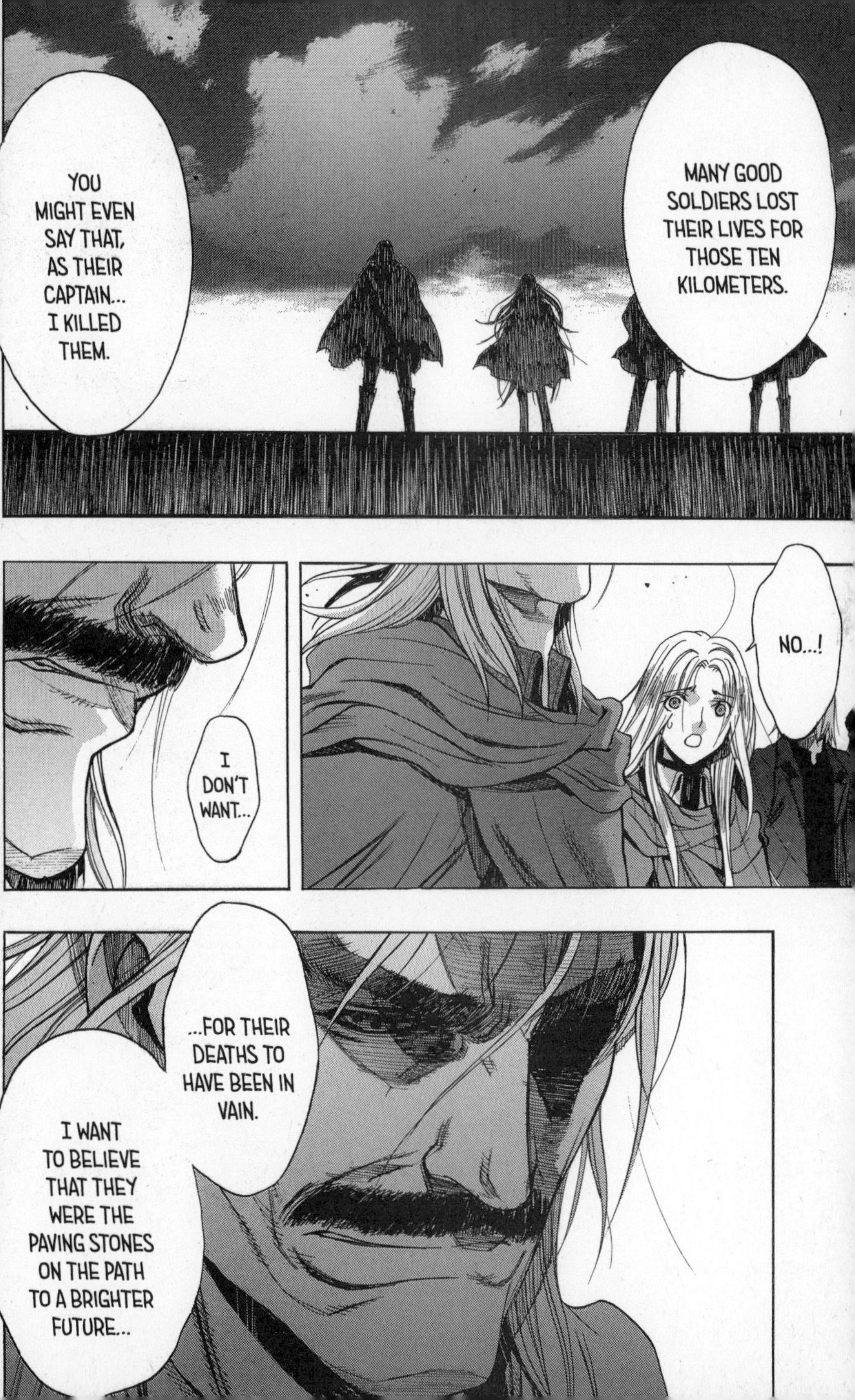
MANY GOOD SOLDIERS LOST THEIR LIVES FOR THOSE TEN KILOMETERS.
YOU MIGHT EVEN SAY THAT, AS THEIR CAPTAIN... I KILLED THEM.
NO...!
I DON'T WANT...
...FOR THEIR DEATHS TO HAVE BEEN IN VAIN.
I WANT TO BELIEVE THAT THEY WERE THE PAVING STONES ON THE PATH TO A BRIGHTER FUTURE...

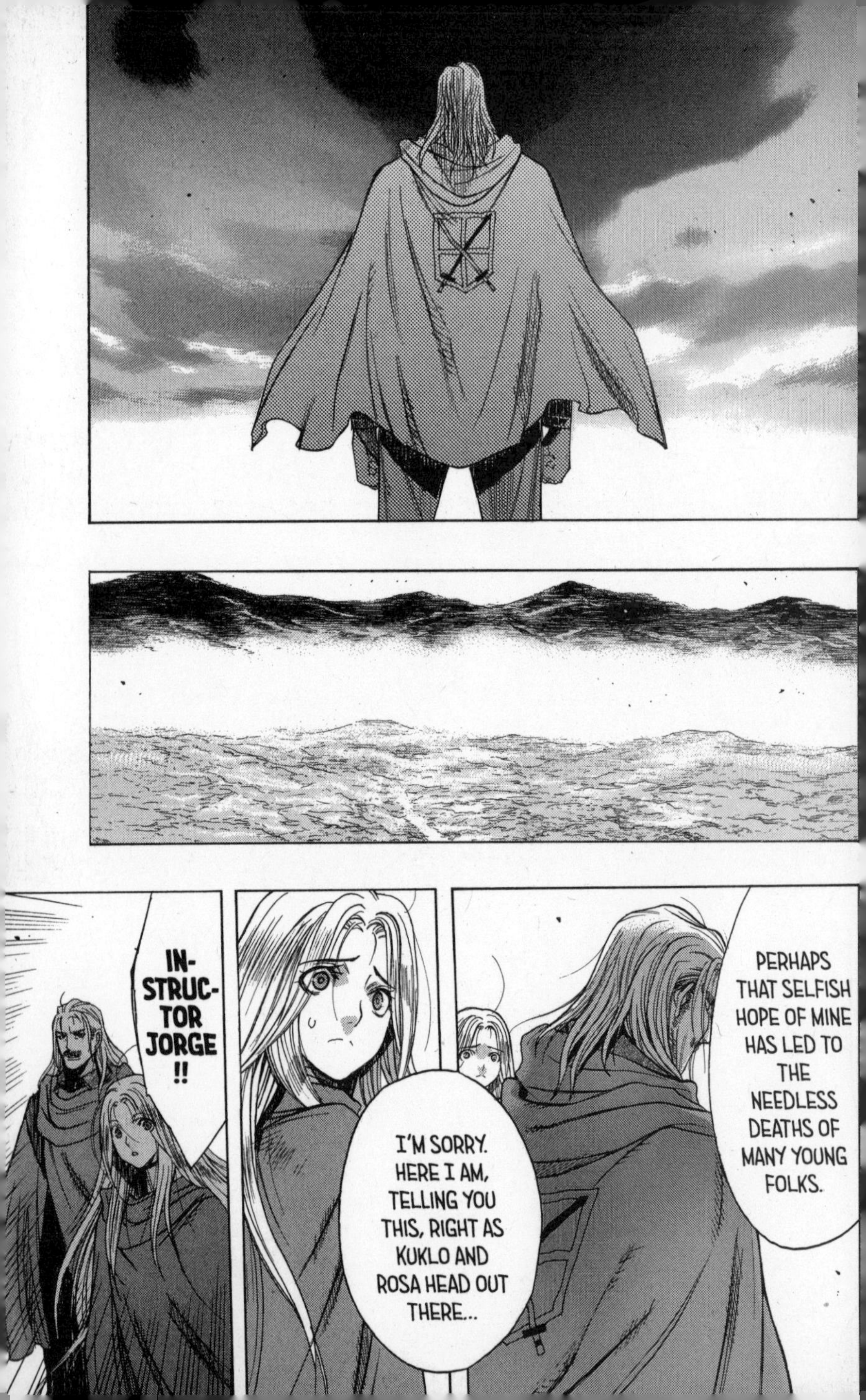
PERHAPS THAT SELFISH HOPE OF MINE HAS LED TO THE NEEDLESS DEATHS OF MANY YOUNG FOLKS.
I'M SORRY. HERE I AM, TELLING YOU THIS, RIGHT AS KUKLO AND ROSA HEAD OUT THERE...
IN-STRUC-TOR JORGE!!

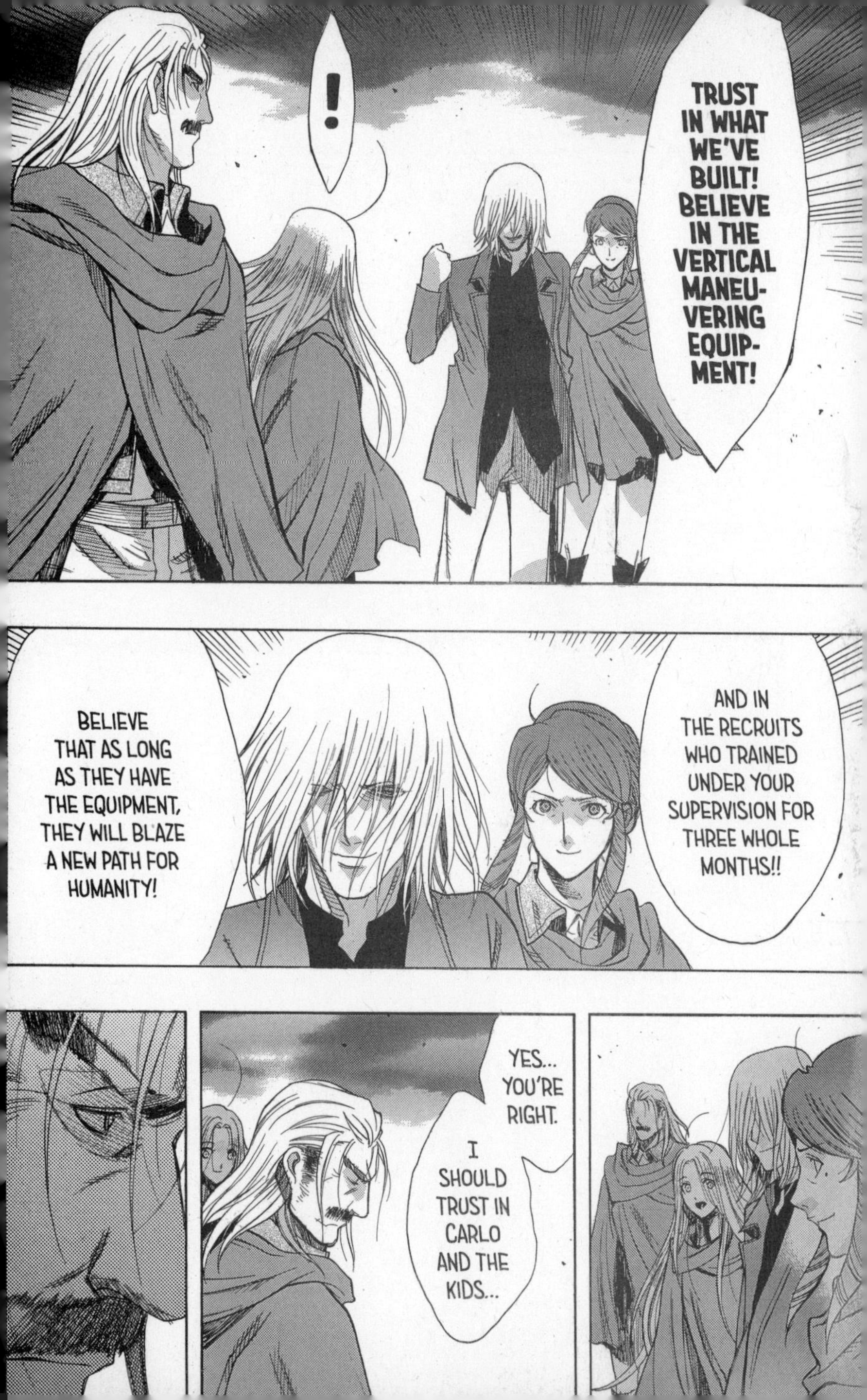
TRUST IN WHAT WE'VE BUILT! BELIEVE IN THE VERTICAL MANEU-VERING EQUIP-MENT!
!
AND IN THE RECRUITS WHO TRAINED UNDER YOUR SUPERVISION FOR THREE WHOLE MONTHS!!
BELIEVE THAT AS LONG AS THEY HAVE THE EQUIPMENT, THEY WILL BLAZE A NEW PATH FOR HUMANITY!
YES... YOU'RE RIGHT.
I SHOULD TRUST IN CARLO AND THE KIDS...

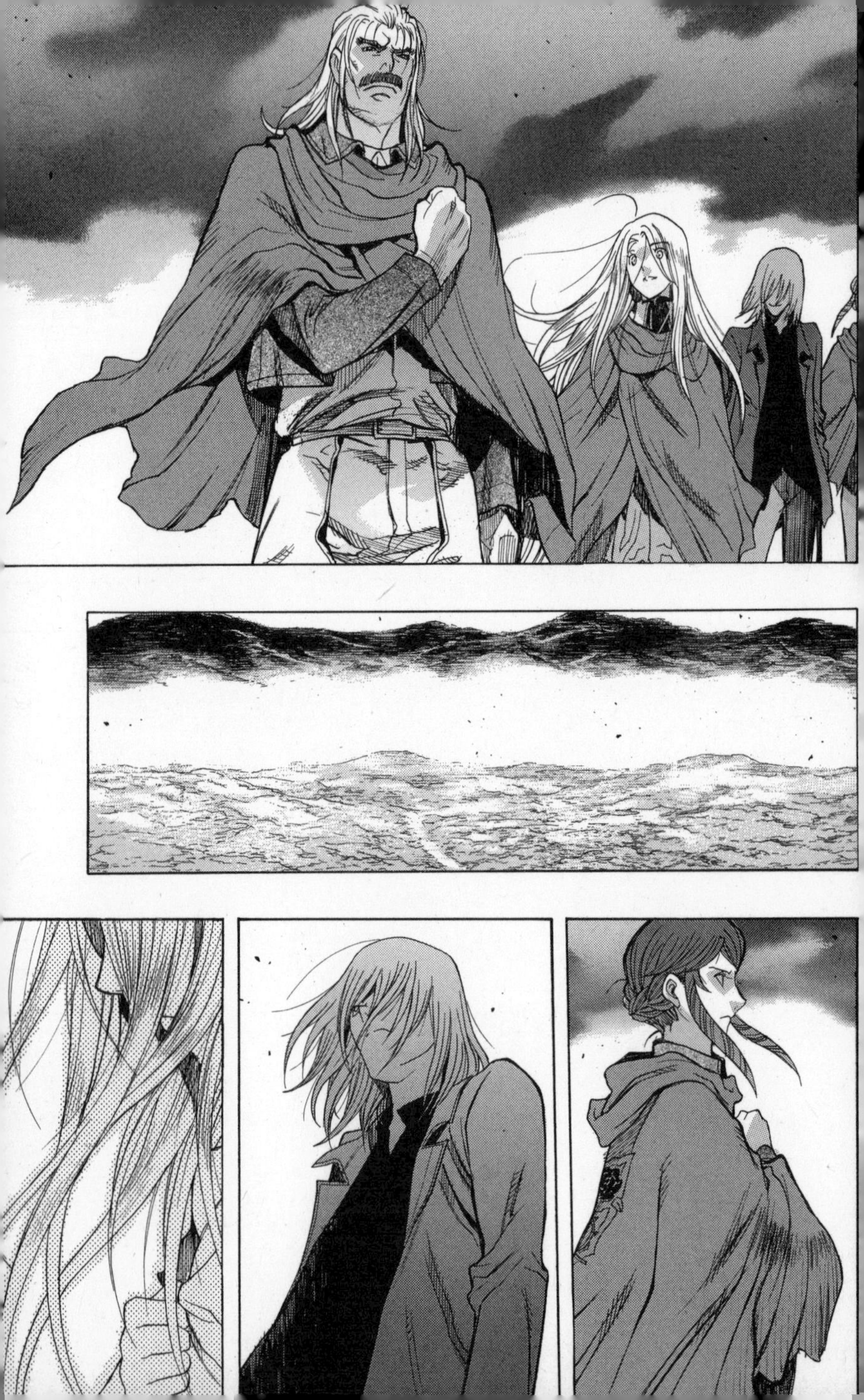

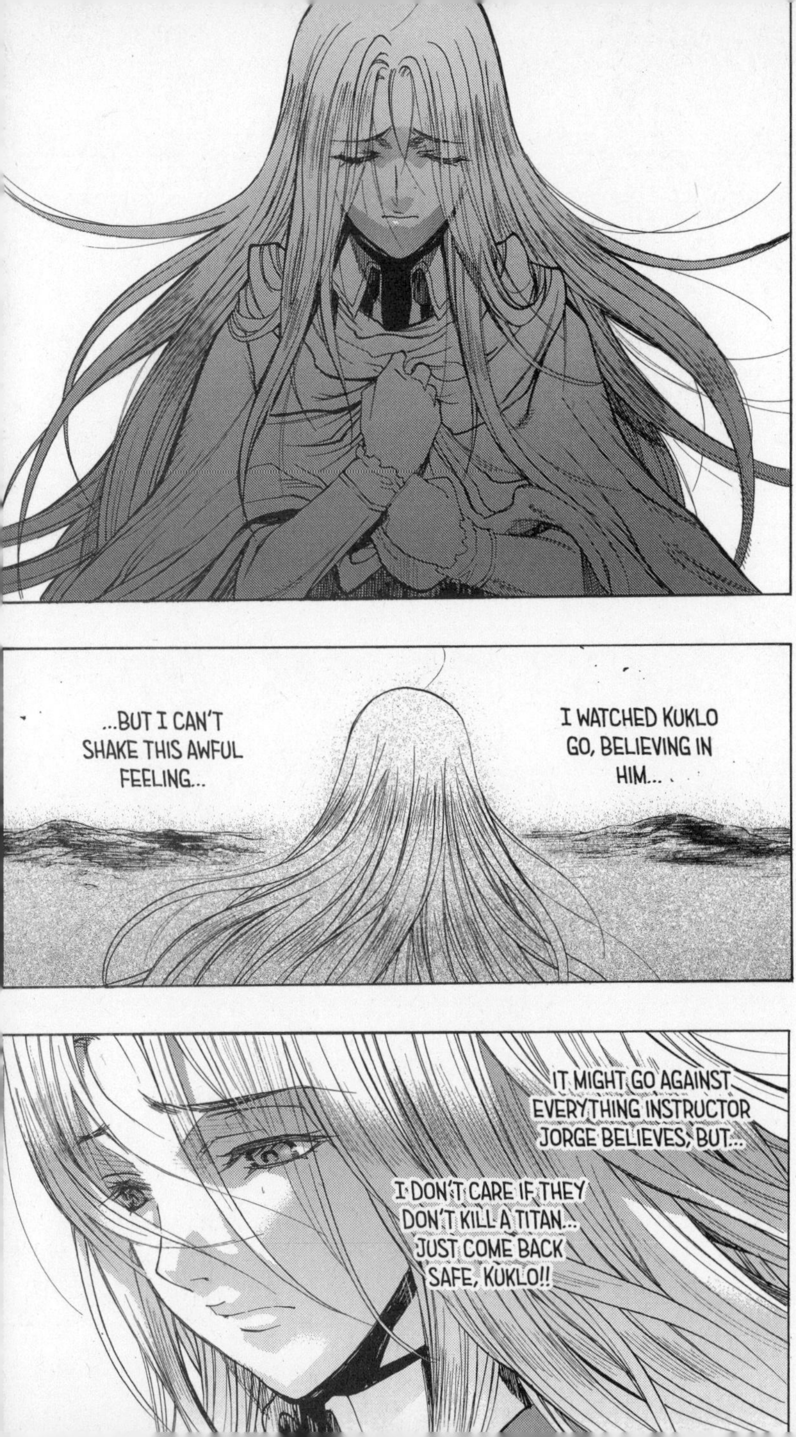
I WATCHED KUKLO GO, BELIEVING IN HIM...
...BUT I CAN'T SHAKE THIS AWFUL FEELING...
IT MIGHT GO AGAINST EVERYTHING INSTRUCTOR JORGE BELIEVES, BUT...
I DON'T CARE IF THEY DON'T KILL A TITAN... JUST COME BACK SAFE, KUKLO!!

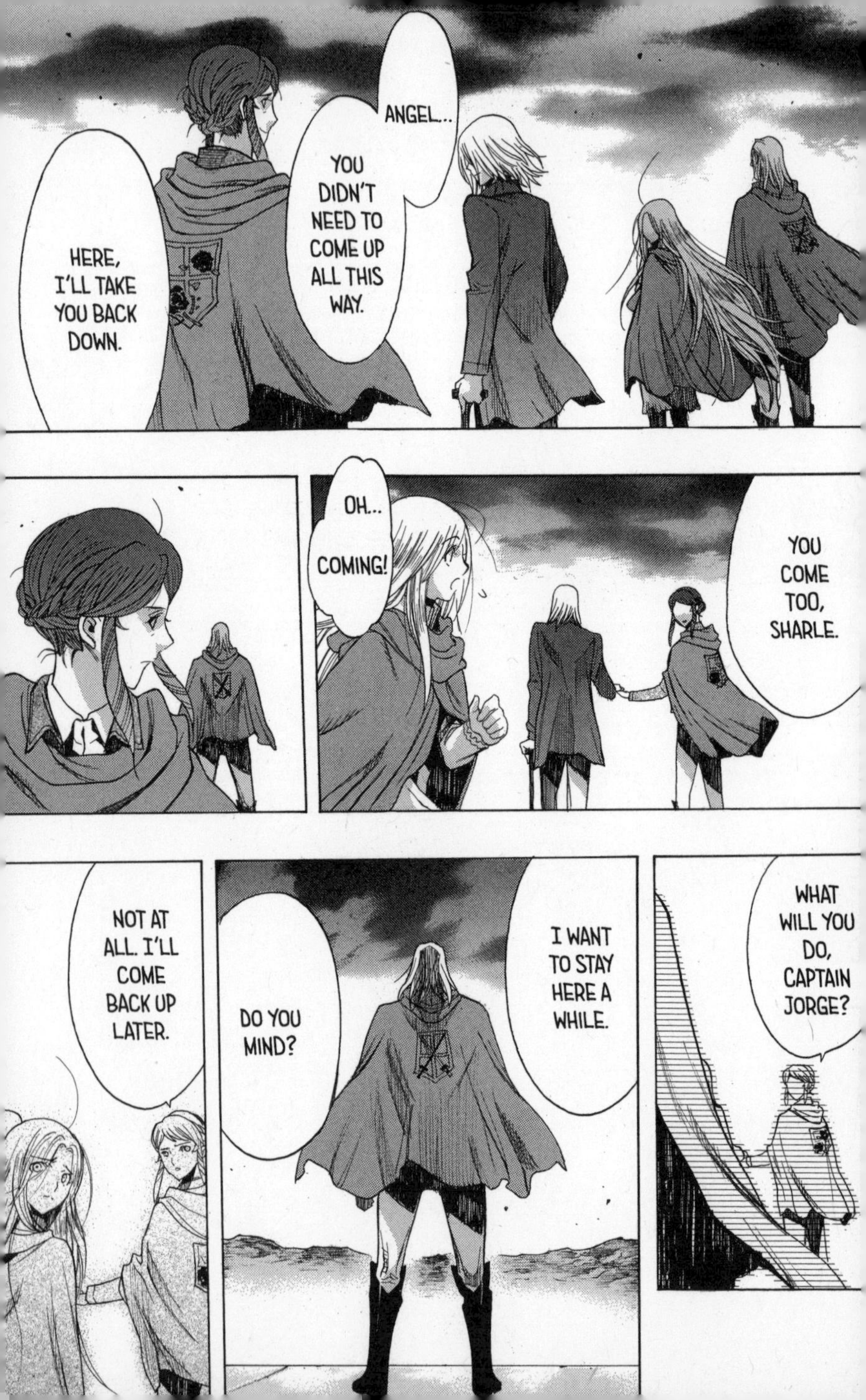
ANGEL...
YOU DIDN'T NEED TO COME UP ALL THIS WAY.
HERE, I'LL TAKE YOU BACK DOWN.
YOU COME TOO, SHARLE.
OH...
COMING!
WHAT WILL YOU DO, CAPTAIN JORGE?
I WANT TO STAY HERE A WHILE.
DO YOU MIND?
NOT AT ALL. I'LL COME BACK UP LATER.

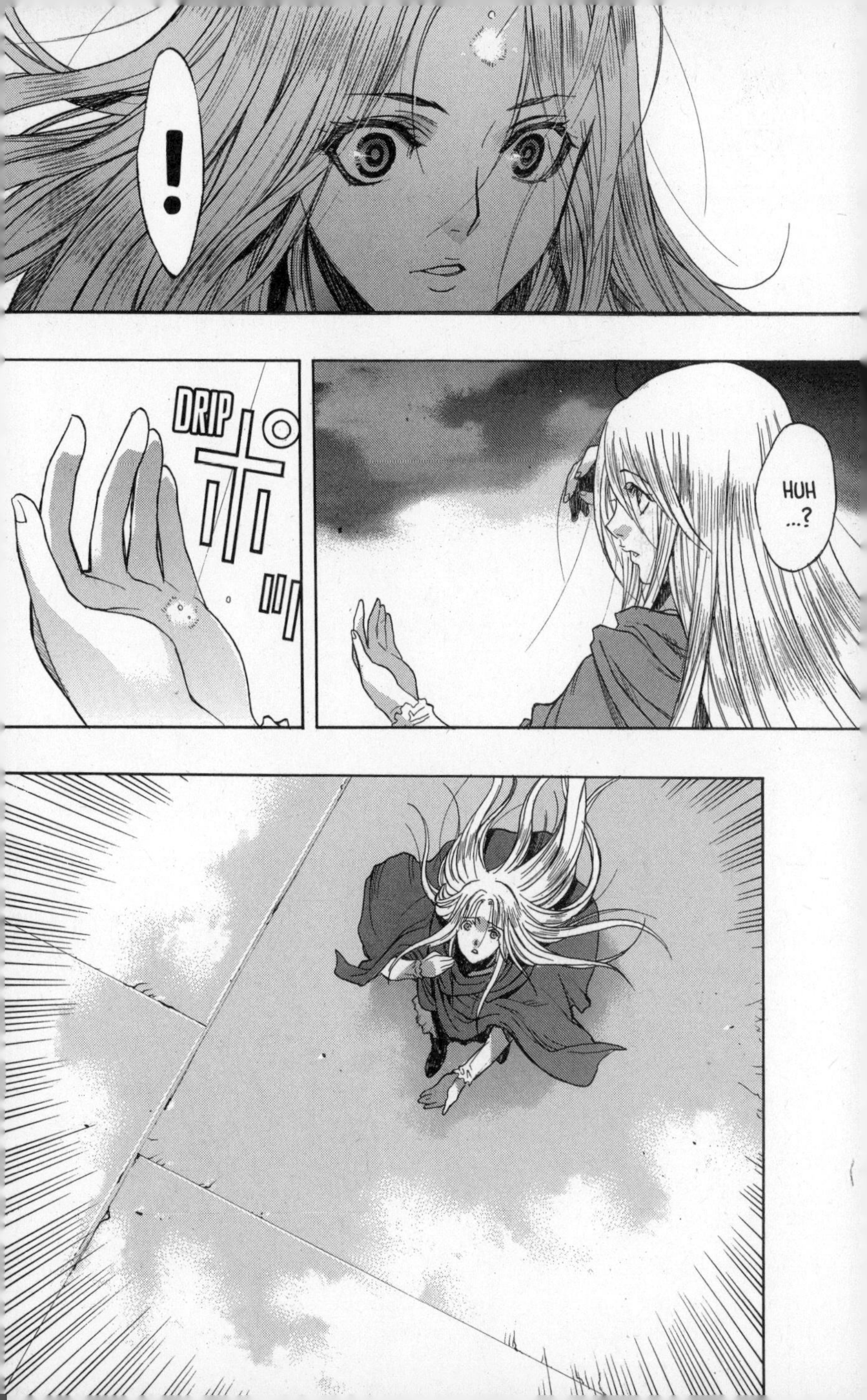
!
HUH ...?
DRIP
ポツ

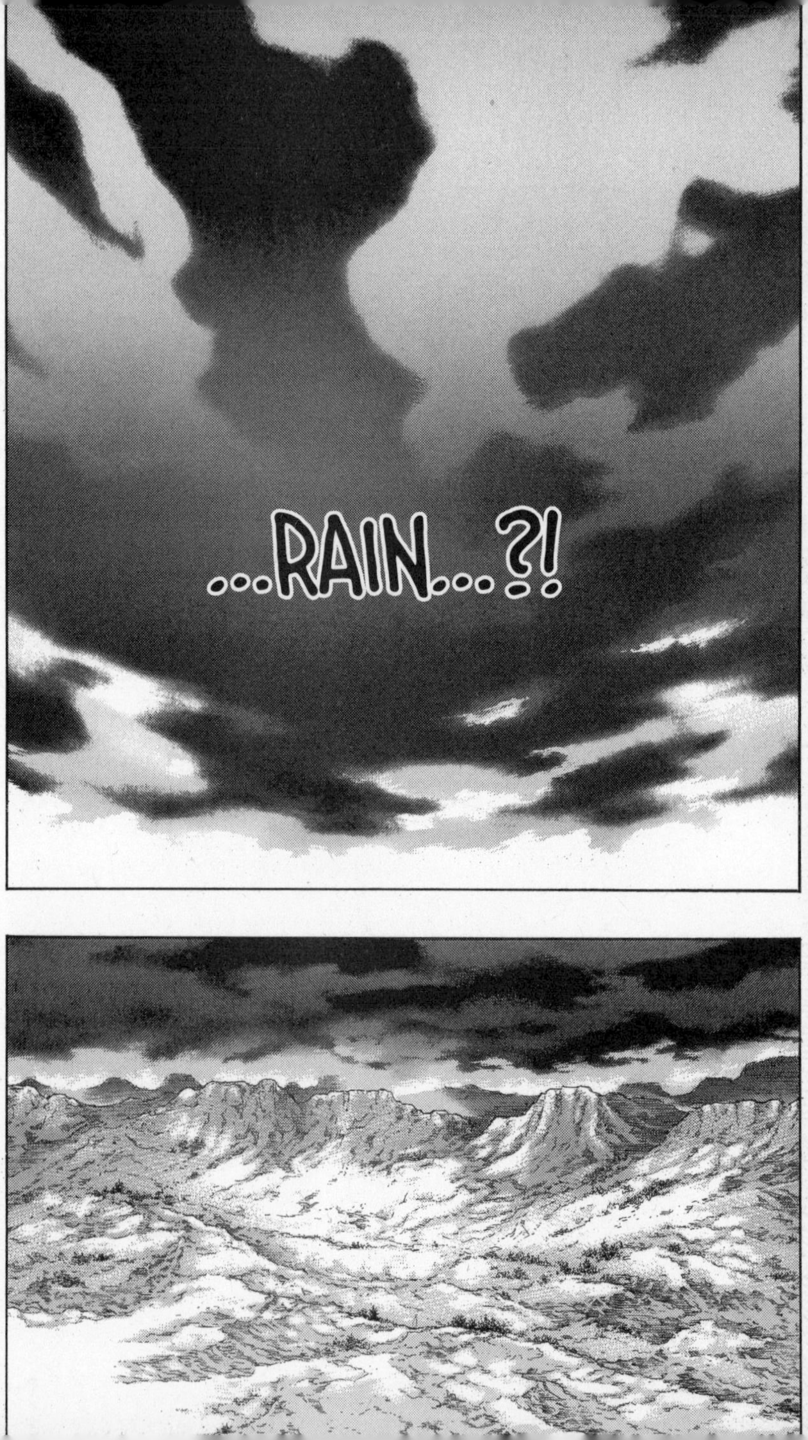
...RAIN...?!

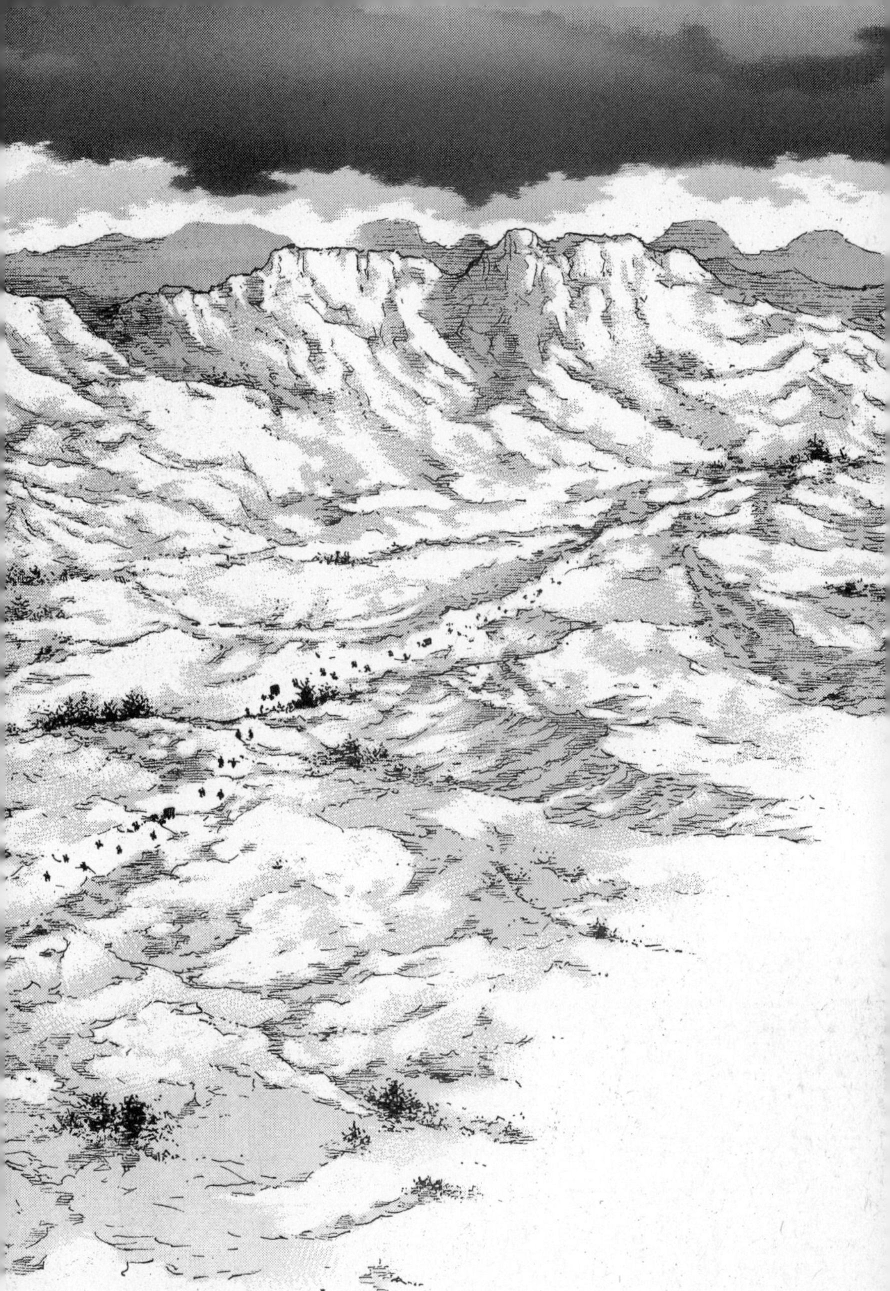

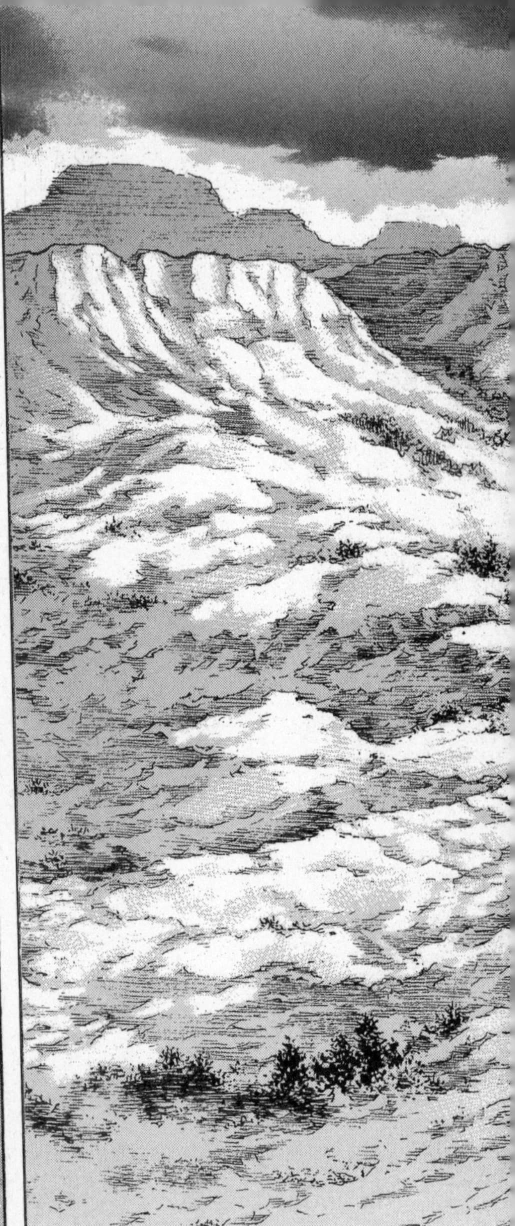

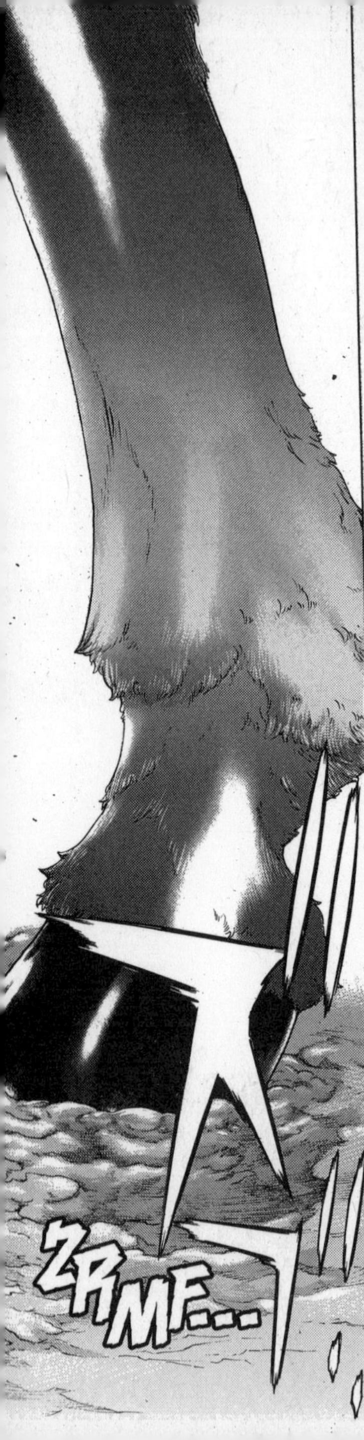
ZRMF...

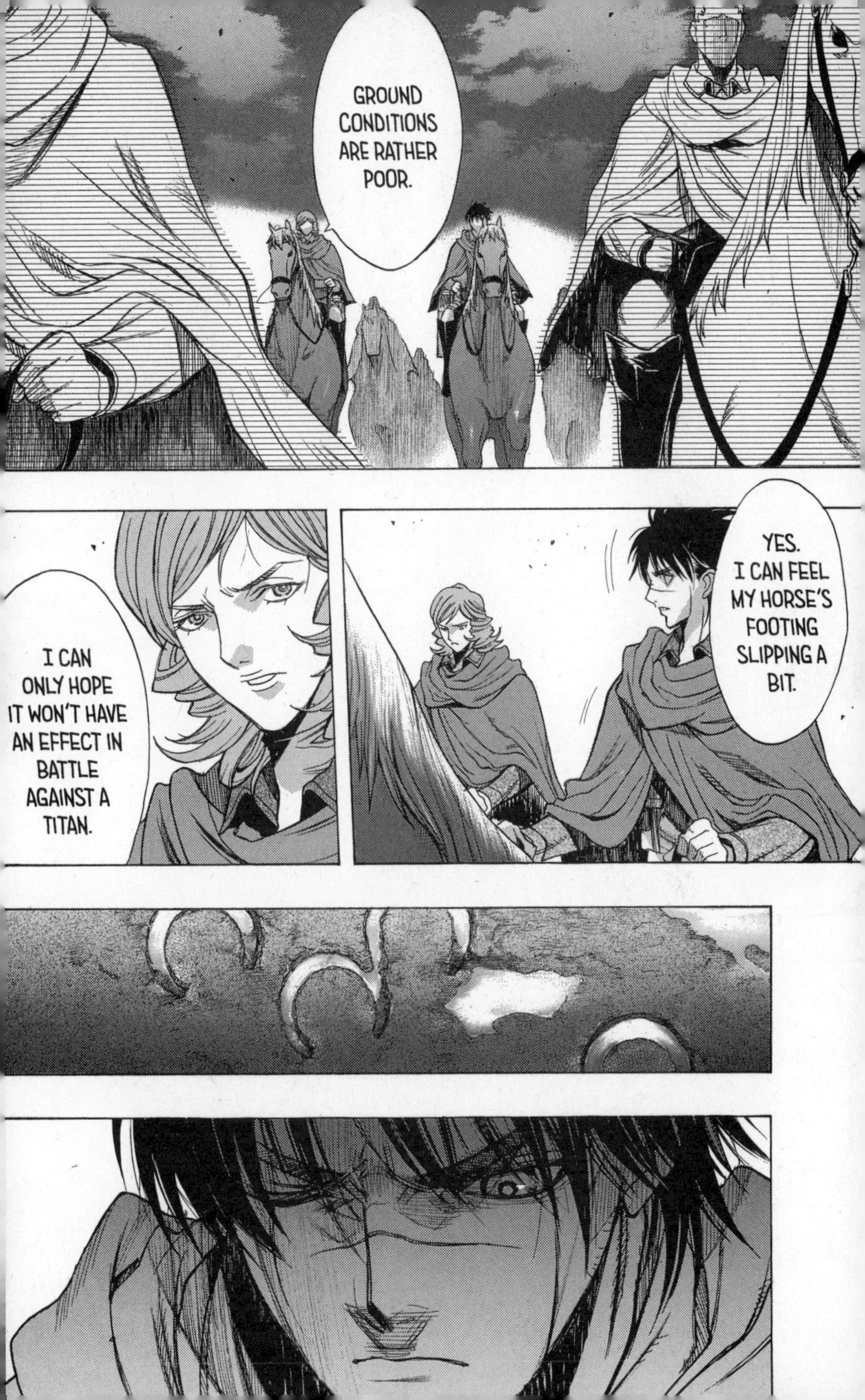
GROUND CONDITIONS ARE RATHER POOR.
YES. I CAN FEEL MY HORSE'S FOOTING SLIPPING A BIT.
I CAN ONLY HOPE IT WON'T HAVE AN EFFECT IN BATTLE AGAINST A TITAN.

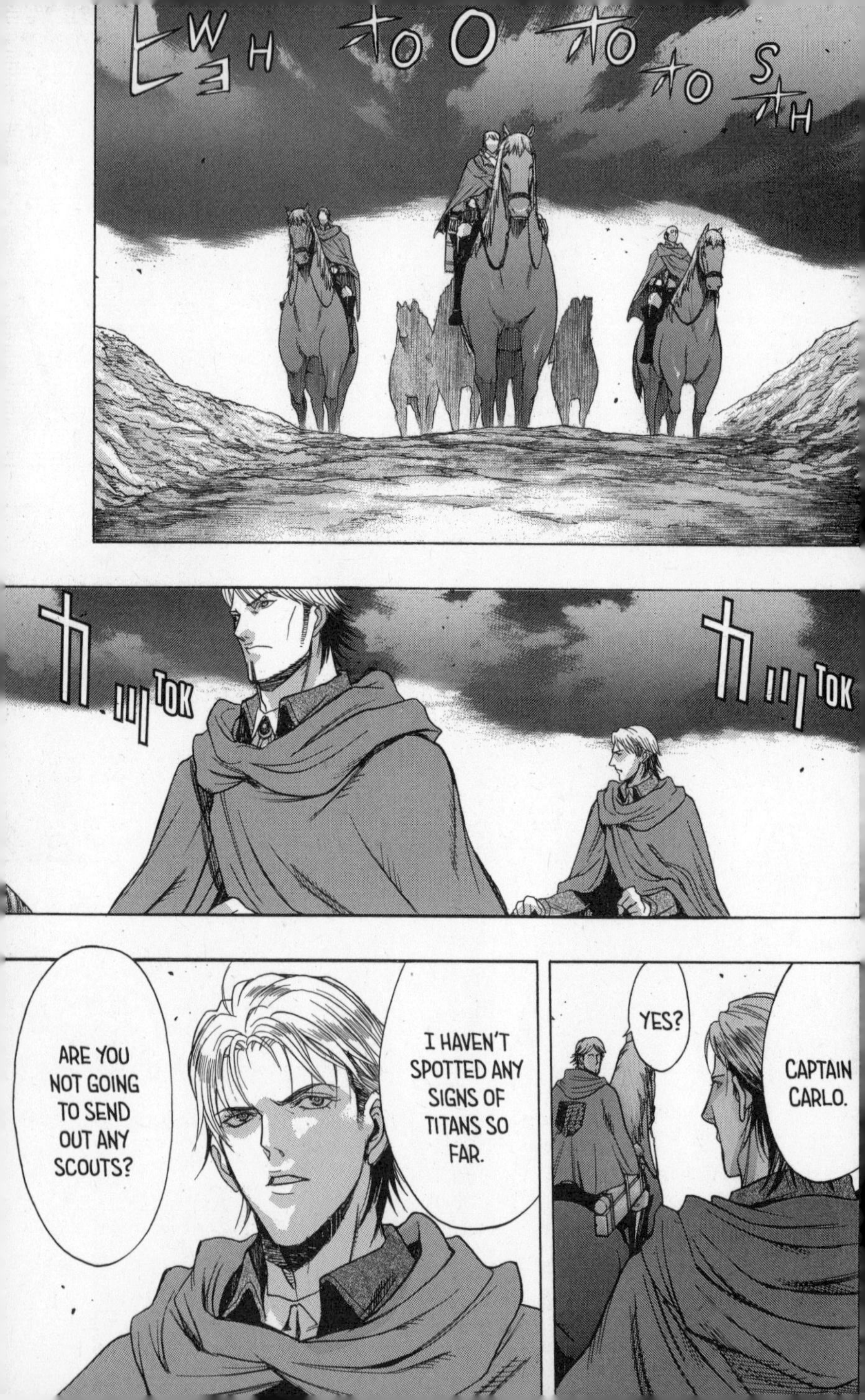
TOK
TOK
CAPTAIN CARLO.
YES?
I HAVEN'T SPOTTED ANY SIGNS OF TITANS SO FAR.
ARE YOU NOT GOING TO SEND OUT ANY SCOUTS?

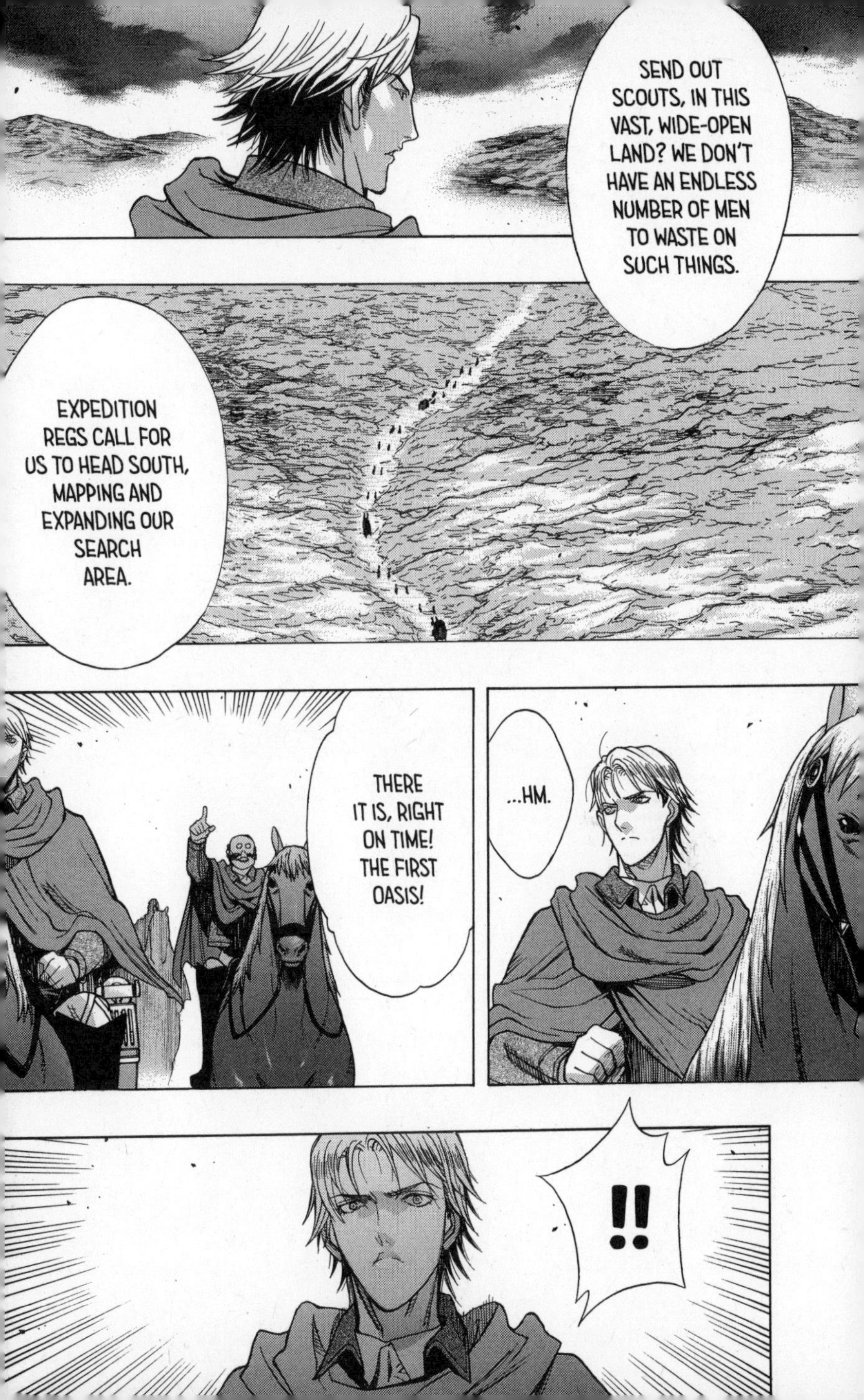
SEND OUT SCOUTS, IN THIS VAST, WIDE-OPEN LAND? WE DON'T HAVE AN ENDLESS NUMBER OF MEN TO WASTE ON SUCH THINGS.
EXPEDITION REGS CALL FOR US TO HEAD SOUTH, MAPPING AND EXPANDING OUR SEARCH AREA.
...HM.
THERE IT IS, RIGHT ON TIME! THE FIRST OASIS!
!!

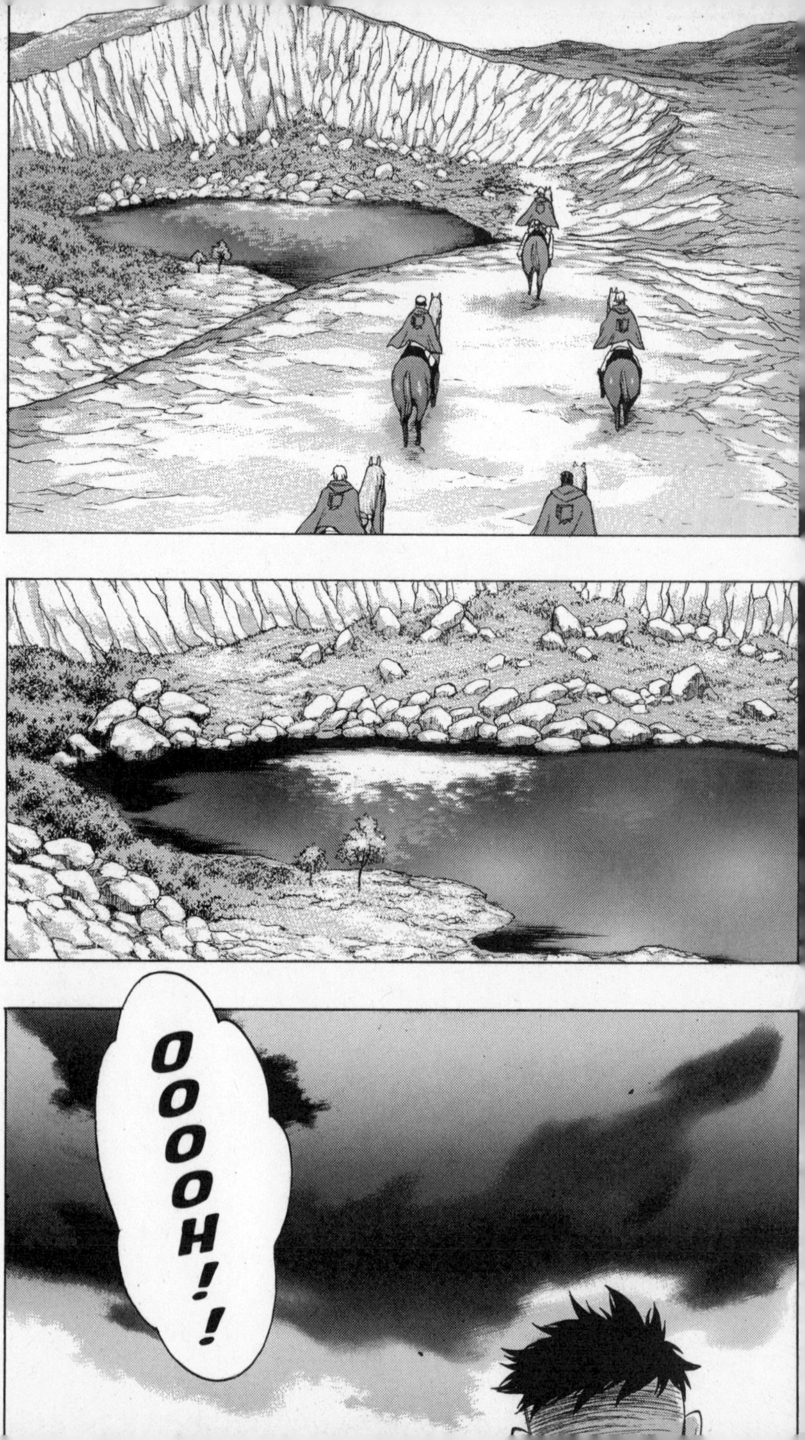
OOOOOH!!

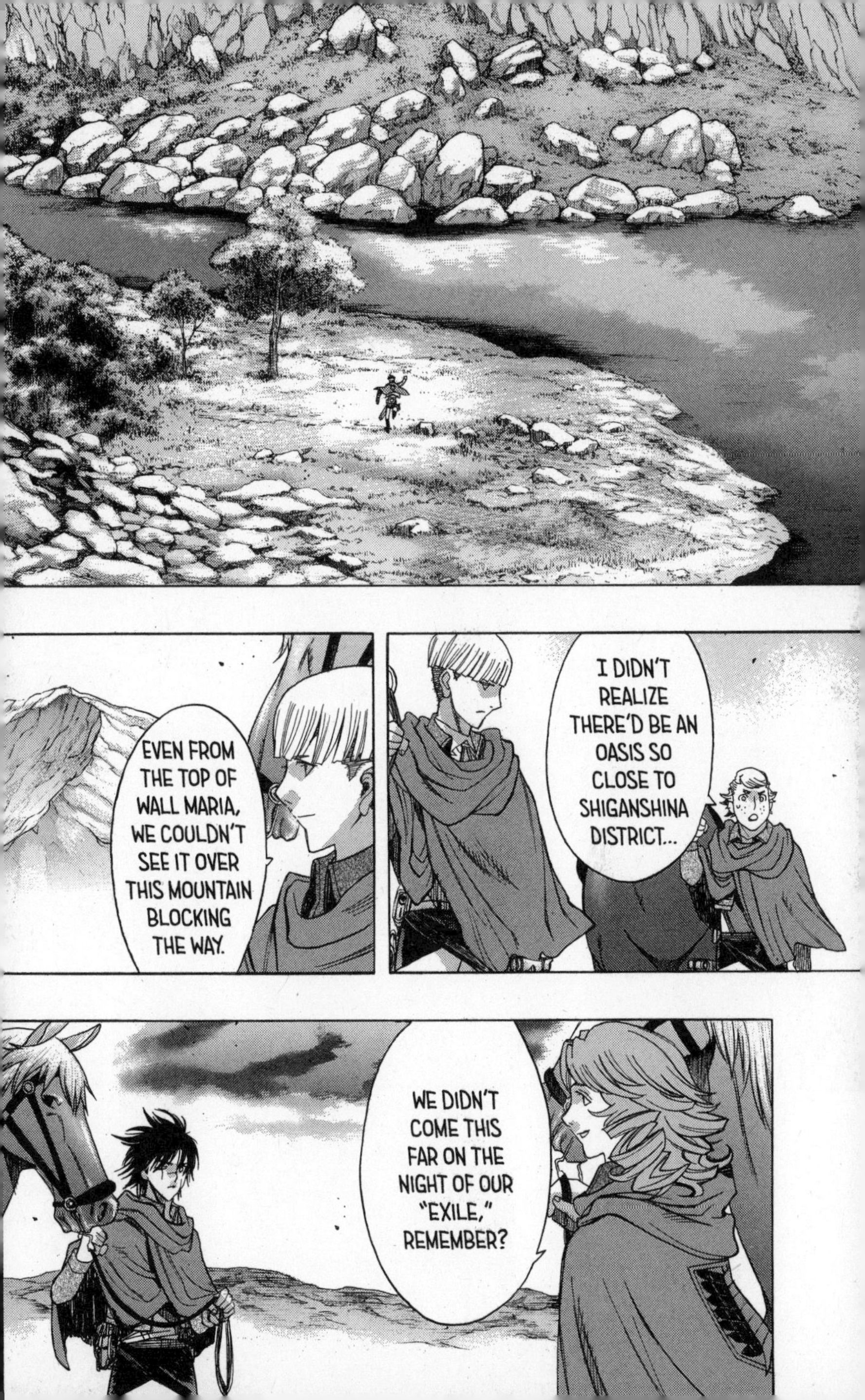
I DIDN'T REALIZE THERE'D BE AN OASIS SO CLOSE TO SHIGANSHINA DISTRICT...
EVEN FROM THE TOP OF WALL MARIA, WE COULDN'T SEE IT OVER THIS MOUNTAIN BLOCKING THE WAY.
WE DIDN'T COME THIS FAR ON THE NIGHT OF OUR "EXILE," REMEMBER?

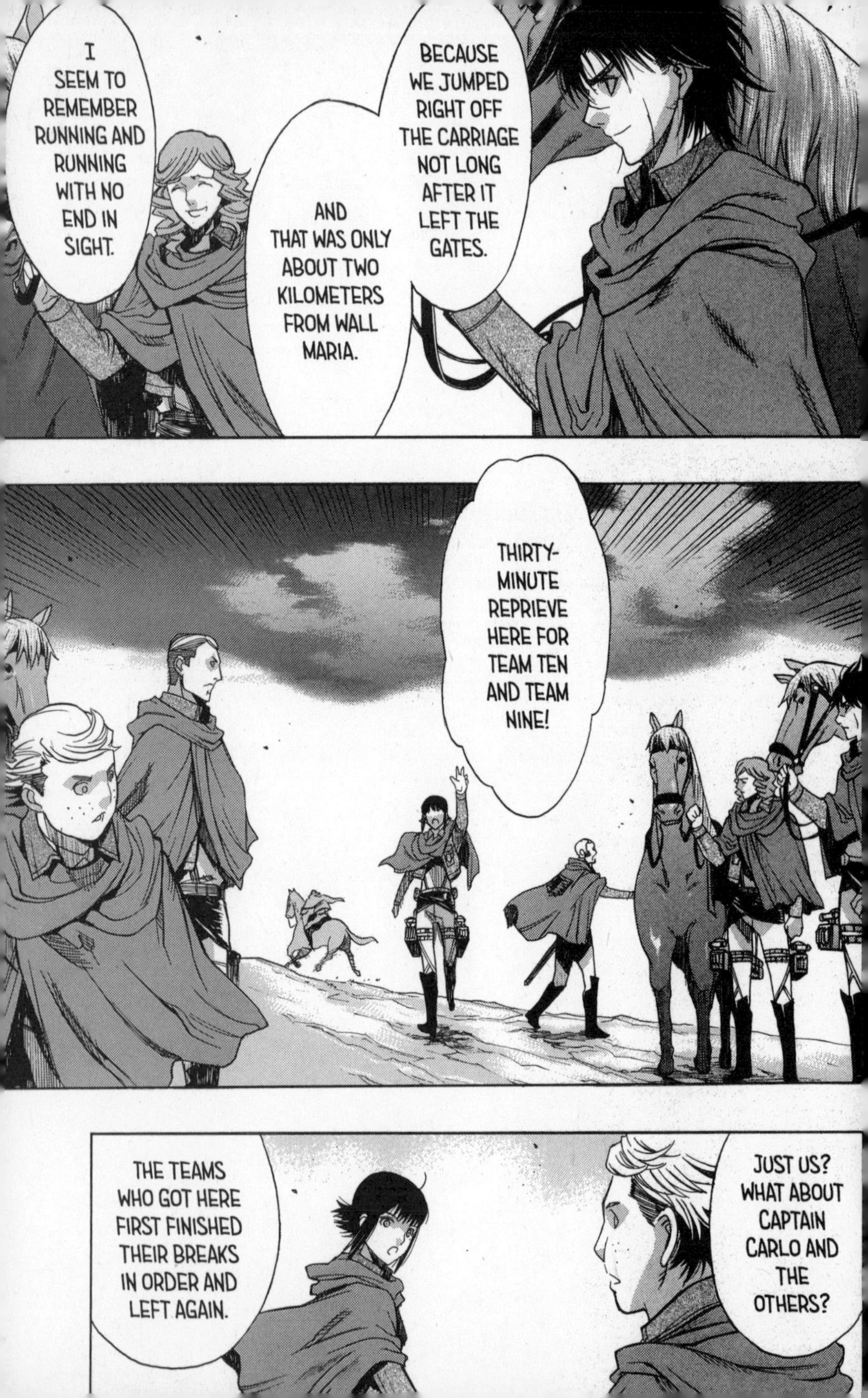
BECAUSE WE JUMPED RIGHT OFF THE CARRIAGE NOT LONG AFTER IT LEFT THE GATES.
AND THAT WAS ONLY ABOUT TWO KILOMETERS FROM WALL MARIA.
I SEEM TO REMEMBER RUNNING AND RUNNING WITH NO END IN SIGHT.
THIRTY-MINUTE REPRIEVE HERE FOR TEAM TEN AND TEAM NINE!
JUST US? WHAT ABOUT CAPTAIN CARLO AND THE OTHERS?
THE TEAMS WHO GOT HERE FIRST FINISHED THEIR BREAKS IN ORDER AND LEFT AGAIN.

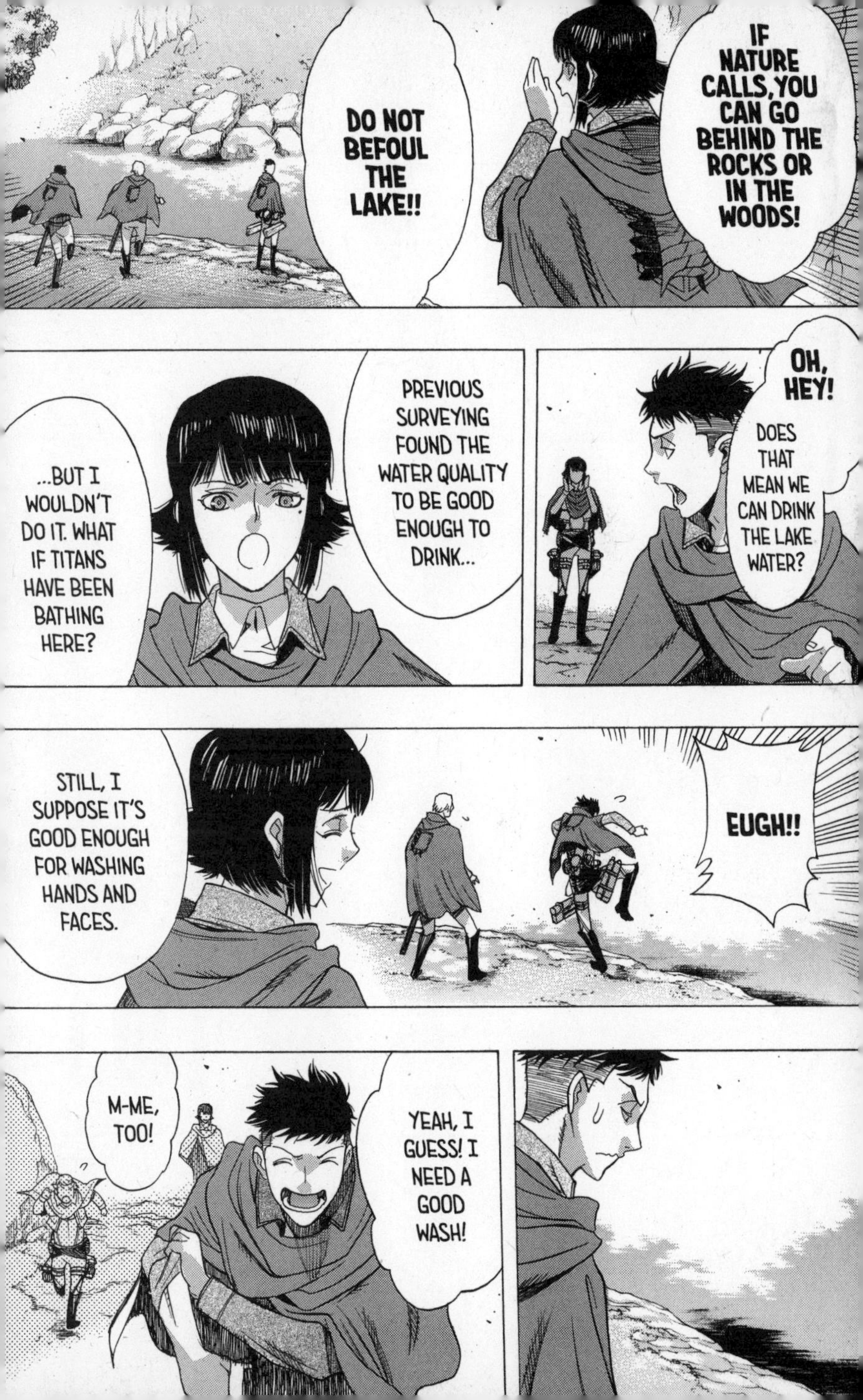
IF NATURE CALLS, YOU CAN GO BEHIND THE ROCKS OR IN THE WOODS!
DO NOT BEFOUL THE LAKE!!
OH, HEY!
DOES THAT MEAN WE CAN DRINK THE LAKE WATER?
PREVIOUS SURVEYING FOUND THE WATER QUALITY TO BE GOOD ENOUGH TO DRINK...
...BUT I WOULDN'T DO IT. WHAT IF TITANS HAVE BEEN BATHING HERE?
EUGH!!
STILL, I SUPPOSE IT'S GOOD ENOUGH FOR WASHING HANDS AND FACES.
YEAH, I GUESS! I NEED A GOOD WASH!
M-ME, TOO!

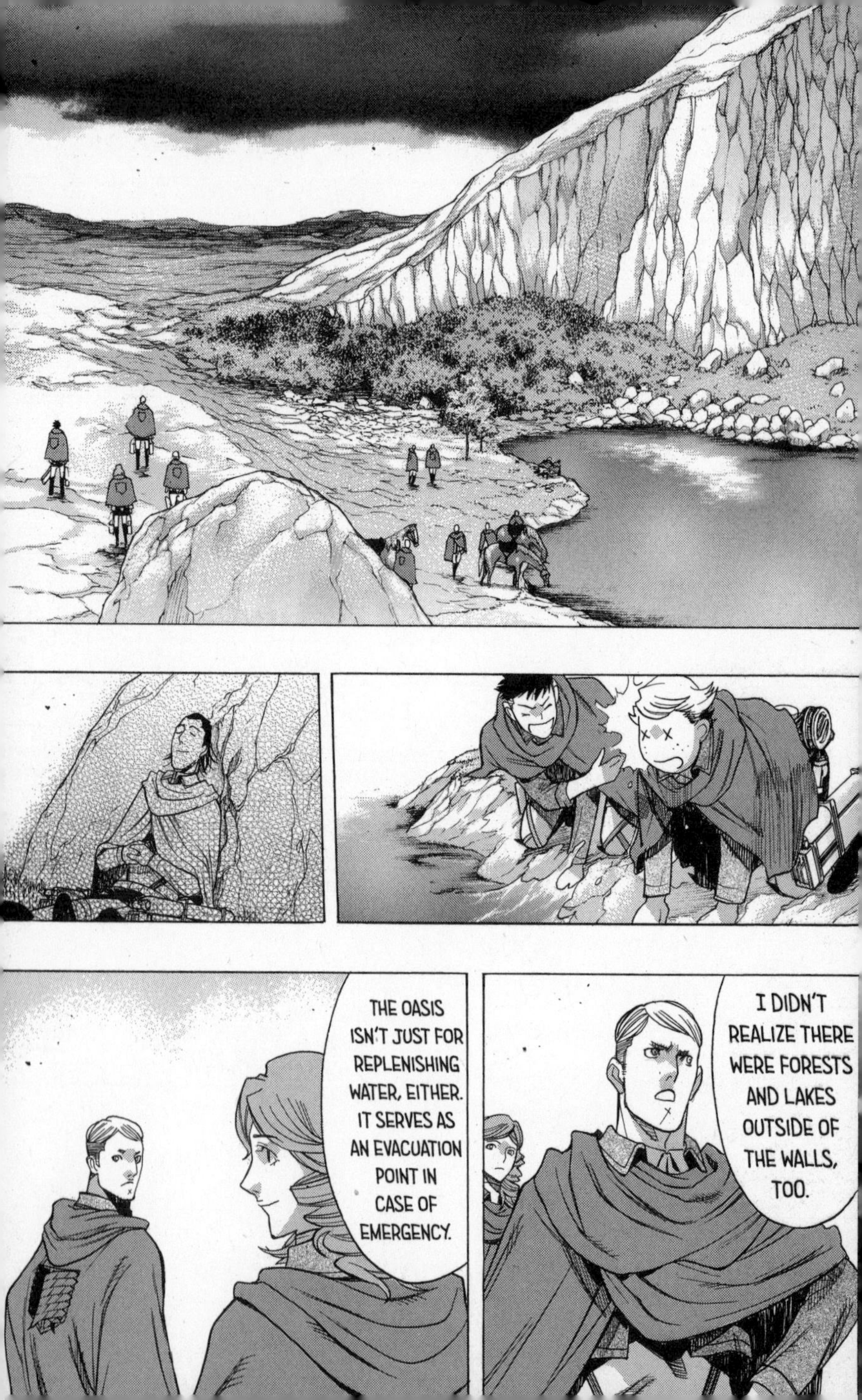
I DIDN'T REALIZE THERE WERE FORESTS AND LAKES OUTSIDE OF THE WALLS, TOO.
THE OASIS ISN'T JUST FOR REPLENISHING WATER, EITHER. IT SERVES AS AN EVACUATION POINT IN CASE OF EMERGENCY.

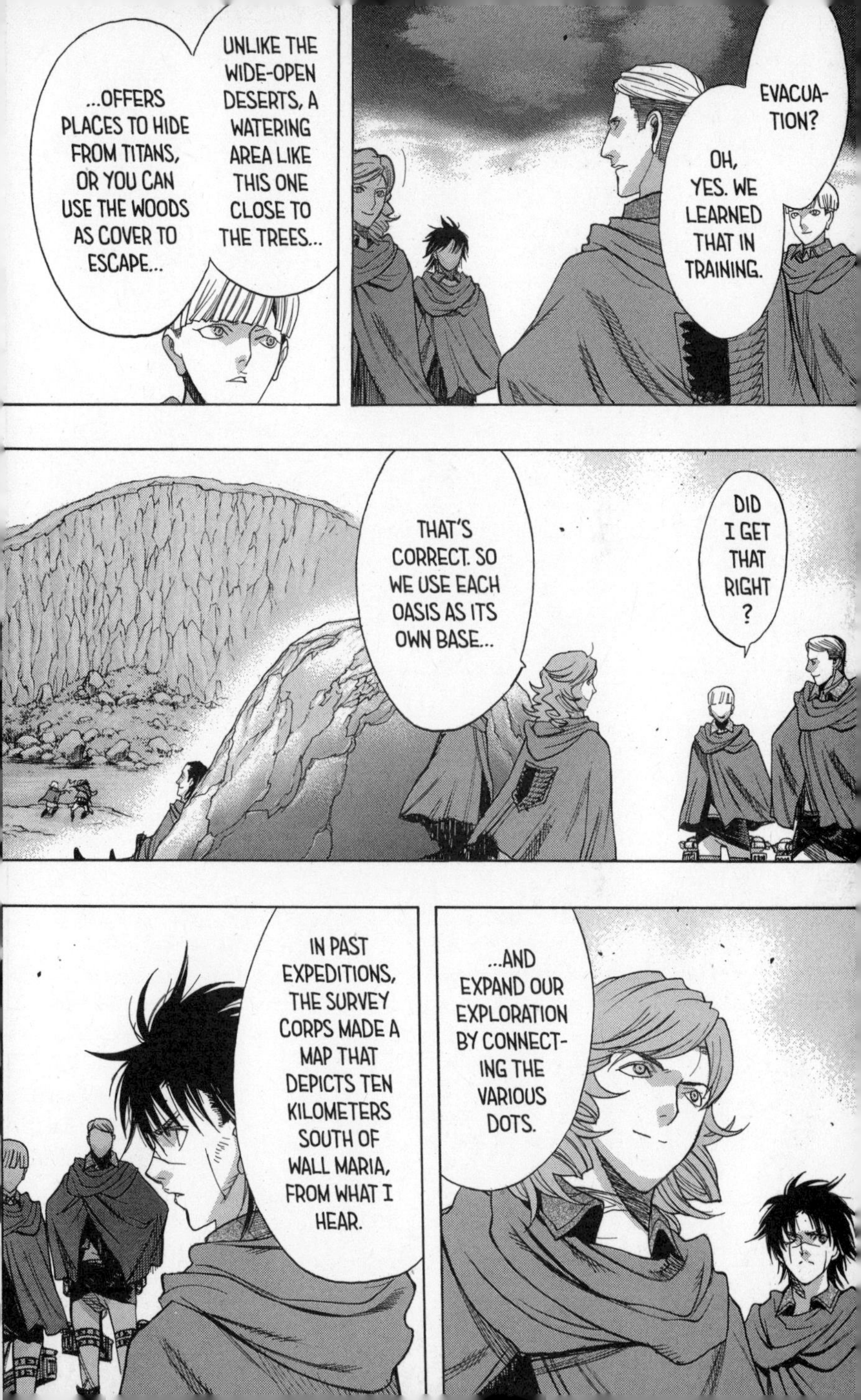
EVACUATION?
OH, YES. WE LEARNED THAT IN TRAINING.
UNLIKE THE WIDE-OPEN DESERTS, A WATERING AREA LIKE THIS ONE CLOSE TO THE TREES...
...OFFERS PLACES TO HIDE FROM TITANS, OR YOU CAN USE THE WOODS AS COVER TO ESCAPE...
DID I GET THAT RIGHT?
THAT'S CORRECT. SO WE USE EACH OASIS AS ITS OWN BASE...
...AND EXPAND OUR EXPLORATION BY CONNECTING THE VARIOUS DOTS.
IN PAST EXPEDITIONS, THE SURVEY CORPS MADE A MAP THAT DEPICTS TEN KILOMETERS SOUTH OF WALL MARIA, FROM WHAT I HEAR.

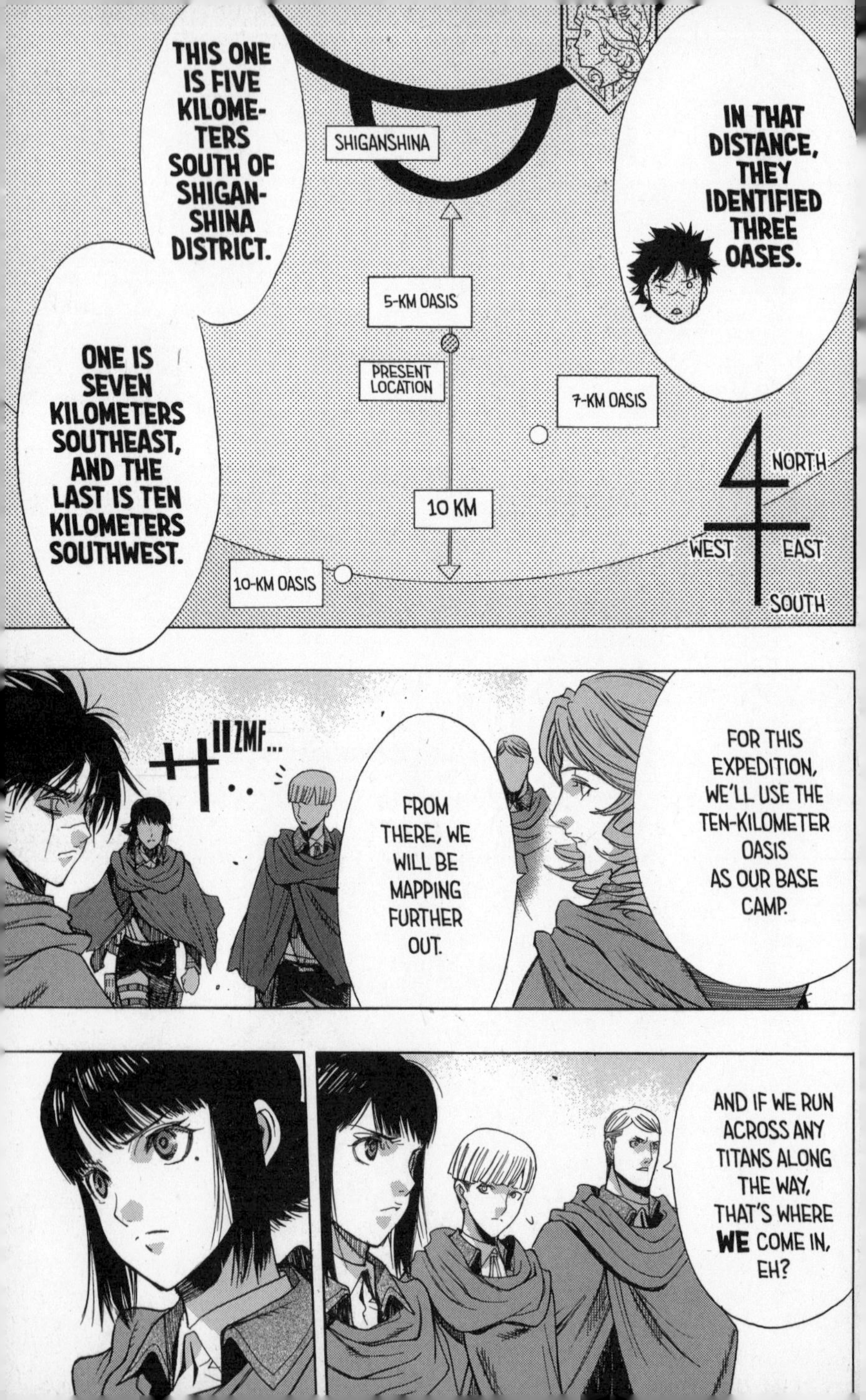
IN THAT DISTANCE, THEY IDENTIFIED THREE OASES.
THIS ONE IS FIVE KILOMETERS SOUTH OF SHIGANSHINA DISTRICT.
SHIGANSHINA
5-KM OASIS
PRESENT LOCATION
7-KM OASIS
NORTH
WEST
EAST
SOUTH
10 KM
10-KM OASIS
ONE IS SEVEN KILOMETERS SOUTHEAST, AND THE LAST IS TEN KILOMETERS SOUTHWEST.
FOR THIS EXPEDITION, WE'LL USE THE TEN-KILOMETER OASIS AS OUR BASE CAMP.
FROM THERE, WE WILL BE MAPPING FURTHER OUT.
HHZMF...
AND IF WE RUN ACROSS ANY TITANS ALONG THE WAY, THAT'S WHERE WE COME IN, EH?

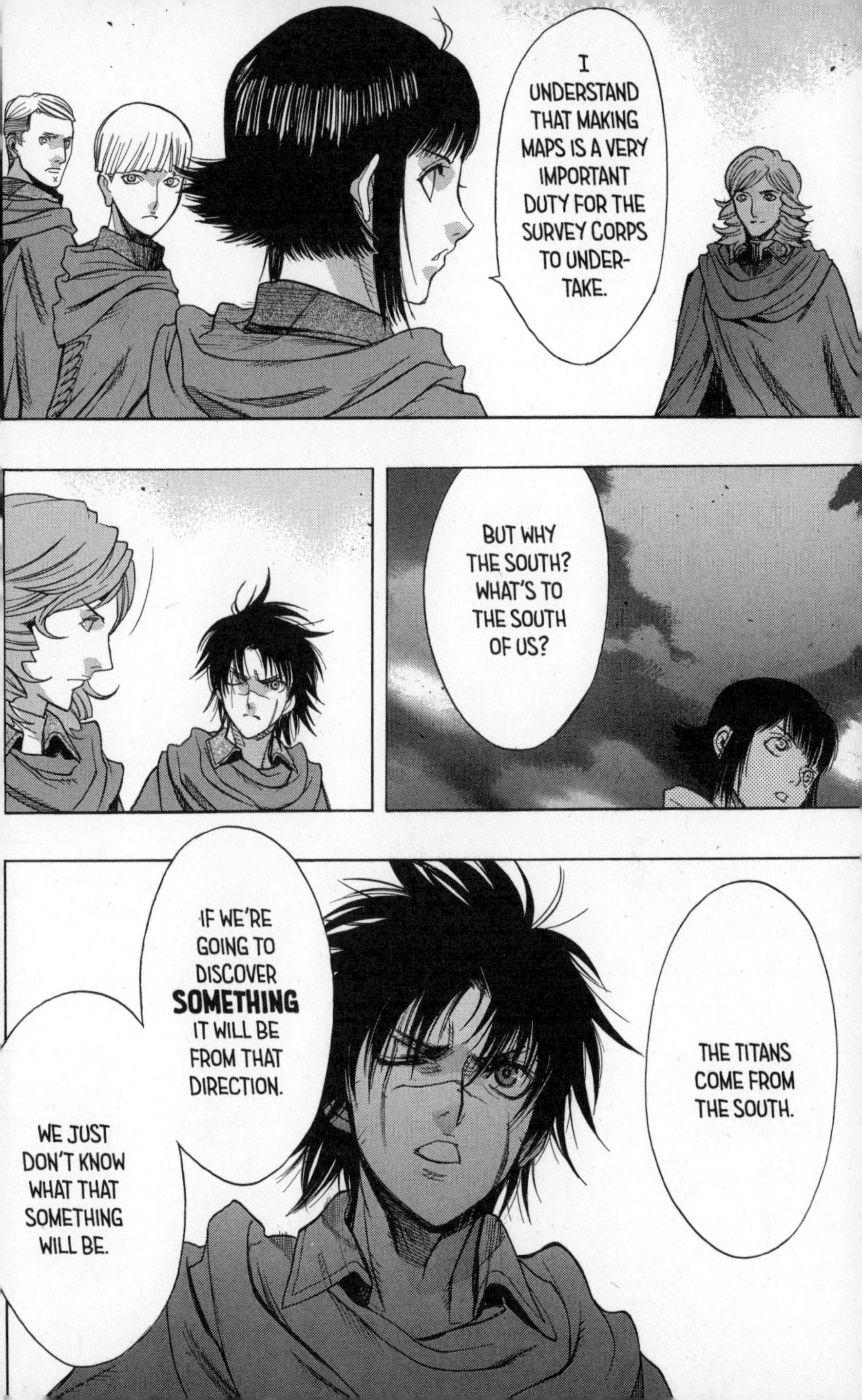
I UNDERSTAND THAT MAKING MAPS IS A VERY IMPORTANT DUTY FOR THE SURVEY CORPS TO UNDER-TAKE.
BUT WHY THE SOUTH? WHAT'S TO THE SOUTH OF US?
THE TITANS COME FROM THE SOUTH.
IF WE'RE GOING TO DISCOVER **SOMETHING** IT WILL BE FROM THAT DIRECTION.
WE JUST DON'T KNOW WHAT THAT SOMETHING WILL BE.

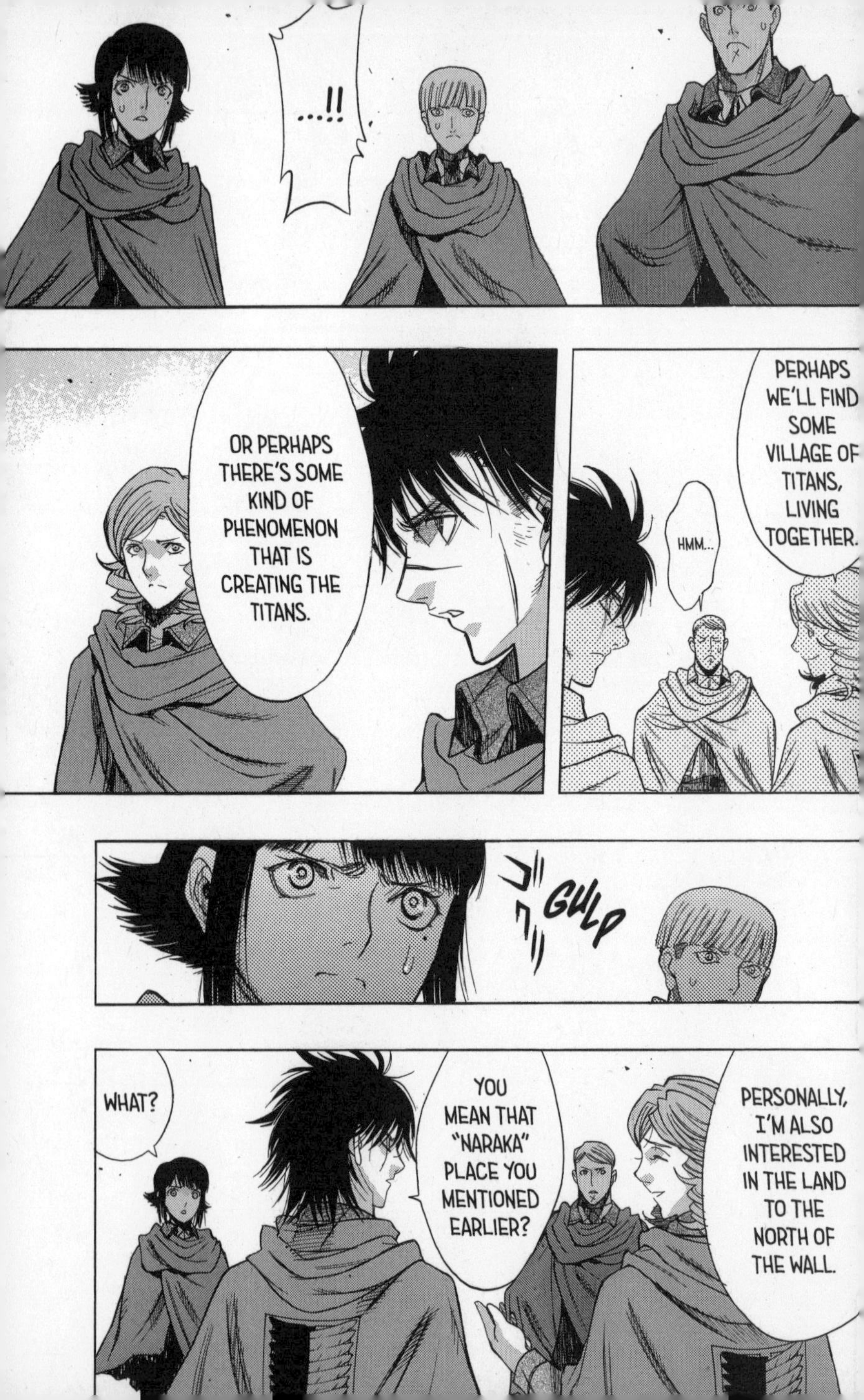
...!!
PERHAPS WE'LL FIND SOME VILLAGE OF TITANS, LIVING TOGETHER.
HMM...
OR PERHAPS THERE'S SOME KIND OF PHENOMENON THAT IS CREATING THE TITANS.
GULP
PERSONALLY, I'M ALSO INTERESTED IN THE LAND TO THE NORTH OF THE WALL.
YOU MEAN THAT "NARAKA" PLACE YOU MENTIONED EARLIER?
WHAT?

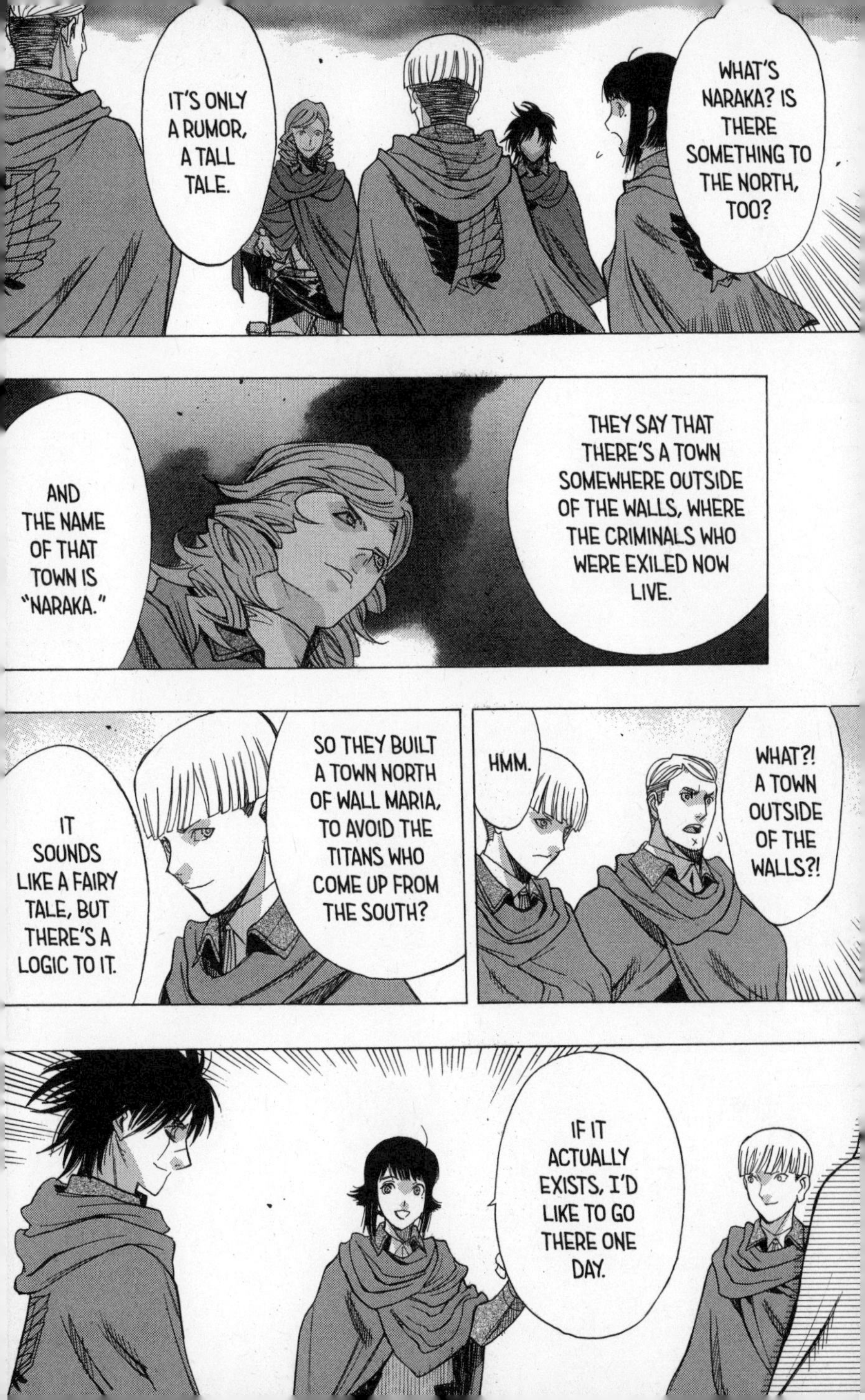
WHAT'S NARAKA? IS THERE SOMETHING TO THE NORTH, TOO?
IT'S ONLY A RUMOR, A TALL TALE.
THEY SAY THAT THERE'S A TOWN SOMEWHERE OUTSIDE OF THE WALLS, WHERE THE CRIMINALS WHO WERE EXILED NOW LIVE.
AND THE NAME OF THAT TOWN IS "NARAKA."
WHAT?! A TOWN OUTSIDE OF THE WALLS?!
HMM.
SO THEY BUILT A TOWN NORTH OF WALL MARIA, TO AVOID THE TITANS WHO COME UP FROM THE SOUTH?
IT SOUNDS LIKE A FAIRY TALE, BUT THERE'S A LOGIC TO IT.
IF IT ACTUALLY EXISTS, I'D LIKE TO GO THERE ONE DAY.

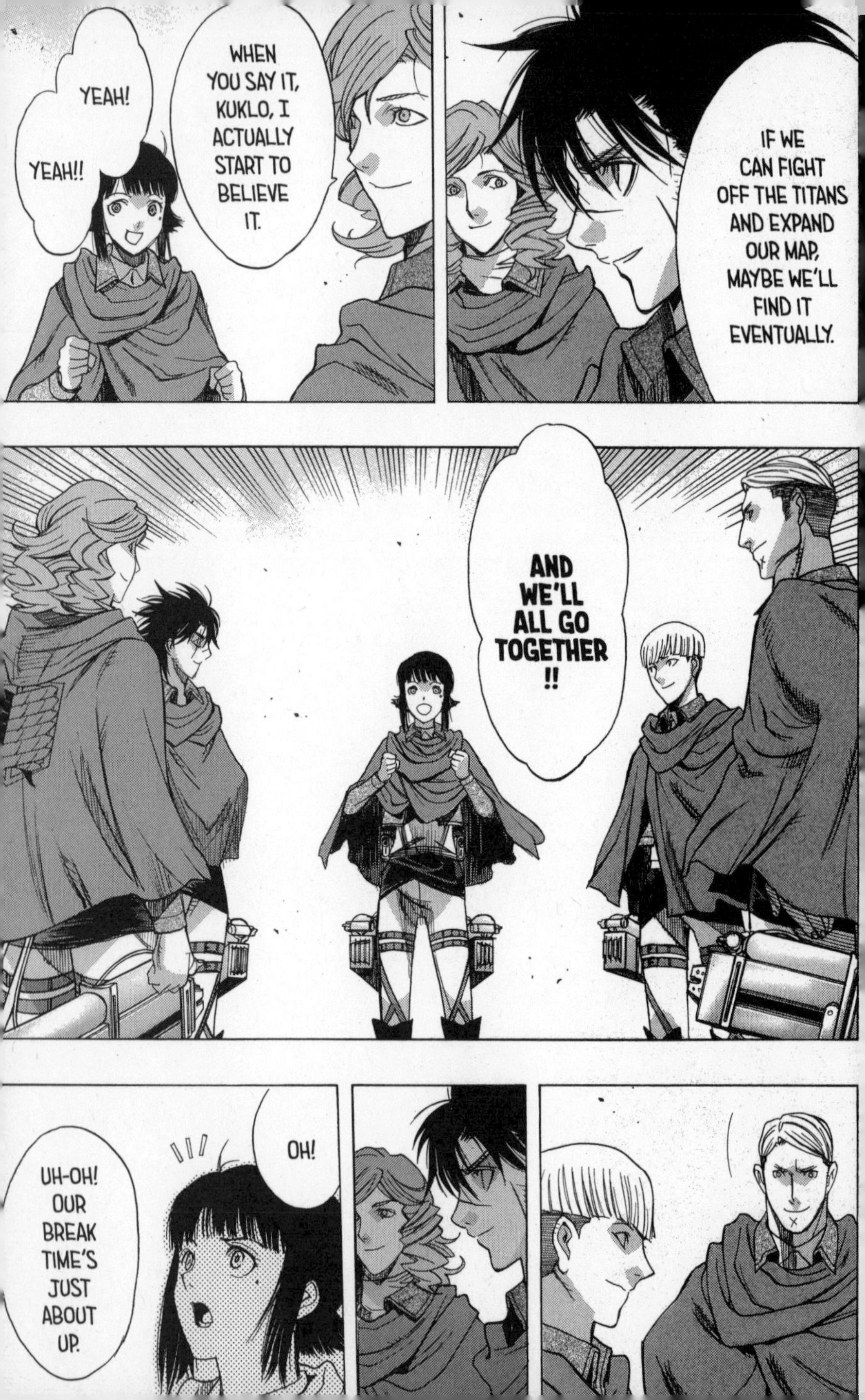
IF WE CAN FIGHT OFF THE TITANS AND EXPAND OUR MAP, MAYBE WE'LL FIND IT EVENTUALLY.
WHEN YOU SAY IT, KUKLO, I ACTUALLY START TO BELIEVE IT.
YEAH!
YEAH!!
AND WE'LL ALL GO TOGETHER!!
OH!
UH-OH! OUR BREAK TIME'S JUST ABOUT UP.

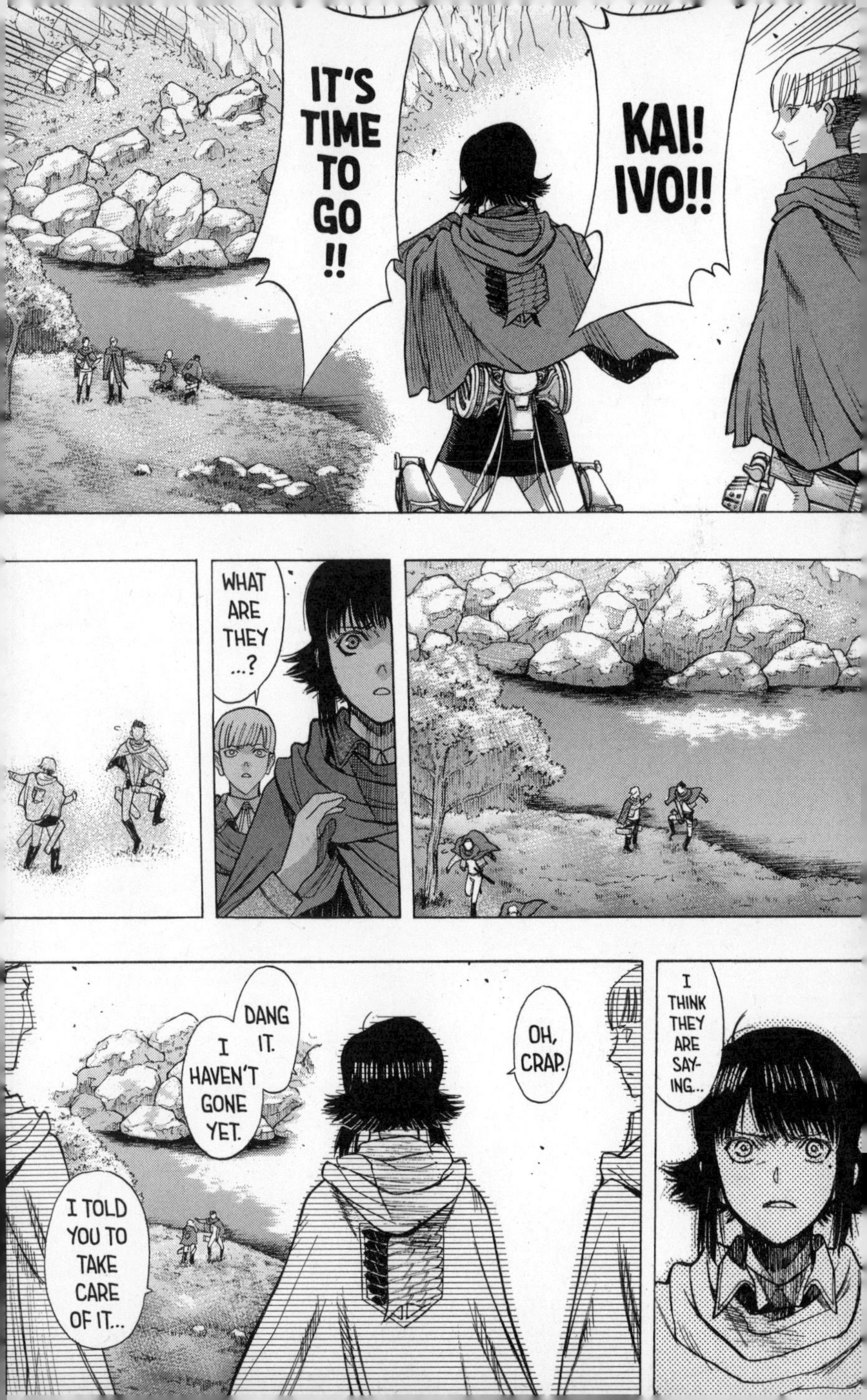
KAI! IVO!!
IT'S TIME TO GO!!
WHAT ARE THEY ...?
I THINK THEY ARE SAY-ING...
OH, CRAP.
DANG IT.
I HAVEN'T GONE YET.
I TOLD YOU TO TAKE CARE OF IT...

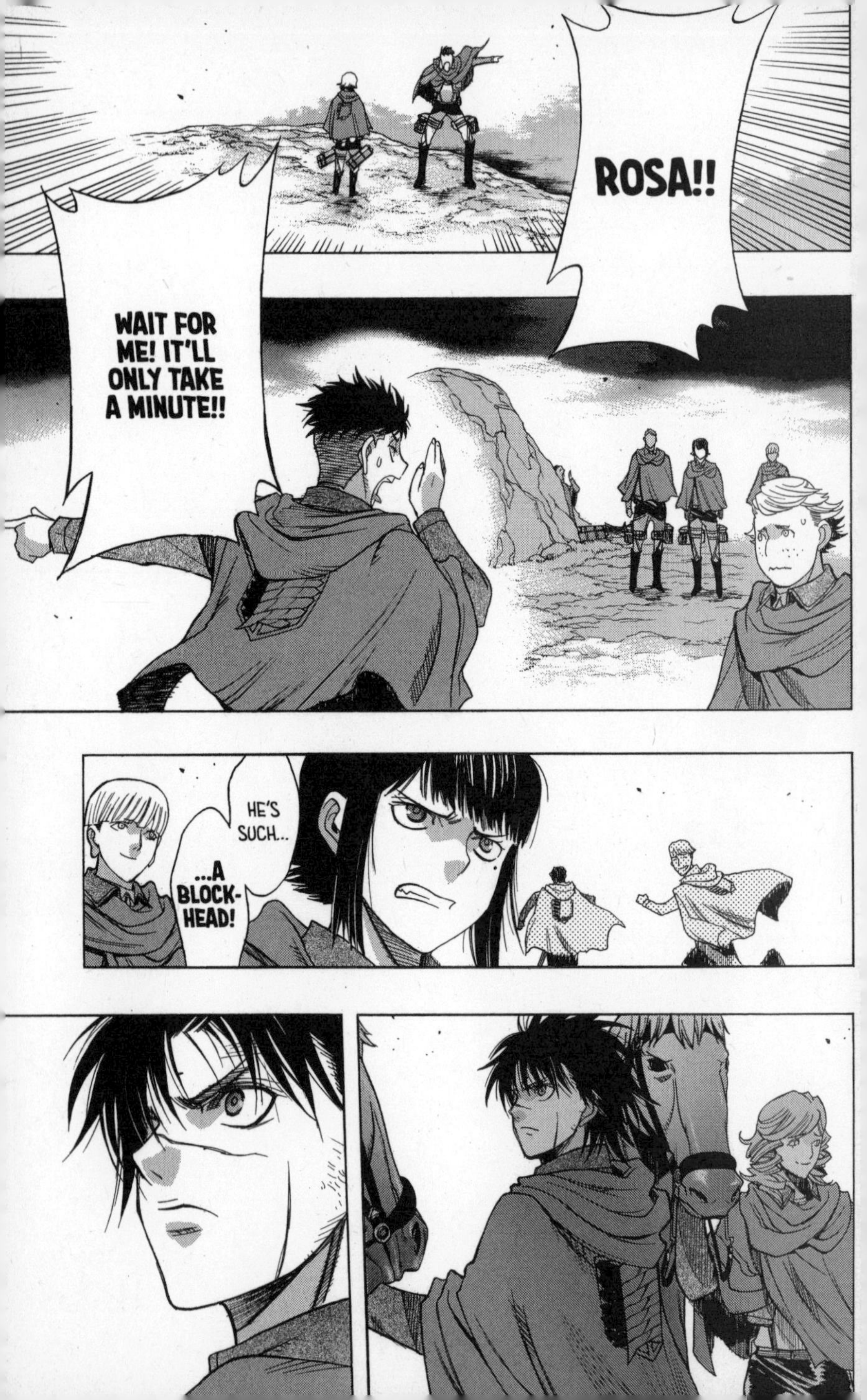
ROSA!!
WAIT FOR ME! IT'LL ONLY TAKE A MINUTE!!
HE'S SUCH...
...A BLOCK-HEAD!

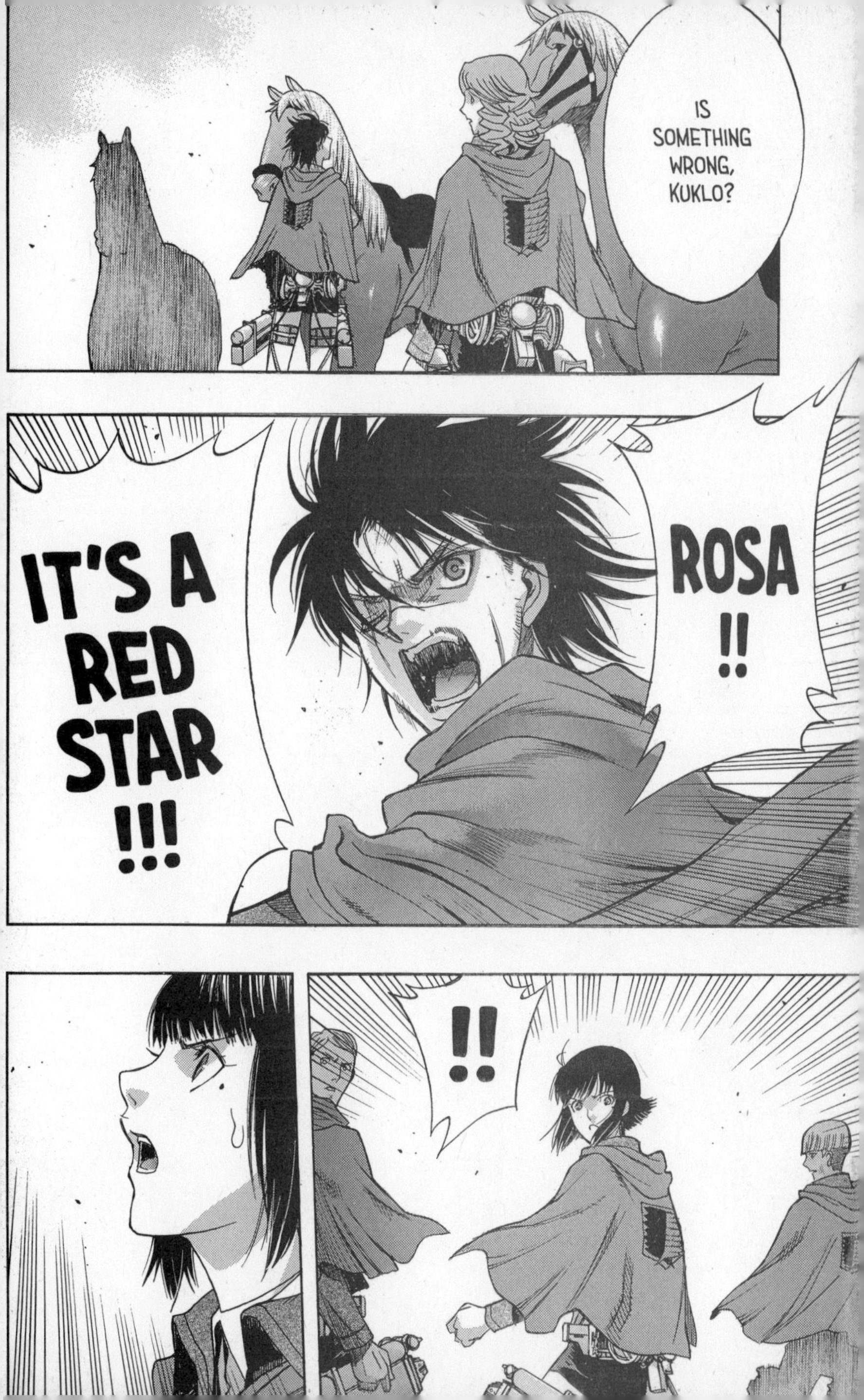
IS SOMETHING WRONG, KUKLO?
ROSA !!
IT'S A RED STAR !!!
!!

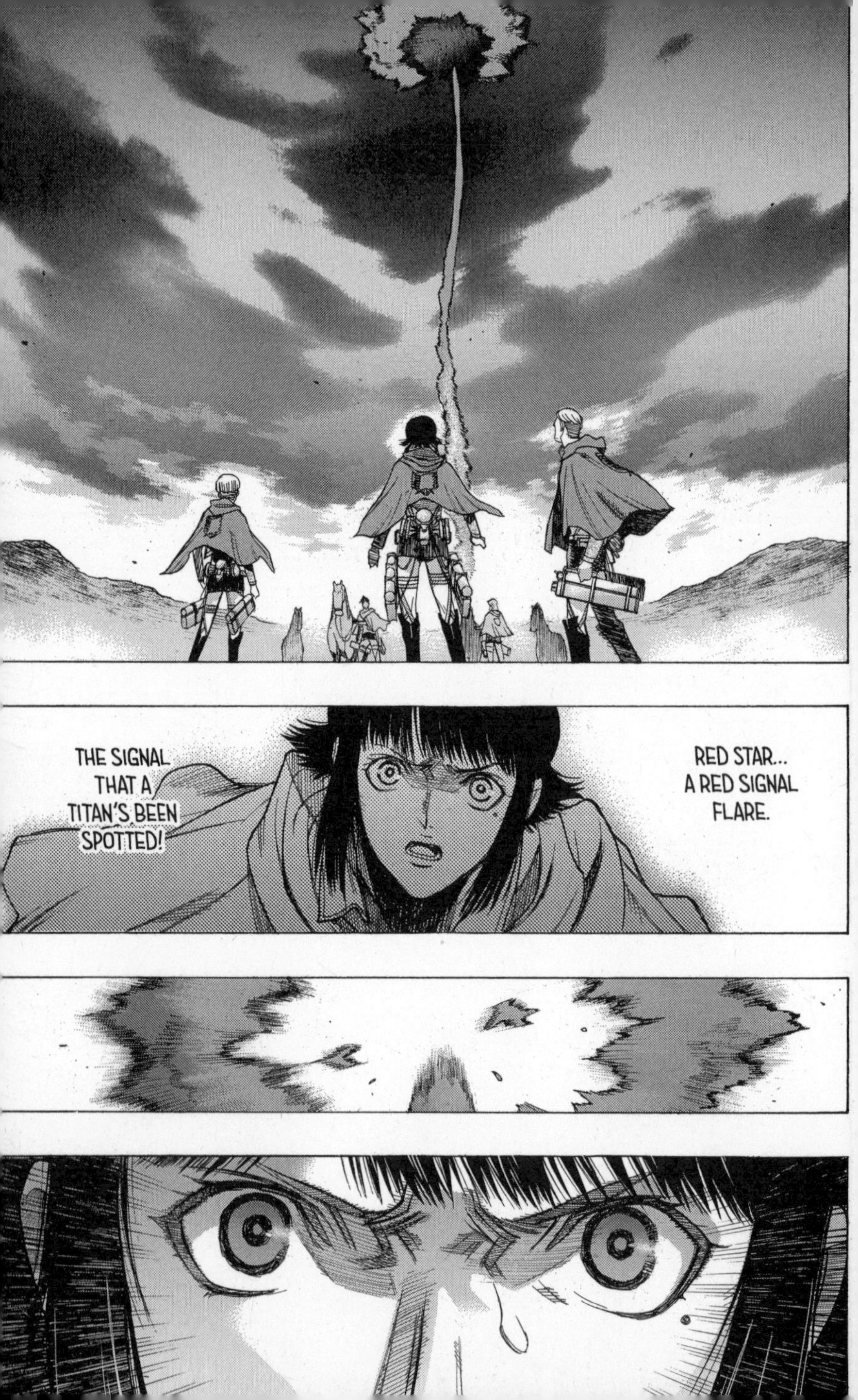
RED STAR... A RED SIGNAL FLARE.
THE SIGNAL THAT A TITAN'S BEEN SPOTTED!

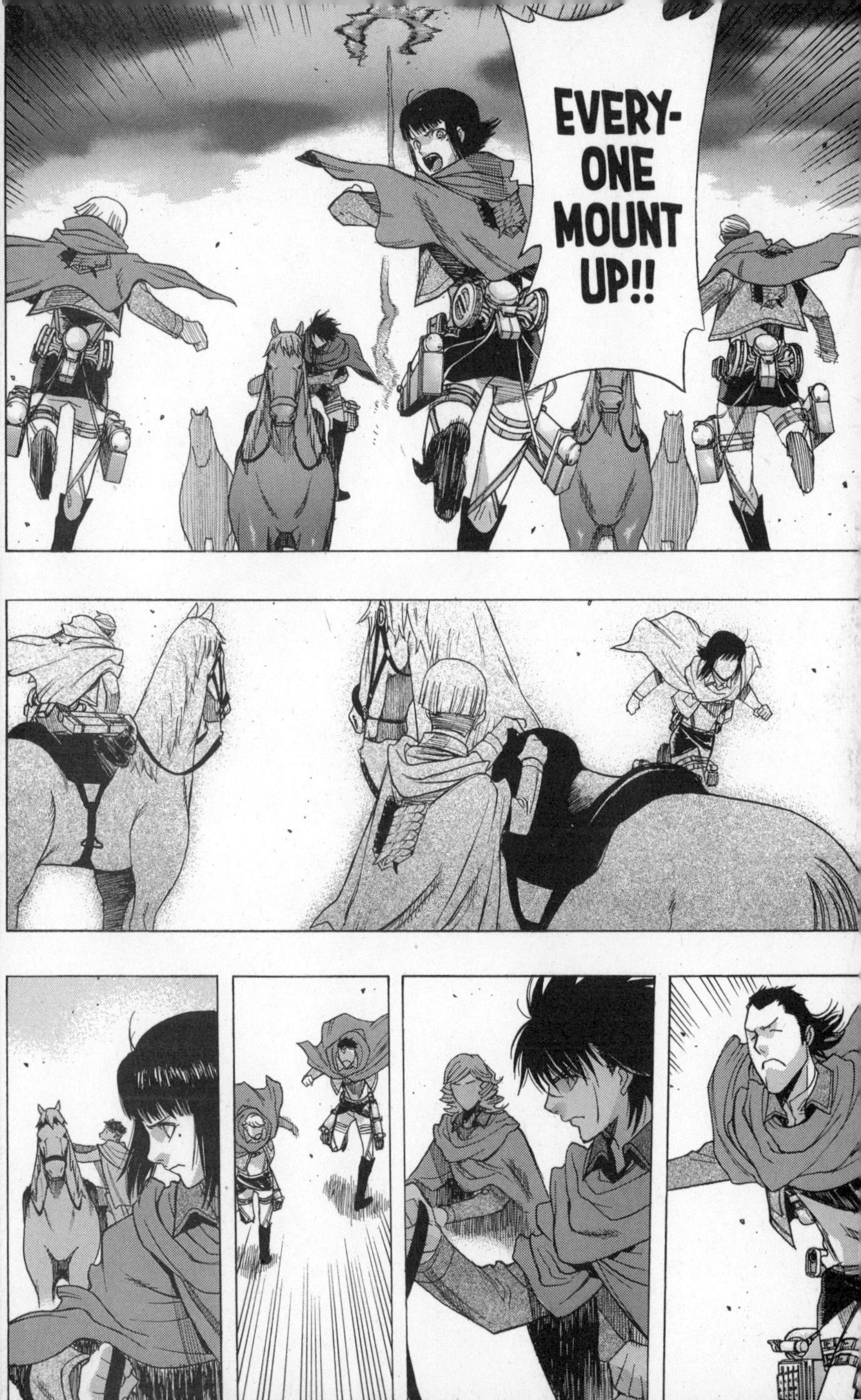
EVERY-ONE MOUNT UP!!

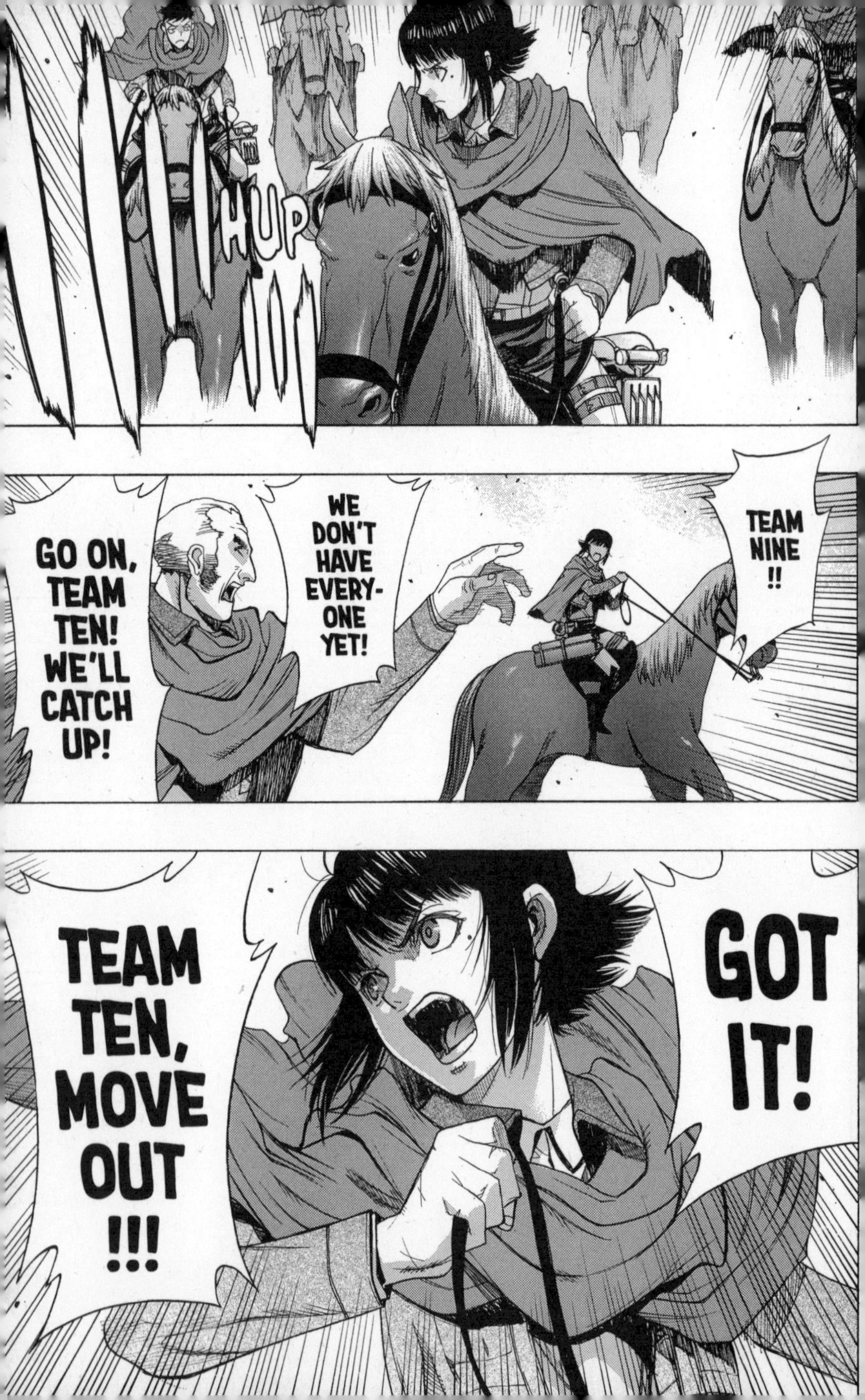
HUP
TEAM NINE !!
WE DON'T HAVE EVERY-ONE YET!
GO ON, TEAM TEN! WE'LL CATCH UP!
GOT IT!
TEAM TEN, MOVE OUT !!!

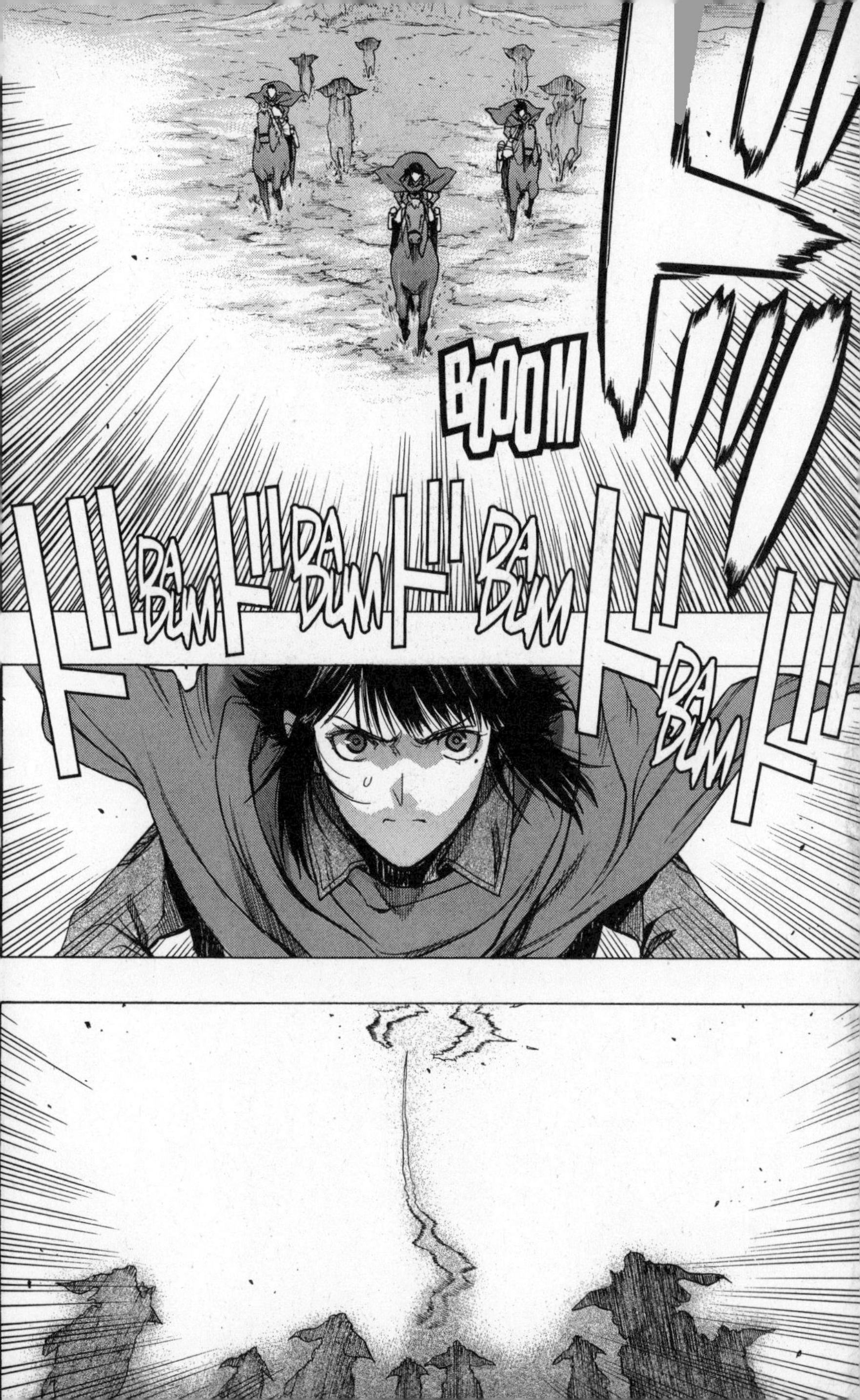
BOOOM
DA BUM
DA BUM
DA BUM
DA BUM

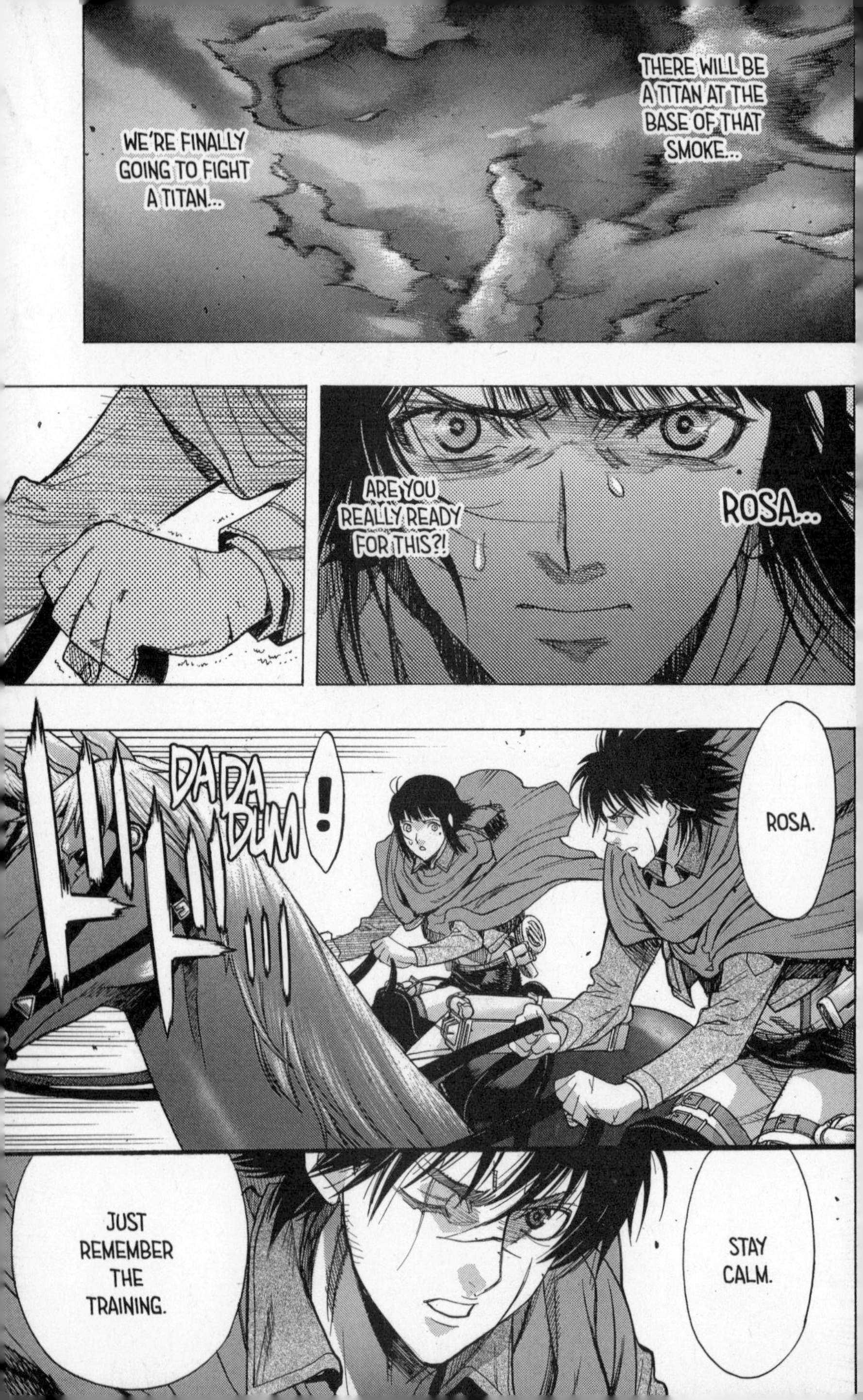
THERE WILL BE A TITAN AT THE BASE OF THAT SMOKE...
WE'RE FINALLY GOING TO FIGHT A TITAN...
ROSA...
ARE YOU REALLY READY FOR THIS?!
ROSA.
!
DADA DUM
STAY CALM.
JUST REMEMBER THE TRAINING.

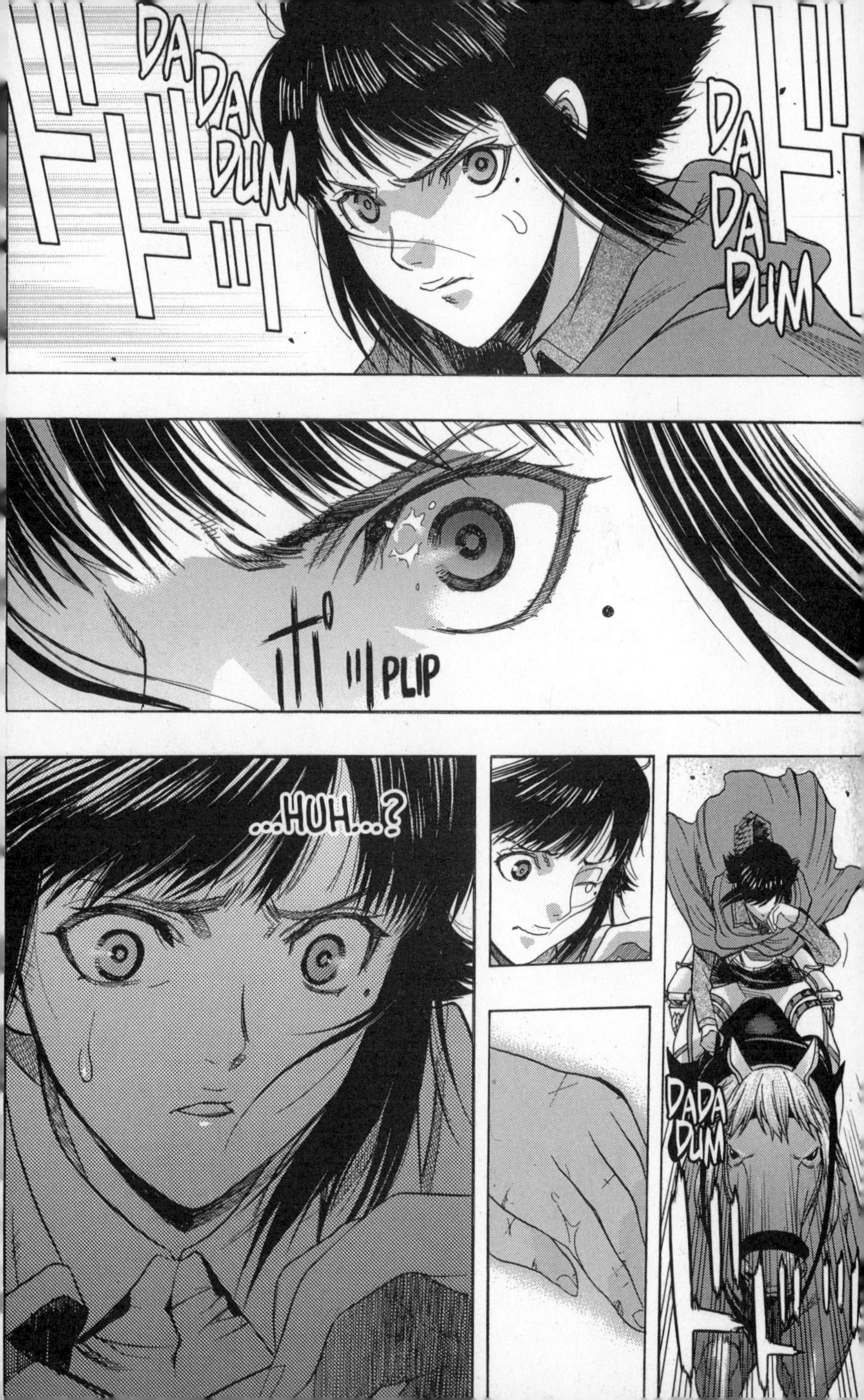
DA
DA
DUM
DA
DA
DUM
PLIP
DADA
DUM
...HUH...?

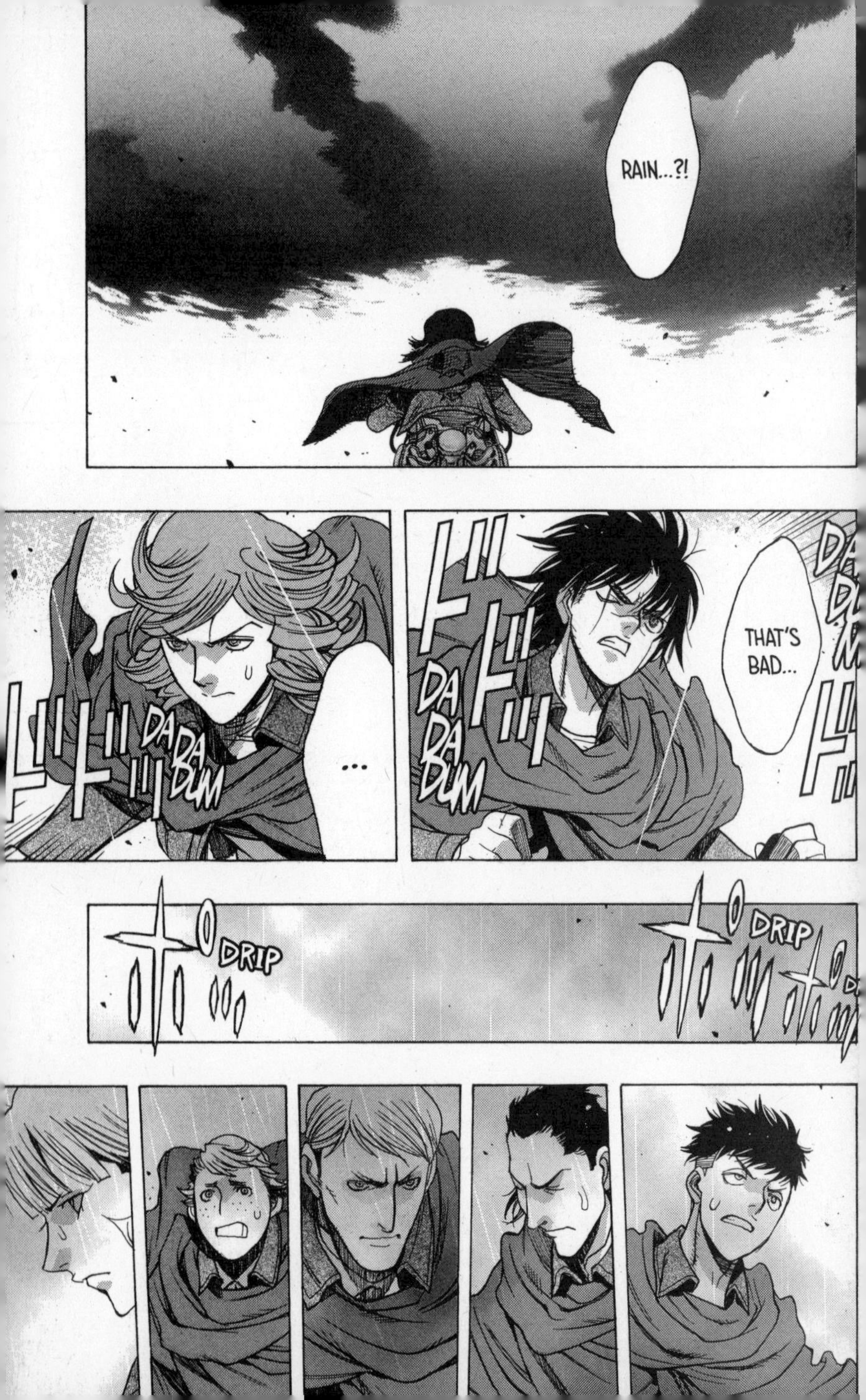
RAIN...?!
THAT'S BAD...
DA DA DUM
...
DA DA DUM
DRIP
DRIP

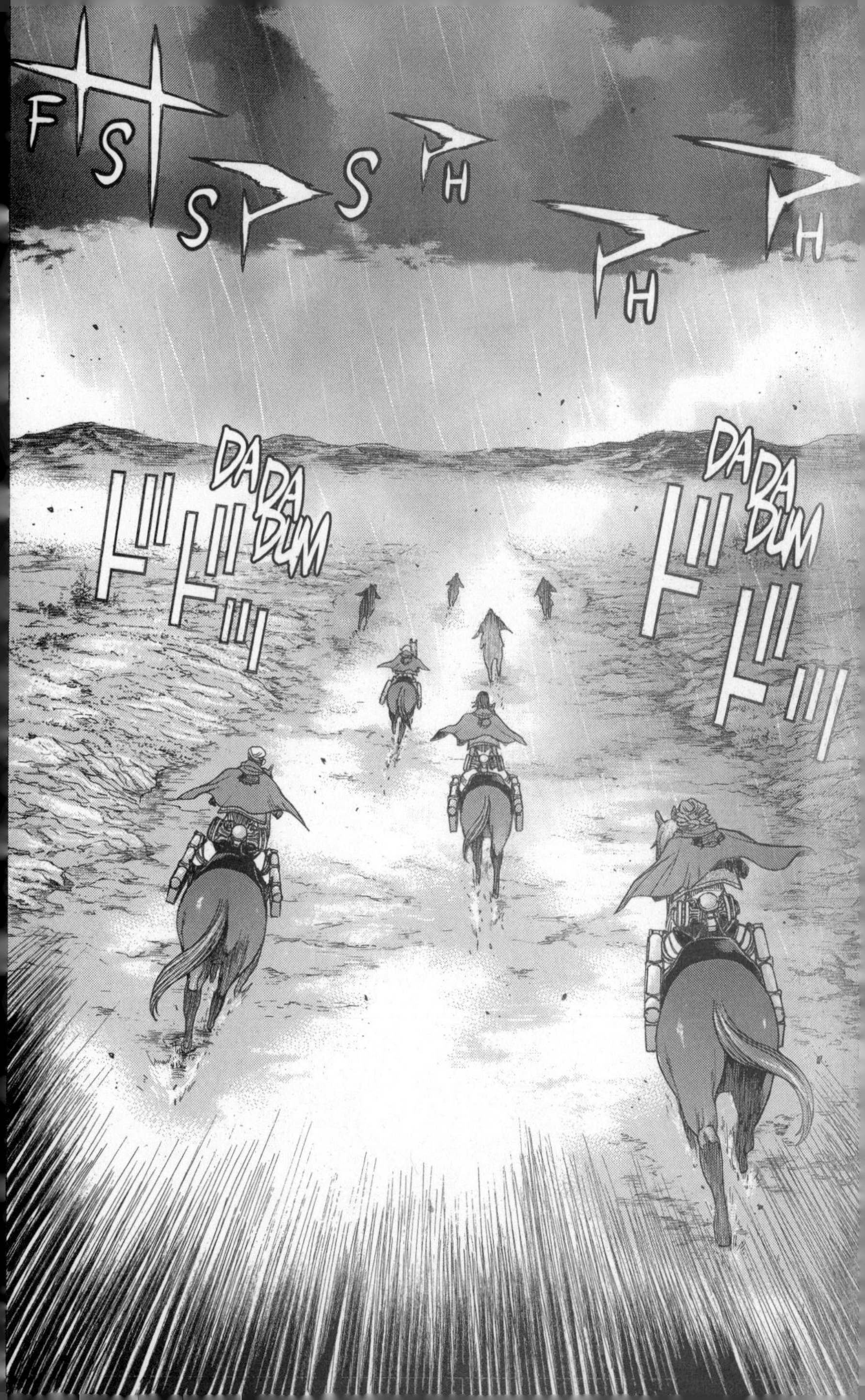
FSSSH
H
H
DADADUM
DADADUM

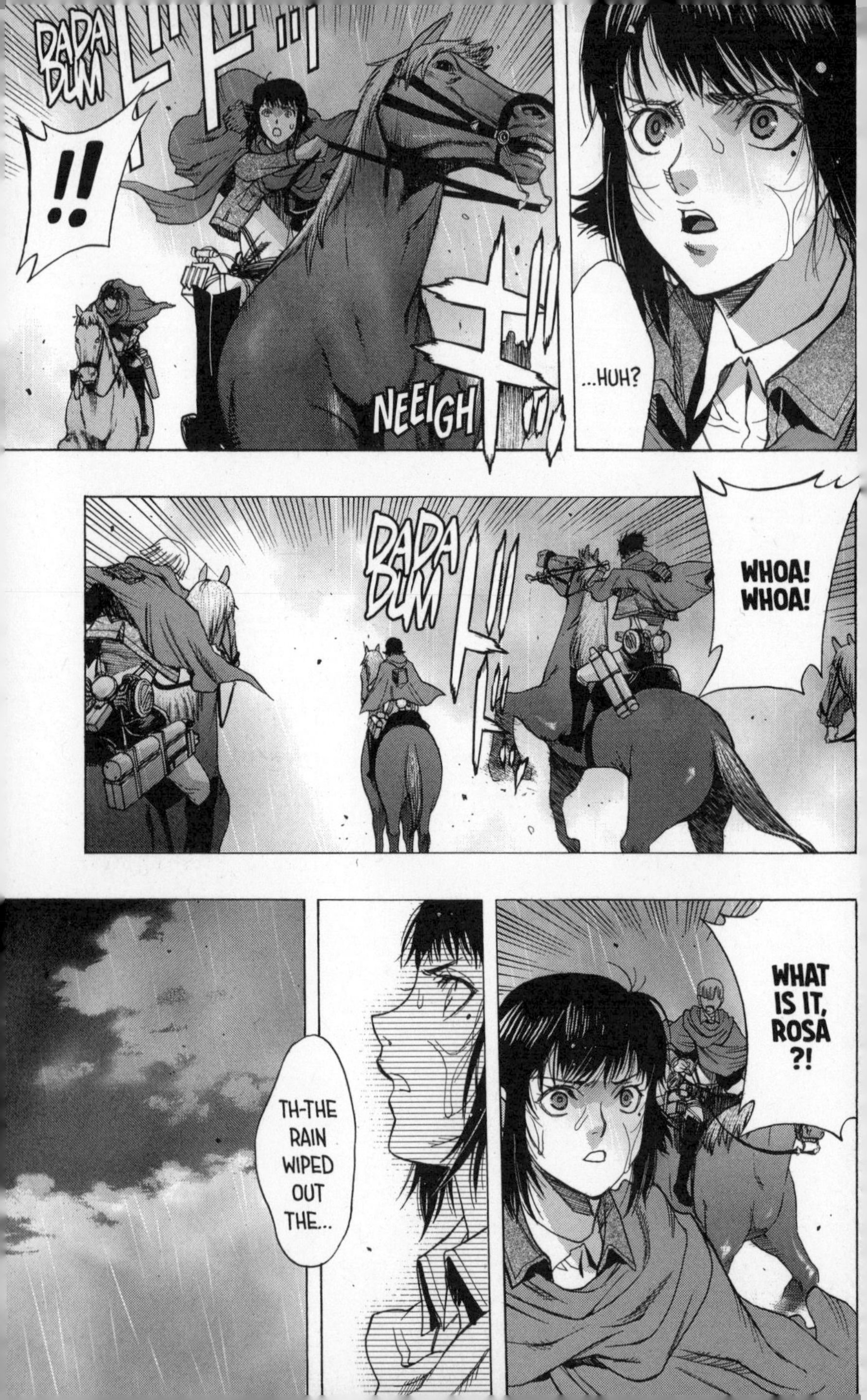
...HUH?
DADA DUM
!!
NEEIGH
WHOA! WHOA!
DADA DUM
WHAT IS IT, ROSA?!
TH-THE RAIN WIPED OUT THE...

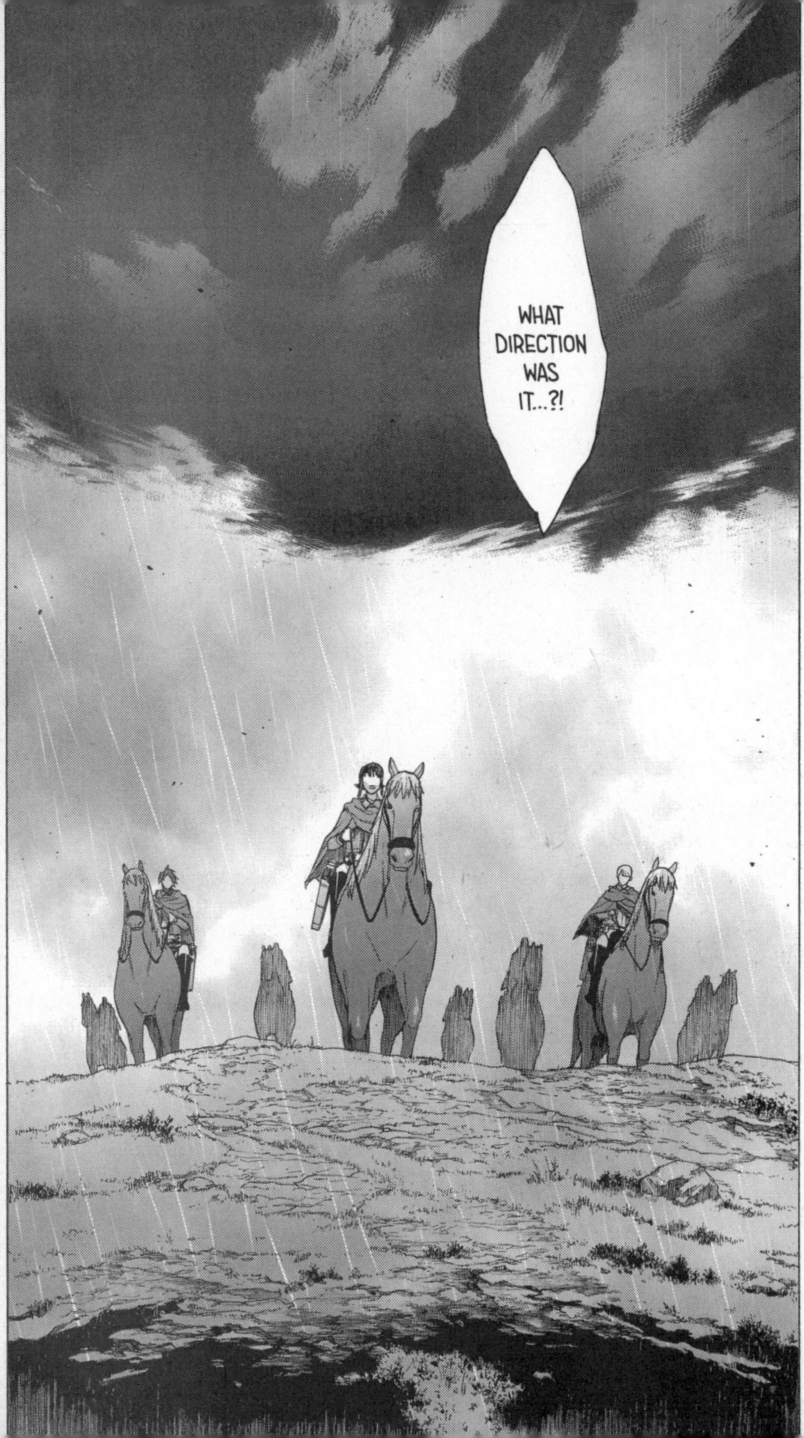
WHAT DIRECTION WAS IT...?!

# Chapter 59: Quagmire Underfoot · End

ATTACK on TITAN

BEFORE THE FALL

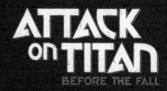

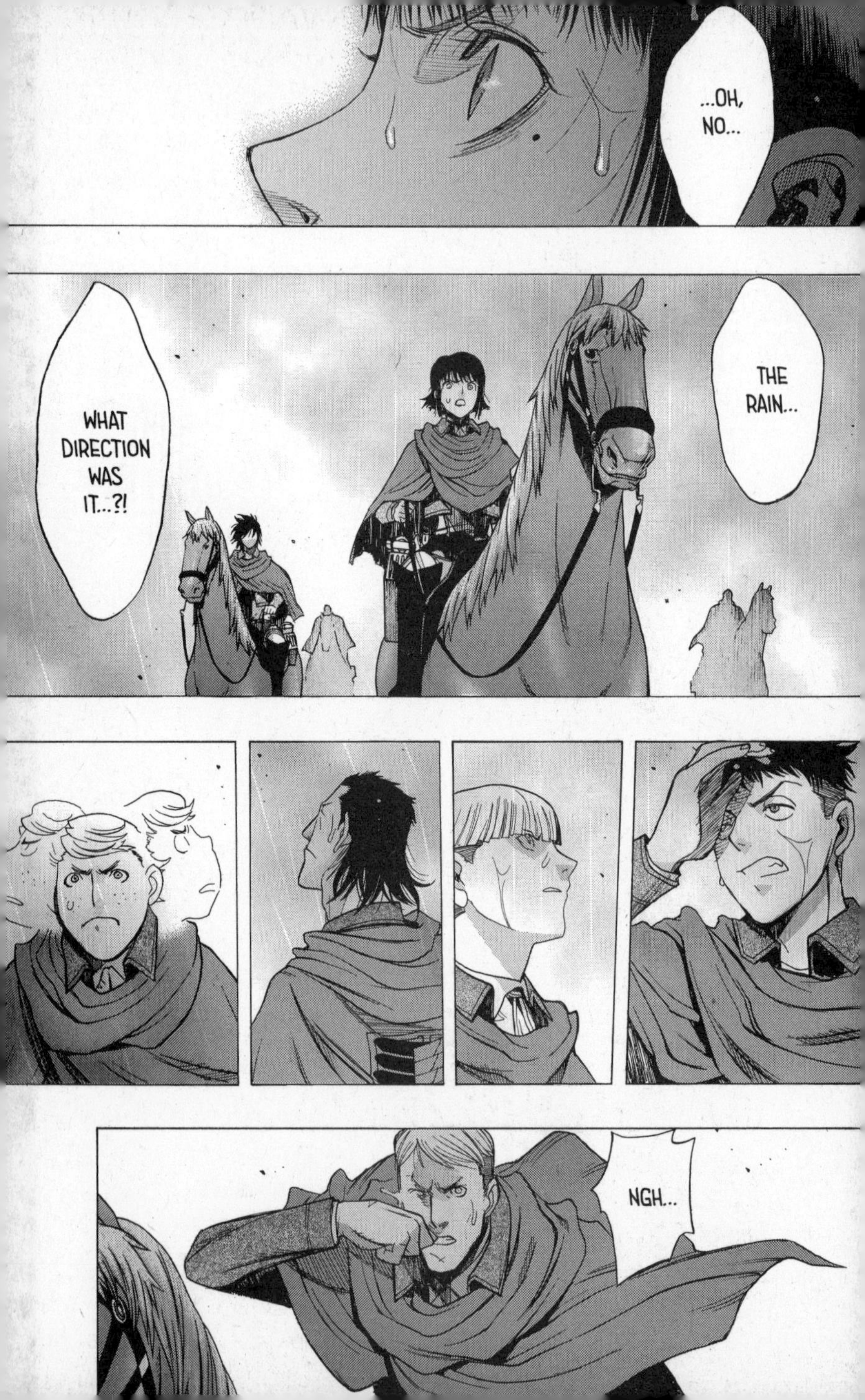
...OH, NO...
THE RAIN...
WHAT DIRECTION WAS IT...?!
NGH...

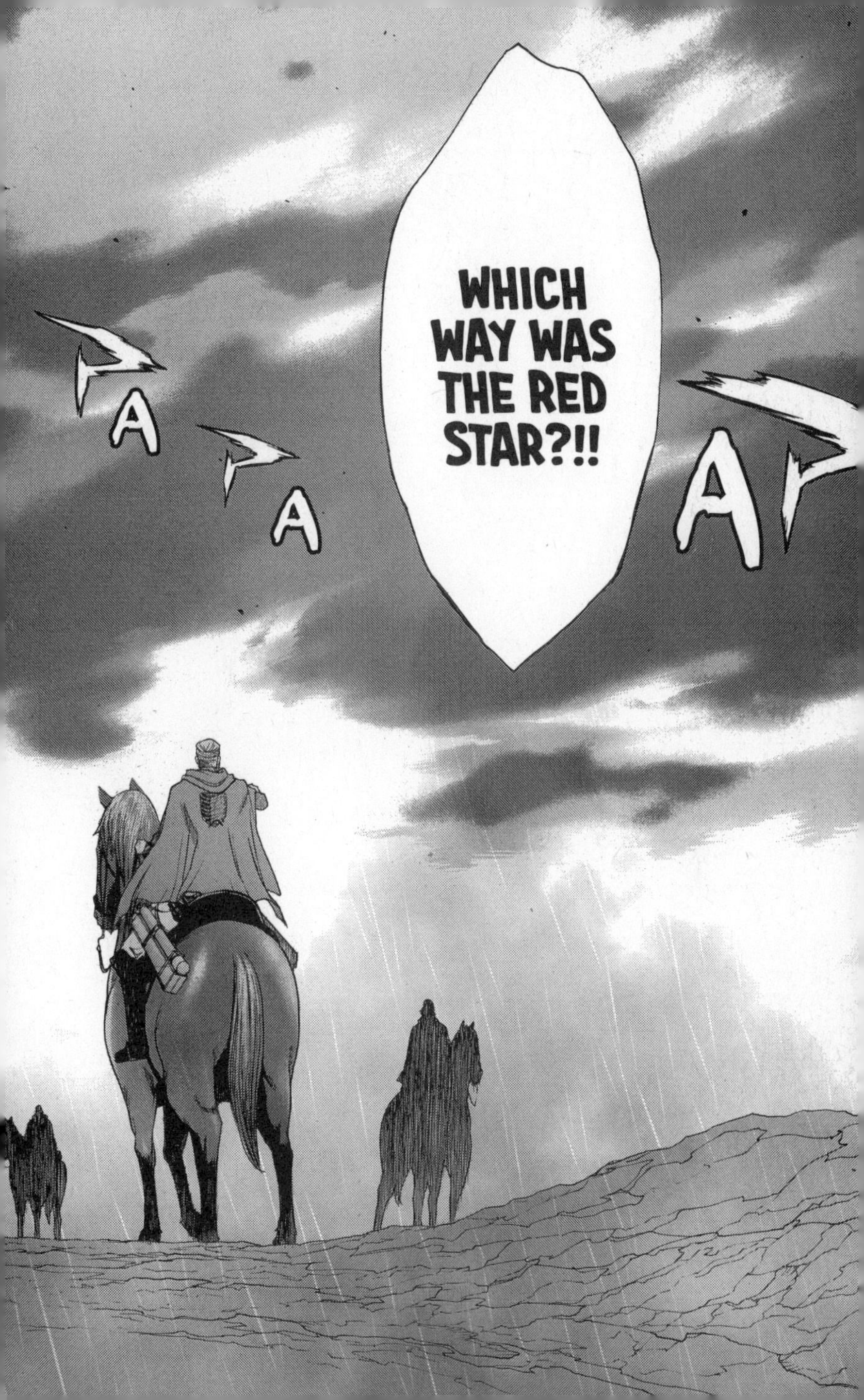
PA
PA
WHICH WAY WAS THE RED STAR?!!
AP

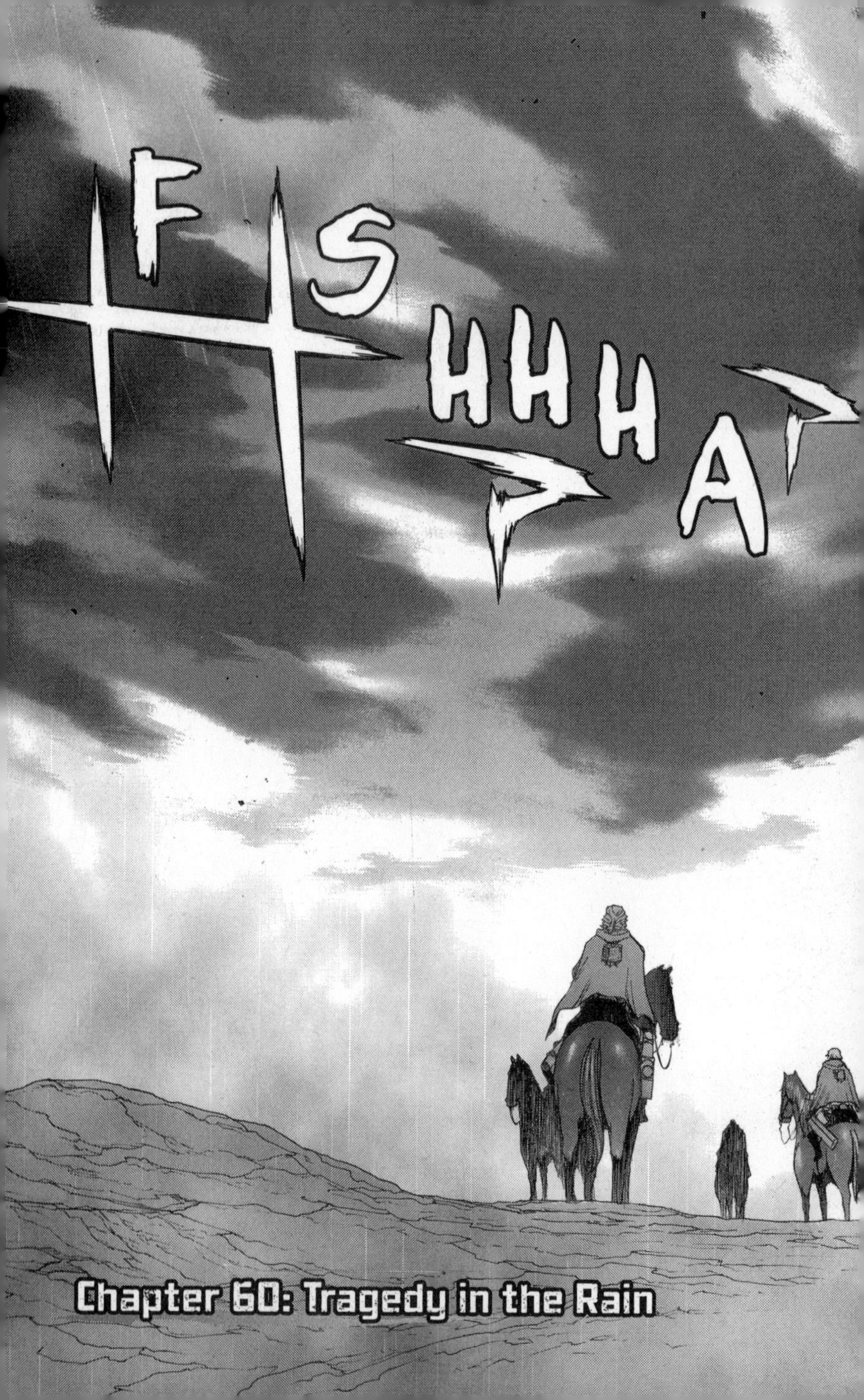
FSSHHHAAA
Chapter 60: Tragedy in the Rain

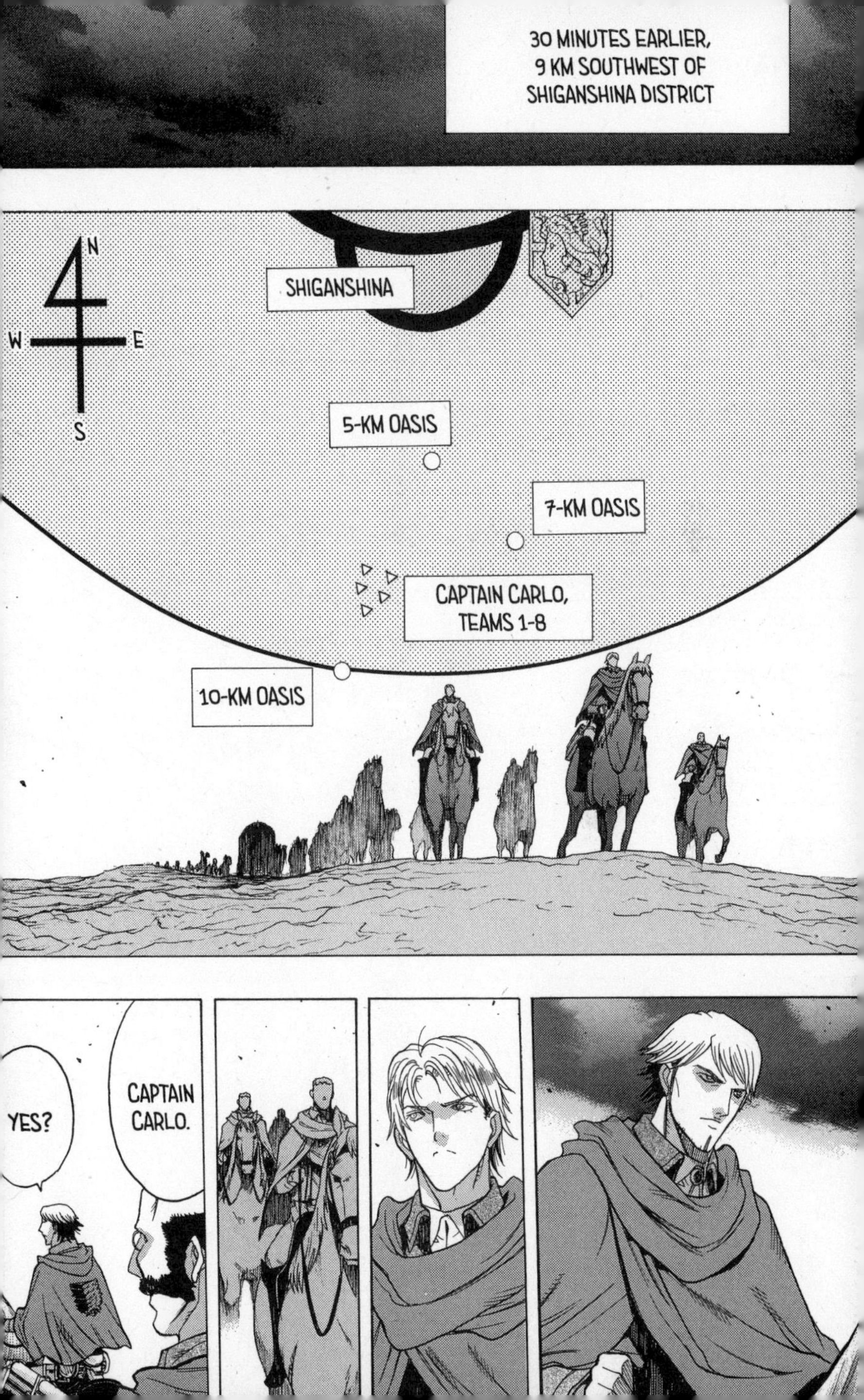
30 MINUTES EARLIER,
9 KM SOUTHWEST OF
SHIGANSHINA DISTRICT
N
W
E
S
SHIGANSHINA
5-KM OASIS
7-KM OASIS
CAPTAIN CARLO,
TEAMS 1-8
10-KM OASIS
CAPTAIN
CARLO.
YES?

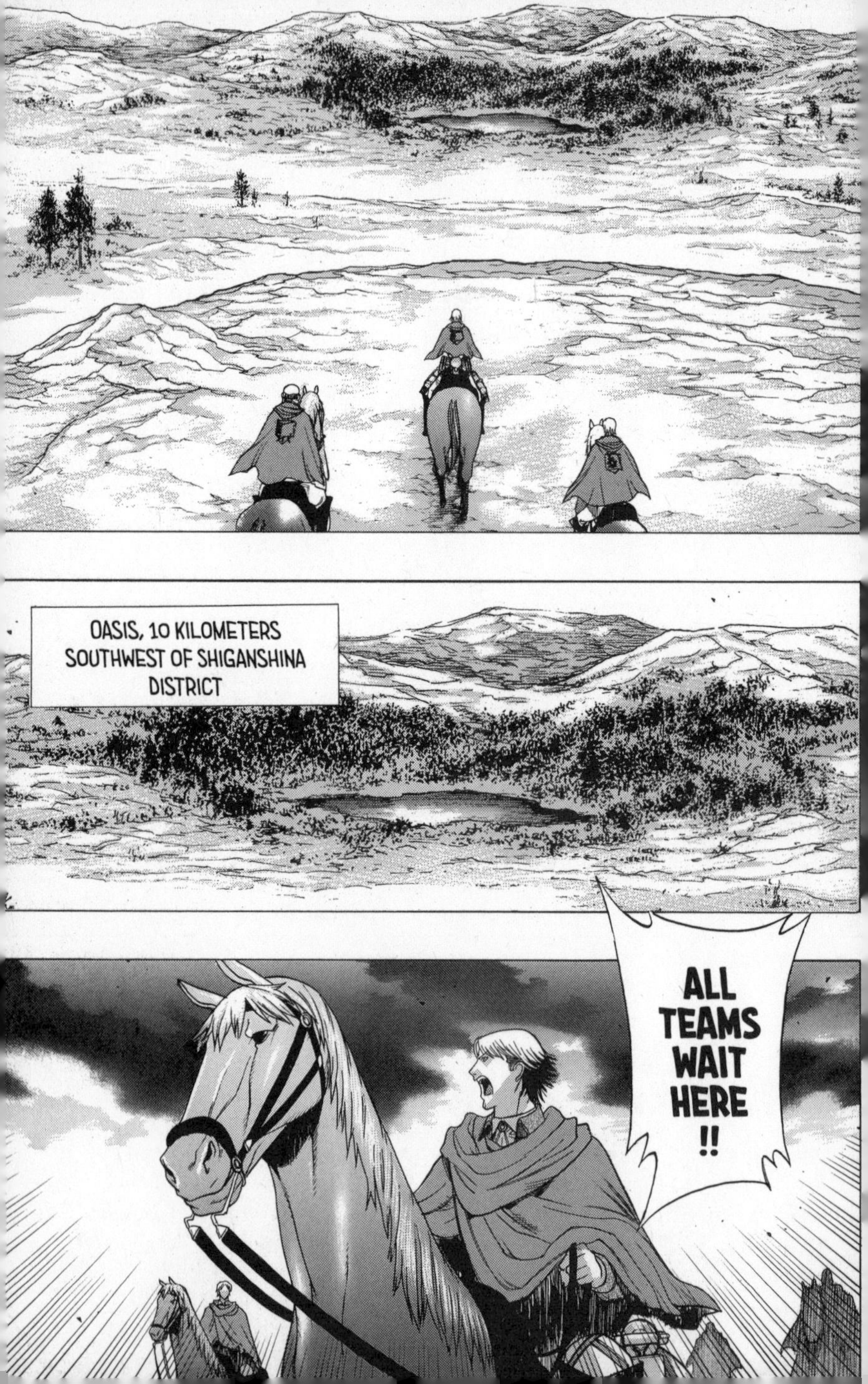
OASIS, 10 KILOMETERS SOUTHWEST OF SHIGANSHINA DISTRICT
ALL TEAMS WAIT HERE !!

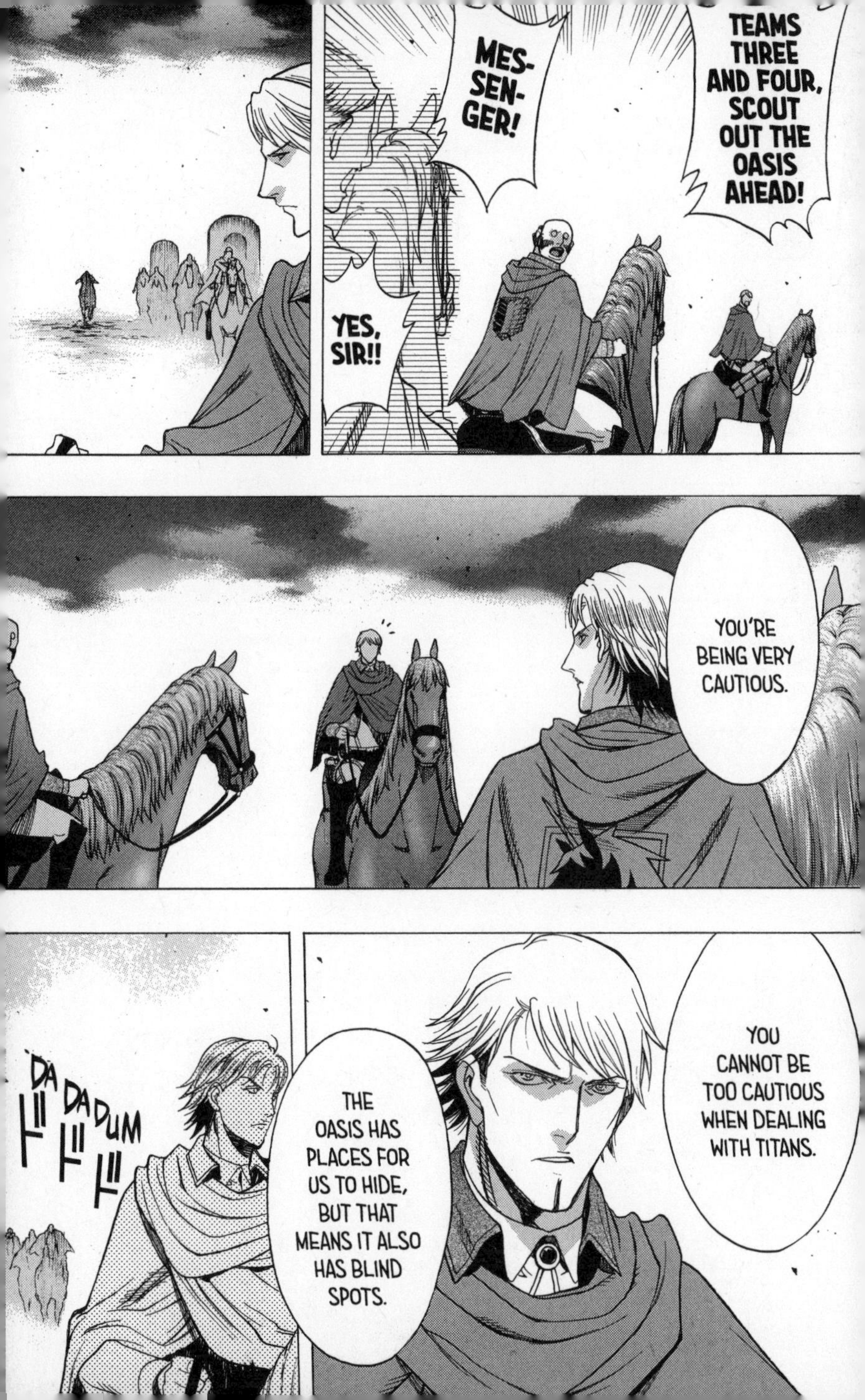
TEAMS THREE AND FOUR, SCOUT OUT THE OASIS AHEAD!
MES-SEN-GER!
YES, SIR!!
YOU'RE BEING VERY CAUTIOUS.
YOU CANNOT BE TOO CAUTIOUS WHEN DEALING WITH TITANS.
THE OASIS HAS PLACES FOR US TO HIDE, BUT THAT MEANS IT ALSO HAS BLIND SPOTS.
DA DA DUM
ドドド

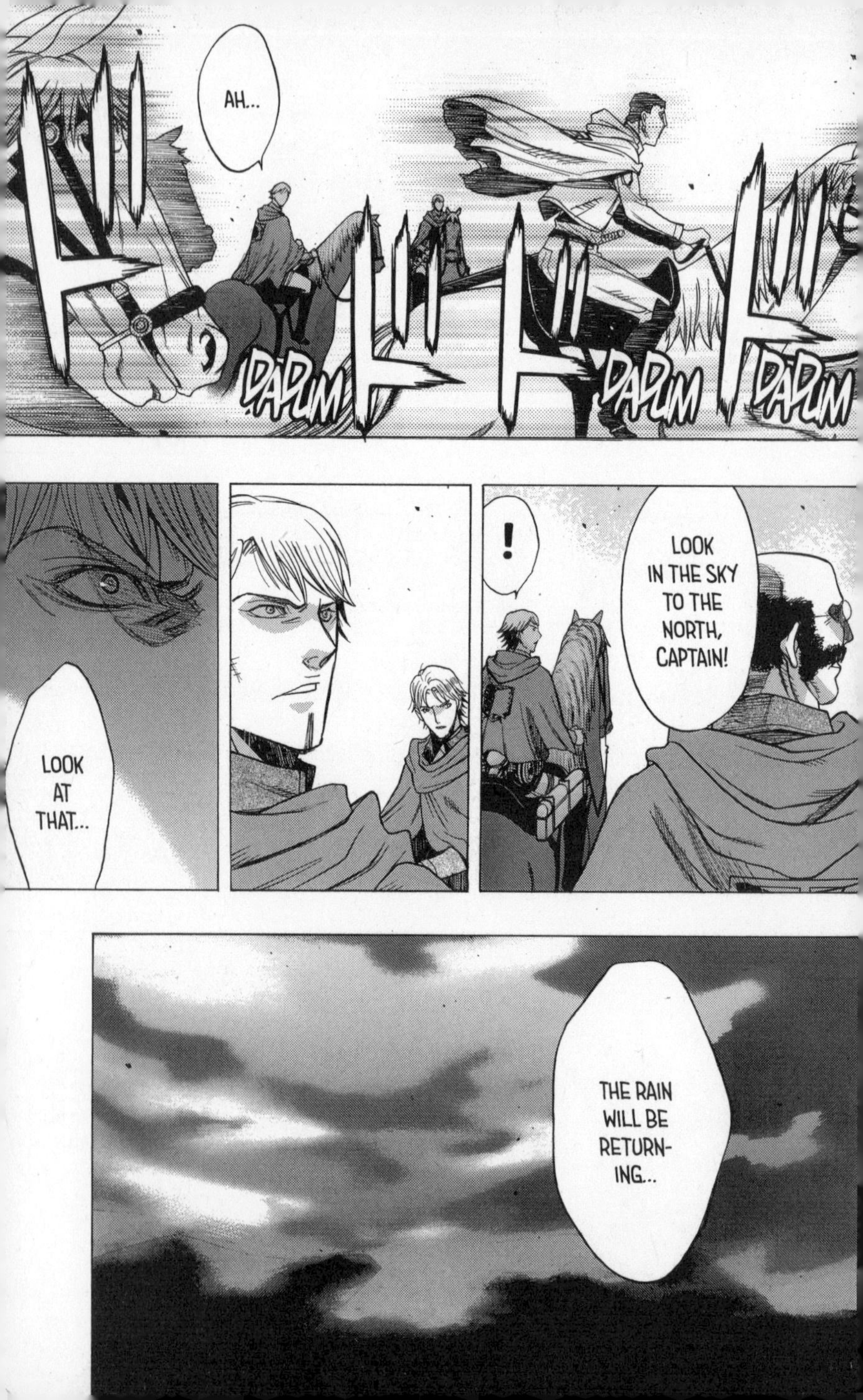
DADUM
DADUM
AH...
DADUM
LOOK IN THE SKY TO THE NORTH, CAPTAIN!
!
LOOK AT THAT...
THE RAIN WILL BE RETURNING...

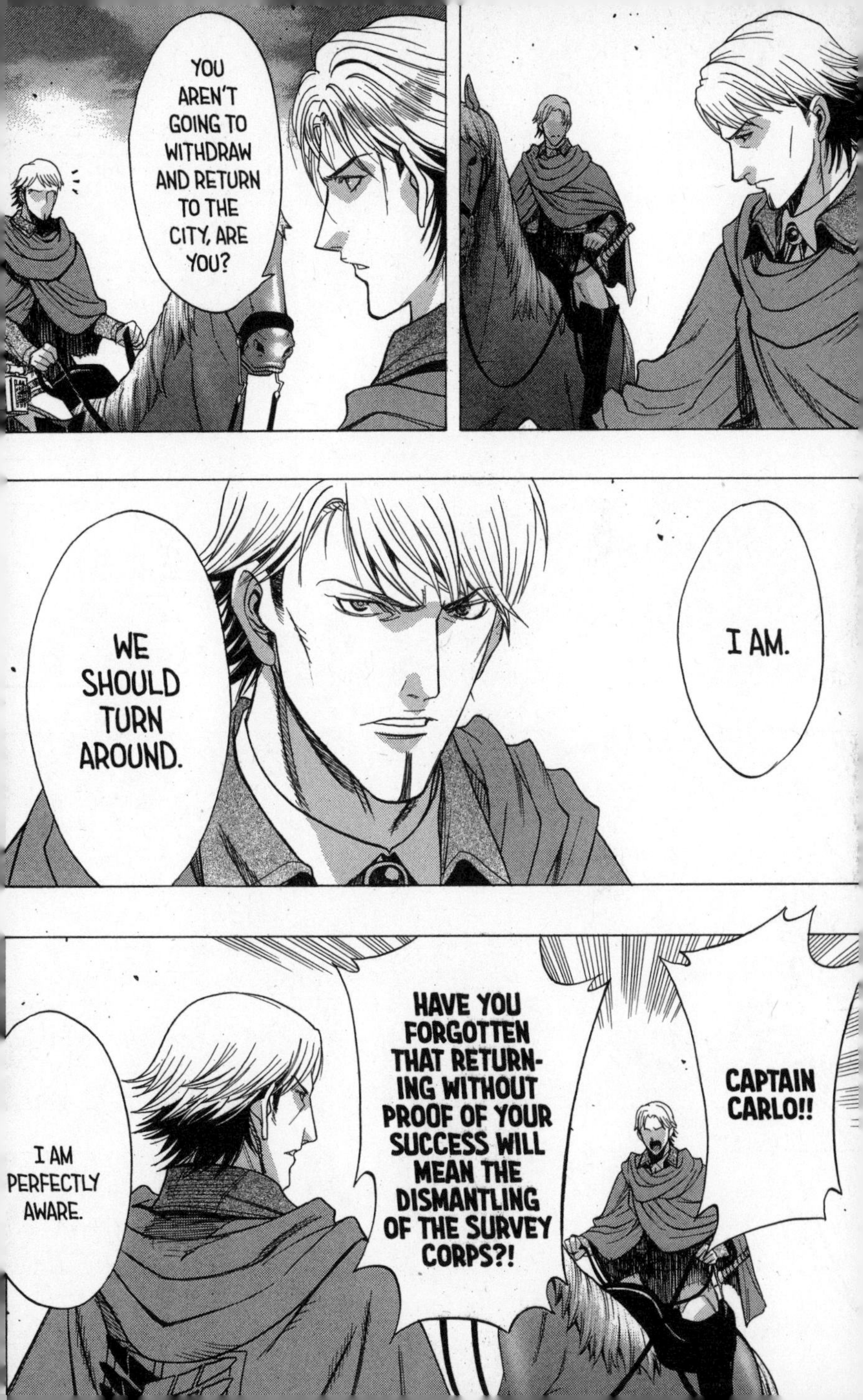
YOU AREN'T GOING TO WITHDRAW AND RETURN TO THE CITY, ARE YOU?
I AM.
WE SHOULD TURN AROUND.
CAPTAIN CARLO!!
HAVE YOU FORGOTTEN THAT RETURNING WITHOUT PROOF OF YOUR SUCCESS WILL MEAN THE DISMANTLING OF THE SURVEY CORPS?!
I AM PERFECTLY AWARE.

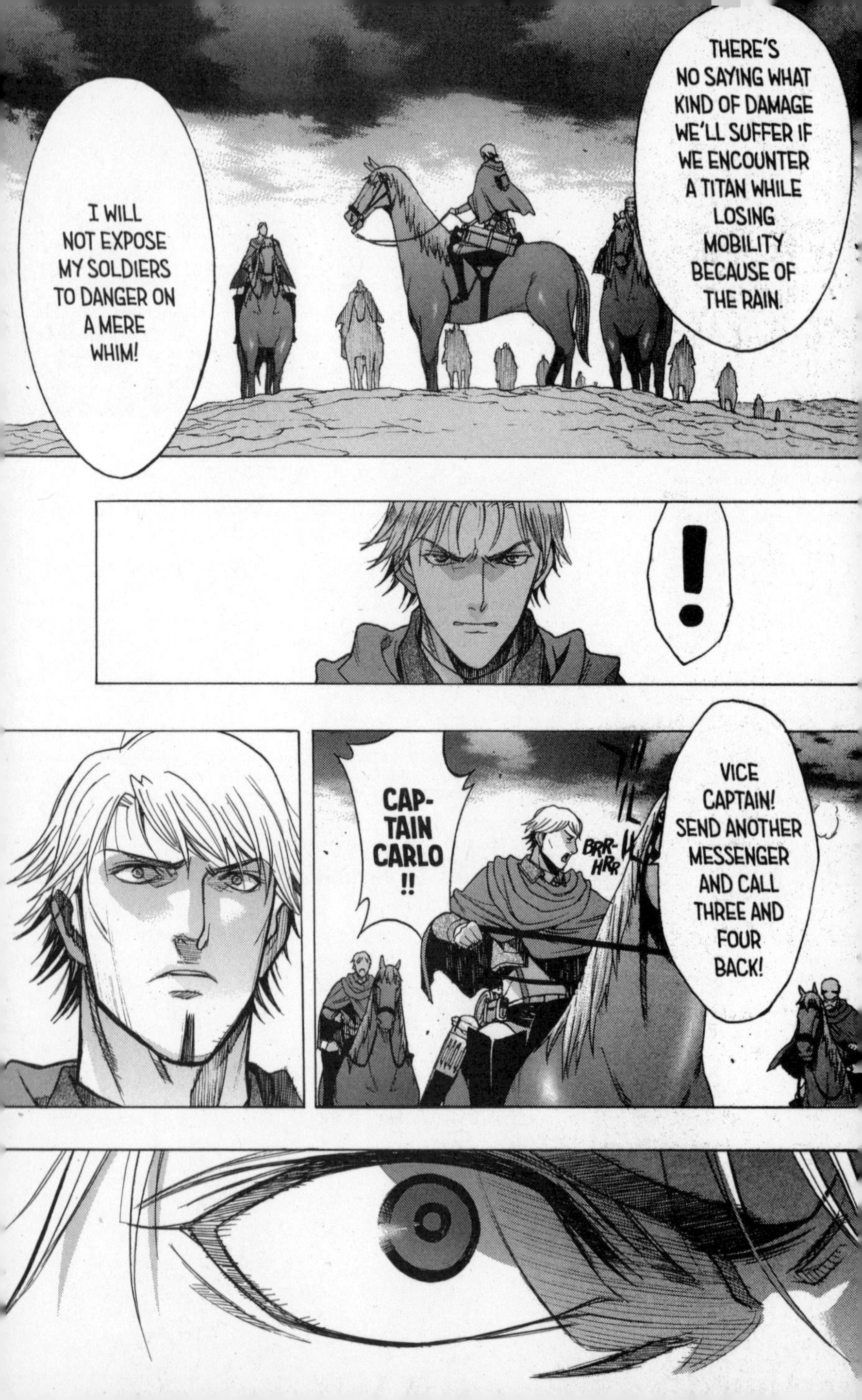
THERE'S NO SAYING WHAT KIND OF DAMAGE WE'LL SUFFER IF WE ENCOUNTER A TITAN WHILE LOSING MOBILITY BECAUSE OF THE RAIN.
I WILL NOT EXPOSE MY SOLDIERS TO DANGER ON A MERE WHIM!
!
VICE CAPTAIN! SEND ANOTHER MESSENGER AND CALL THREE AND FOUR BACK!
BRR-HRR
CAP-TAIN CARLO!!

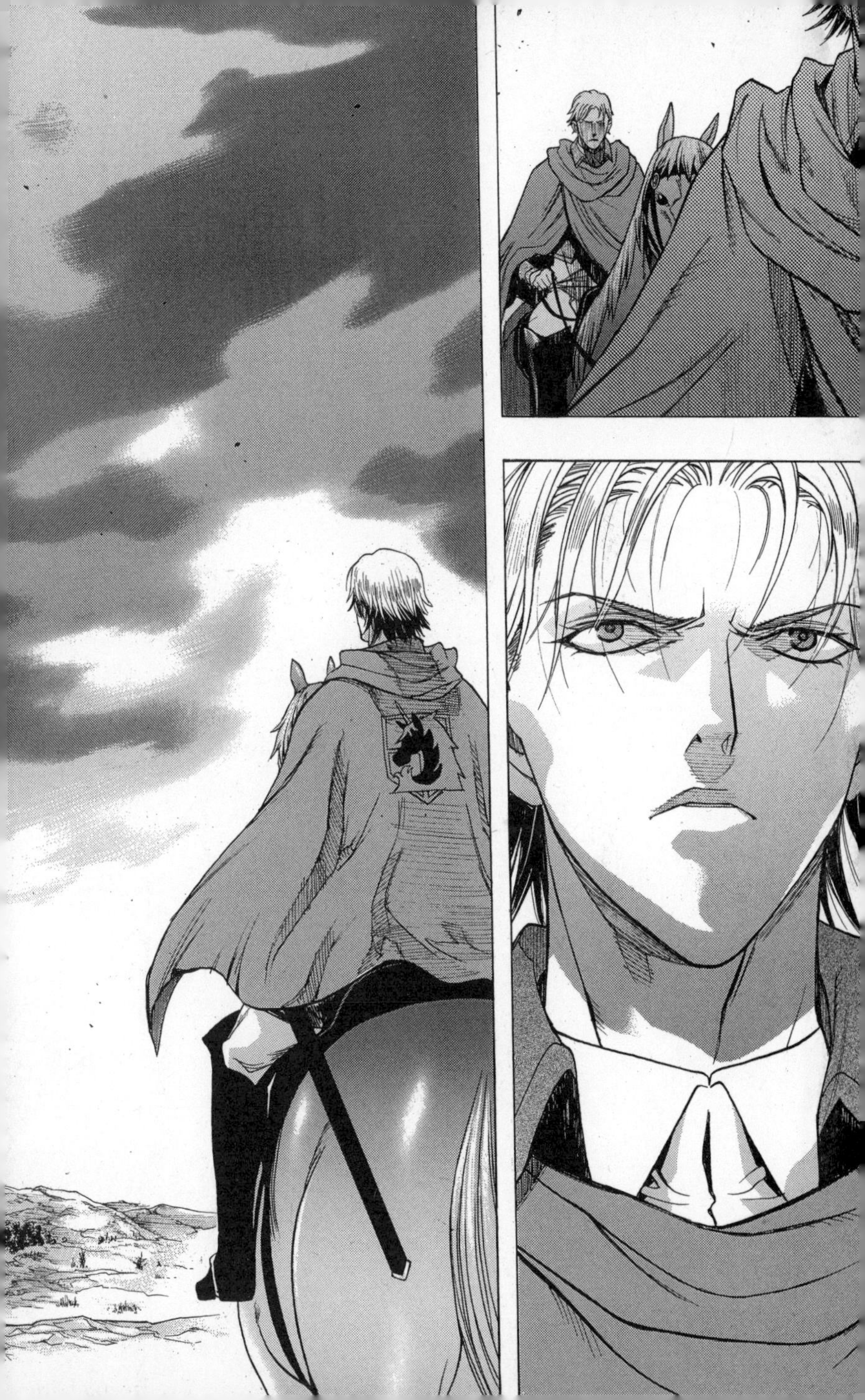

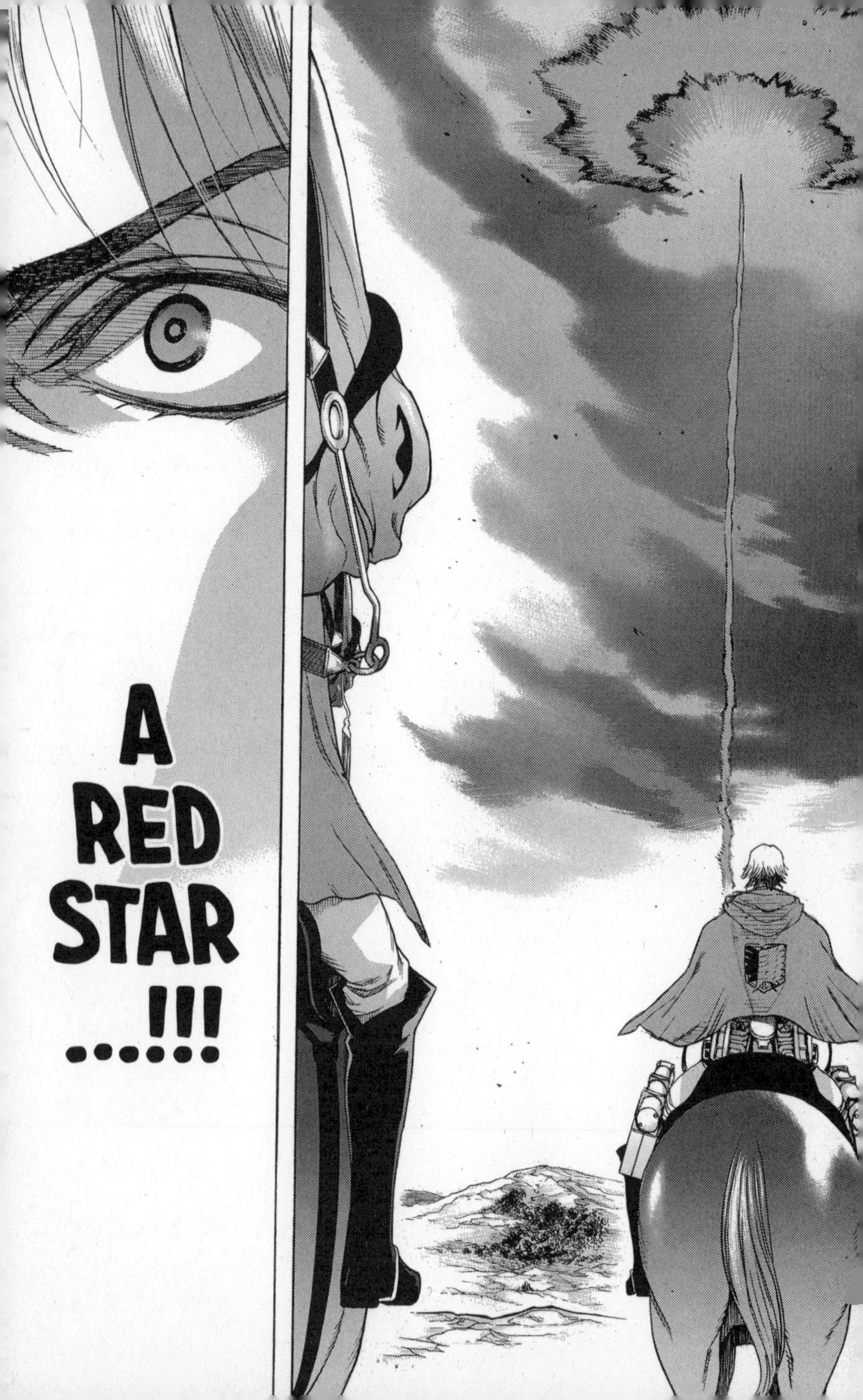
A RED STAR ...!!!

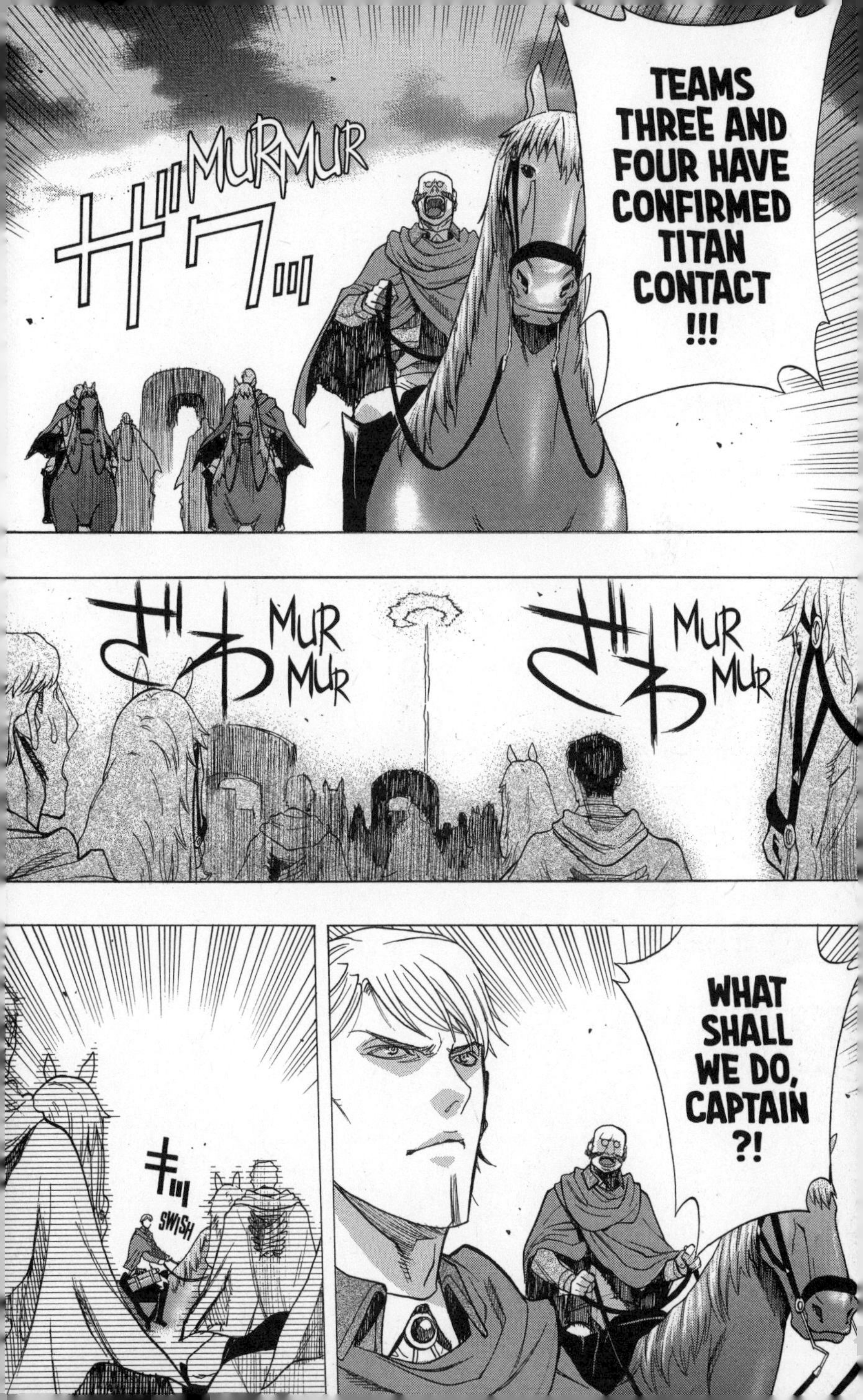
TEAMS THREE AND FOUR HAVE CONFIRMED TITAN CONTACT !!!
MURMUR
MUR MUR
MUR MUR
WHAT SHALL WE DO, CAPTAIN ?!
SWISH

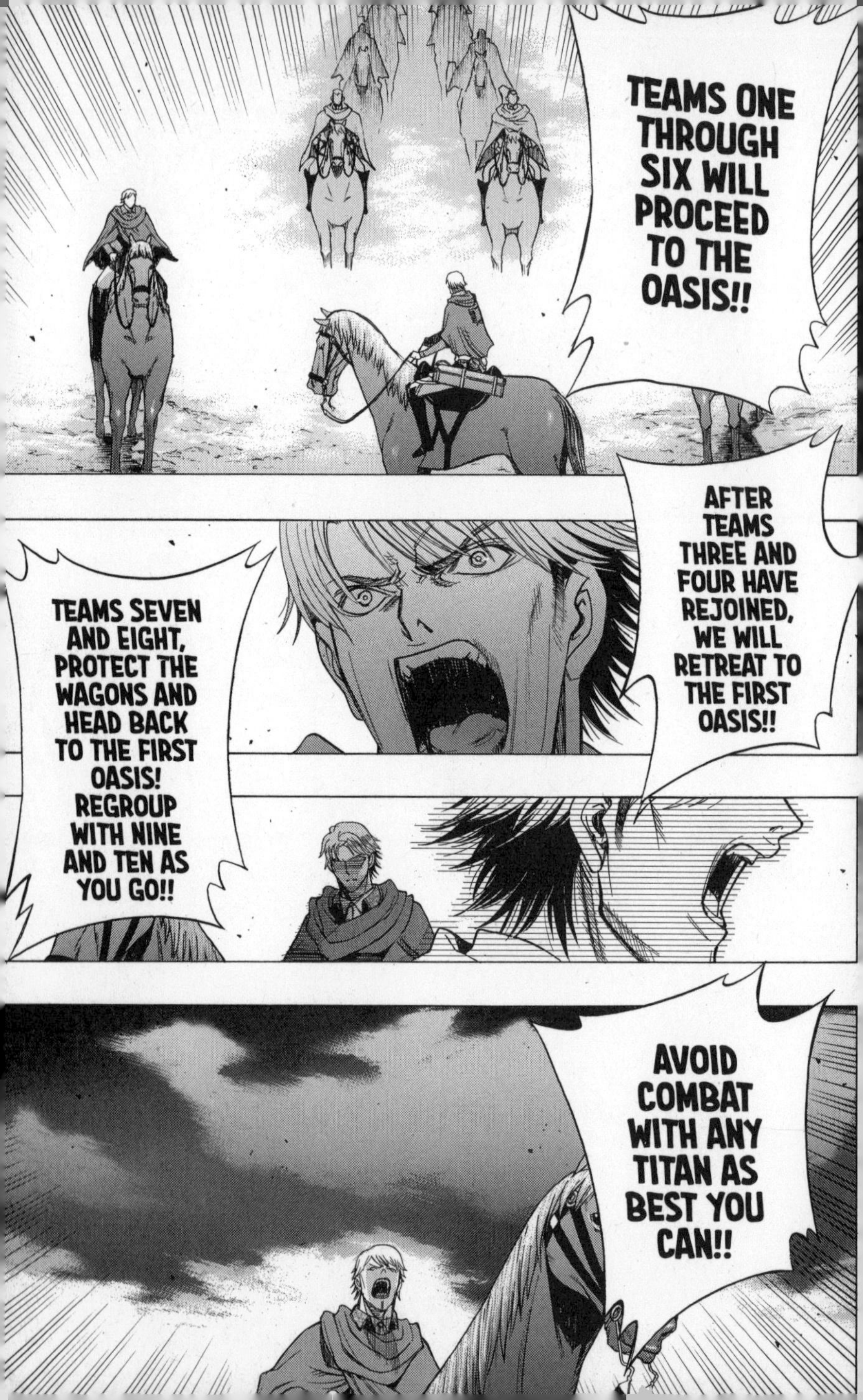
TEAMS ONE THROUGH SIX WILL PROCEED TO THE OASIS!!
AFTER TEAMS THREE AND FOUR HAVE REJOINED, WE WILL RETREAT TO THE FIRST OASIS!!
TEAMS SEVEN AND EIGHT, PROTECT THE WAGONS AND HEAD BACK TO THE FIRST OASIS! REGROUP WITH NINE AND TEN AS YOU GO!!
AVOID COMBAT WITH ANY TITAN AS BEST YOU CAN!!

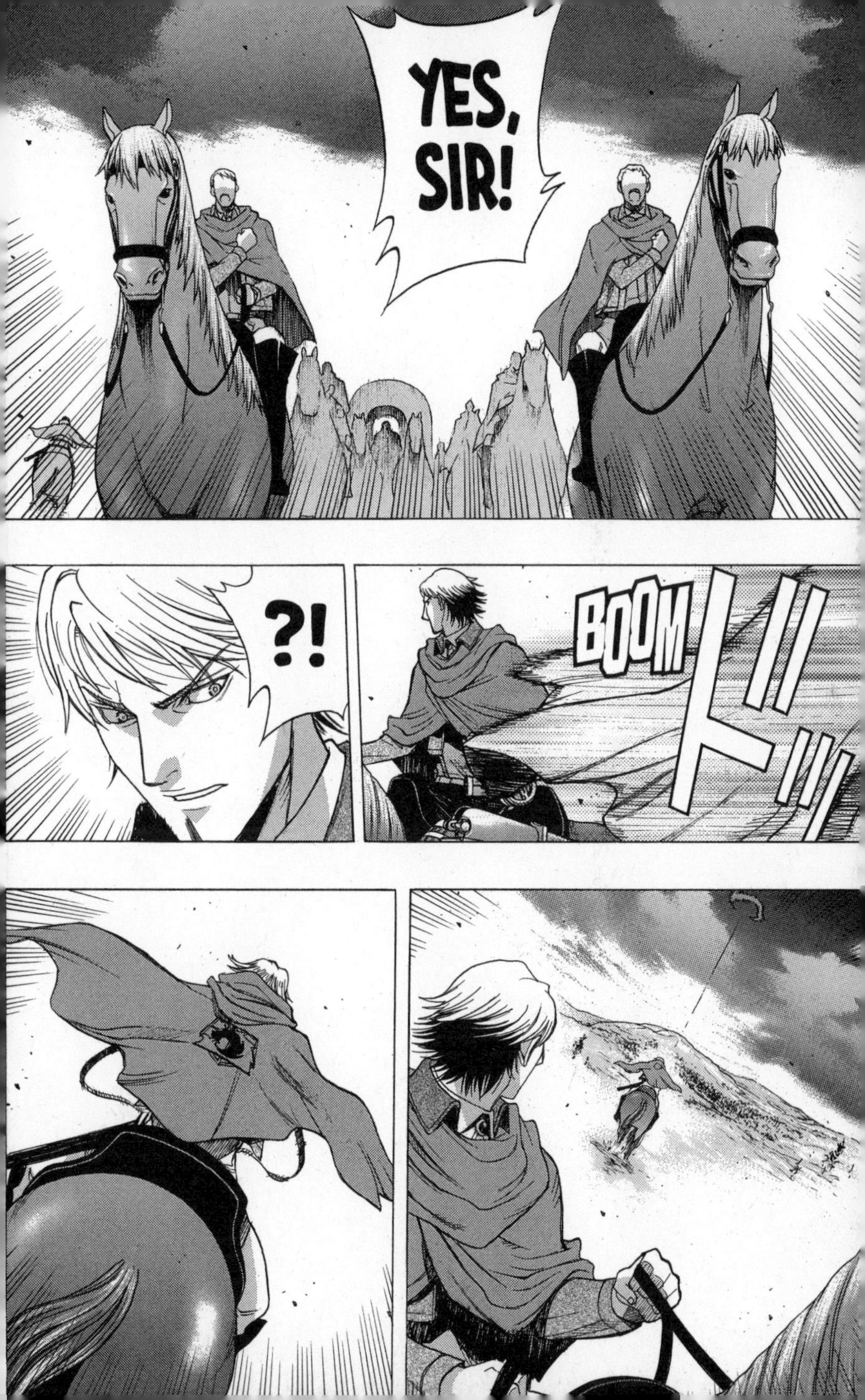
YES, SIR!
BOOM
?!

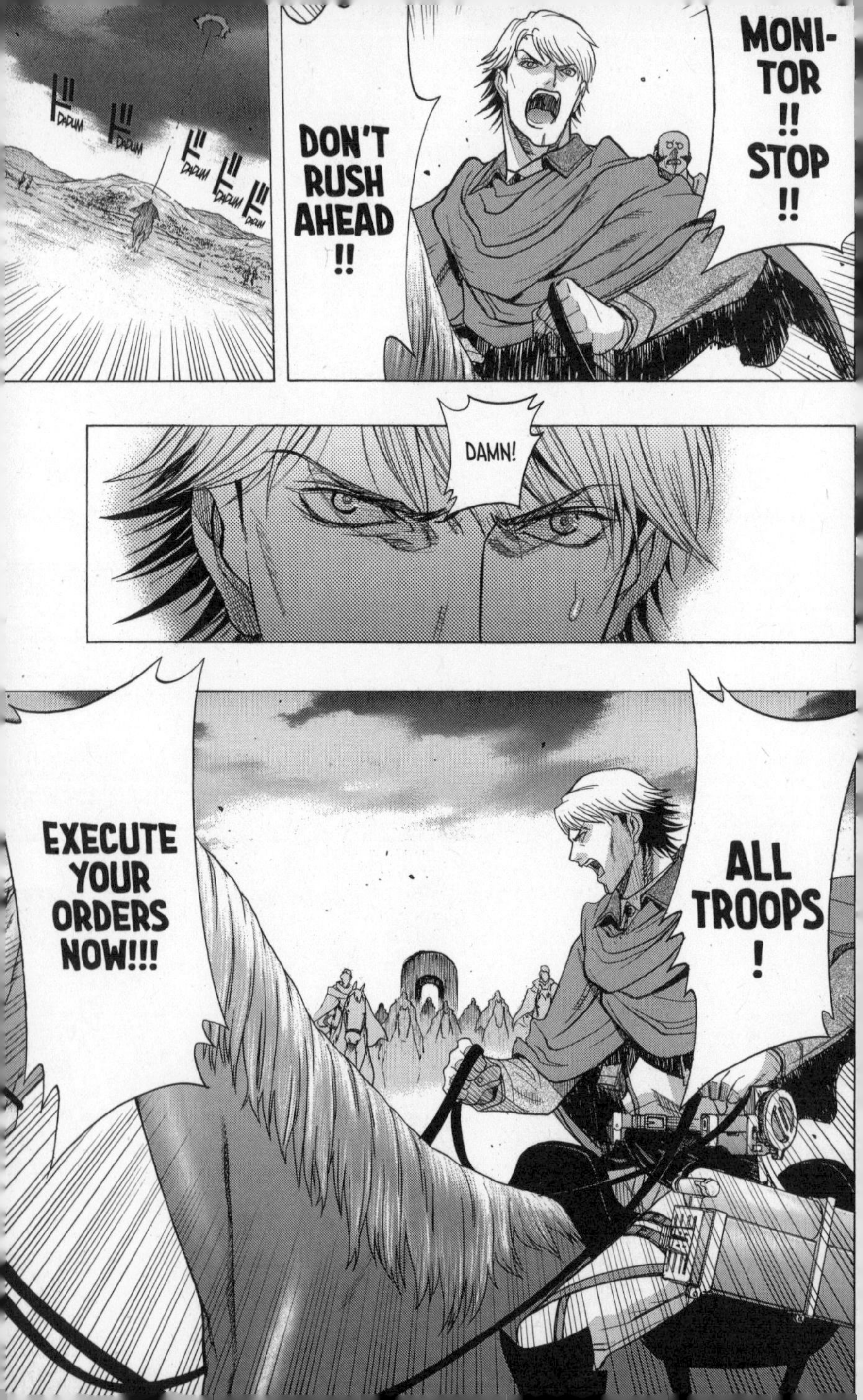
MONI-TOR!! STOP!!
DON'T RUSH AHEAD!!
DAPUM DAPUM DAPUM DAPUM DAPUM
DAMN!
ALL TROOPS!
EXECUTE YOUR ORDERS NOW!!!

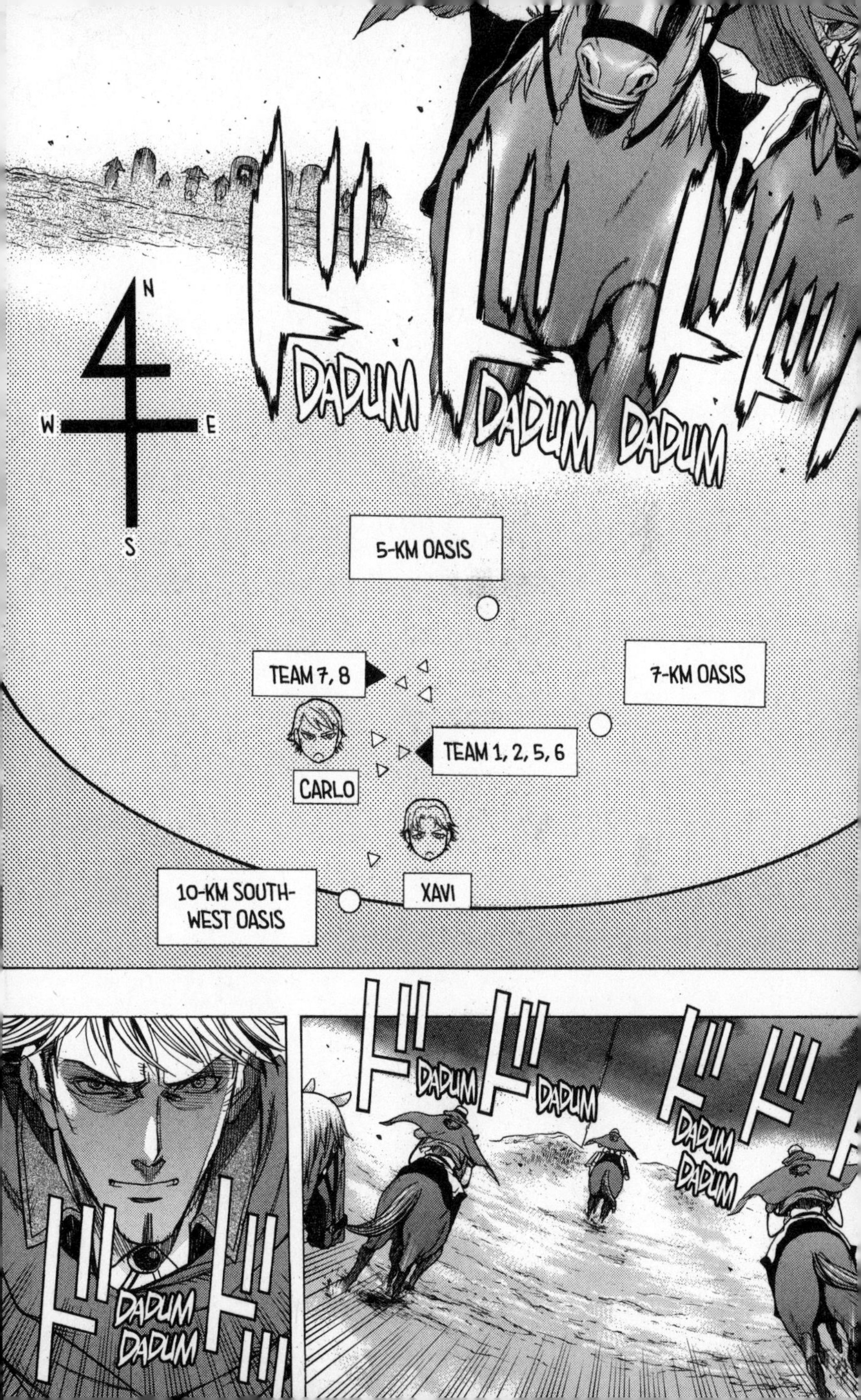
DADUM
DADUM
DADUM
N
W
E
S
5-KM OASIS
7-KM OASIS
TEAM 7, 8
TEAM 1, 2, 5, 6
CARLO
XAVI
10-KM SOUTH-WEST OASIS
DADUM
DADUM
DADUM
DADUM
DADUM
DADUM

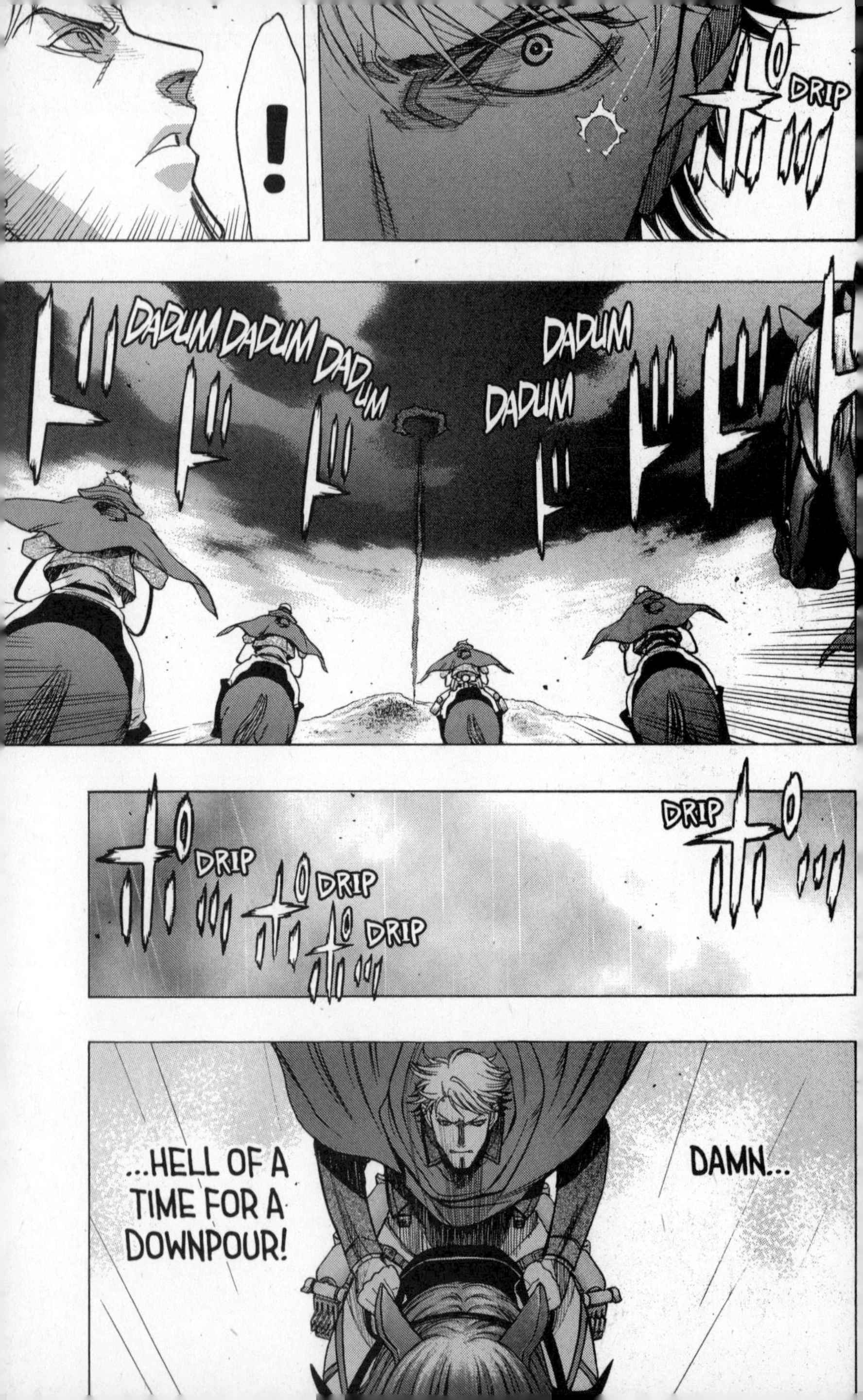
DRIP
!
DADUM
DADUM
DADUM DADUM DADUM
DRIP
DRIP
DRIP
DRIP
DAMN...
...HELL OF A TIME FOR A DOWNPOUR!

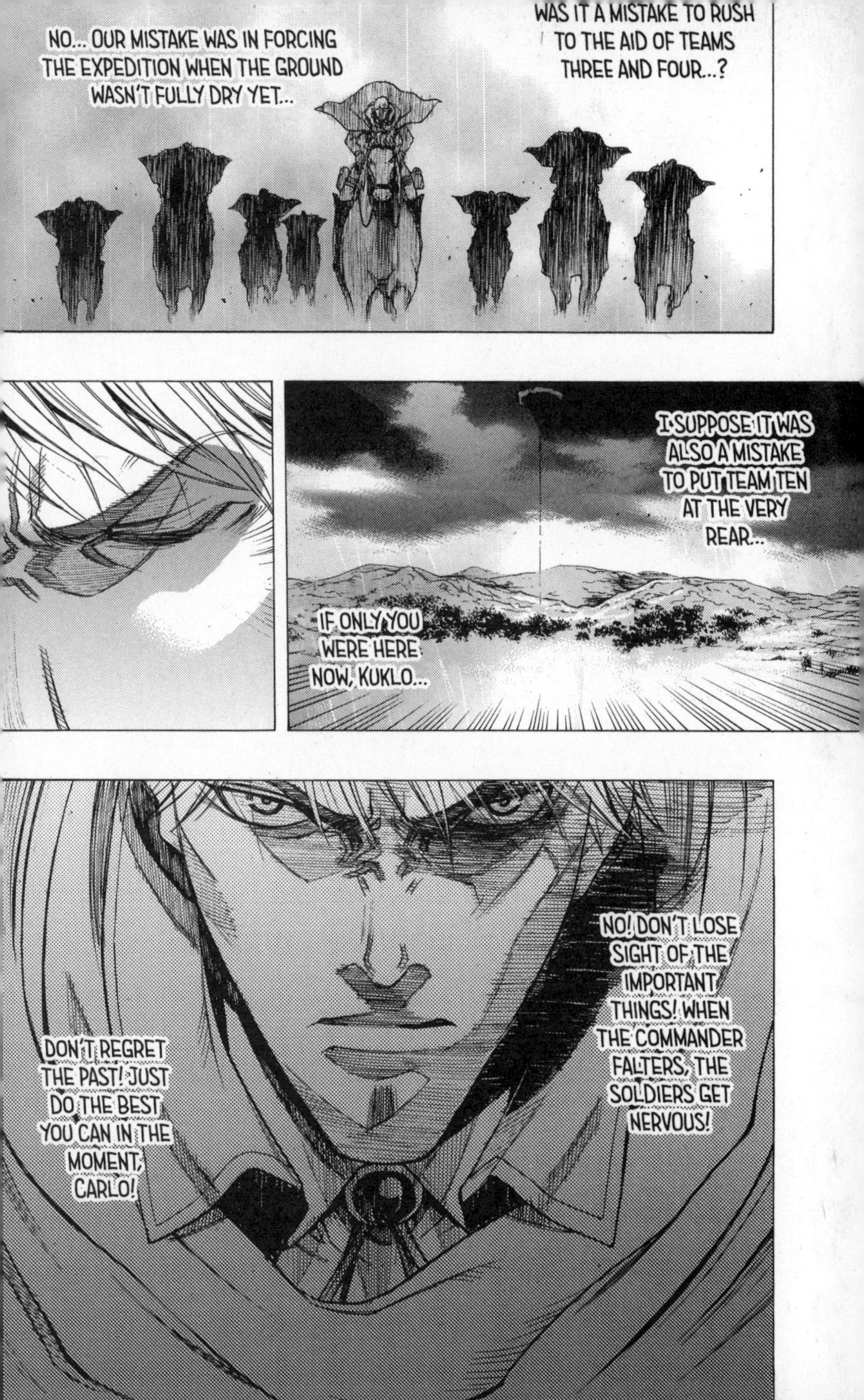
WAS IT A MISTAKE TO RUSH TO THE AID OF TEAMS THREE AND FOUR...?
NO... OUR MISTAKE WAS IN FORCING THE EXPEDITION WHEN THE GROUND WASN'T FULLY DRY YET...
I SUPPOSE IT WAS ALSO A MISTAKE TO PUT TEAM TEN AT THE VERY REAR...
IF ONLY YOU WERE HERE NOW, KUKLO...
NO! DON'T LOSE SIGHT OF THE IMPORTANT THINGS! WHEN THE COMMANDER FALTERS, THE SOLDIERS GET NERVOUS!
DON'T REGRET THE PAST! JUST DO THE BEST YOU CAN IN THE MOMENT, CARLO!

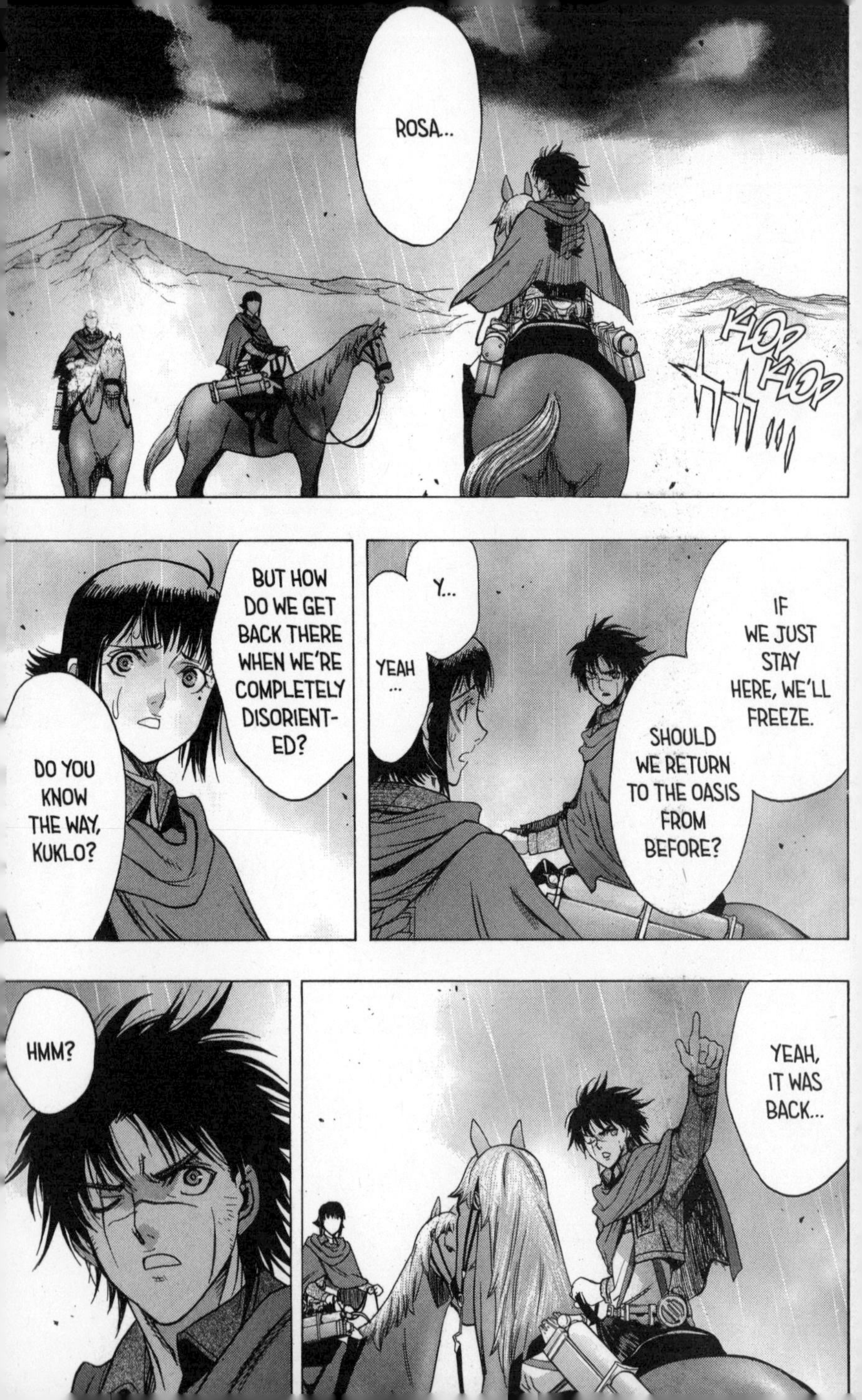
ROSA...
KLOP KLOP
IF WE JUST STAY HERE, WE'LL FREEZE.
SHOULD WE RETURN TO THE OASIS FROM BEFORE?
Y...
YEAH ...
BUT HOW DO WE GET BACK THERE WHEN WE'RE COMPLETELY DISORIENT-ED?
DO YOU KNOW THE WAY, KUKLO?
YEAH, IT WAS BACK...
HMM?

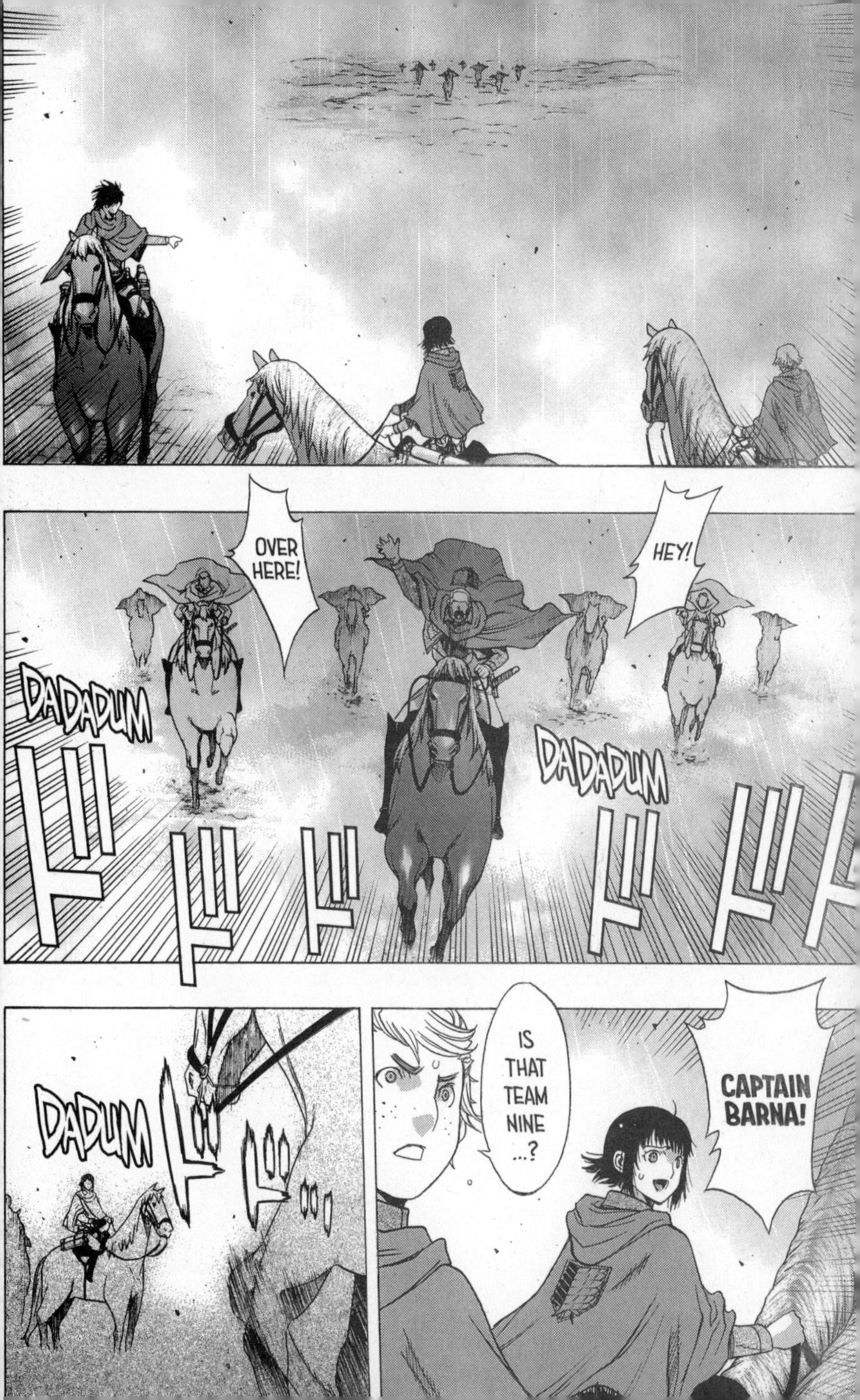
HEY!
OVER HERE!
DADADUM
DADADUM
CAPTAIN BARNA!
IS THAT TEAM NINE ...?
DADUM

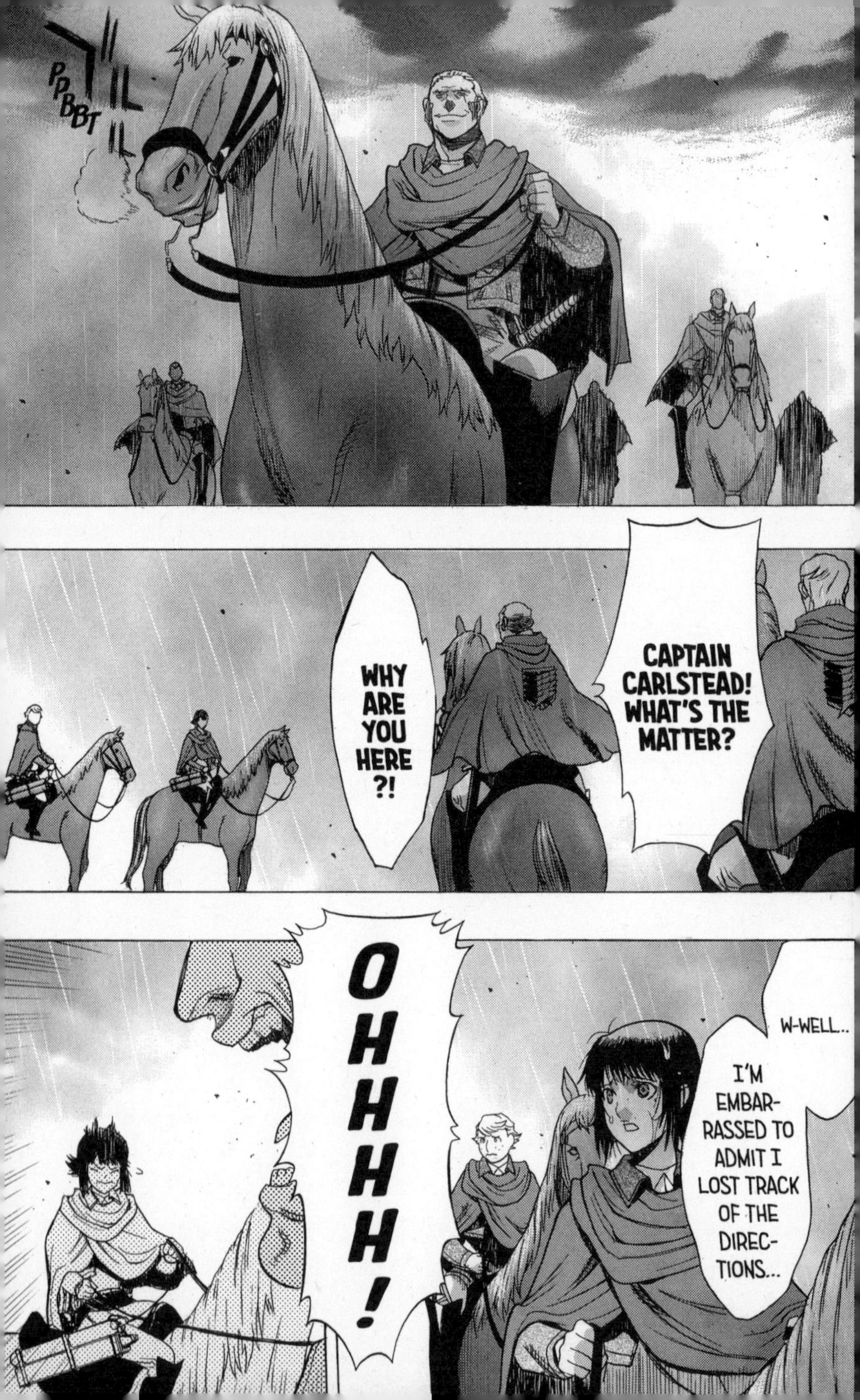
PPBBT
CAPTAIN CARLSTEAD! WHAT'S THE MATTER?
WHY ARE YOU HERE ?!
W-WELL...
I'M EMBARRASSED TO ADMIT I LOST TRACK OF THE DIRECTIONS...
OHHHHH!

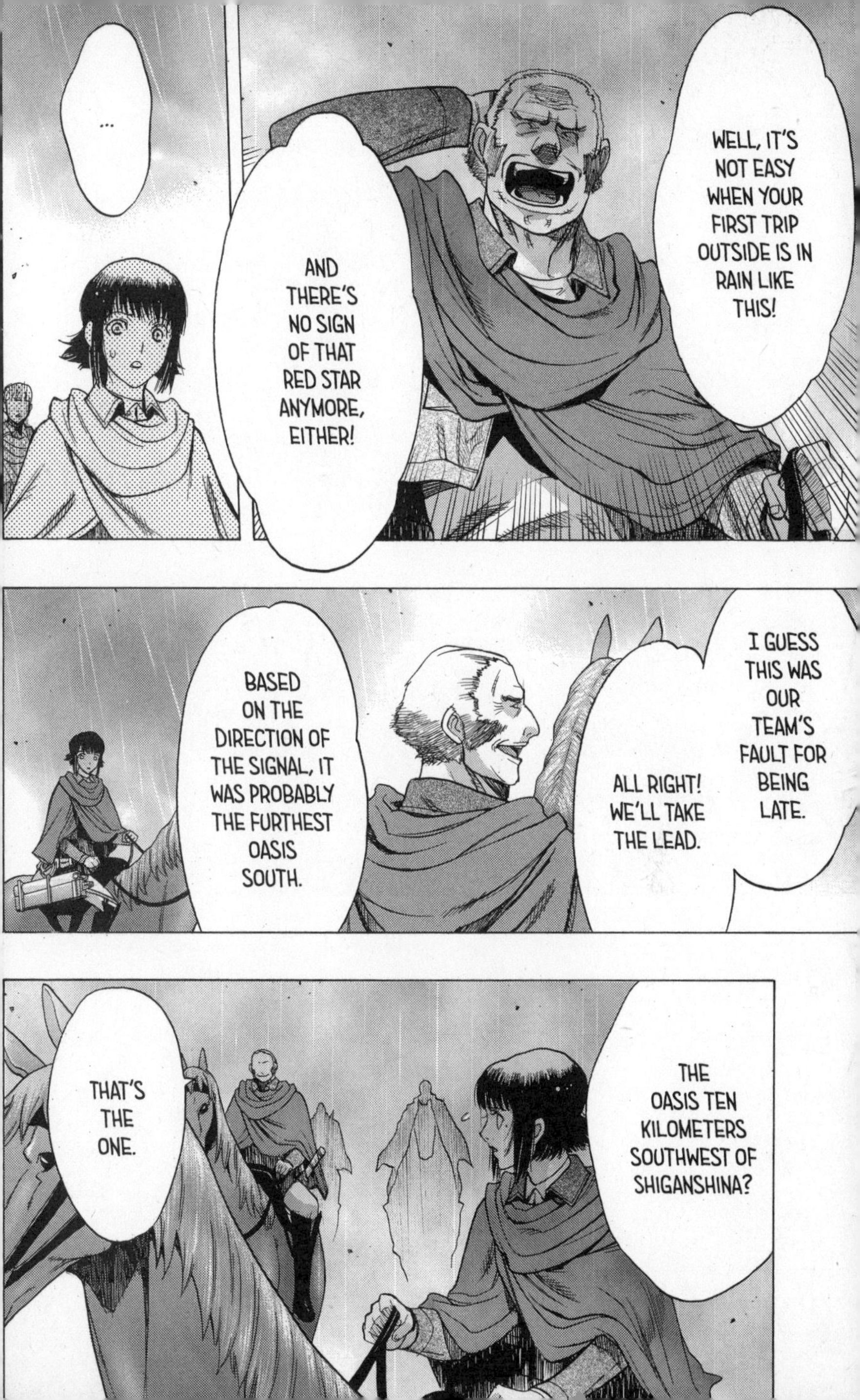
WELL, IT'S NOT EASY WHEN YOUR FIRST TRIP OUTSIDE IS IN RAIN LIKE THIS!
AND THERE'S NO SIGN OF THAT RED STAR ANYMORE, EITHER!
...
I GUESS THIS WAS OUR TEAM'S FAULT FOR BEING LATE.
ALL RIGHT! WE'LL TAKE THE LEAD.
BASED ON THE DIRECTION OF THE SIGNAL, IT WAS PROBABLY THE FURTHEST OASIS SOUTH.
THE OASIS TEN KILOMETERS SOUTHWEST OF SHIGANSHINA?
THAT'S THE ONE.

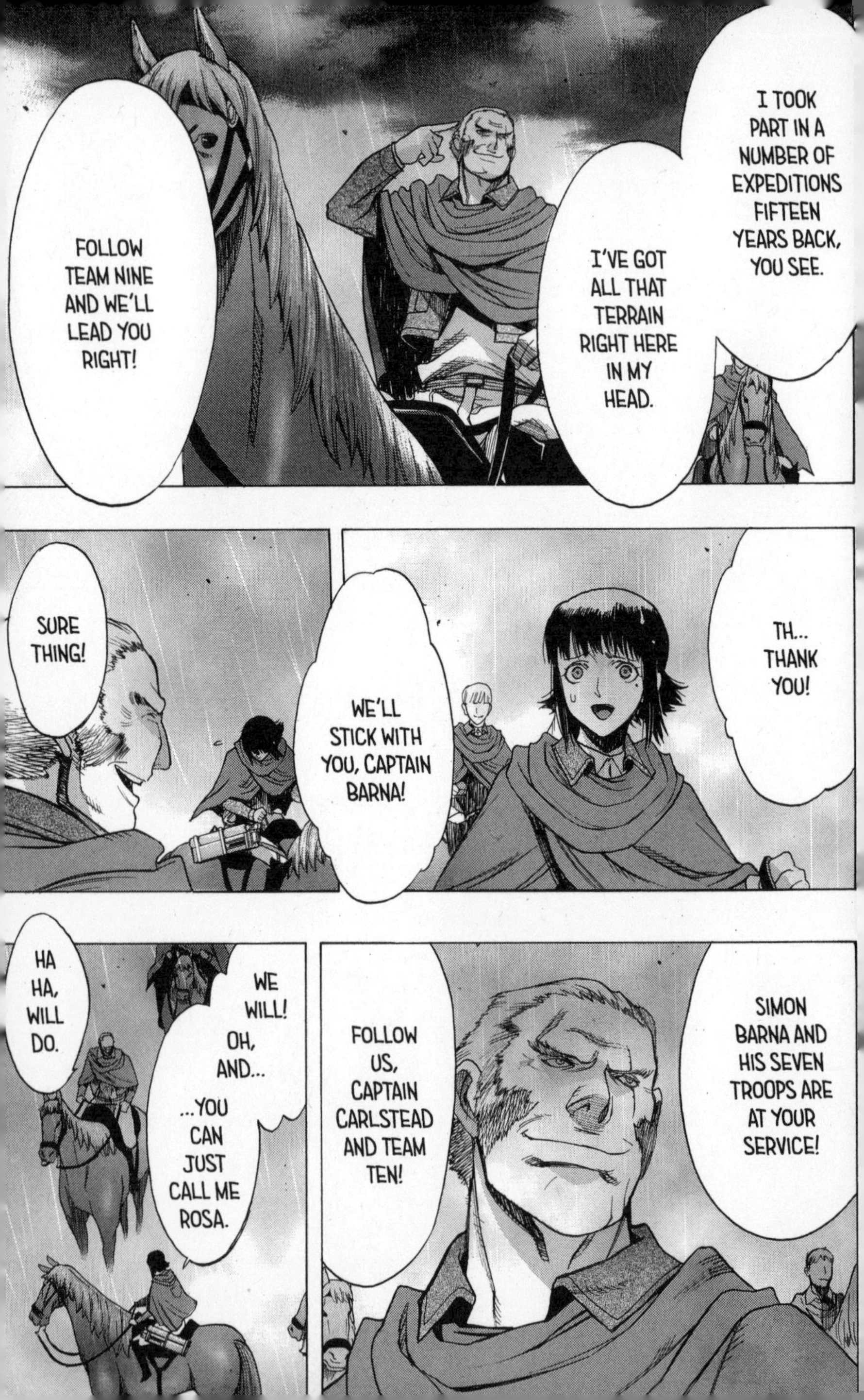
I TOOK PART IN A NUMBER OF EXPEDITIONS FIFTEEN YEARS BACK, YOU SEE.
I'VE GOT ALL THAT TERRAIN RIGHT HERE IN MY HEAD.
FOLLOW TEAM NINE AND WE'LL LEAD YOU RIGHT!
TH... THANK YOU!
WE'LL STICK WITH YOU, CAPTAIN BARNA!
SURE THING!
SIMON BARNA AND HIS SEVEN TROOPS ARE AT YOUR SERVICE!
FOLLOW US, CAPTAIN CARLSTEAD AND TEAM TEN!
WE WILL! OH, AND...
...YOU CAN JUST CALL ME ROSA.
HA HA, WILL DO.

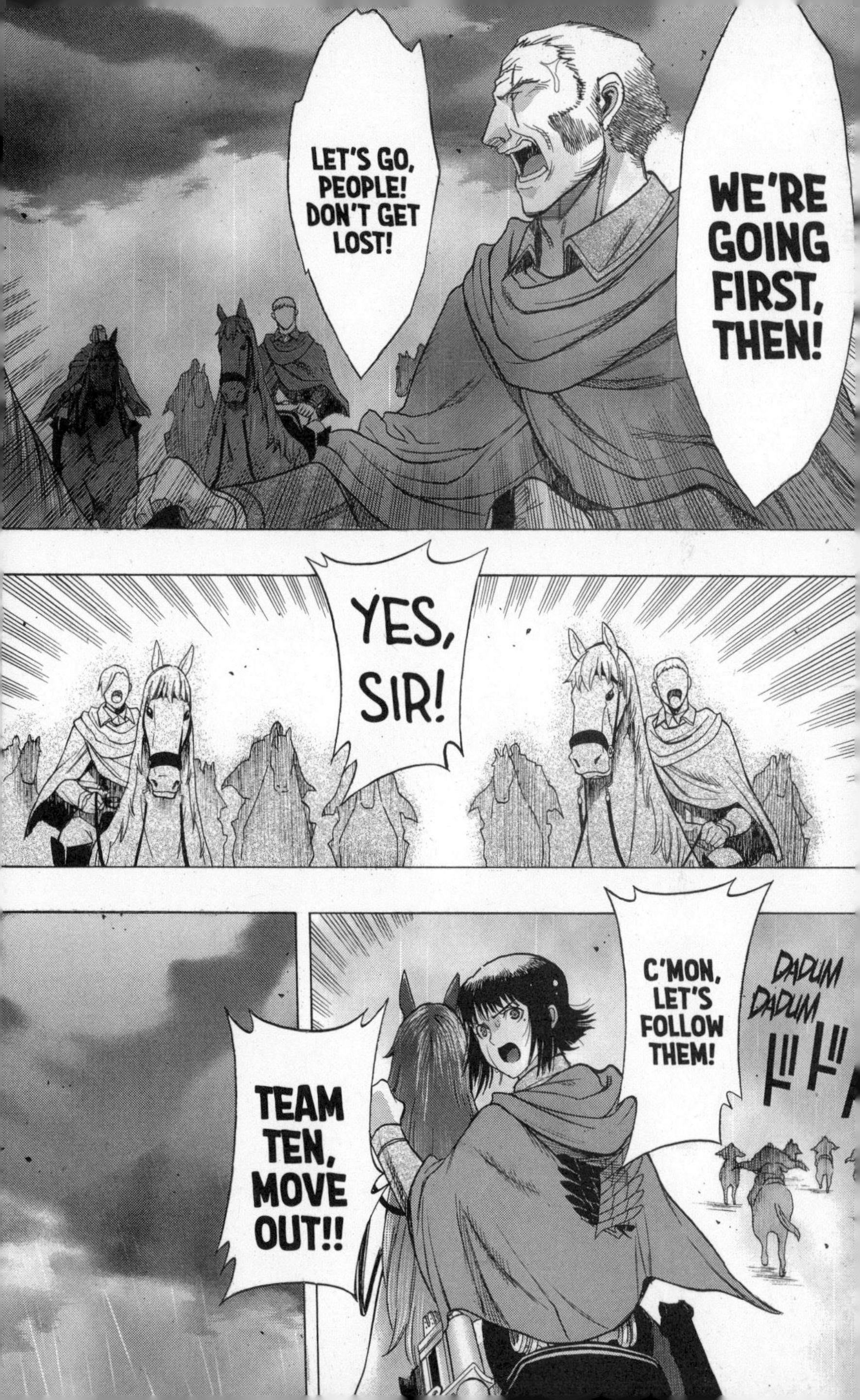
WE'RE GOING FIRST, THEN!
LET'S GO, PEOPLE! DON'T GET LOST!
YES, SIR!
C'MON, LET'S FOLLOW THEM!
DADUM DADUM
ドド
TEAM TEN, MOVE OUT!!

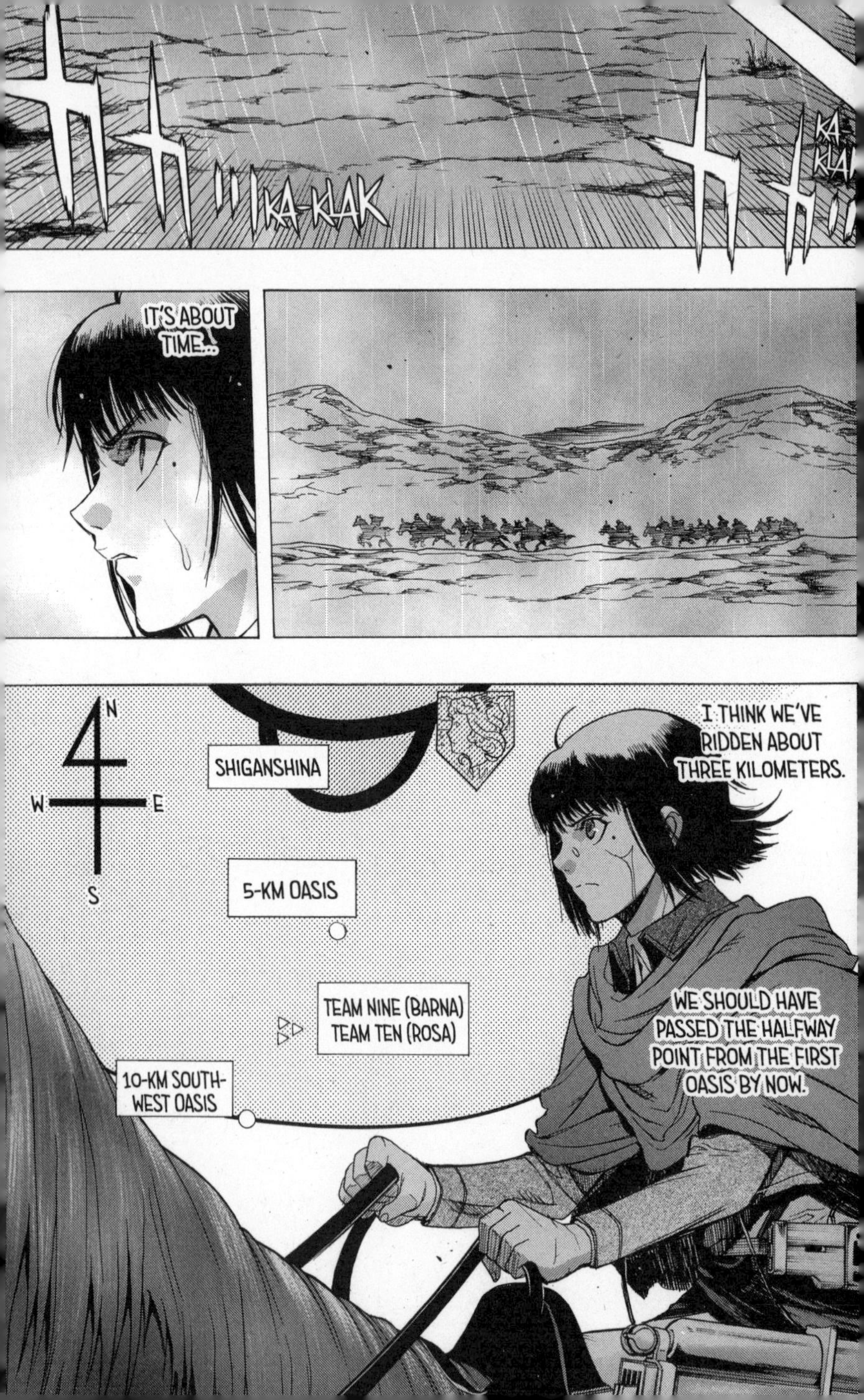
KA-KLA
KA-KLAK
IT'S ABOUT TIME...
I THINK WE'VE RIDDEN ABOUT THREE KILOMETERS.
N
SHIGANSHINA
W
E
S
5-KM OASIS
WE SHOULD HAVE PASSED THE HALFWAY POINT FROM THE FIRST OASIS BY NOW.
TEAM NINE (BARNA)
TEAM TEN (ROSA)
10-KM SOUTH-WEST OASIS

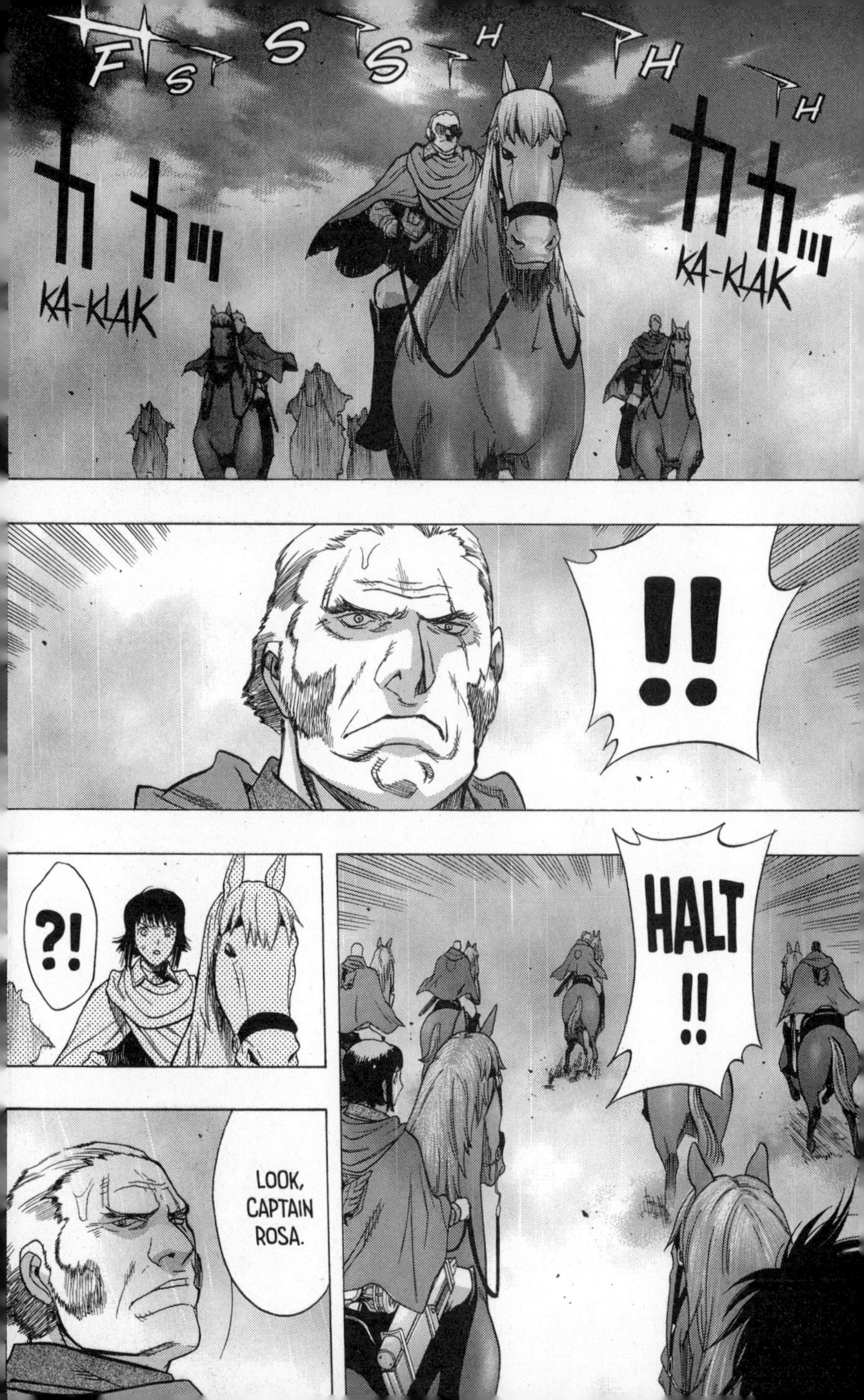
FSSSHHH
カカッ
KA-KLAK
カカッ
KA-KLAK
!!
HALT !!
?!
LOOK, CAPTAIN ROSA.

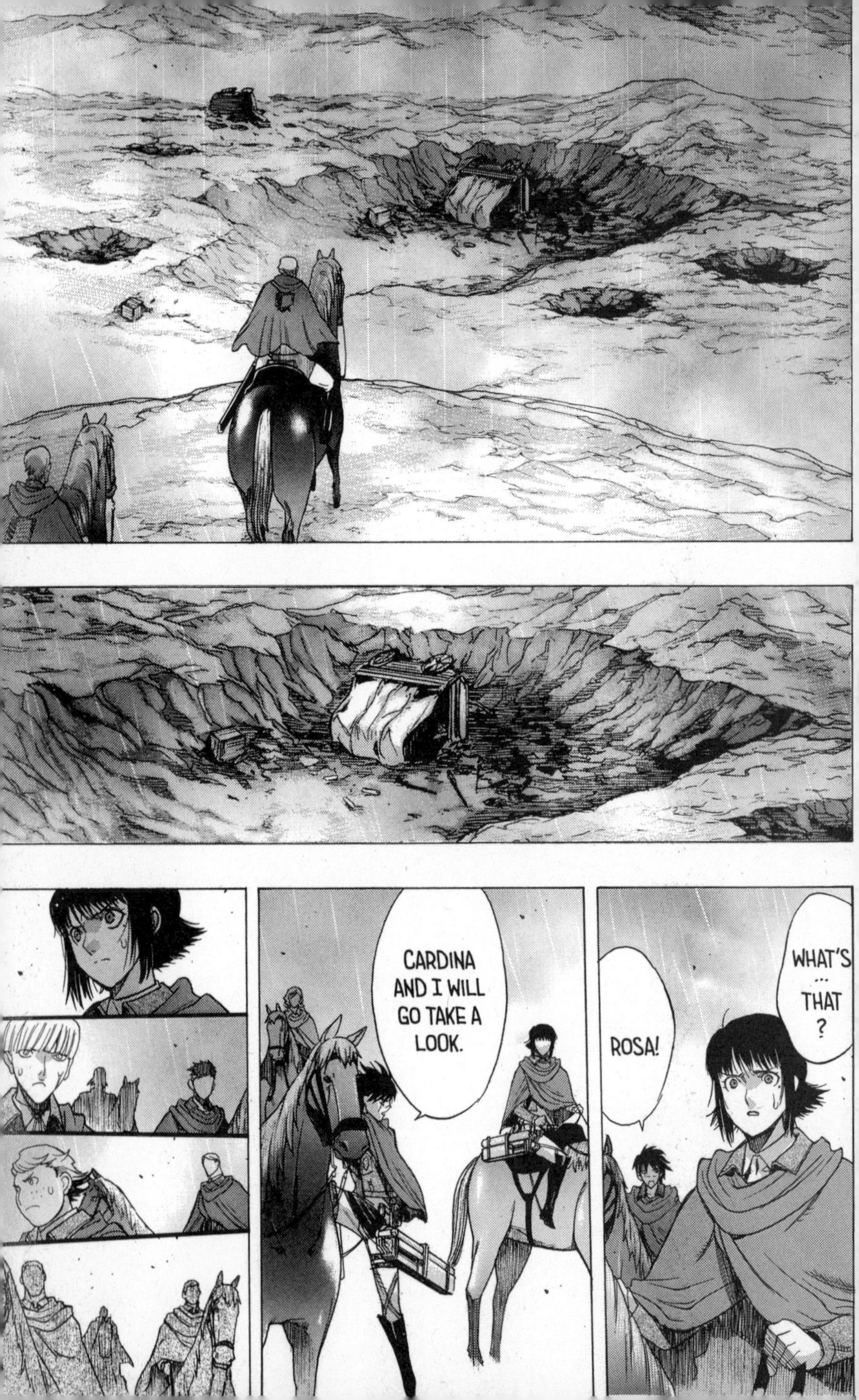
WHAT'S ... THAT?
ROSA!
CARDINA AND I WILL GO TAKE A LOOK.

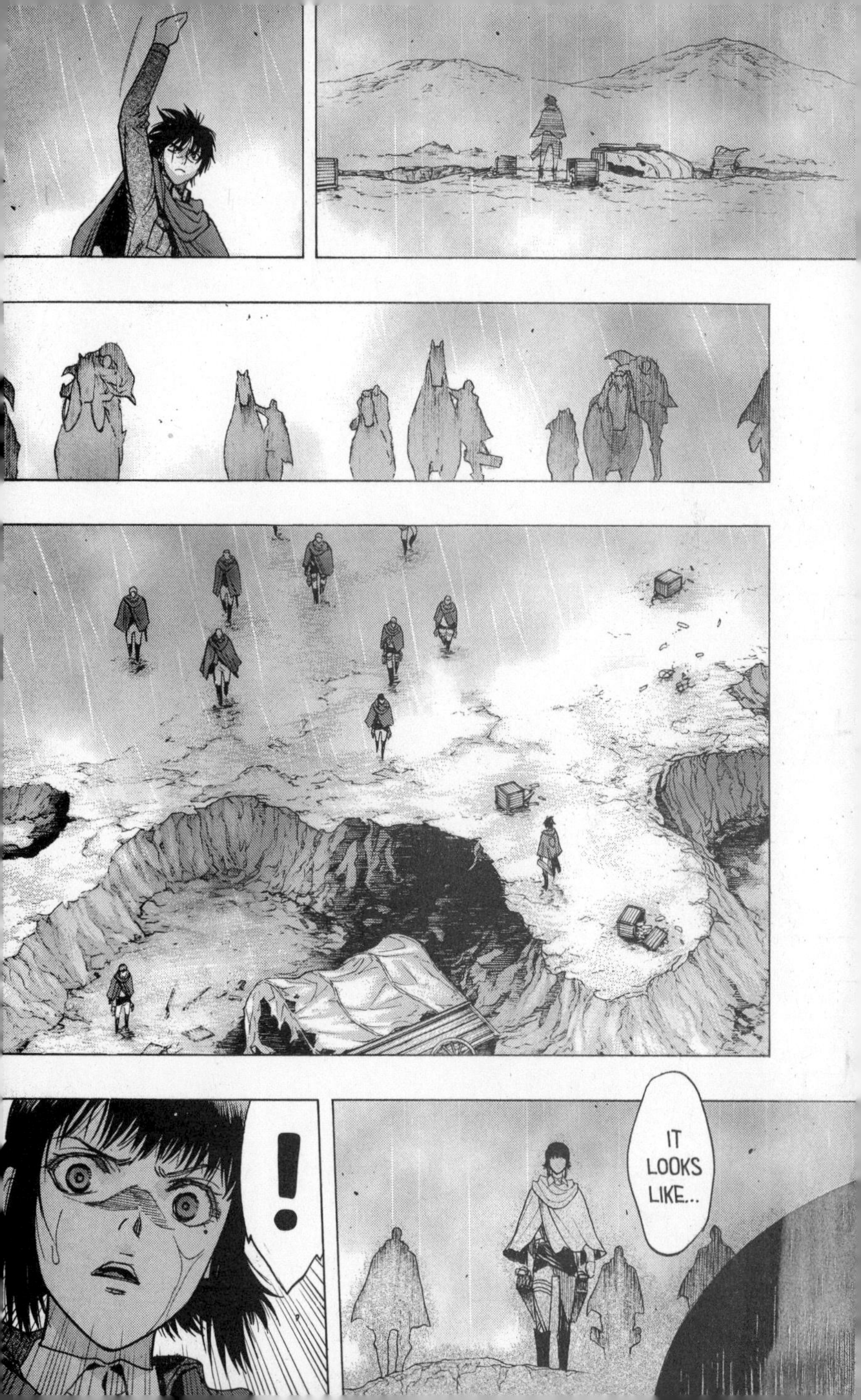
IT LOOKS LIKE...
!

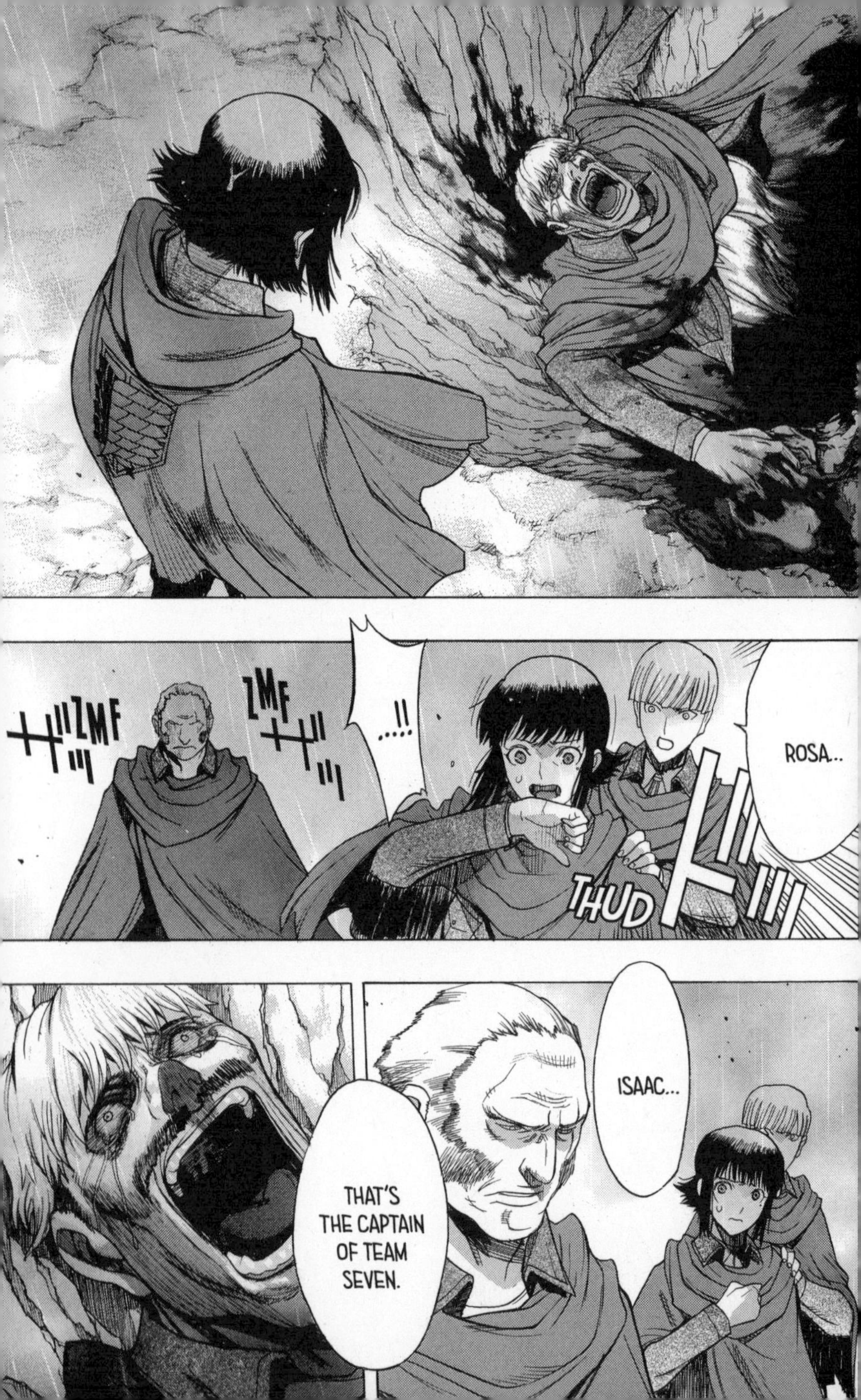
ROSA...
THUD
...!!
ZMF
ZMF
ISAAC...
THAT'S THE CAPTAIN OF TEAM SEVEN.

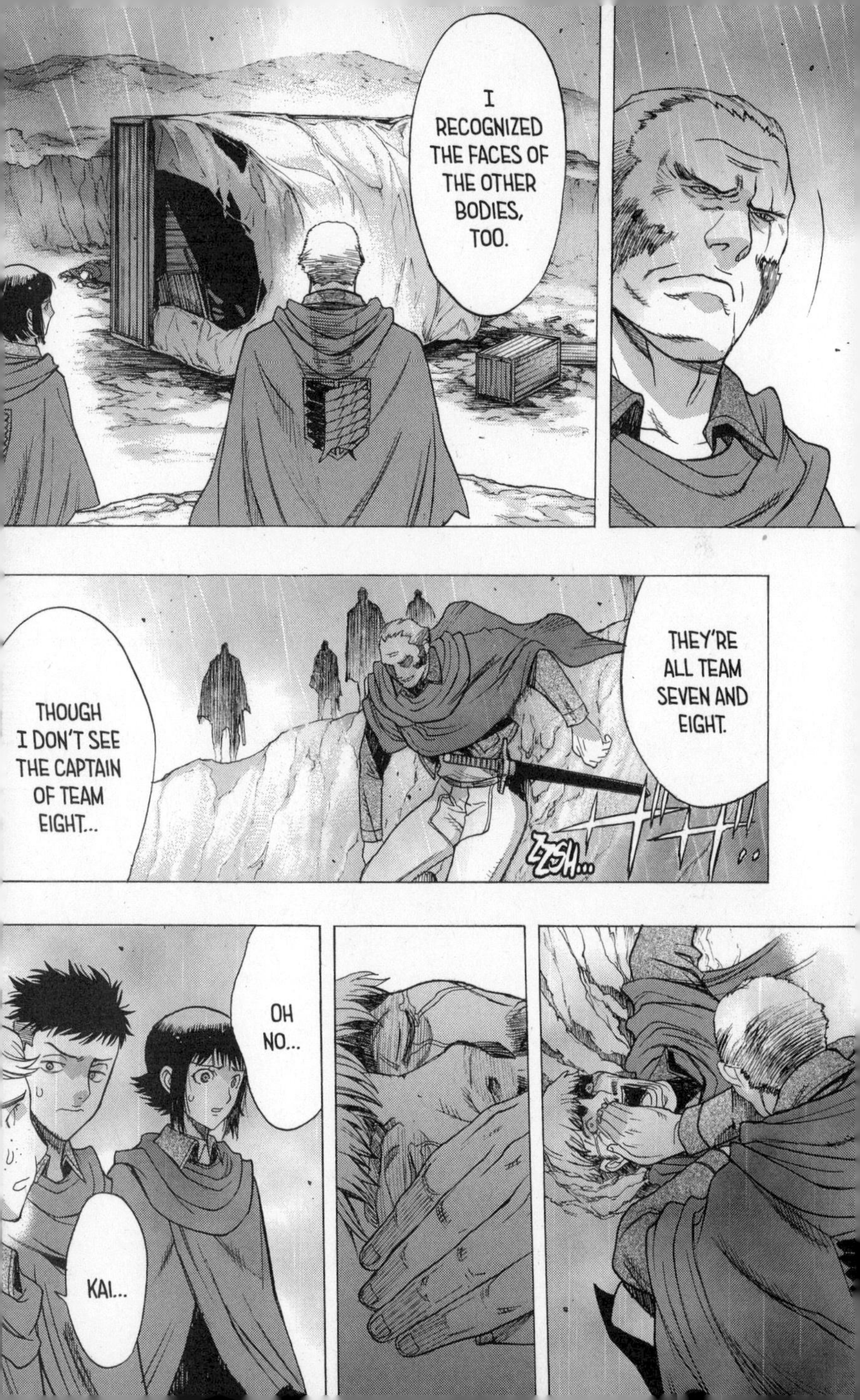
I RECOGNIZED THE FACES OF THE OTHER BODIES, TOO.
THEY'RE ALL TEAM SEVEN AND EIGHT.
ZZSH...
THOUGH I DON'T SEE THE CAPTAIN OF TEAM EIGHT...
OH NO...
KAI...

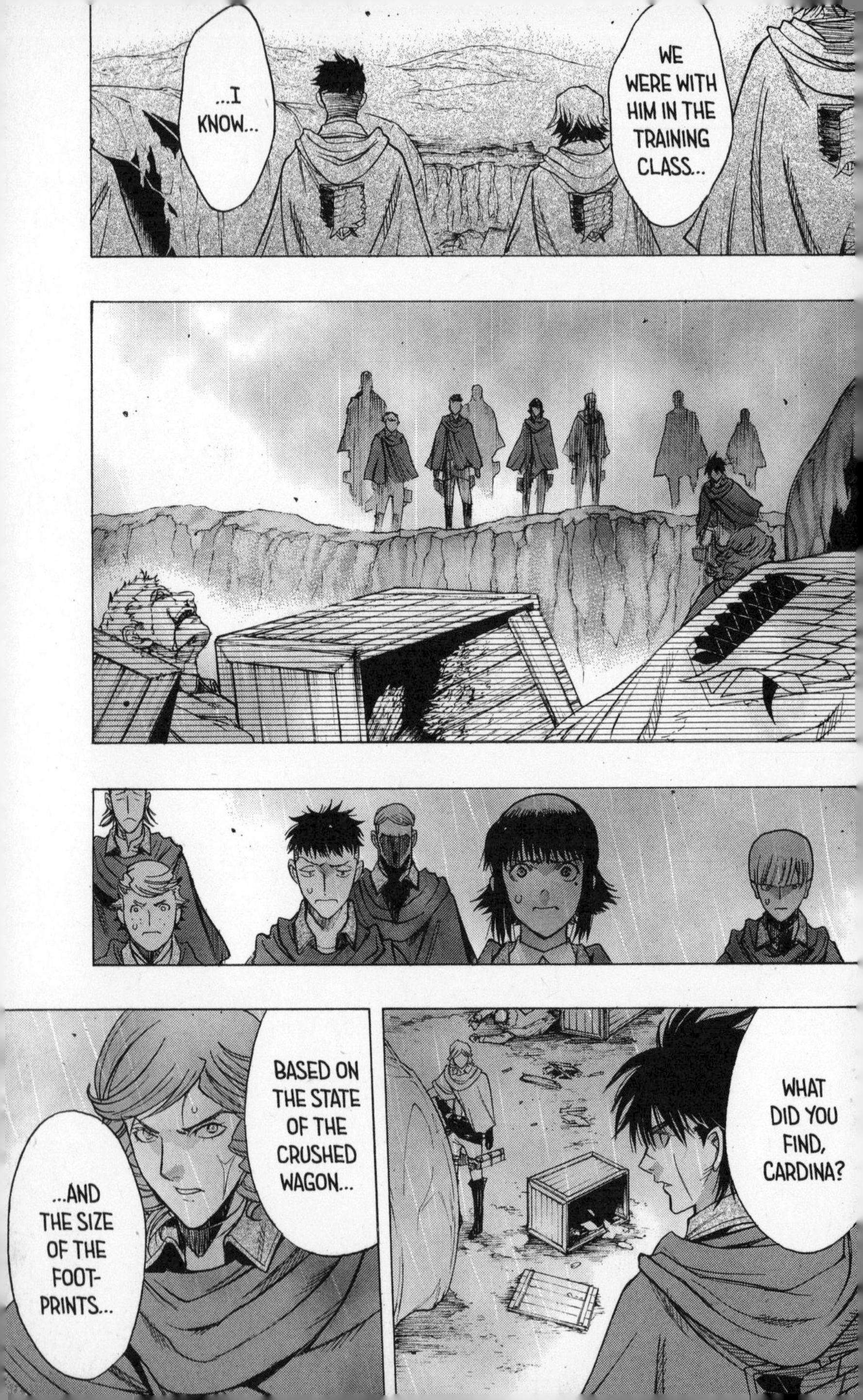
WE WERE WITH HIM IN THE TRAINING CLASS...
...I KNOW...
WHAT DID YOU FIND, CARDINA?
BASED ON THE STATE OF THE CRUSHED WAGON...
...AND THE SIZE OF THE FOOT-PRINTS...

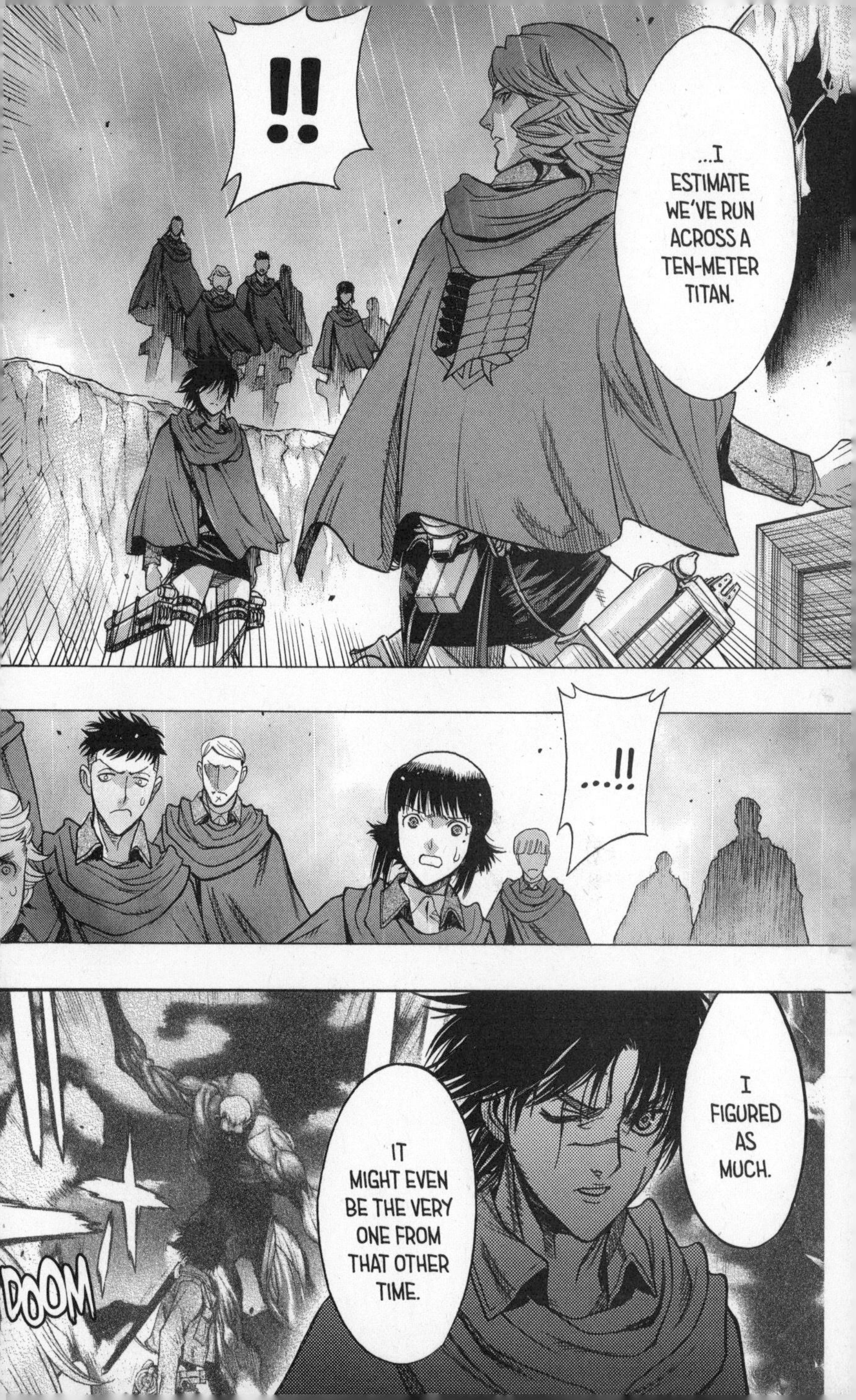

...I ESTIMATE WE'VE RUN ACROSS A TEN-METER TITAN.
!!
...!!
I FIGURED AS MUCH.
IT MIGHT EVEN BE THE VERY ONE FROM THAT OTHER TIME.
DOOM

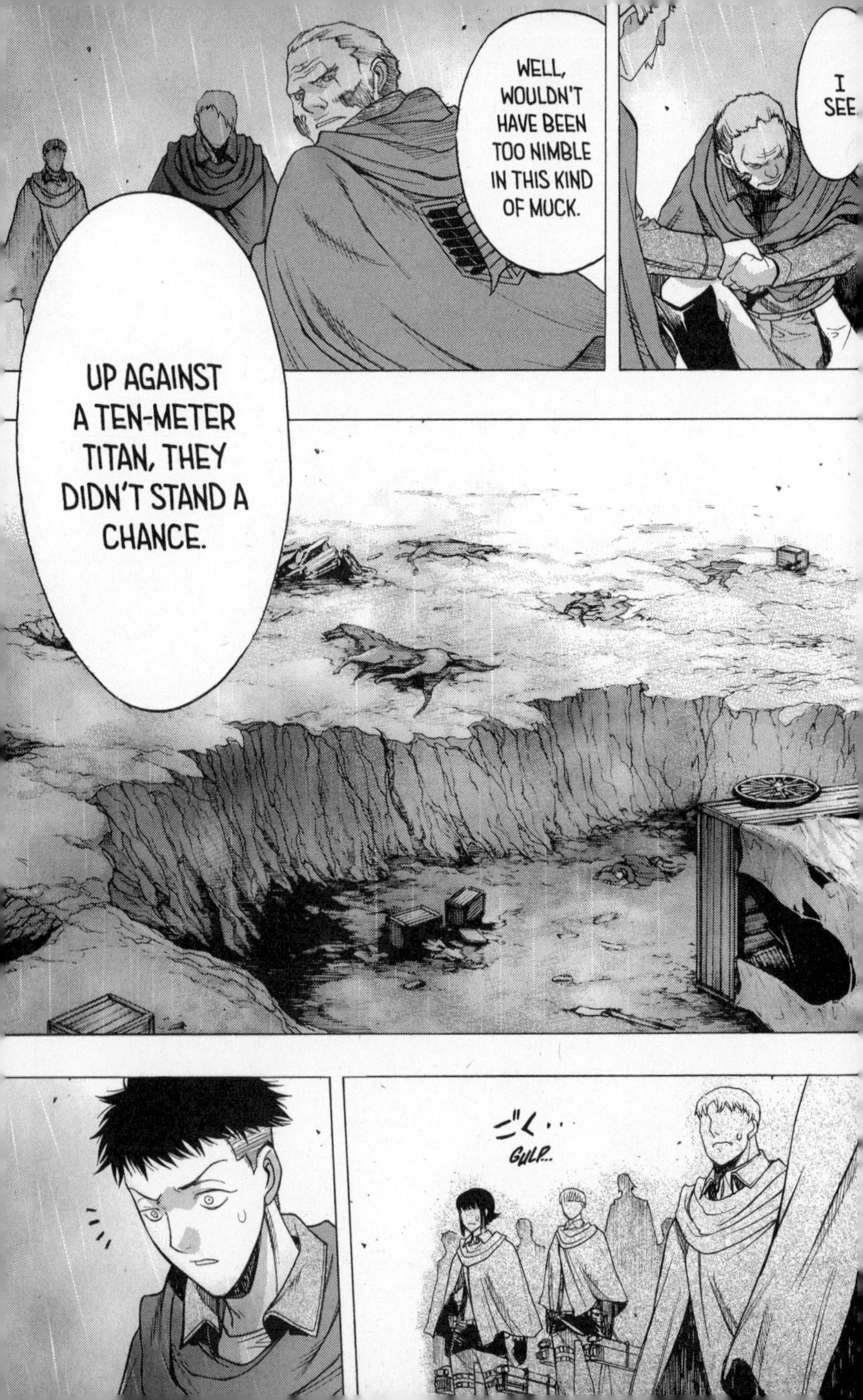
I SEE
WELL, WOULDN'T HAVE BEEN TOO NIMBLE IN THIS KIND OF MUCK.
UP AGAINST A TEN-METER TITAN, THEY DIDN'T STAND A CHANCE.
ごく…
GULP...

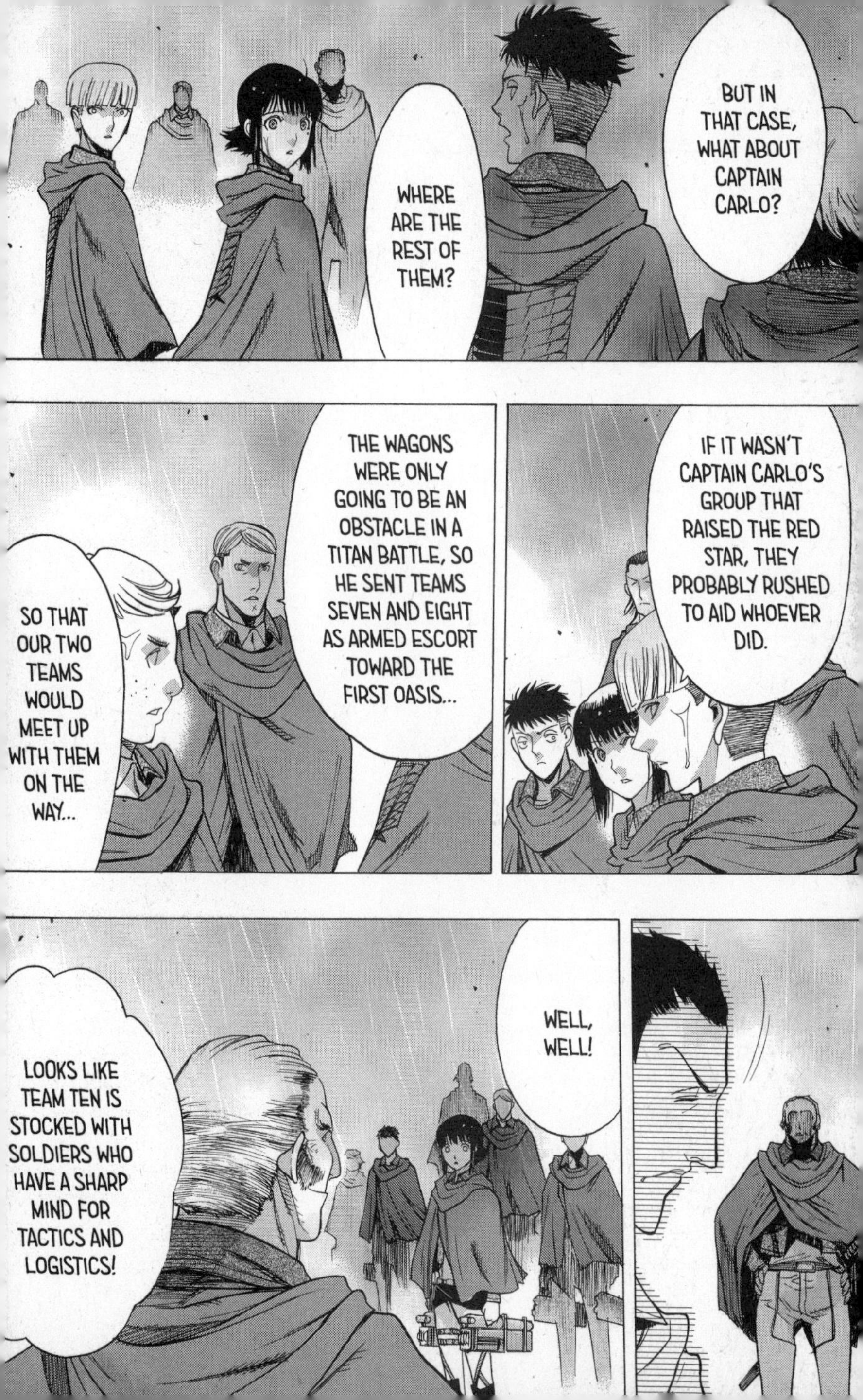
BUT IN THAT CASE, WHAT ABOUT CAPTAIN CARLO?
WHERE ARE THE REST OF THEM?
IF IT WASN'T CAPTAIN CARLO'S GROUP THAT RAISED THE RED STAR, THEY PROBABLY RUSHED TO AID WHOEVER DID.
THE WAGONS WERE ONLY GOING TO BE AN OBSTACLE IN A TITAN BATTLE, SO HE SENT TEAMS SEVEN AND EIGHT AS ARMED ESCORT TOWARD THE FIRST OASIS...
SO THAT OUR TWO TEAMS WOULD MEET UP WITH THEM ON THE WAY...
WELL, WELL!
LOOKS LIKE TEAM TEN IS STOCKED WITH SOLDIERS WHO HAVE A SHARP MIND FOR TACTICS AND LOGISTICS!

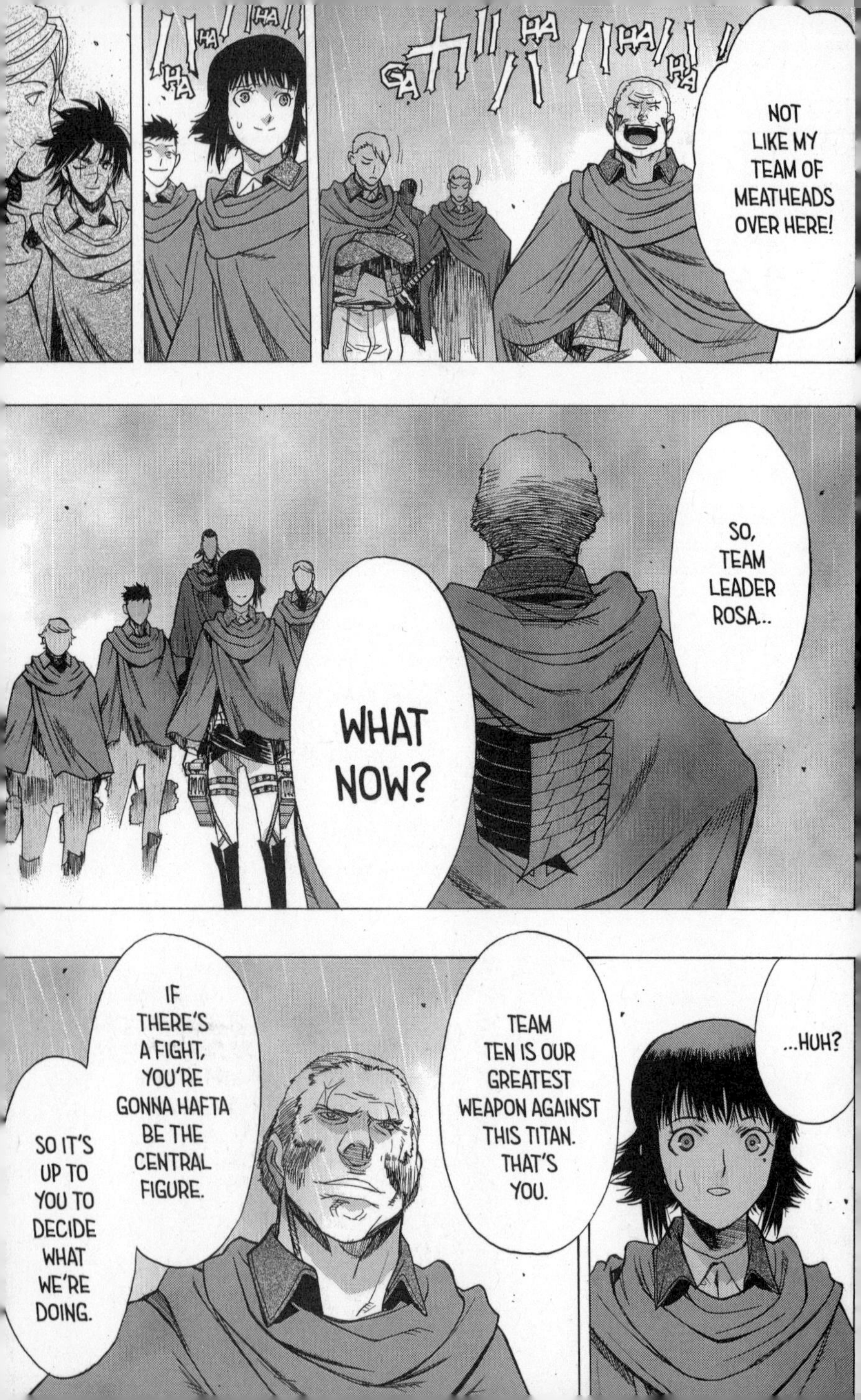
NOT LIKE MY TEAM OF MEATHEADS OVER HERE!
SO, TEAM LEADER ROSA...
WHAT NOW?
...HUH?
TEAM TEN IS OUR GREATEST WEAPON AGAINST THIS TITAN. THAT'S YOU.
IF THERE'S A FIGHT, YOU'RE GONNA HAFTA BE THE CENTRAL FIGURE.
SO IT'S UP TO YOU TO DECIDE WHAT WE'RE DOING.

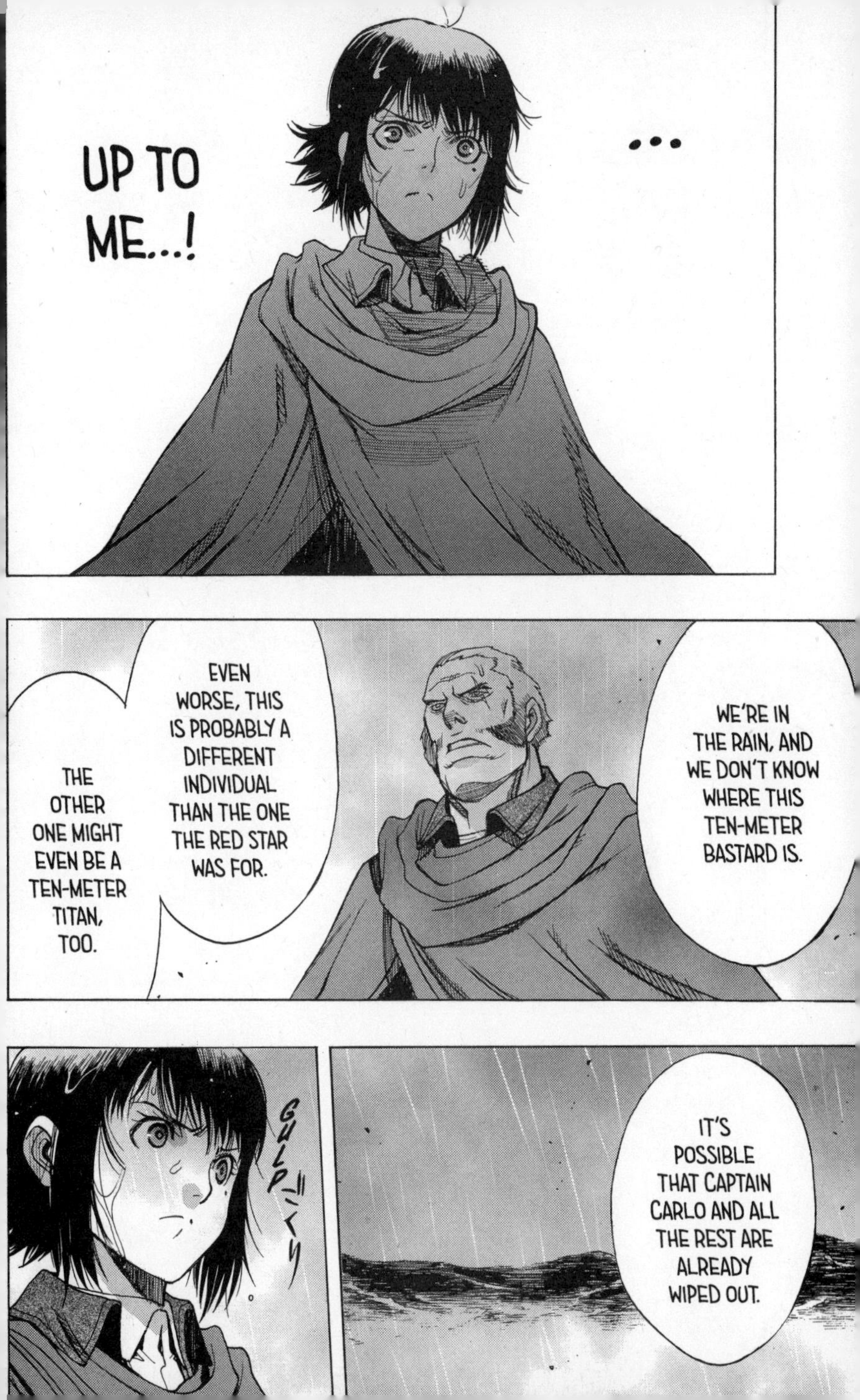
...
UP TO ME...!
WE'RE IN THE RAIN, AND WE DON'T KNOW WHERE THIS TEN-METER BASTARD IS.
EVEN WORSE, THIS IS PROBABLY A DIFFERENT INDIVIDUAL THAN THE ONE THE RED STAR WAS FOR.
THE OTHER ONE MIGHT EVEN BE A TEN-METER TITAN, TOO.
IT'S POSSIBLE THAT CAPTAIN CARLO AND ALL THE REST ARE ALREADY WIPED OUT.
GULP

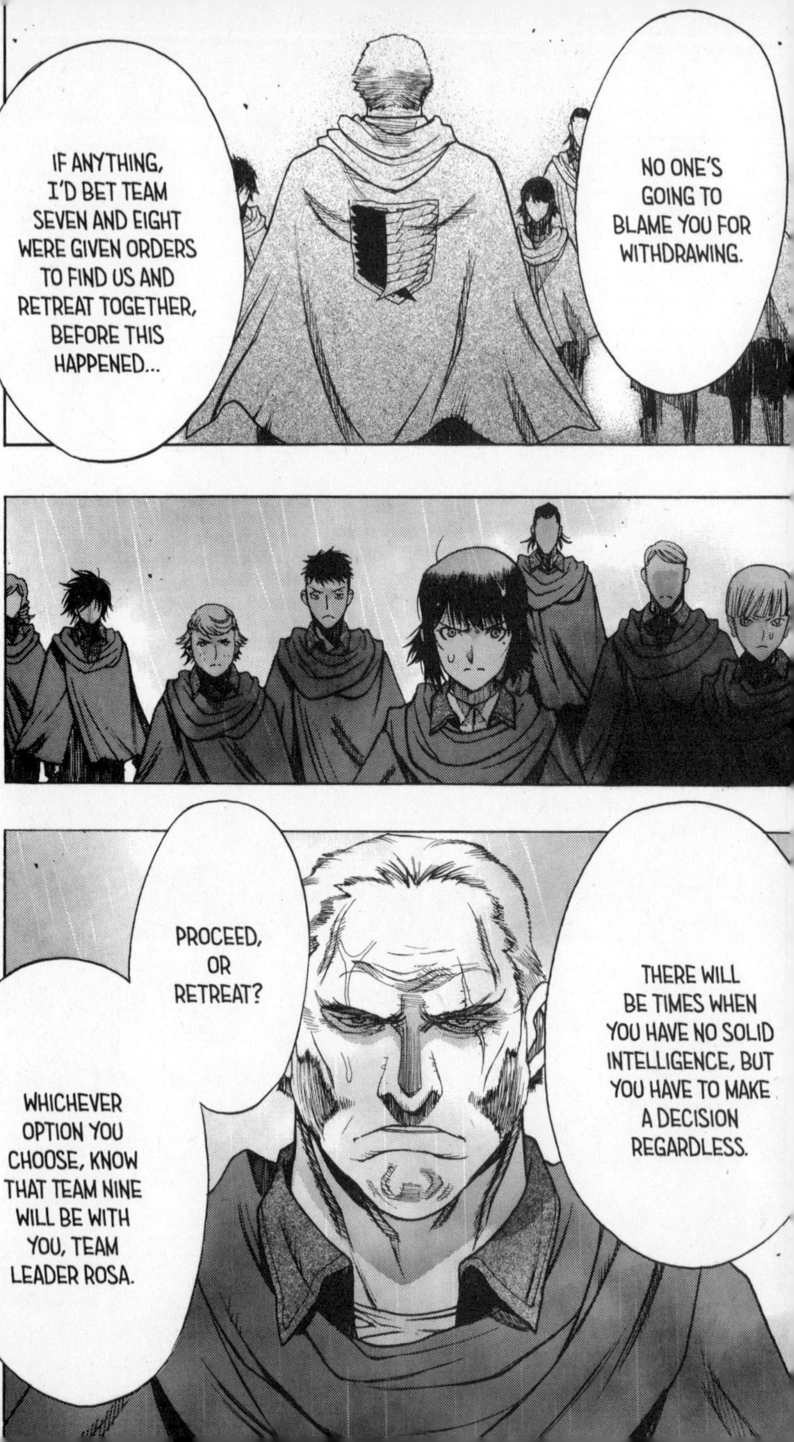
NO ONE'S GOING TO BLAME YOU FOR WITHDRAWING.
IF ANYTHING, I'D BET TEAM SEVEN AND EIGHT WERE GIVEN ORDERS TO FIND US AND RETREAT TOGETHER, BEFORE THIS HAPPENED...
THERE WILL BE TIMES WHEN YOU HAVE NO SOLID INTELLIGENCE, BUT YOU HAVE TO MAKE A DECISION REGARDLESS.
PROCEED, OR RETREAT?
WHICHEVER OPTION YOU CHOOSE, KNOW THAT TEAM NINE WILL BE WITH YOU, TEAM LEADER ROSA.

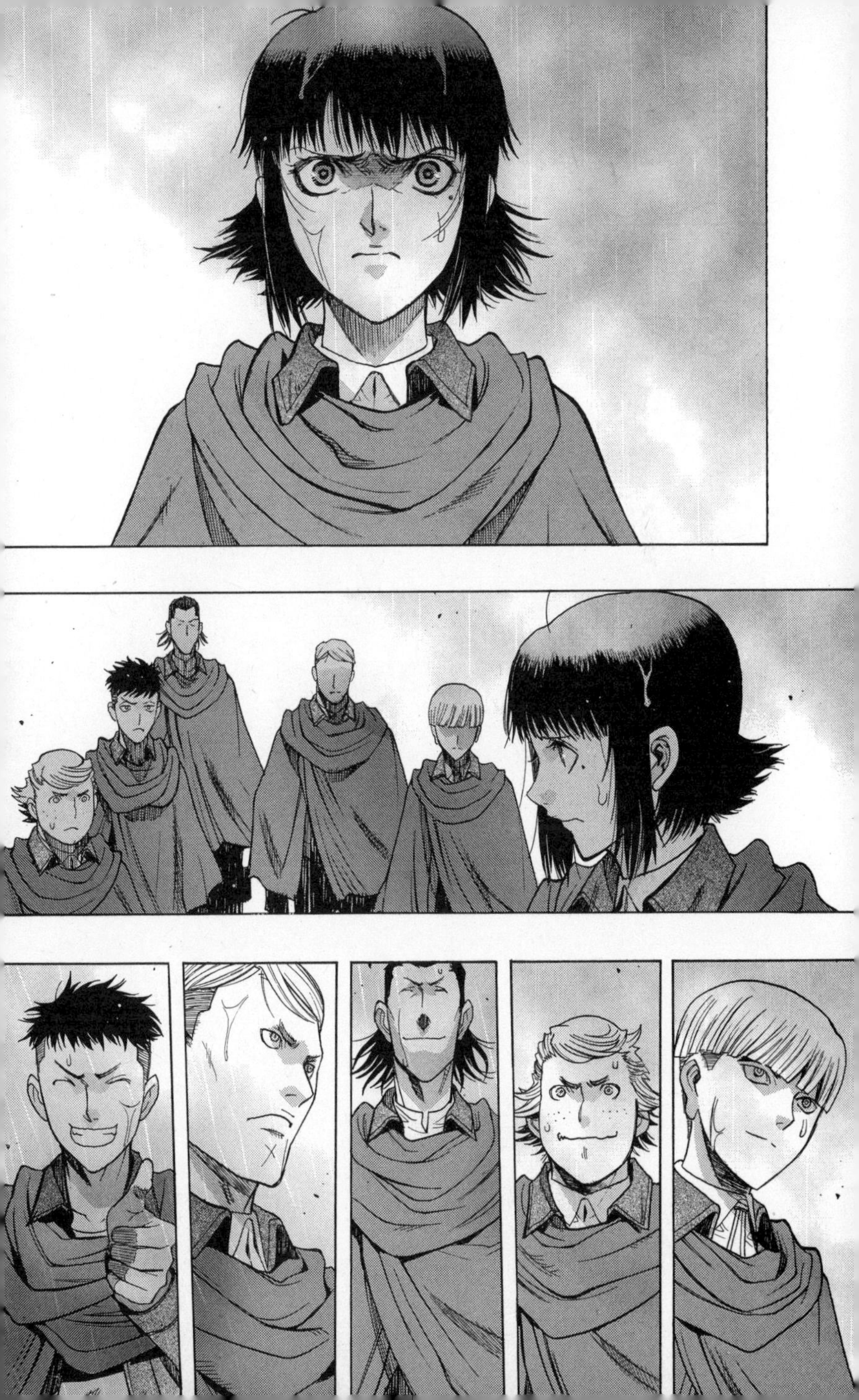

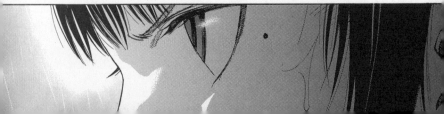

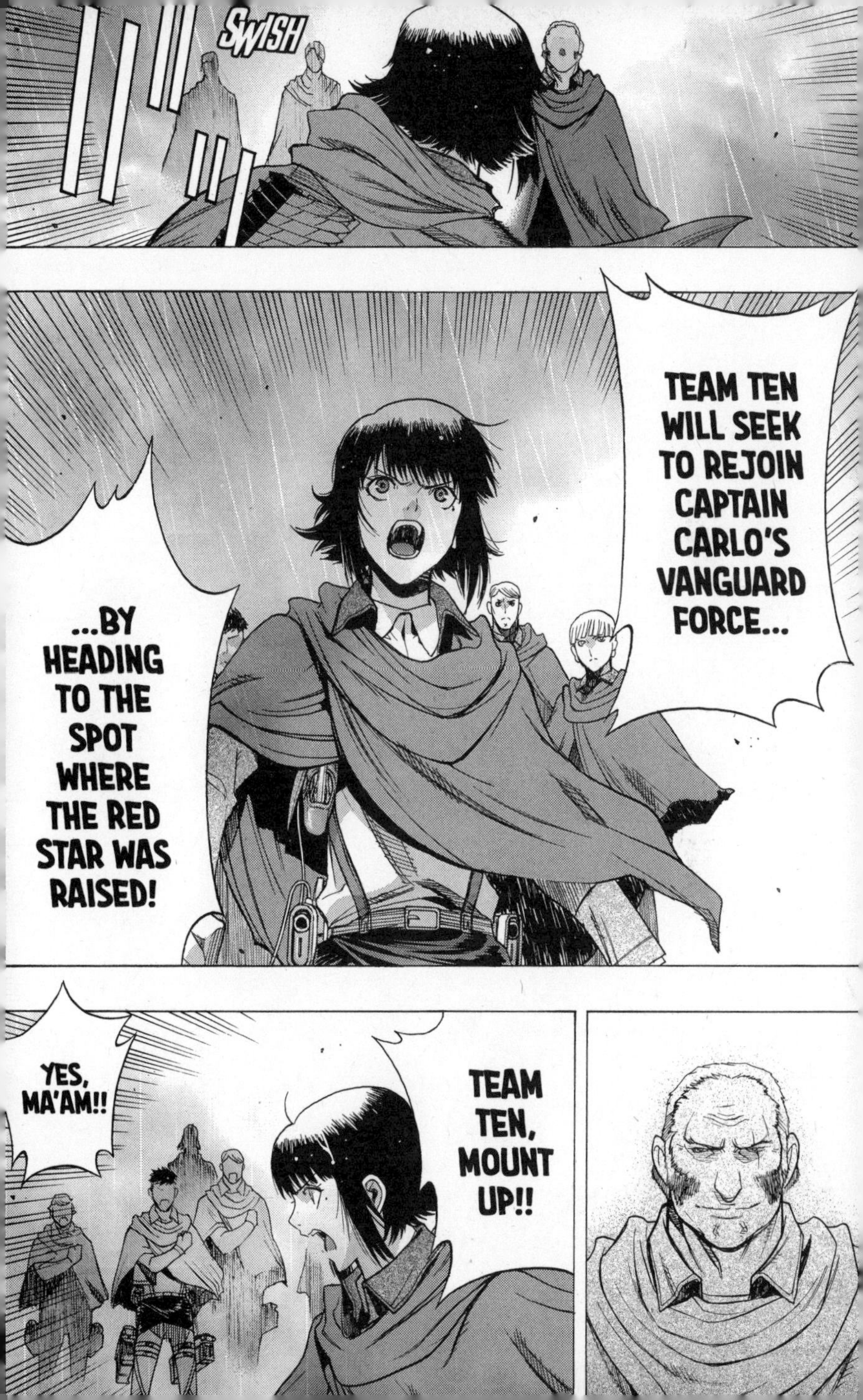
SWISH
TEAM TEN WILL SEEK TO REJOIN CAPTAIN CARLO'S VANGUARD FORCE...
...BY HEADING TO THE SPOT WHERE THE RED STAR WAS RAISED!
TEAM TEN, MOUNT UP!!
YES, MA'AM!!

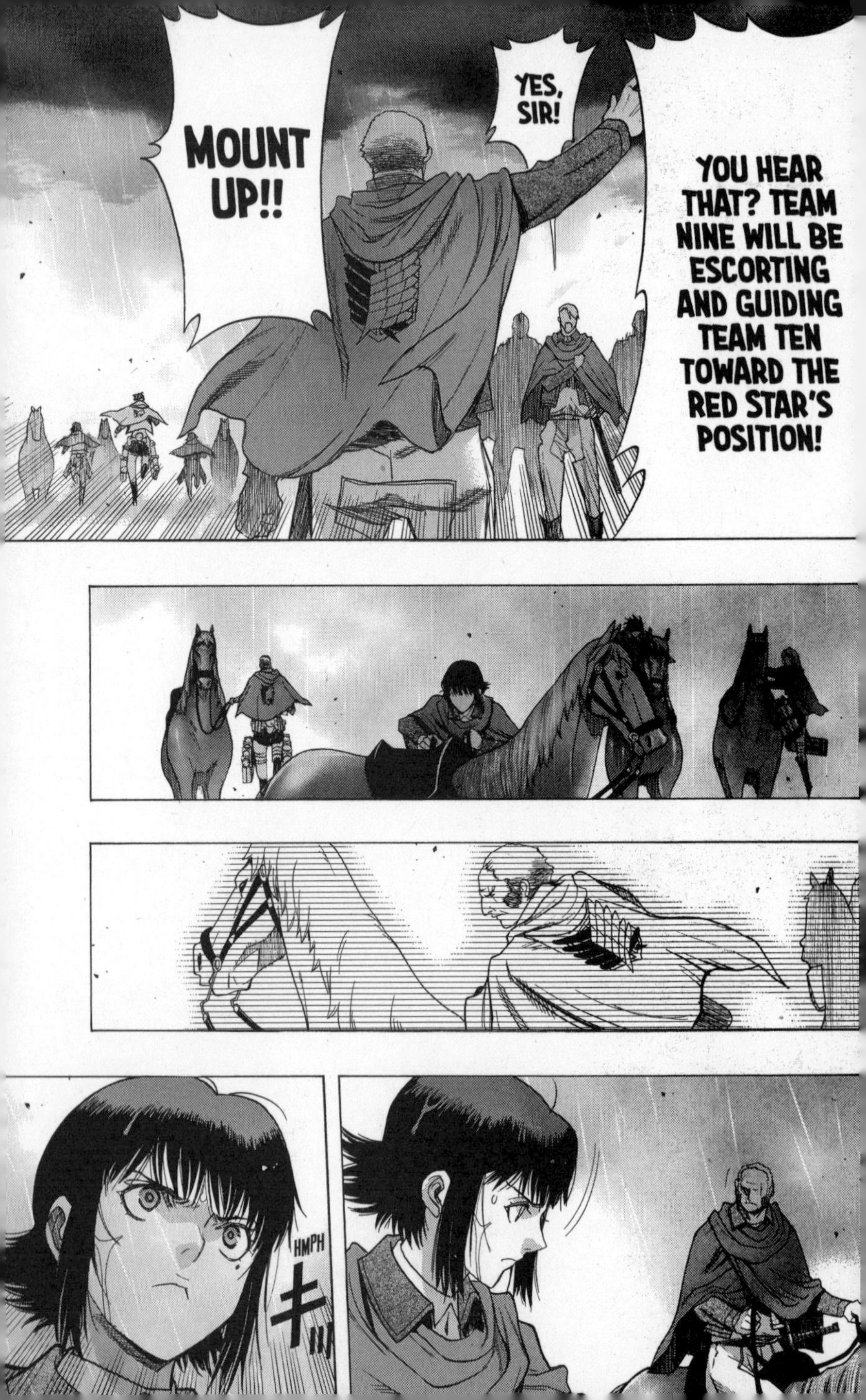
YOU HEAR THAT? TEAM NINE WILL BE ESCORTING AND GUIDING TEAM TEN TOWARD THE RED STAR'S POSITION!
YES, SIR!
MOUNT UP!!
HMPH

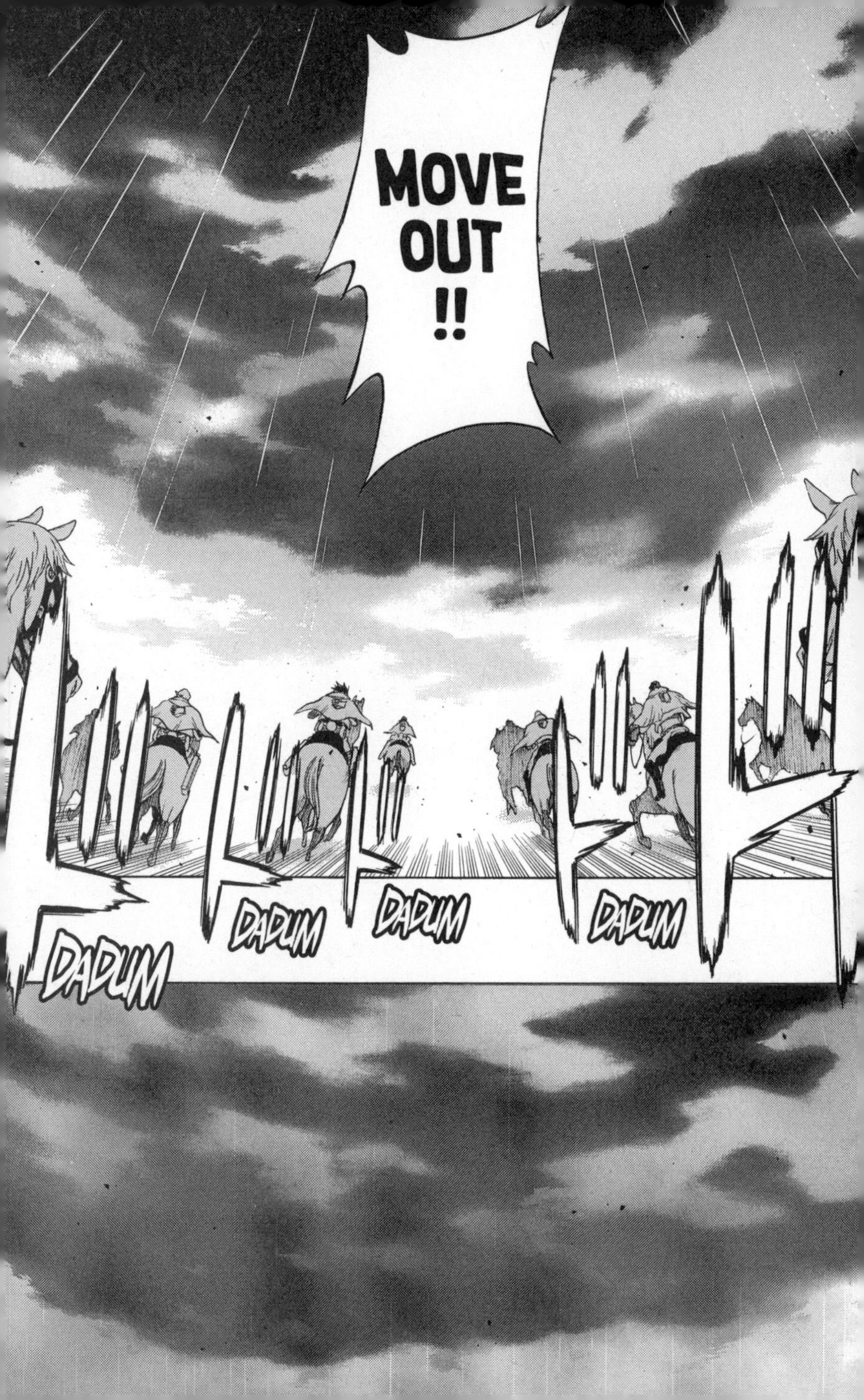
MOVE OUT!!
DADUM
DADUM
DADUM
DADUM

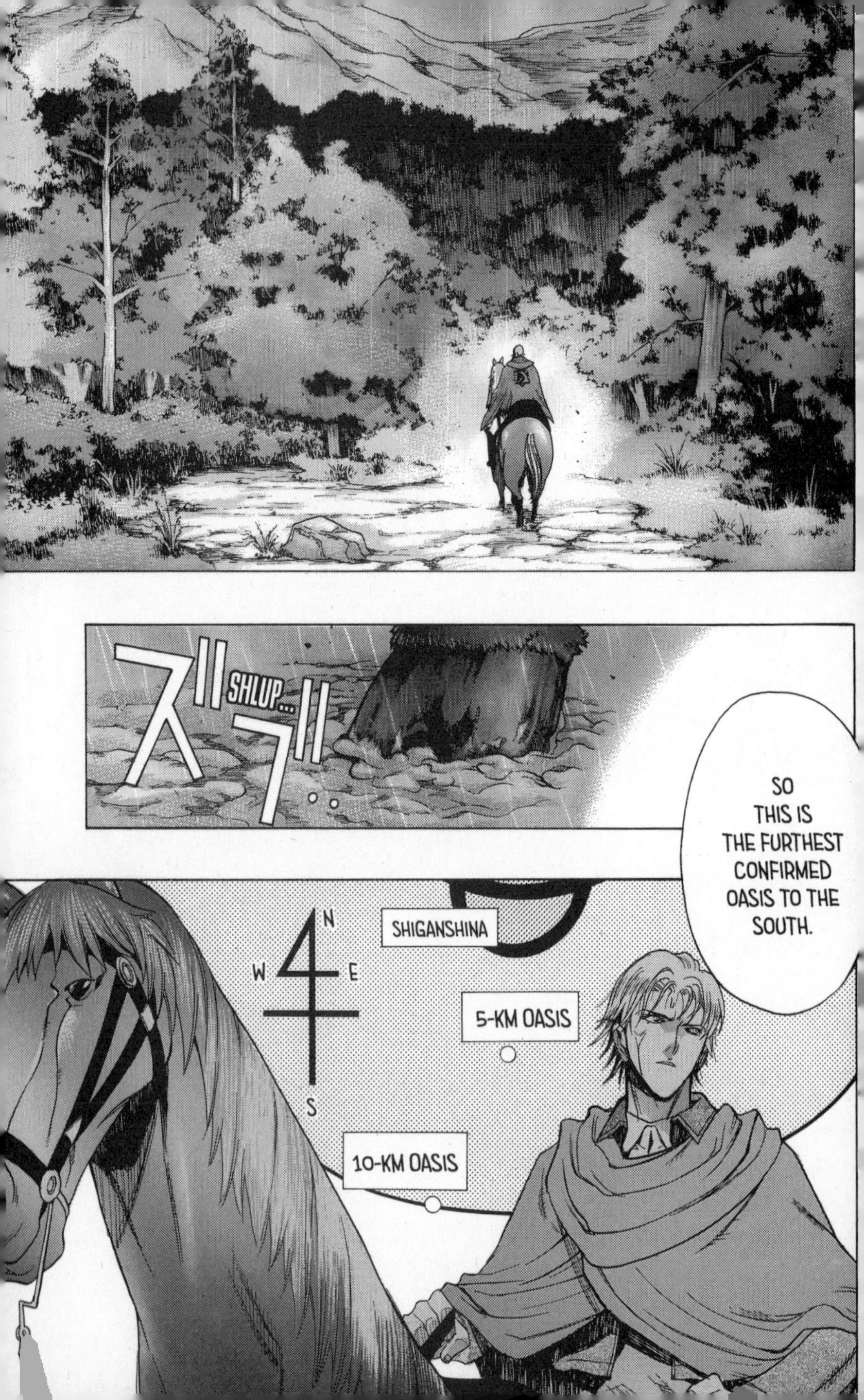
SHLUP...
SO THIS IS THE FURTHEST CONFIRMED OASIS TO THE SOUTH.
N
W
E
S
SHIGANSHINA
5-KM OASIS
10-KM OASIS

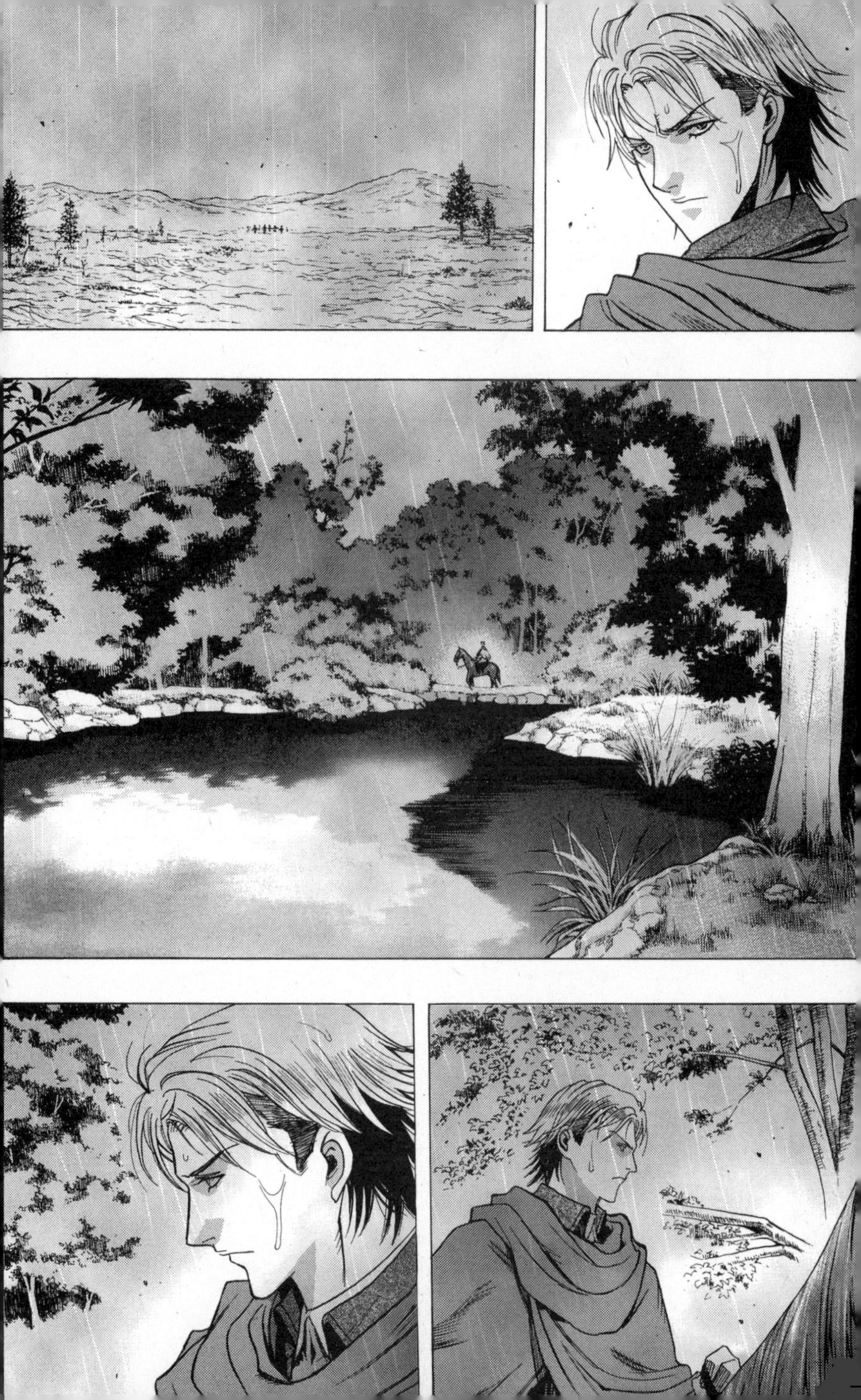

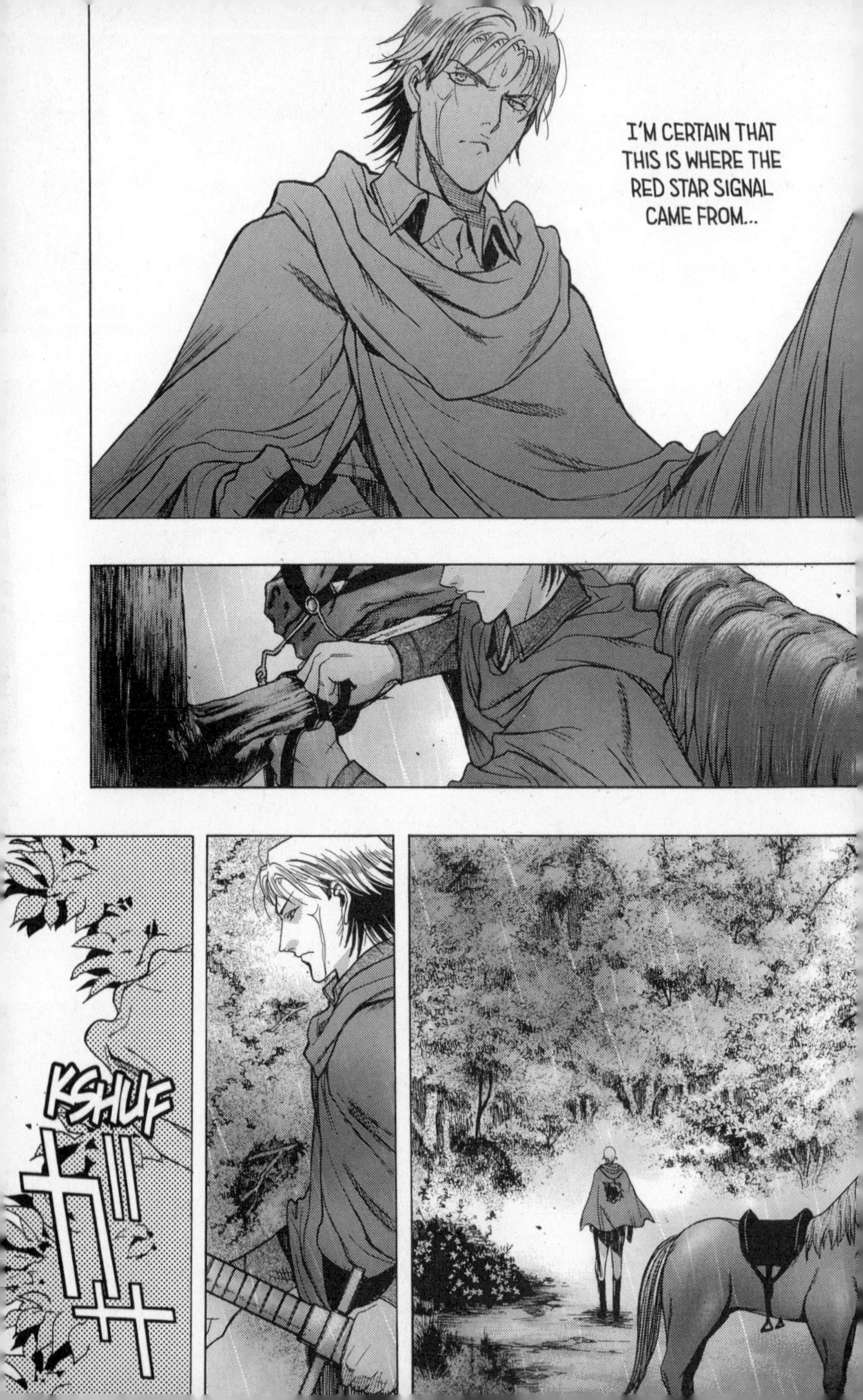
I'M CERTAIN THAT THIS IS WHERE THE RED STAR SIGNAL CAME FROM...
KSHUF

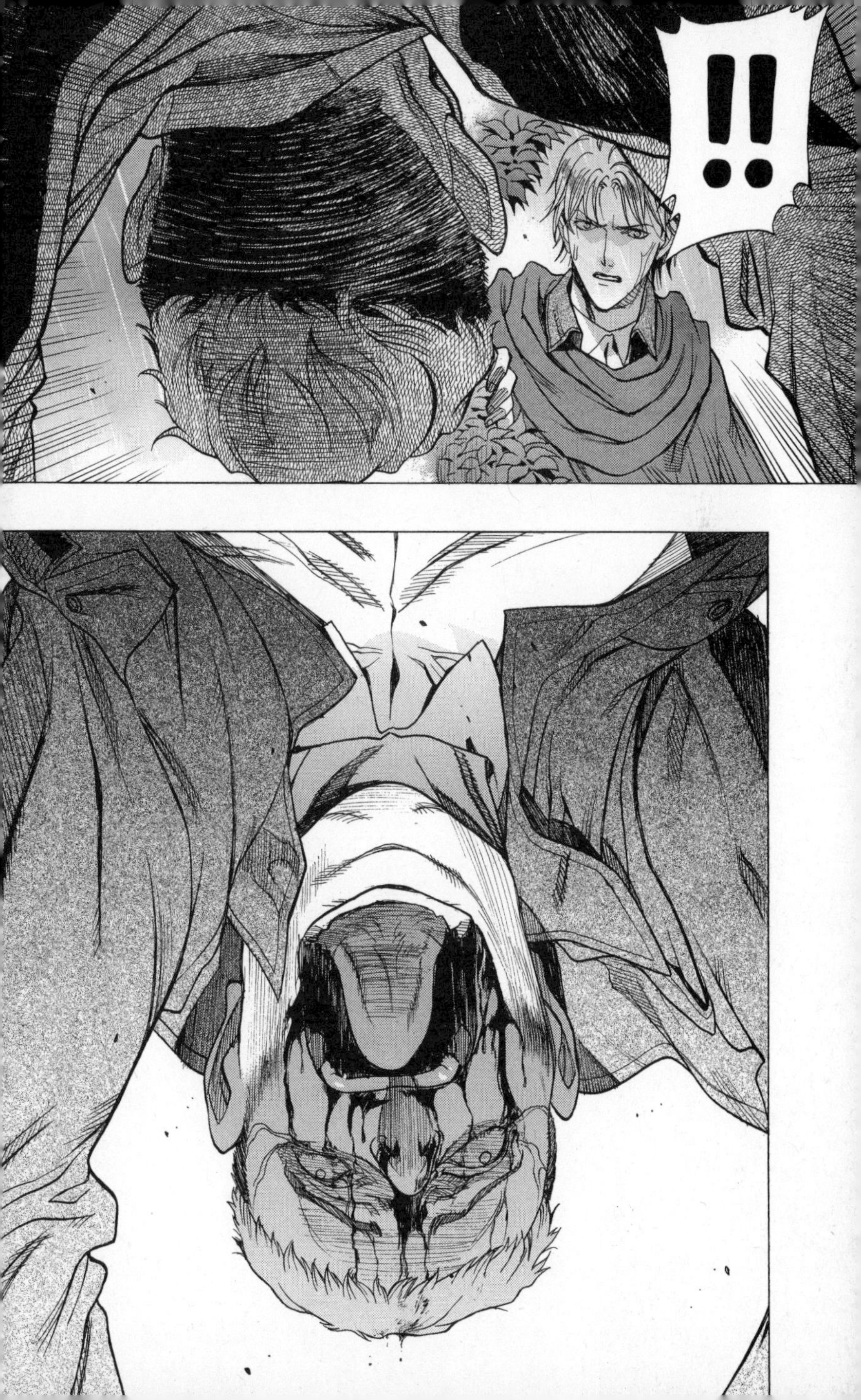
!!

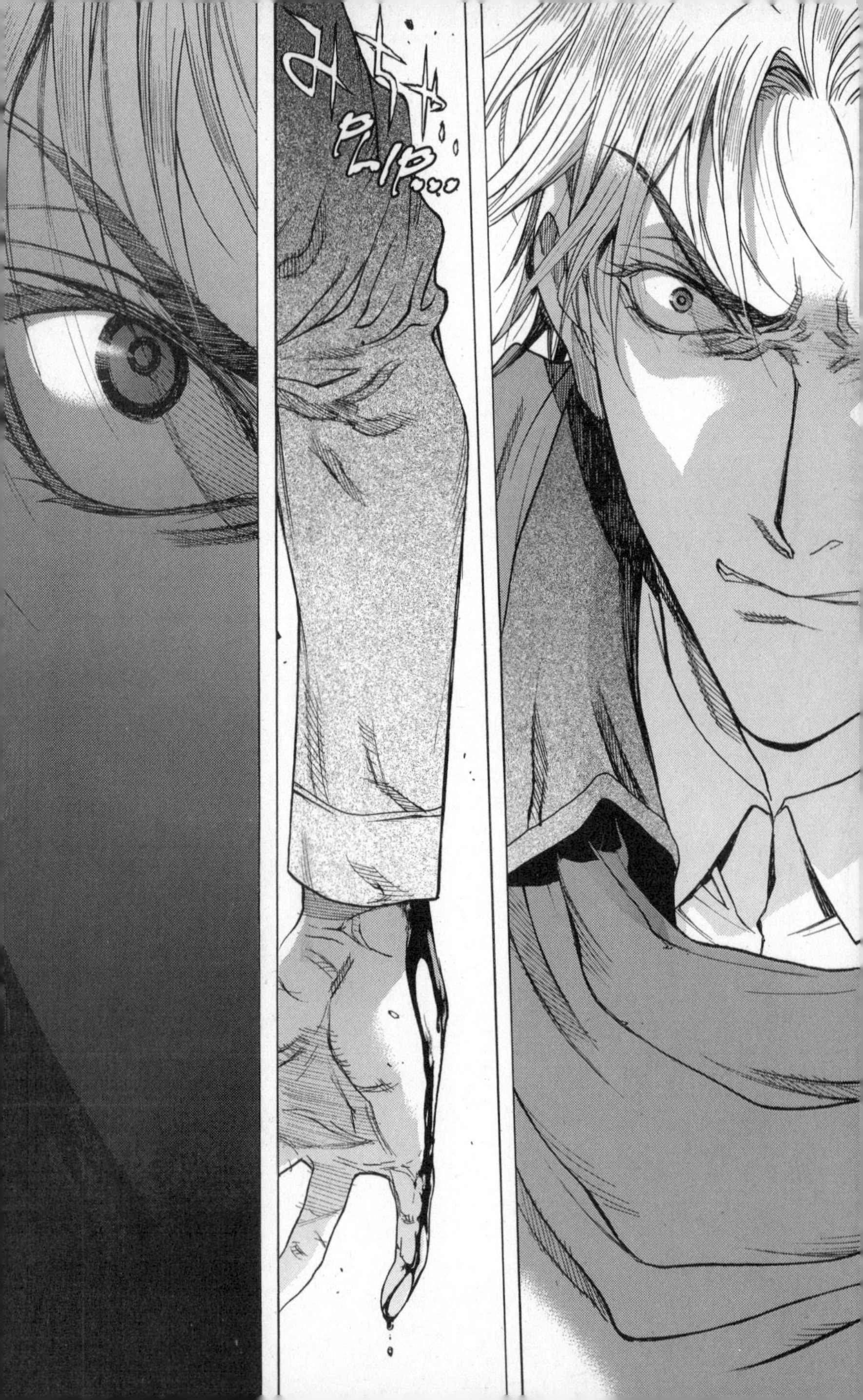
みちゃ
ぬりゅ…

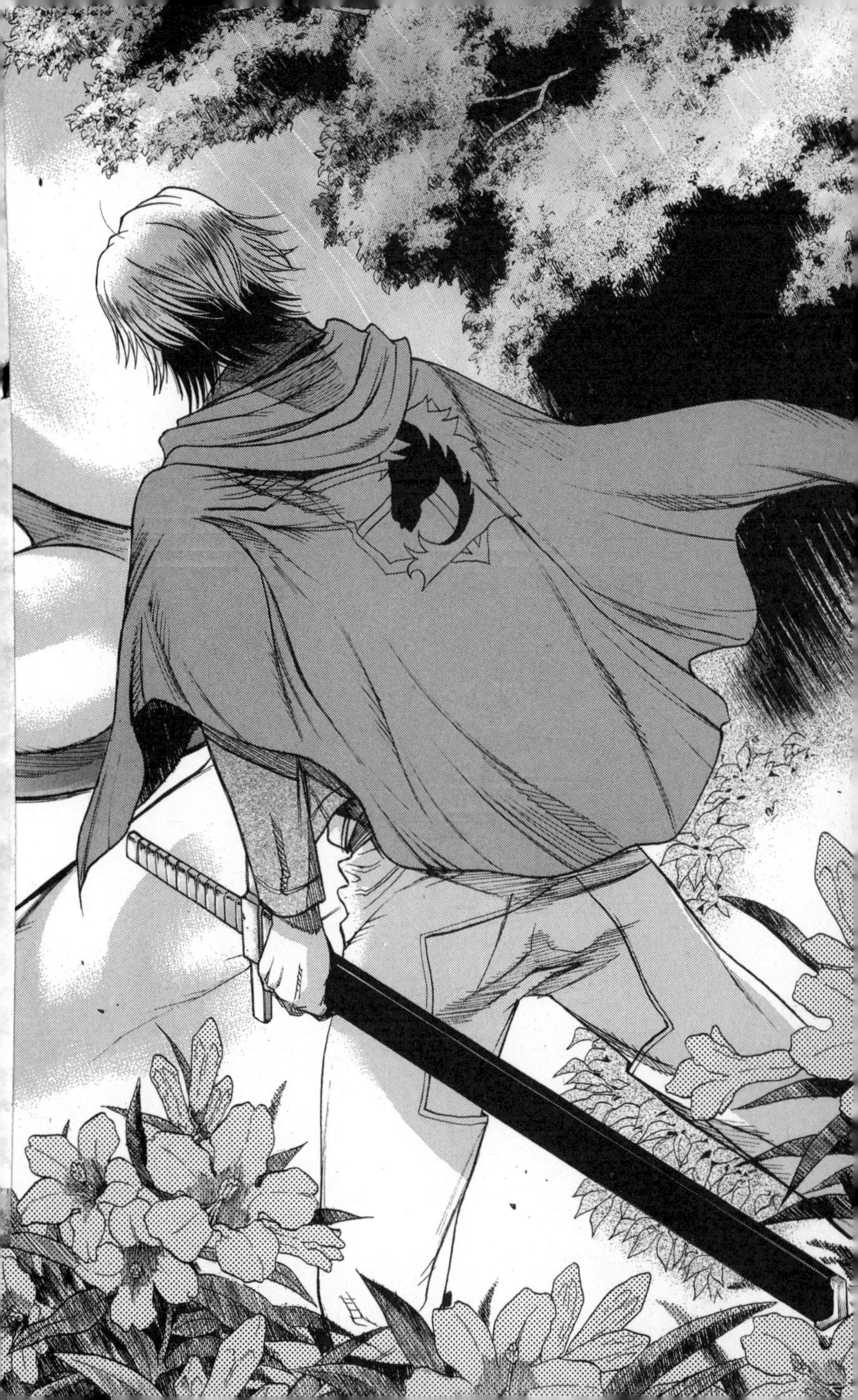

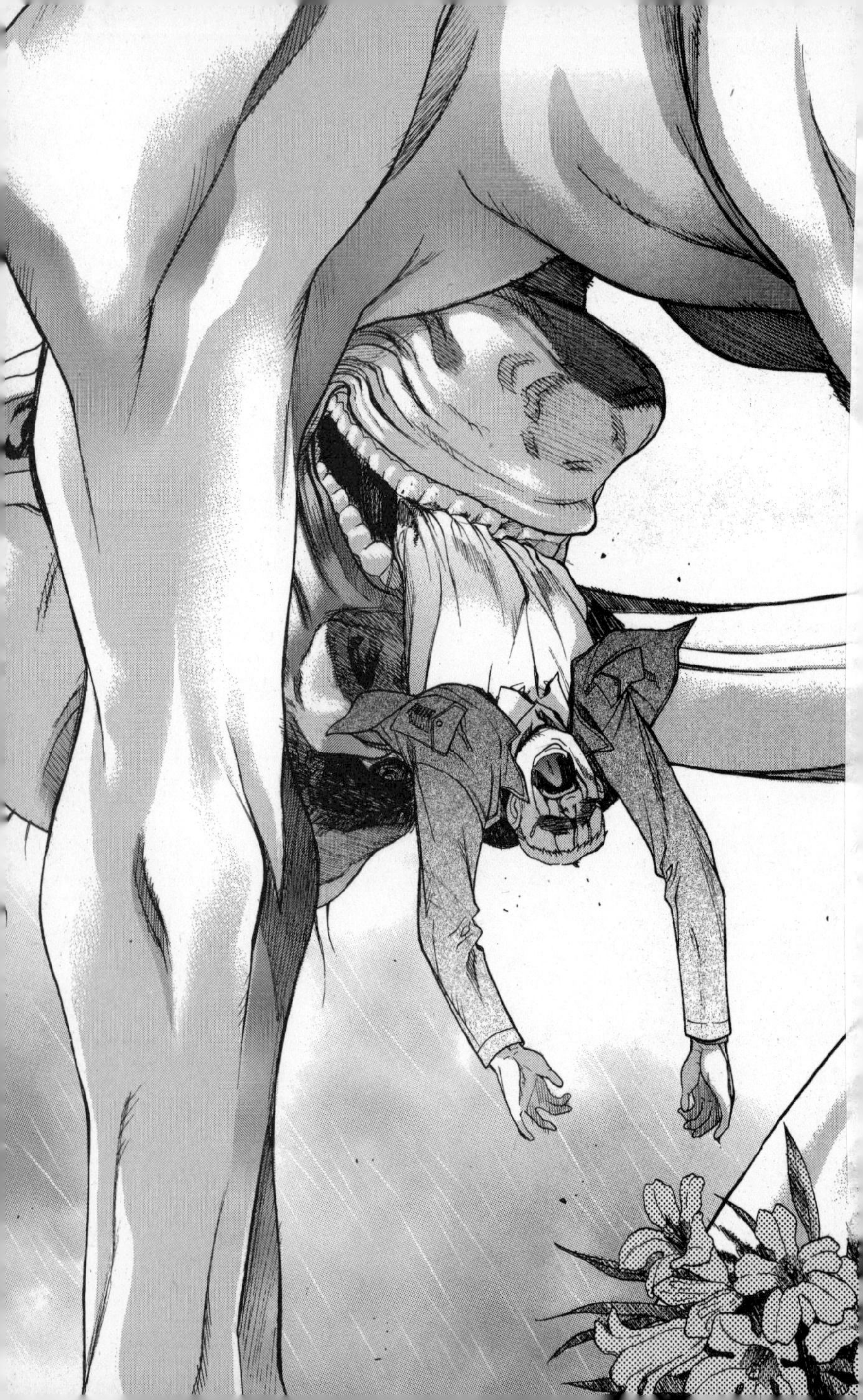

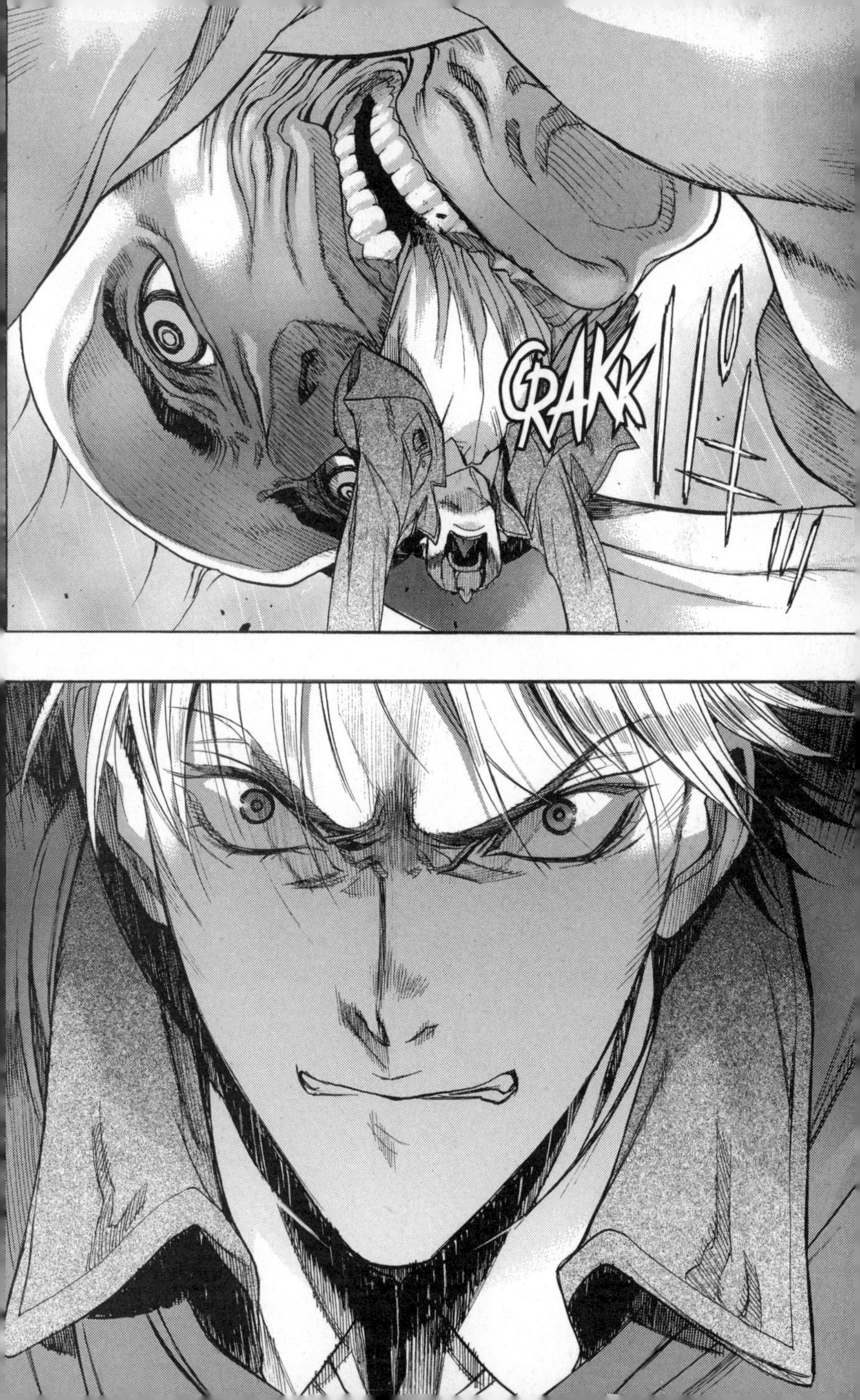
CRAKK

TO BE CONTINUED

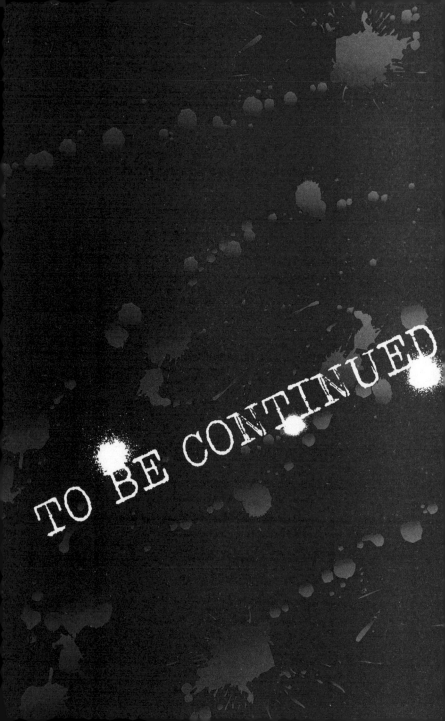

# Translation Note

NARAKA, PAGE 146

THE NAME FOR A TYPE OF REALM IN THE BUDDHIST
AFTERLIFE. A NARAKA IS SOMETHING LIKE PURGATORY
IN WHICH THE DEAD MUST LIVE OUT A SET PERIOD OF
TIME, UNDERGOING HELLISH TORMENT, UNTIL THEIR
KARMA IS CONSUMED AND THEY CAN BE REBORN
INTO A HIGHER PLANE OF LIFE. ALSO KNOWN
AS "NARAKU" IN JAPANESE.

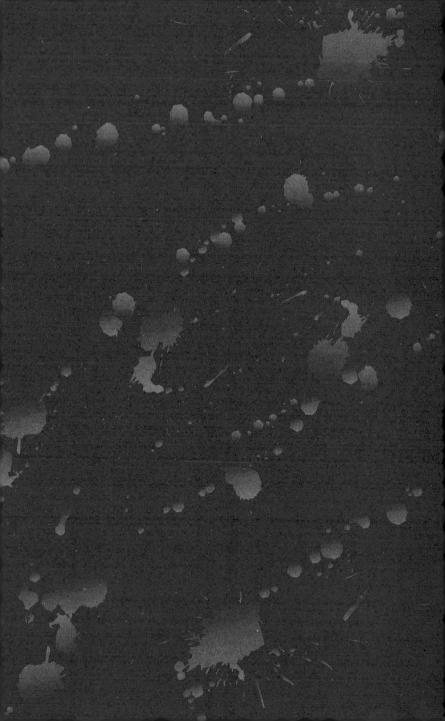

FIND YOUR NEW FAVORITE SHONEN!
FIRE FORCE
THAT TIME I GOT REINCARNATED AS A
SLIME
KC KODANSHA COMICS
A NEW SERIES FROM THE CREATOR OF SOUL EATER, THE MEGAHIT MANGA AND ANIME SEEN ON TOONAMI!
"One of the most fun, new action-based series I've read in quite a while."
—AiPT!
© Atsushi Ohkubo/Kodansha, Ltd. All rights reserved.
AN AWESOME RPG FANTASY FOR FANS OF SO I'M A SPIDER, SO WHAT? AND THE DEVIL IS A PART-TIMER!
"A fun adventure that fantasy readers will relate to and enjoy."
—AiP
© Fuse/Taiki Kawakami/Kodansha, Lt
All rights reserved.

DELUXE EDITION

# BATTLE ANGEL ALITA

**After more than a decade out of print, the original cyberpunk action classic returns in glorious 400-page hardcover deluxe editions, featuring an all-new translation, color pages, and new cover designs!**

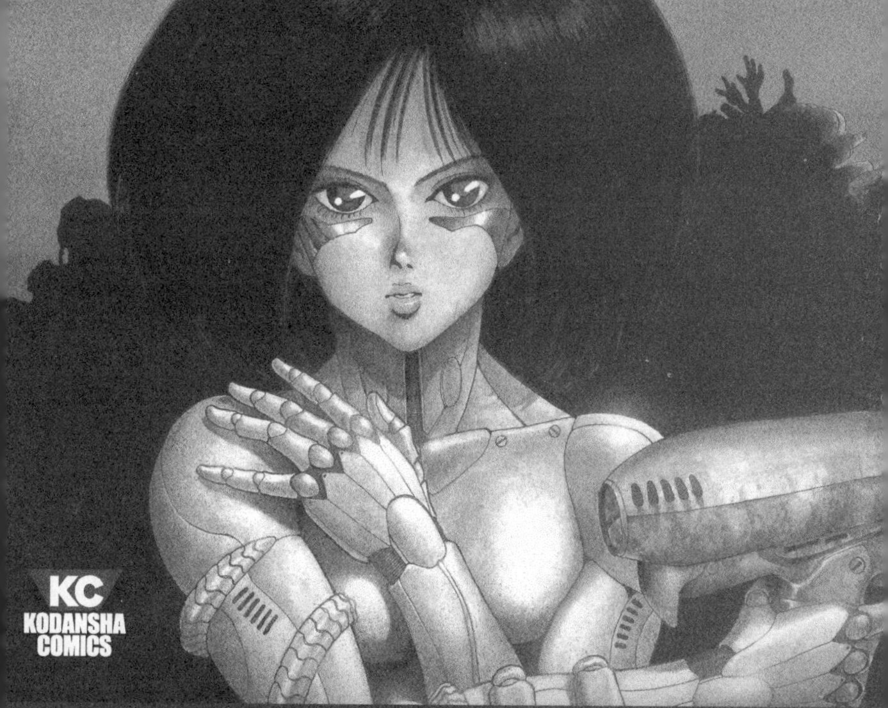

KC KODANSHA COMICS

Far beneath the shimmering space-city of Zalem lie the trash-heaps of The Scrapyard... Here, cyber-doctor and bounty hunter Daisuke Ido finds the head and torso of an amnesiac cyborg girl. He names her Alita and vows to fill her life with beauty, but in a moment of desperation, a fragment of Alita's mysterious past awakens in her. She discovers that she possesses uncanny prowess in the legendary martial art known as panzerkunst. With her newfound skills, Alita decides to become a hunter-warrior - tracking down and taking out those who prey on the weak. But can she hold onto her humanity in the dark and gritty world of The Scrapyard?